Tiananmen Fictions Outside the Square

In the series ASIAN AMERICAN HISTORY AND CULTURE
edited by Sucheng Chan, David Palumbo-Liu,
Michael Omi, K. Scott Wong, and Linda Trinh Võ

TIANANMEN FICTIONS
OUTSIDE THE SQUARE

The Chinese Literary Diaspora
and the Politics of Global Culture

BELINDA KONG

Temple University Press
PHILADELPHIA

Temple University Press
Philadelphia, Pennsylvania 19122
www.temple.edu/tempress

Published 2012

LIBRARY OF CONGRESS CATALOGING-IN-PUBLICATION DATA

Kong, Belinda, 1976–
  Tiananmen fictions outside the square : the Chinese literary diaspora and the politics
of global culture / Belinda Kong.
      p.   cm. — (Asian American history and culture)
  Includes bibliographical references and index.
  ISBN 978-1-4399-0758-0 (cloth : alk. paper)
  ISBN 978-1-4399-0759-7 (pbk. : alk. paper)
  ISBN 978-1-4399-0760-3 (e-book)
    1. Chinese literature—Foreign countries—History and criticism.   2. China—
History—Tiananmen Square Incident, 1989.   3. Authors, Chinese—Foreign
countries.   4. Chinese diaspora in literature.   I. Title.
PL3033.K66   2012
895.1'3009—dc23
                                                                                2011043063

∞ The paper used in this publication meets the requirements of the American
National Standard for Information Sciences—Permanence of Paper for Printed
Library Materials, ANSI Z39.48–1992

Printed in the United States of America

2 4 6 8 9 7 5 3 1

THE
AMERICAN
LITERATURES
INITIATIVE

A book in the American Literatures Initiative (ALI), a collaborative
publishing project of NYU Press, Fordham University Press, Rutgers
University Press, Temple University Press, and the University of Virginia
Press. The Initiative is supported by The Andrew W. Mellon Foundation.
For more information, please visit www.americanliteratures.org.

Contents

Acknowledgments

In book time, this work is more a young adult than a newborn, and it owes its origins, growth, and personality to a whole network and history of influential figures. I want to first thank my family, James and Yong Wilshire, for their support of my academic pursuits throughout the years, however remote academe may strike them at times. This project has its roots in my dissertation, so I also want to express my gratitude to my advisers at the University of Michigan: my co-chairs, Simon Gikandi and Lydia Liu, for vast area expertise and professional guidance; Yopie Prins, for gentle encouragement and advocacy; Christi Merrill, for believing in language, in style, and helping me retain the faith years later; and David Porter, for generous mentorship, critical rigor, and sheer humaneness. And in memory of Lemuel Johnson, my first adviser, who embodied the model scholar in my early graduate school years and who introduced me to an ideal of universal singularity, in all its impossible density. I'd like to think this is a book he would have seen his influence in.

At Bowdoin College, many people have contributed to this book's development and realization, and I want to extend my heartfelt thanks to them. My students, especially in the "Writing China from Afar" and "Forbidden Capital" classes, have been incredible interlocutors and kept my feet firmly grounded during the writing process. My wonderful colleagues in the English Department and the Asian Studies Program fostered a supportive intellectual environment that was invaluable to a junior scholar teaching at a liberal arts college for the first time. Marilyn Reizbaum and Aviva Briefel in particular lent their astute eye and professional wisdom to seeing this book go forward. Special thanks to Shuqin Cui for unstinting mentorship and encouragement, for reading part of the manuscript and posing challenging questions of gender and cross-cultural translation that I'm still thinking through. Above all, I am deeply indebted to several friends and colleagues in my writing group who went above and beyond the call of duty and fellowship by reading substantial portions of the manuscript and offering sympathetic camaraderie as much as critical feedback along the way. Without them, this would have been a far lonelier journey. Jeffrey Selinger provided an incisive perspective from outside my discipline and much-needed honesty when my prose fell flat; Vyjayanthi Ratnam Selinger gave ever-canny suggestions on both macro and micro levels and helped me stay true to my vision toward the end; Rachel Sturman, with what seemed indefatigable and heroic intellectual energy, tendered trenchant and probing advice at many stages and has been inspirational by her example as much as counsel; and Hilary Thompson, with brilliance and profundity, always saw where I was coming from, where I might want to go, and the forking paths that led there or beyond.

My appreciation extends to the staff at Temple University Press: to Amanda Steele and Gary Kramer, for their expert assistance in shepherding the manuscript to press, and especially to my editor, Janet Francendese, for intuitively understanding my project's goals right from the outset and for dedicating such extraordinary care to its materialization. As part of the American Literatures Initiative, this book benefits from the generous funding of the Andrew W. Mellon Foundation as well. I also want to give warm thanks to the series editor, David Palumbo-Liu, and to my second reader, Rob Wilson, for their detailed and insightful comments, which have pushed me in new directions and substantially deepened the intellectual engagements of the book. In addition, William Irwn Thompson read parts of the manuscript with a keen poet's eye and saved me from many goofy mixed metaphors. My sincere thanks, too, to Chen Guang, for his good-hearted support and brave example, for permitting me to include his artwork here, and for instantiating what Tiananmen could mean at its highest potential. Finally, to Hilary, may we always muse among the vegetables.

TIANANMEN FICTIONS OUTSIDE THE SQUARE

Chen Guang, *Duan 1*. Oil on canvas, 2007. Courtesy of the artist.

Introduction: Tiananmen in Diaspora and in Fiction

Post-Tiananmen Literary Diaspora

In our memories of Tiananmen, two images of power square off. Hannah Arendt, countering Mao Zedong two decades prior, as much as foresaw this. While Mao maintained that "power grows out of the barrel of a gun," Arendt optimistically proposed that true power "always stands in need of numbers" and resides in the "living power of the people" (*On Violence* 41–42). These two theses find their historical embodiment and confrontation in 1989 Beijing. On one side, we recall masses parading through the streets and students occupying the Square; on the other, army tanks grinding down blockaded boulevards. This global iconography has ensured Tiananmen's legacy, as a parable of regime violence as much as a tragedy in the human annals of popular protest. Whatever genre we invoke, recollections of Tiananmen almost always employ a political lexicon, for above all the episode has come to be enshrined as a political myth, the grand clash between totalitarianism and democracy at the near-end of the Cold War era. Its bloody dénouement presents a most spectacular challenge of, even refutation to, the Arendtian hypothesis, a crux case for any theory of power in contemporary times. With good reason, then, has Tiananmen been conceived primarily in political terms, as an event with global political import. Accordingly, its legacy has been expressed most often in the language of failure.

What remains largely unrecognized is the significance of Tiananmen for literature—as an event whose tremendous *generative* power persists today, more than two decades later, not just for China but also for the

West. Indeed, the fates of their respective literatures have become irrevocably intertwined in the wake of June 4. This book examines the myriad literary effects of Tiananmen, with a focus on fiction. Its central thesis is that, more than any other episode in recent world history, Tiananmen has brought about, and into stark relief, a distinctly *politicized* Chinese literary diaspora.

First, this process can be observed purely on the level of representational content. Since 1989, the subject of Tiananmen has entered into the realm of literature, with history going hand in hand with fiction, giving rise to a body of Tiananmen narratives that continues to swell in number. Given that the topic remains under official censorship by the communist government, the majority of these works have been published outside the People's Republic of China (PRC). (As I will elaborate below, fiction writers within the PRC who attempt to address Tiananmen have necessarily resorted to evasive narrative strategies, and it is this necessary recourse to evasion, rather than an absence of authorial intent or a difference in political attitude, that most clearly distinguishes mainland from diasporic publications.) Whether originally written in Chinese or not, these works now circulate predominantly in cultural and linguistic contexts beyond the national boundaries of the protest movement's actual occurrence. If Tiananmen was first and foremost a national event in the spring of 1989, its representational afterlife has been catapulted beyond the nation—that is to say, it has become transnational, by necessity. In turn, precisely because the topic can be publicly, openly, and directly addressed only outside the PRC, Tiananmen has functioned as a particularly productive node for the diasporic literary imagination. After twenty-some years, as more and more writers seek to represent this incident, Tiananmen itself has become one of the hallmarks of diasporic literary identity. Writing Tiananmen thus constitutes a preeminently diasporic enterprise, one that spurs the expansion of diasporic literature even as it consolidates the literary diaspora's identity. As one scholar asserts, "In the years since the crackdown, Beijing 1989 has become one of the most popular time-space coordinates onto which overseas Chinese writers project their fictional worlds, making the portrayal of the Tiananmen Square Massacre one of the central themes in contemporary Chinese American and transnational Chinese fiction" (Berry 353).[1] On this level, the term "post-Tiananmen literary diaspora" can be construed quite narrowly, as a specific reference to those writers who give voice to Tiananmen's history via literary forms.

But more broadly, beyond representational content, the post-Tiananmen literary diaspora can be understood as a sociological phenomenon of mass migration that underpins the literature itself. Ever since Deng Xiaoping's Open Door Policy in 1978, there had been a steady stream of students and intellectuals from the PRC to the West, but on the heels of Tiananmen, this flow suddenly turned, as one scholar puts it, into "a massive hemorrhage" (L. L. Wang 208). In the exodus immediately following the military crackdown on June 4, the most eye-catching group of evacuees comprised those top student leaders of the protest movement such as Wuer Kaixi, Chai Ling, and Li Lu (numbers 2, 4, and 17 respectively on the PRC government's "21 most-wanted students" list), who managed to be smuggled out of the country and rapidly rose to celebrity status in the West just months after the massacre. Of slightly less visibility were the fugitive intellectuals who actively supported the students, including the astrophysicist Fang Lizhi, the cultural critic Su Xiaokang, and the novelist-journalist Zheng Yi, all of whom fled China within the next two years and eventually found refuge in the United States. There they joined other intellectuals such as the illustrious investigative reporter Liu Binyan, who had been a visiting scholar in the United States since 1988 and who was barred from reentering the PRC after he publicly denounced the massacre on American national television. In the years to come, these two cohorts of high-profile exilic dissidents would produce the most explicit and by now familiar diasporic writings on Tiananmen, including Liu Binyan's coauthored account of the movement, *"Tell the World"* (1989); Fang Lizhi's political essays, composed during his period of asylum inside the Beijing U.S. embassy and collected in *Bringing Down the Great Wall* (1990); Su Xiaokang's autobiographical *A Memoir of Misfortune* (2001); as well as a host of memoirs by former student leaders such as Li Lu's *Moving the Mountain* (1990), Shen Tong's *Almost a Revolution* (1990), and Zhang Boli's *Escape from China* (2002). Based on intensely personal experiences or reflections and often informed by a testimonial or authenticating impulse, this trove of memoirs, essays, and analyses generically anchors Tiananmen in first-person real-life encounters, constructing the episode as, above all, one of witnessing and truth-telling.

Much less recognized, however, is the vital and enduring impact of Tiananmen on Chinese literature at large. June 4 not only catalyzed a wave of political evacuation but also propelled several generations of creative writers into the diaspora. Consider the sphere of poetry. For an older generation of poets linked to the 1978–79 Democracy Wall movement and the underground magazine *Today* (*Jintian*), Tiananmen was decisive. Bei Dao, who happened to have been on an invited conference trip to Berlin in 1989, was subsequently forced into exile and spent the next decade or so drifting from country to country, alone and separated from his family. Yang Lian, who was a visiting scholar at the University of Auckland since earlier that year, joined an international protest against the Chinese government and consequently lost his Chinese citizenship; he was then granted political asylum in New Zealand and in due course settled in London. Gu Cheng, also a visiting scholar at Auckland at the time, lived in self-imposed exile in New Zealand from 1989 until his suicide in 1993. Duo Duo, who was working for a small Beijing newspaper and who personally witnessed the protests in the Square, was fortuitously aboard a flight to London on June 4; thereafter for the next dozen years, he too was banned from the PRC. Together, these and other poets of the Democracy Wall generation embodied a group of self-identified dissident writers who were driven into exile by Tiananmen.[2] "In the ruins of Tiananmen Square," one scholar notes, a "poetics of nightmare" surfaced in their works (Barnstone 37). Yet Tiananmen also contributed to what another critic calls "a robust growth" of Chinese poetry in the diaspora in the post-1989 era, as these exilic poets were joined by a later set including Wang Jiaxin, Song Lin, Zhang Zao, Zhang Zhen, and Bei Ling, all of whom settled down to write in the West in the 1990s, many as immigrants or scholars rather than political exiles (Yeh 283–84).

Indeed, on a macro view, the more protracted literary legacy of Tiananmen, if also more subtle and less easily pinpointed, is to be felt in the *voluntary* rather than coerced acts of writers—a premise that lies at the core of my study. Aside from enforced banishment, June 4 has induced considerable emigration or naturalization elsewhere on the part of those who may or may not have been activist during the 1989 protest movement. Gao Xingjian, for instance, had already moved to France in 1987, but he withdrew his membership from the Chinese Communist Party (CCP) after the massacre and was later branded a persona non grata by the Chinese government; thereafter, he continued to live in Paris and acquired French citizenship in 1997. Ma Jian, who had been residing in Hong Kong since 1986 but returned to Beijing in 1989 to see the demonstrations for himself, left for Germany after Hong Kong's 1997 handover and now lives in London. Both Gao and Ma had published in the PRC in the 1980s but had moved away to avoid official suppression of their works, so their reasons for departure were as much professional as political. For both, though, June 4 was a key impetus for not returning.

At the same time, the massacre compelled countless international students who were already enrolled in graduate programs overseas to stay abroad. Many of them would go on to pursue creative writing and become celebrated authors in the diaspora. In the United States alone, there were some thirty thousand Chinese international graduate students in 1989, and President George Bush's offer of temporary asylum to these students after June 4 substantially altered the demographics of Chinese America (L. L. Wang 196). In the field of literature, Ha Jin is perhaps the best-known case.[3] He had been studying comparative poetics at Brandeis since 1985 and had originally intended to return to China after graduation to teach at the university level, but after watching television images of the Beijing bloodshed, he decided to remain in the United States and is now a professor of English at Boston University. Similarly, Qiu Xiaolong, who had been a visiting scholar at Washington University since 1988, resolved to stay on in the United States and begin a writing career in English after the massacre. Shouhua Qi, arriving in early 1989 as a master's student at Illinois State University, likewise decided to continue writing in the United States following June 4 and now teaches English literature in Connecticut. Comparable stories unfolded in Canada. Ting-xing Ye, on scholarship at York University since 1987, decided not to return to China after her studies ended in 1989 and went on to become an author of young-adult fiction in English, settling near Toronto. Ying Chen, in a slightly different scenario, left Shanghai in the spring of 1989 just before the crackdown and remained in self-imposed exile in Montreal, first to study creative writing at McGill University and later to become an established Francophone novelist. Nor are these trajectories unique to the Americas. A notable European counterpart to Ha Jin is Dai Sijie, who had been studying in France on a scholarship since 1984 and who remained there after June 4 to become an acclaimed filmmaker and best-selling novelist in French.

Finally, a significant contingent of emigrants left the PRC shortly after the massacre to become professional writers in the West, with many of them in interviews and essays attributing their departures at least in part to Tiananmen. Among them are Yan Geling, who came to the United States at the end of 1989 and now lives in the San Francisco Bay area; Diane Wei Liang, who also left in 1989, first for the United States and then for London, and now holds dual British and American citizenship; Liu Hong, who left in the same year for Britain; Sheng Xue, who likewise left the same year and now lives in Toronto; Shan Sa, who went to France in 1990; and Hong Ying, who moved to Britain in 1991. As June 4 set the initial conditions for an epochal exodus out of the country, the post-Tiananmen years saw a definite burgeoning of Chinese emigrant authors in the West. That the trend persisted into the 1990s, albeit in a more diffuse manner, is suggested by the advent of a younger generation of writers such as Annie Wang and Yiyun Li, who came to the United States in 1993 and 1996 respectively, and who have risen to literary prominence in the first decades of the twenty-first century. As the post-Tiananmen era now enters its third decade, the ranks of Chinese diaspora writers will continue to grow, even as their orientations inevitably evolve in the shifting milieus of globalization. In this broadest sense, the post-Tiananmen literary diaspora can be said to encompass not just those writers who left the PRC or chose to stay abroad in the few years after June 4, but also those who continue to follow this trajectory into the new millennium under the long shadow of the massacre.

Demographic considerations alone, though, can stretch limit points to infinity and make categories lose coherence. Of greater import to my argument is that Tiananmen has substantially altered the *disposition* of the Chinese literary diaspora by galvanizing its politics. To be sure, the Chinese literary diaspora is a long-standing and vast phenomenon that predates 1989, and those who write post–June 4 by no means constitute a wholly new or cohesive group. Yet, after the massacre, we can detect in diasporic literature an intensified engagement with matters of political power, a new kind of negative identificatory tug-of-war with the communist state. If Tiananmen had the effect of temporarily politicizing the Chinese diaspora at large during that Beijing spring (recall the mass demonstrations and vigils in Chinese communities worldwide in 1989 in support of the pro-democracy activists), this politicization has endured in much contemporary diasporic literature.

My book spotlights this key political variant of the literary diaspora following June 4. The authors within this configuration, though geographically located abroad, nonetheless continue to imagine and write about China in their works. Yet, instead of simply indulging in homeland nostalgia, they now marshal the cultural authority of world literature, especially in the West, in order to critique the excesses of communist state power. Much more so than in preceding decades, these writers are supremely preoccupied with challenging authoritarianism and the communist regime's discursive monopoly on Chineseness. In the massacre's wake, they exhibit a much stronger tendency to actively dispute and disrupt the PRC government's constructions of what it means to be Chinese, and to reconstruct this identity more heterogeneously for the world. Their task is not a straightforward one, however. Particularly on the subject of Tiananmen, diaspora authors straddle a fine line. While they extend counternarratives against the official PRC version of this history and multiply antihegemonic visions of China as a site of diverse and competing political actors, they also risk perpetuating Cold War perceptions of China as a brutal totalitarian country by artistically resurrecting an episode of violent state repression and failed protest. Viewed in the polarizing terms of liberal democracy versus communist totalitarianism, West versus East, the global cultural impact of Tiananmen literature, and of this politicized literary diaspora, may well seem bounded by a tension between anticommunist contestation and potential neo-orientalism. My study, though, strives to reach beyond this agonistic viewpoint by highlighting the capacity of a diaspora to serve as a third, transformative space.

First, in terms of cultural identity, diaspora writers assume a seminal role in defining the parameters and meanings of Chineseness after 1989. No longer is the definition of Chineseness solely or even primarily the activity of those living within the PRC, nor are the geopolitical regions of Taiwan and Hong Kong the main alternative spots for self-representation. Instead, the cultural geography of Chineseness has been considerably re-drawn. Abundant work has already been done by scholars to lay the foun-dation in the broader theoretical project of decentering or deessentializ-ing the category of Chineseness, whether via the vocabulary of diaspora, transnationalism, hybridity, or the global (Tu; Wang G., "Chineseness"; Ong and Nonini; Ong, *Flexible*; Ang; Ma and Cartier; Ng and Holden; L. Chen, *Writing*; Shih; Tsu and Wang). Perhaps earliest in this regard was Tu Wei-ming, who posited in the early 1990s a notion of "cultural China" as encompassing three interactive "symbolic universes: (1) mainland China, Taiwan, Hong Kong, and Singapore, (2) overseas Chinese communities throughout the world, and (3) the international communities of scholars, students, officials, journalists, and traders who provide a global forum for China-related matters." As Tu states, his expansive formulation was aimed to "challenge the claims of political leadership (in Beijing, Taipei, Hong Kong, or Singapore) to be the ultimate authority in a matter as significant as Chineseness" (viii). My study concentrates on the second symbolic uni-verse on Tu's grid, but as each chapter will show, this universe never exists in isolation but always in symbiotic relation with the first and third. While Tu's neo-Confucianist, capitalist-oriented, and origin-recentering model has been vehemently rejected from several quarters (Dirlik, "Critical" 318–20; Nonini and Ong 8–9; Ang 42–44; Cheah 121–26), there is nevertheless wide consensus among scholars about the plurality of ways to be Chinese in the world today—including, as it were, the very negating of Chinese-ness. And as I will elaborate in chapter 2, not by chance did these scholarly rearticulations of Chineseness proliferate post-Tiananmen, and we can view this phenomenon as an elongated, if oblique rather than reductively causal, ramification of June 4 on diasporic intellectual discourse.

Additionally, the presence of Chinese diaspora writers working within the national and linguistic spaces of the non-Sinophone world has recon-figured contemporary literature in a number of geographic areas. As I argue elsewhere, the influx of the post-Tiananmen generation of Chinese writers into the United States has significantly transformed the terrains of Asian American literature, as exemplified by the work of Ha Jin (B. Kong 145–47). This literary impact can also be discerned in other Anglophone countries, particularly England, where a contingent of renowned Chinese emigrant writers resides today. Aside from Ma Jian and Hong Ying, who both write in Chinese, there are the English-language best-selling Jung Chang, Xinran, and most recently, Guo Xiaolu. In Europe, Gao Xingjian, Dai Sijie, and Shan Sa have done the same for Francophone literature, while Lulu Wang's debut Dutch-language novel was a smash hit in Holland. If the term "Chinese diaspora" has customarily referred to the Sinophone world circumscribing the PRC, Taiwan, Hong Kong, and sometimes Malaysia and Singapore, my study transfers critical attention toward the ascendance of cultural agents displaced from those traditional hubs and now scattered across multiple Western milieus.

Furthermore, Chinese diaspora writers help to guard against the forgetting of June 4 by mediating between the official silence inside the PRC and the attenuation of world memory at large. The 1989 Beijing movement was extraordinary from the perspective of world politics, but as an occasion of mass demonstrations or state aggression, it was not exceptional, even in twentieth-century Chinese history. The 1919 May Fourth student movement was its most well-known predecessor and the 1976 Tiananmen Incident its most recent, but in between were the much less-remembered Tiananmen Square antigovernment protests of 1925 and the ensuing massacre of civilians by army troops in 1926 (Spence 298–303). June 4 therefore has its lineage. What partly distinguishes this latest Tiananmen is its global dimension in an age of technology and speed. Unlike its precursors, the 1989 incident unfolded via media venues that enabled it to become an international drama almost instantaneously. As Fang Lizhi observed from his Beijing asylum within months of the crackdown, this specific Tiananmen would be "the first exception" to the "Technique of Forgetting History" enforced by the CCP since its coming into power, for unlike previous instances of national persecution and disasters that had been systematically erased from the historical record by the regime, in 1989, for "the first time," thanks to the presence of foreign journalists inside China and their instrumental role in positioning the world as "opinion makers," "Chinese Communist brutality was thoroughly recorded and reported, and . . . virtually the whole world was willing to censure it" (274). As one scholar further comments on the long-term effects of Tiananmen's global mediatization: "The media spotlight placed on Beijing during the spring of 1989 created repercussions that continue to affect how China is seen globally, how it sees itself, and how the Chinese outside the People's Republic see themselves" (Marchetti xi). Yet what Fang's optimistic projection could not anticipate is that this very rapidity of information dissemination entails a kind of imagistic compression, so that the lived reality of one locale can come to be flattened into a series of easily consumable images transmitted across the globe—the most famous example being the Tank Man. One key theme of this book, then, is that the globalized imagistic propagation of June 4 has been extremely uneven, for world memory proves itself to be all too susceptible to globalization's vicissitudes and its attendant sporadic amnesia. If 1989 can be comprehended as the first Tian-anmen to bear out Paul Virilio's thesis about human experience in the age of "glocalization"—on his wry metaphor, "a constricted planet that is becoming just one vast floor" (23)—then it has also fallen prey to what he calls "a bug in the memory," as the human perceptual horizon shrinks from the skyline to the television box, from "the *line* of the visible horizon" to "the *square* horizon of the screen" (26). Particularly in the context of China's current economic ascent onto the world stage, issues of human rights and political freedom have frequently and tactically been forgotten by world governments and institutions in favor of market interests. In this climate, diaspora writers of Tiananmen may reflect and reproduce global changes in their writings, but they all deliver a reminder, so that 1989 will not go the way of 1925–26.

This is not to say, however, that all Tiananmen writers travel the same ideological path, or that they even agree in their basic assessment of the pro-democracy movement. A potential mistaken assumption here may be that all diaspora writers are equally sympathetic to or supportive of the student activists. Actually, far from it. Another theme running through these pages is that Tiananmen has become a heatedly disputed matter over which sundry groups now vie for representational and discursive power, not just within the PRC but in the diaspora. June 4 might have united Chinese communities worldwide against the communist government in the moment of 1989, but since then, the topic has turned increasingly into a point of fracture, between artists and activists as much as intellectuals and former student leaders (see especially chapters 1 and 4). It is within this fraught circumstance of conflicting diasporic judgments, more than a world polarized between East and West, that writers take on the task of representing Tiananmen. Together, the authors here impart an array of diasporic positions political and philosophical, ethical and aesthetic.

Nonetheless, it merits underscoring that all the writers in this study, their dislocation notwithstanding, are extremely privileged subjects. On one end of the displacement spectrum are those vulnerable illegal trans-migrants whom one scholar calls the "clandestine diaspora" (L. Ma 23). On the opposite end is this literary diaspora, comprising highly visible individuals who have found success and fame in their emigrant or trans-national lives. Without substantial social and cultural capital, these writ-ers simply cannot enter into the Tiananmen discourse in the first place, much less adopt a voice of authority about this history and its relation to Chinese identity. Indeed, they instantiate a claim on "China" with every act of writing Tiananmen. If the critic C. T. Hsia put forth the oft-cited thesis some forty years ago that modern Chinese writers display an "ob-session with China" (533–54), the post-1989 literary diaspora has partly inherited this attitude—perhaps even more so than those writers who stay on in the PRC, given the atrophy of the intelligentsia's authority there from the 1990s onward. The intellectual proclivity for "China obsession," we might say, has become partly diasporized in June 4's wake. Nowhere is this diasporic inheritance more apparent, and more fertilized, than in Tiananmen fictions, which literally move toward or situate themselves at the Square, that symbolic seat of national political power. Little surprise, then, that one scholar would say of many post-Tiananmen exilic intellectuals that they are "stuck by a notable lack of peripheral thinking" and have not "entirely changed their 'centrist' frame of mind—the elitist belief that they can ultimately influence the reformist leaders in the Party to their way of thinking" (L. Lee 233). As one facet of diasporic intellectuals' cultural production, Tiananmen literature is not always so rigidly oriented as this remark would suggest, but the gravitational heart of this canon does undoubtedly lie in the land left behind, weighed with an imaginative if not always emotional nostalgia. Despite the varying degrees to which these writers personify and perform Chineseness, the place they have chosen as their "contingent and arbitrary stop" of fictional self-positioning, what Stuart Hall calls a "'cut' of identity" (230), is not one of radical rupture but firmly harkens back to origin's center. What this book delineates is one geometry of their diasporic stopovers, with each chapter outlining one side of the diasporized Square. This is not to say that all diaspora authors necessarily resort to national allegories, that all post-Tiananmen roads lead to Fredric Jameson's notorious thesis on third-world literature's inevitable allegorical impulse (69), but it is instructive to keep in mind that Tiananmen fictions give traction to the Jamesonian theory precisely because of their authors' elite status.

Ultimately, perhaps due to this very eliteness, the writers here all possess the means of self-advocacy that permit them to shed light on the creative and transformative potential of not just the Chinese literary diaspora but of diasporic subjects in general. The need to recognize this agency is arguably more pressing than ever before, as the diasporic condition now operates as a principal rather than supplemental feature of human existence. Although the large-scale dispersal of peoples is millennia old, numerous social scientists have recently shown that human migration experienced a revolution in the late twentieth century, resulting in a contemporary world order much more profoundly shaped by diasporas than ever before (Van Hear 1–5; L. Ma 1–2; Parreñas and Siu 1). According to the Global Commission on International Migration (GCIM), the number of those who live outside their country of birth skyrocketed from 82 million in 1970 to 175 million in 2000 to nearly 200 million in 2005, and of all diasporas, the Chinese one is the world's largest, estimated at 35 million at the dawn of the new millennium (83–84).[4] Excluding the populations of Hong Kong and Macau since their repatriation to the mainland but inclusive of generations born abroad, the latest count of overseas Chinese given by Taiwan's Overseas Compatriot Affairs Commission hovered at 39.5 million at the end of 2010. An excessive focus on magnitude, though, can breed misconceptions. Indeed, some scholars object to the very use of the term "diaspora" to categorize non–mainland Chinese populations, wary of its potential connotations of homogeneity and unity that could reinforce the PRC's hegemonic claims on identity as much as Western racialized views of Asian otherness (Wang G., *Don't* 240–45; Wang G., "Single" 38–41; Shih 23–28). At the same time, scholars who do adopt the term have severally pointed out that definitions of "diaspora" in migration studies can sometimes be too caught up in mass statistics, or else overly constricted by criteria of forced expulsion or economic exploitation, crises and catastrophes (Van Hear 5–6; L. Ma 2–4; Goh 1–7). This image of diasporas as victim populations, as nameless hordes of the dispossessed and persecuted, can obscure an appreciation for diasporic subjects' ability to re-create and transmute not only themselves but the milieus into which they are dispersed. My book's spotlight on Tiananmen fictions illumines exactly this reanimating capacity. A diaspora, after all, comprises not just bodies in motion but also the production of culture in transit. For the diaspora authors here, literature offers a forum to fine-tune, modify, or forge anew the world's understanding of China, Chineseness, and Tiananmen. These writers do not simply bear out an inescapable identity that predetermines them or a wounded psyche that haunts them. On the contrary, they resignify "diaspora" as much as "Chineseness" via plural roles: as architects of political counter-discourses about the homeland state, as remakers of cultural identity in transplanted environments, and as mediators of historical memory and human rights between the PRC and the rest of the world. Indeed, Tiananmen allows these writers to persistently activate literature's manifold uses. As the PRC grows ever more visible as a global power today, Tiananmen fictions offer a timely focal point for reinvigorating critical interrogations of the functions of literature, not merely within China or the West, but in the overlapping spaces of the quickly converging first and second worlds.

Four Tiananmen Fictions

As mentioned above, diasporic memoirs and personal essays constitute the most recognizable genres of writing on Tiananmen. This study, however, is not narrowly concerned with life-based narratives for which firsthand experience serves as the prime justification. It should be clarified from the outset that by "Tiananmen fictions" I refer not to works by those who personally participated in the demonstrations or witnessed the massacre and then converted their memories into autobiographical stories. In fact, two of the authors here, Gao Xingjian and Ha Jin, were not located in the PRC in 1989 and learned of the incident only from afar, via television images and news reports. The other two did repeatedly visit the Square that spring, but Ma Jian left Beijing about a week before the crackdown to tend to his comatose brother in their hometown of Qingdao, and Annie Wang was not in the Square herself during its final evacuation. Moreover, Wang was too young and Ma too old to be counted within the ranks of college student protestors, together sandwiching the Tiananmen generation from either side. This book, then, centers on writers who were *not* insiders of the movement or eyewitnesses of June 4.

Indeed, the role of the witness is a complicated one for the historiography of Tiananmen. More than twenty years later, the massacre has become an episode cloaked in mythologies spun from both hemispheres, misrepresented by the PRC's official erasure of it as much as the international community's fixation on eyewitness accounts, however inflated, however mutually contradictory. Where free expression is absent, especially when the media fail and the cameras go black, into the void steps the witness. Tiananmen is hence an event heavily saturated with testimonial claims. I will expound on this matter in chapter 4, in relation to what one commentator calls the actual "geography of the killing" behind the misnomer "the Tiananmen Square massacre" (Munro 811). Yet, despite the mounting significance of the political witness in international arenas since World War II, particularly in instances of mass atrocities and certainly with what transpired in the early hours of June 4, this book does not rely on the figure of the witness as the sole mediator of history or the principal purveyor of historical knowledge. An overdependence on the witness can lead to a moral and intellectual complacency on our part, where we feel obviated from the need to probe further for history's continuities, meanings that exceed mere facticity to impinge on our present and future. Biographical authenticity will thus not be taken as the legitimating criterion for evaluating representations of Tiananmen here, and the works examined in turn will not premise themselves on the truth-claims of personal life experience.

Instead, I am interested in the multifarious ways that Tiananmen has come to be written in the diaspora, not as an individually lived event but as a collective historical idea that has found an afterlife in literature. Here I borrow Walter Benjamin's concept of *afterlife* as the non-organic continued life of something that "has a history of its own, and is not merely the setting for history," a continuation that is at once "a transformation and a renewal" ("Task" 71, 73). Benjamin's perspective enables us to conceive of a temporality of Tiananmen that is itself living history, as that which has not yet lapsed but survives into our time, manifesting ever-newer meanings for the changing present. My objective is to tease out the nonbiographical, nonpast knowledges of Tiananmen as provided through fiction, and the ways fiction compels us to think beyond strictly historical or Chinese contexts to new dilemmas that confront the post-1989 world. Indeed, fiction yields a special efficacy for charting an event's afterlife, since its province is often that of meaning's distillation and life's renewal, in a realm less bound by the stringencies of organic decay.

The four works I concentrate on—Gao Xingjian's *Taowang* (*Escape*) (1989), Ha Jin's *The Crazed* (2002), Annie Wang's *Lili* (2001), and Ma Jian's *Beijing Coma* (*Beijing zhiwuren*) (2008)—are exemplary in this regard.[5] Eminent figures in the diaspora, these four authors exemplify the increased propensity of the post-Tiananmen literary diaspora to critique communist state power, for they all highlight various sites where this power exerts itself most violently—on individual freedom for Gao, intellectual labor for Jin, female sexuality for Wang, the biological body for Ma. More crucially, their Tiananmen fictions mark major moments in the evolving afterlife of the diasporic imagination of June 4, together reflecting the ongoing development of global concerns since 1989. Each text proffers a discrete conceptual angle onto the Square: the existentialist (Gao), the aporetic (Jin), the global-capitalist (Wang), and the biopolitical (Ma). Accordingly, each work prompts an investigation into a distinct nexus of issues and problems that go far beyond the singular events of Tiananmen, from human displacement and political responsibility to diasporic trauma and melancholia, and ever more proximately to our time, from the challenges posed by global capital and its determinations on transnational subjectivity to the biopolitical dangers facing those who remain behind in globalizing authoritarian countries. The unique theoretical arc I chart via these four texts, then, should profoundly illustrate that the perceptual horizon of the post-Tiananmen literary diaspora is far from provincial. This diaspora evolves alongside planetary realities, and Tiananmen endures as not an unshakable specter but a continually revitalizable history that allows writers to ponder, struggle with, and elucidate contemporary global questions.

In chapter 1, I consider the 2000 Nobel Laureate in Literature, Gao Xingjian, and his play *Taowang* (*Escape*), the first full-length fictional work on Tiananmen to come out of the Chinese diaspora. Born in 1940, nine years before the establishment of the PRC, Gao is the oldest writer in this study and also the one with the greatest generational distance from the Tiananmen students. His imaginary approach to the Square of 1989 is freighted with a long personal history of encounters with China's national upheavals and political repression, a trajectory that has culminated in his philosophy of existentialist flight. Hence, in *Taowang*, the June 4 massacre is not an occurrence unique to the Chinese communist regime or even an archetypal instance of totalitarian state violence but an allegory for human existence within any polis, any community. For Gao, the tanks of Beijing denote the most extreme form of collectivities' oppression of the individual, but they differ from the pro-democracy movement only in degree and not in kind. In the face of both modes of collective power, the singular human must flee in order to preserve integrity and freedom of the self. As I will argue, Gao's universalizing of the Square empties Tiananmen of its concrete social and political import, abstracting it into a human condition that takes place everywhere and nowhere. The conceptual insights afforded by his play are thus mostly negative, leading to a quietist view of political action and of humanity. Yet his very contextualizing of Tiananmen within these philosophical discourses behooves us to seek alternative models of exile, of the human, and of politics as such. Tiananmen through Gao's fiction therefore brings to the fore the critical challenge of theorizing dislocation and dispossession, and the relationship between the human and the polis—perennial preoccupations of diasporas, to be sure.

While Gao's play takes place in an unnamed country and city, the other three Tiananmen fictions of this study all solidly anchor themselves in the real geography of the post-Mao PRC, albeit each with its own inventive accents and alterations. In chapter 2, I turn to Ha Jin, one of the most prominent Asian American writers today. Of the four works here, Jin's *The Crazed* most closely approximates the tenets of contemporary diaspora theory, especially in the novel's representation of the Square as a site of failed arrival, a destination that the protagonist approaches but never gets to. In literary criticism and cultural studies, conceptual models of diaspora proliferated in the early 1990s, as numerous postcolonial critics drew on ideas from deconstruction for political critiques of the nation and empire. Jin's arrival in the United States in 1985 as a graduate student of comparative poetics, and his subsequent continuation in American academe after June 4, coincides with this institutional emergence of deconstructive diaspora theory. *The Crazed* hence marks a historical moment in the development of Tiananmen literature, a product of Jin's postemigrant status in the 1990s U.S. academy. So too, although the novel shares with Gao's play a self-distancing from the scene of the massacre, Jin, unlike Gao, casts this narrative absence as a form of diasporic rather than existential alienation, that is, as a sign of his own removal from the ostensible setting of the carnage. The Square, for Jin, epitomizes China's core, in both its hope and horror, an origin from which he has irreversibly, if mournfully, detached himself. Indeed, from his long-distance vantage point in the United States, most of Jin's oeuvre can be interpreted as a compulsive attempt to imaginatively return to the lost homeland, whose heart at Tiananmen is now accessible only as a fictional gap or aporia. Thus, I also read Jin's novel through a paradigm of diasporic melancholia, interweaving theories of diaspora with those of trauma to illuminate his distinctive mode of aesthetically vanishing the Square.

I confine my analysis of diaspora theory to this chapter so as to highlight that no one formulation of "diaspora" is sufficient to explicating all four diasporic texts here, much less all diasporic texts in total. Likewise with trauma theory. While recent work by a number of critics adopting the overarching frame of historical trauma has been valuable for our understanding of twentieth-century Chinese literature and culture (Yang, *Chinese*; B. Wang; Berry), including the Tiananmen authors I address here (G. Xu; Schaffer and Smith; Schaffer and Song), my study aims to supplement this perspective by drawing out the multifaceted and shifting complexities of Tiananmen fictions. As will become evident in my appraisal of Jin, any application of trauma theory to diaspora writers must also grapple with the problem of remote witnessing—or nonwitnessing—which is in turn entangled with the dynamics of diasporic perception and politics. Furthermore, as my analyses of the other texts will reveal, it is simply not the case that every Chinese author fits the mold of a melancholic victim of the massacre, inexorably caught in the throes of writing and rewriting a primal scene of diasporic trauma. Tiananmen fictions are not mere symptoms. Despite the primacy I assign to June 4 as a major condensation point for the literary diaspora, the faculty I wish to emphasize in these writers is their creative vitality. The diasporic life Tiananmen has yielded them and the afterlife they engender for Tiananmen are reciprocal, symbiotic.

This vitality will become even more apparent in the second half of the book with Annie Wang's *Lili* and Ma Jian's *Beijing Coma*, two works that unhinge Tiananmen from its strictly historical basis. In chapter 3, I discuss Wang's novel in relation to more specific diaspora theories of femininity, globalization, and neo-orientalism. While Jin formalizes his diasporic distance from origin via a narrative that ends in a moment of failed arrival at the Square, Wang by contrast explicitly thematizes this distance as a cultural-political confrontation between American and Chinese perceptions of China. In other words, Wang concretizes Gao's existential and Jin's diasporic alienation as a geopolitical difference. Of all the Tiananmen writers here, she is the youngest, and the only one who is younger than the Tiananmen student generation: born in 1972, she was sixteen at the time of June 4 and grew to adulthood only in the post-massacre period. As a sign of her generational belatedness, her novel's portrait of late-1980s Beijing anachronistically invokes the hypercapitalist atmosphere of the 1990s instead of the cautious liberalization of the previous decade. Yet this anachronism usefully resituates Tiananmen within a more current framework of the PRC's globalization, enabling Wang to tackle issues of a contemporary Chinese neocoloniality within the global capitalist order.

Consequently, she is also the writer who most thoroughly internationalizes the representation of the Square, and her text the one that deals most
overtly with its own diasporic condition vis-à-vis its Western readership.
At the same time, her novel relentlessly uncovers the inequalities internal to Chinese society itself, especially along axes of gender and class. *Lili*
is thus at once a feminist critique of Chinese nationalism's patriarchy, a
demythologizing of student elitism, and a redefinition of mass politics as
material consumption and cultural mimicry in the era of global capital.
Wang's fiction occupies the symbolic space and time of Tiananmen to lay
bare the unequal power relations between as well as within nations, the
geopolitics as well as the social power reproductions of capitalist China.

This literary interrogation of power against the symbolic backdrop of
Tiananmen will get taken up again by Ma Jian in *Beijing Coma*. With
this latest novel, Tiananmen as history comes to fruition in literature.
In chapter 4, I culminate my study with the text that stays most faith-
ful to Tiananmen's reality but simultaneously elevates it most fully into
the realm of myth. Of all extant Tiananmen fictions, Ma's is the one that
stays closest to the student movement, bringing Tiananmen back full circle from Gao's intellectual-philosopher, Jin's teacher-scholar, and Wang's
woman-hooligan to the core of the protests' origins: student life. Moreover,
where the other works here underscore the necessity or outcome of flight,
Ma's alone insists on the conceptual return to—and reoccupation of—the
Square as the symbolic place of the CCP's despotic past and present as
well as that of Chinese democracy's future struggle. Both Ma and Jin were
born in the mid-1950s, children of the first PRC generation, and both are
disenchanted heirs to the communist promise. But unlike Jin, Ma has become a passionate and outspoken advocate of Chinese democracy and human rights. He therefore embodies a significant mode of cultural politics
in the post-Tiananmen literary diaspora, and *Beijing Coma* represents his
vigorous intervention into the contested terrains of diasporic Tiananmen
discourse. In this last chapter, I will recapitulate the controversial historiography of the massacre as well as recent international criticisms of the
"radical" student leadership, so as to refocus attention away from moral
censure toward political legacy. In this context, Ma's novel plays a critical
role, for it brilliantly reconfigures Tiananmen through the lens of totalitarian state biopower, exposing the ways the communist state manages and
controls its vast population through techniques of governing bodies and
biological life. In his epic vision, June 4 epitomizes the half-century-long
genealogy of communism's cannibalistic biopolitics, one that stretches
from actual instances of politicized cannibalism in the Cultural Revolution
to capitalist modes of state predation in the new millennium and forward
into the Beijing Olympics moment. The Square of 1989, though, remains

the most visible instant of biopolitical sovereignty, so it is here that Ma imaginatively lingers, even as he unhinges this biopolitical paradigm from its historical space and time and reincarnates it as a general condition over the PRC today. From Gao's and Jin's absent Square to Wang's globalized one, where the Square was nowhere or else utterly porous, we come at last to a ubiquitous Square with no exits. Yet in Ma's fiction, the most terrifying circumstance is not a repetition of history but the banishing of all repetition, not the reenactment of totalitarian biopower but the forgetting of all biopolitical action, not another military mobilization but a spiritual death of student life altogether. Ultimately, a Square with no students hereafter is equivalent to a Square where the tanks have never ceased to triumph. This latest diasporic portrayal of Tiananmen may be the darkest, most dystopic and nightmarish one yet.

By chance, the Tiananmen fictions selected here are all published with near-decade lapses from the massacre and from each other. Gao completed *Taowang* in a flurry just months after June 4, whereas *The Crazed* and *Lili* were both published at the turn of the millennium, and *Beijing Coma* first appeared (in English translation) in 2008, almost two full decades after 1989. By various reports, Jin, Wang, and Ma all spent ten years on their respective texts. It would seem that Tiananmen inspires either stunningly swift or painstakingly prolonged artistic efforts, and that every ten years' passing prompts yet another diaspora writer to revisit the Square and re-create its relevance anew, just as the historical massacre symbolized one era's end and another's beginning in the PRC. It may be said, then, that Tiananmen represents an epochally charged and an ever-resilient and timely flash point for unresolved dilemmas, ones that impinge on but are not restricted to Chineseness in our time. This, in any case, is the metanarrative of the present study. Each of the four works chosen raises a constellation of issues that press on not just the Chinese literary diaspora but also the ever more compressed human world we inhabit in common. The focus on Tiananmen compels these writers as much as their global readers to consider persistent problems of existential exile and displacement, historical trauma and witnessing, as well as the more modern crises brought on by globalization and totalitarianism such as capitalist neoimperialism and state sovereign biopower. No one set of terms, however, can wholly encompass Tiananmen's significations. So, in each chapter I explore at length a cluster of theoretical concepts and their associated debates—including Hannah Arendt's notion of the human and the polis and Edward Said's of exile and the intellectual (Gao); deconstruction-inflected theories of diaspora such as Stuart Hall's and trauma studies' psychoanalytic extensions of Freudian melancholia (Jin); Rey Chow's model of postcolonial orientalism and autoethnography and Aihwa Ong's of capitalist transnationalism and flexible citizenship (Wang); and finally, Walter Benjamin's thesis on the historical emergency, Michel Foucault's on modern biopower, and Giorgio Agamben's on exceptionality and bare life (Ma). These conceptual engagements can elucidate not just Tiananmen and its fictions but also the post-Tiananmen epoch that is our present, for ultimately, I want to suggest that these issues are not simply interlinked but evolving, that they reflect an accreting progression of global concerns in the post-Tiananmen world. That critical discourses have shifted from vocabularies of humanism and displacement to those of transnationalism and globalization in the past two decades may be one indicator of this development. The old terminology is not so much superseded as redefined and recontextualized—which is precisely the story of Tiananmen fictions.

Other Tiananmens

This book, then, does not purport to be a comprehensive survey into all genres of writing on Tiananmen, nor does it give an exhaustive analysis of all Tiananmen literature. Indeed, such monumental tasks seem increasingly daunting, if not impossible, with each passing year. While 1989 recedes ever more remotely in chronological time, its resuscitation by writers the world over has by contrast endowed it with a constant literary present. If anything, literary references and especially casual allusions to it have proliferated over time, in works by both Chinese diaspora writers and others, so that a complete inventory of Tiananmen's entry into world literature would become a scholarly exercise of a very different sort than the one undertaken here, something akin to an encyclopedic catalogue. Still, there are edifying insights to be derived from such an enterprise, so let me briefly telescope these by sketching a few categories of other Tiananmen representations, in literature as well as visual culture, if only to make more salient my own textual choices.

In poetry, there is a sizable corpus in both Chinese and non-Chinese languages, and this genre well deserves a separate study. A thorough tally of Tiananmen poetry, though, would include not just explicitly Tiananmen-related pieces but also those implicitly tied to the incident. To take one telling example: in Bei Dao's poetry, while direct references to June 4 are not many—the 1990 "Requiem" ("Diao wang") being his most overt homage to the massacre's victims—it is nonetheless periodically and obliquely resurrected in numerous poems years later such as "deny" ("Fouren") (1995) and "June" ("Liuyue") (2000), poems that commemorate unnamed anniversaries and in which images of the dead or of a square, and themes of memory's erasure or return, none too subtly harken back to 1989. Through these images and themes, and given his trademark poetics of ambiguity, Tiananmen can even be said to atmospherically permeate Bei Dao's post-1989 writing. To consider another farther-flung example: in Chinese American poet Marilyn Chin's English-language volume *The Phoenix Gone, The Terrace Empty* (1994), the last section is entitled "Beijing Spring" and dedicated to "the Chinese Democratic Movement," but just two poems in the section ("Tienanmen, the Aftermath" and "Beijing Spring") deal with Tiananmen, whereas the other pieces accrue June 4 relevance only indirectly, associatively. Structural placement, contextual proximity, paratextual resonance, circumstantial inspiration—all these factors come into play in the identification and assessment of Tiananmen poetry in the expansive sense. Even a strictly themed anthology such as the 2007 *Liusi shiji* (June 4 collected poetry), the first literary compilation devoted entirely to the topic of Tiananmen and assembling more than 150 Chinese poems on June 4, appears in print only after a highly selective vetting: as the editors report, they had initially collected a total of 5,341 poems (Jiang i). Hence, while Wang Dan rightly notes in the volume's preface that, "up until now, we have not had one historical document that comprehensively lays bare the June 4 Incident from the angle of literature" ("*Liusi*" iii), it is clear from the anthology's compilation that the genre of poetry alone defies scholarly efforts at comprehensiveness.

In novels and drama too, Tiananmen has been extensively disseminated, as more and more writers across the globe incorporate the events of Beijing spring into their works from 1989 onward. The extent of address ranges widely, though we can extrapolate some patterns of engagement. First, a common marginalization of Tiananmen can be observed in a number of works by notable authors, whether emigrant, overseas-born, or non-Chinese. (On this score, ethnicity and nativity do not seem to dictate aesthetic handling.) Some touch on Tiananmen only tangentially. Japanese American playwright Wakako Yamauchi's *The Chairman's Wife* (1990), for one, teasingly opens in the late afternoon of June 4, 1989, against sounds of fluctuating sirens and a chorus of "distorted, toneless, surreal" voices repeatedly whispering "Tiananmen" (103), but otherwise the play centers on the interior psychic drama of Jiang Qing (Chiang Ching in the text) in her prison hospital cell. Hong Kong Anglophone writer Xu Xi's short story "Manky's Tale," collected in *History's Fiction* (2001), also uses the protest movement as a political backdrop against which to unfold a more micro plot, in this case the intergenerational tension between a dying patriarch and his jazz musician son. And in a sharp departure from *Lili*, Annie Wang's yuppie column-turned-novel *The People's Republic of Desire* (2006) mentions Tiananmen only twice, first as a prefatory aside about the new capitalist China's cultural amnesia, then midway through the book as the enigmatic reason behind the narrator's parents' divorce. In effect, the novel enacts what it thematizes, as national history surfaces as tidbits of domestic drama and background data on personality profiles.

In several other works by Chinese diaspora authors, Tiananmen appears at greater length but nevertheless functions as a thematically minor if structurally seminal episode, either to propel the main plotline forward or to supply narrative closure. One well-known example is the Internet novel *Beijing Story* (*Beijing gushi*), written by an anonymous Chinese graduate student in New York in the late 1990s under the alias Beijing Comrade (Beijing Tongzhi) and the basis of Hong Kong director Stanley Kwan's film *Lan Yu* (2001). In the pivotal ninth chapter, the young hero's near brush with death on the eve of June 4 serves as a turning point in the homosexual romance plot, since it cements the hitherto fickle and self-doubting narrator's love for him. But as one critic points out, although the military crackdown represents the novel's "narrative hub," the young man's death at the end—not from government assault but a random cab accident—suggests a censure less of June 4 itself than of post-Tiananmen China's "economic mobility and capitalist freedoms" (Berry 316, 318). In a similar episodic bracketing of Tiananmen, Ting-xing Ye's *Throwaway Daughter* (2003) contains two middle chapters set in June 1989 in which a Chinese adoptee and her Canadian family watch television footage of the Beijing bloodshed, a traumatic experience that precipitates the nine-year-old protagonist's eventual journey to China in search of her birth parents. For the rest of the novel, however, Tiananmen has little bearing on the protagonist's discoveries about her family history and is barely mentioned again. Alternately, in Alex Kuo's *Chinese Opera* (1998) and Liu Hong's *Startling Moon* (2001), the massacre transpires toward the end of both narratives, as a sudden eruption of destructive force that provokes the characters to private and romantic resolutions, but aside from personal affairs, the incident functions largely to drive the characters out of China and bring the plots to closure. Despite their disparities, all these works share a peculiar peripheralizing of Tiananmen, treating it as evocative backdrop or loose allegory, an ancillary scene or a strategic plot twist, or else a rapid denouement to the dominant storyline. Nonetheless, these works contribute to a growing corpus of global Tiananmen fictions, and they all train world attention on the historical repressiveness of the communist regime by circulating primarily outside the PRC, among mostly non-Sinophone audiences. Even *Beijing Story*, which originally spread via the Chinese Internet, has since the early 2000s been multiply translated by online fans and is now popular among English Internet readers.

On the other hand, a number of fictional works do allot sustained narrative space to Tiananmen, and whether composed by emigrant or overseas-born Chinese or non-Chinese writers, their chief circuit too lies outside the PRC. One prevalent theme concerns cross-cultural relations, with Tiananmen demarcating the possibilities and limits of East-West fellowship. An early example here is *Forbidden City* (1990), by the Canadian young-adult-fiction author William Bell. The novel revolves around the Chinese friendships formed by a teenager from Toronto traveling in Beijing, first with his government monitor and tour guide, then with a female student activist, but both friendships end tragically when the latter two are killed in the massacre and the ensuing clampdown. Strongly embedded in the text is a humanist plea for cross-racial bonds and empathy, for cultivating knowledge of cultural others and identifying with their plight. This message is encapsulated in the conclusion when the protagonist's father, a cameraman for the Canadian Broadcasting Corporation, confesses to having been absorbed merely by the news value of the incident until his own son went missing in the chaos.

The interplay between cross-cultural conflict and understanding, if within racial bounds, also emerges pervasively in Tiananmen works by ethnic Chinese authors in North America. Many of these conjure the events of 1989 Beijing to explore the complex affiliations, sometimes meaningful but often replete with dissonances, between mainland Chinese and Chinese American identities. Alex Kuo's *Chinese Opera* and Ting-xing Ye's *Throwaway Daughter* present good examples, as does C. Y. Lee's *Gate of Rage* (1991): in all three novels, motifs of returning to a native or ancestral land, of seeking cultural roots, or of repairing fractured family histories can be traced, if with vastly different emotional tenors and narrative results. Another noteworthy work in this connection is Elizabeth Wong's *Letters to a Student Revolutionary* (1991). Born in California to immigrant parents, Wong draws on her own exchange of letters with a young woman from the PRC in the years prior to 1989 as the premise for her Tiananmen drama. The play tracks a ten-year correspondence between two women who share "youth, gender, and race" but "widely divergent" notions of freedom (Uno 261), and the action culminates in the abrupt severance of their relationship after the June 4 crackdown, projected onto the stage via a rapid slide show. In the epilogue, however, China and America overlap in a common forgetting of the massacre, as the former launches into its "policy of selective historical amnesia" and the latter reverts to its "shopping and the concerns of everyday living" (308). Cultural and national disparities collapse in a general failure of memory. The PRC and the United States converge as well in Terrence Cheng's *Sons of Heaven* (2002). Born in Taipei and raised in New York, Cheng too imports into 1989 Beijing an American presence and plays on the two cultures' possible congruencies via two estranged brothers, one a graduate of Cornell University who joins in the student demonstrations, the other a People's Liberation Army (PLA) soldier who is ordered to suppress the protest movement. Supplementing their perspectives is a third, that of Deng Xiaoping, whose suffering during the Cultural Revolution is recounted with psychological density through a series of flashbacks. By the novel's end, the returnee dissident transfigures into the heroic Tank Man, the soldier, too, turns rebel and manages to reunite with his younger brother, and the penultimate image of the older sibling resting his head on the younger's lap becomes superimposed onto Deng's final memory of his crippled son on his own lap. With these and other mirroring details, Cheng insinuates that, ultimately, all three men are victims of state persecution, in the long history of the communist wounding of Chinese masculinity, even as their fundamental humanity shines through. In all these works, Tiananmen affords diasporic writers an opportunity to meditate on cultural inheritance and difference, framed within the push-pull of identity and the possibility of national-cultural transcendence.

Yet Tiananmen also lends itself to some ironic diasporic visions of China, several of which exhibit special skepticism toward the hyperbolic claims of Chinese masculinity. "Manky's Tale," for instance, can be read as Xu Xi's subtle commentary on postcolonial Hong Kong's uneasy filiations with the Chinese fatherland and its politics, where the pro-democracy students' vehement revolt against the communist leaders doubles as an incongruous analogue to the protagonist's repressed aggression toward his dying father. In counterpoint to the mainland students who lay authoritative claim to the nation's future, the indecisive protagonist and his enfeebled father both seem to suffer from a deficit of masculine and patriotic self-assurance, in the setting of a colony transitioning between empires. With more sardonic sting, the short story "Plain Moon" ("Su Yue") (1991), by Taiwan emigrant and New York–based writer Gu Zhaosen, showcases the personal duplicity and domestic betrayal that can hide behind the lofty public rhetoric of democracy and nationalism. The tale focalizes through its eponymous heroine, a love-starved immigrant from Hong Kong and a low-wage worker in a garment factory in New York City who naively idolizes an international student activist from China and offers to secure permanent residency status for him in the United States via marriage, only to learn soon after that he has all along carried on a romantic liaison with his fiancée from Shanghai. In a particularly wry detail, Gu has the unfaithful husband use a Wuer Kaixi lecture as cover for a secret tryst, suggestively rendering Plain Moon, in one critic's apt phrase, "a belated victim of the [Tiananmen] Incident" (D. D. Wang, "Chinese" 256). Treachery recurs in Diane Wei Liang's more sensationalist detective novel *Paper Butterfly* (2008), in which an embittered former student protestor, after being betrayed to the authorities by his best friend in 1989 and then jailed for eight years in a reform labor camp, devolves into a child-kidnapper and near-murderer who accidentally kills his ex-girlfriend in his quest for vengeance. Liang's figure of the male activist turned hatred-filled and revenge-obsessed criminal, someone who brings pain and death to innocent women around him, constitutes an exceptionally banalizing and debased portrait of the Tiananmen student in literature.

More typical is the delicate satire of Gu's story, or else, on the part of feminist writers, a more incisive critique of Chinese cultural misogyny. These texts can be read in opposition to the conventional iconography of Beijing spring and the student movement, which, as scholars have pointed out, often couples revolution with romance (D. D. Wang, "Chinese" 256; Berry 307–8). For example, one work that liberally borrows the trope of romantic love is An Tian's *Tiananmen qingren* (Tiananmen lover) (2004), by a former student activist now residing in Vancouver: the novel follows a sensitive young man from his participation in the Beijing protests to his exilic life in Canada and eventual career as a medical doctor there, but through it all, he remains inescapably haunted by, and emotionally loyal to, the woman he had been secretly infatuated with in 1989 but who had been crushed by a tank outside the Square on June 4. Against this sentimental tale of undying love in the face of horrific death, Gu's story can be read as a gentle "parody" (D. D. Wang, "Chinese" 256), but several women writers' stress on female sexuality and patriarchal power takes on a harder edge. I will discuss the gendered dimension of Tiananmen at greater length in chapter 3 with Annie Wang's *Lili*, but this novel has an important precursor in Hong Ying's *Summer of Betrayal* (*Beipan zhi xia*) (1992). Herself a renowned exemplar of the post-Tiananmen literary diaspora, Hong Ying is innovative for locating June 4 at the beginning rather than the conclusion of her narrative. In the initial chapter, the protagonist flees the slaughter in the Square only to find, upon her arrival at her boyfriend's apartment, that he has cheated on her with his supposedly estranged wife. This dual moment of political and sexual betrayal triggers a tortuous search for identity, and to some measure the protagonist finds both self-expression and liberation through poetry and sex. In the penultimate scene of an orgy with her bohemian friends, she declares triumphantly that she has become "the art of sex, its lyrics," her naked body "as pure and unblemished from top to bottom as her eyes" (176), but the finale renders this triumph ambiguous. As the police show up to break up the party and everyone hurriedly dresses, the protagonist alone remains defiantly bare, challenging the officers with her nudity, but in the same instant, her friends implicitly abandon her when they otherize her as an epileptic madwoman and then stand passively by as she alone gets arrested for "indecent behavior" under martial law (181). We might read this scene as Hong Ying's feminist revision of the Tank Man tableau, with its highly phallic imagery. The subject of criminalized female sexuality will be taken up again by Wang's *Lili*, but resituated in a more contemporary framework of China's globalization. Carrying forward her predecessor's feminist critique, Wang will locate the Asian female body in relation to not just communist state power and Chinese cultural misogyny but also Western neo-orientalism and transnational capital. For now, we can say that the works summarized above all summon Tiananmen to accentuate the heterogeneity of Chinese identities, particularly along the axis of gender.

So, while the canon of Tiananmen fictions cannot be said to be voluminous, it is certainly thriving and becoming ever more sizable and diffuse. Ultimately, though, these other works lack features paramount for my study. First and foremost, the four texts here strike me as conducting the most substantive and trenchant inquiry into the power-politics relation that lies at the heart of 1989's events. They may enfold themes raised by other works, but they do so by unequivocally linking their narratives to Tiananmen, reviving this history to grapple with or distill fundamental issues of state power and the politics of confrontation. In addition to this concerted engagement, they facilitate an examination into Tiananmen's evolving applicability to the post-1989 world at large. Finally, I zero in on these writers—rather than those born or long established abroad—because they allow me to isolate with greater empirical concreteness the sociohistorical phenomenon I call the post-Tiananmen literary diaspora. Insofar as all four share a comparable trajectory of leaving China or becoming diasporic as a result of June 4, they cast into acute relief the dynamic transactions between texts and contexts, home and diaspora.

On this last point, it merits emphasizing that the distinction between homeland and diaspora is not an absolute one. While my book focuses on diasporic perspectives, Tiananmen is by no means the exclusive concern of diaspora authors alone. Although the topic is censored by the PRC government, many writers within the country do wrestle with giving it literary embodiment. These efforts, however, necessitate disguise, circuity, subterfuge. Instead of blatant references to the protest movement and the massacre such as those omnipresent in the Tiananmen works penned abroad, we find in mainland fictions a host of evasive maneuvers and layers of camouflage. Even the boldest writers will be cautious to cloak any allusion to June 4, making it plain enough to cue the searching eye but veiled enough to deflect political scrutiny.

The best-known example here is veteran novelist Mo Yan's *The Republic of Wine* (*Jiuguo*) (1992), which uses the trope of cannibalism to unleash a biting satire against cultural gourmandise and official corruption. The book's connection to Tiananmen is oft-noted: Mo Yan started writing it only three months after the crackdown, but it could not be published on the mainland until three years later, after the Taiwanese edition appeared in print (Goldblatt v). So, although no scenes of student protests or mass killings occur in the novel, its central preoccupation with Chinese civilizational gluttony, Party venality, and the contemporary writer's crisis of authorial identity can all be interpreted through the lens of Tiananmen, as a "piercing" look into the "quotidian decay of social and individual life" that underpinned the calamity of June 4 (Yang, "*Republic*" 7). In chapter 4, I will elaborate on the literary uses of cannibalism as a political metaphor, especially for the communist state's vicious devouring of its own people, in relation to Ma Jian's *Beijing Coma*; certainly, Ma owes Mo Yan a literary debt for the Tiananmen resonance of this motif. For the latter, though, Tiananmen can only be hinted at, and one evocative marker of it may be the cryptic character of the protagonist's son. Of this character we know almost nothing except that he is, significantly, a student—and a student whose attitude toward his Party-lackey father is unapologetically sullen, rebellious, and antagonizing. In the multilayered web of the novel, the figure of the boy does not simply belong to an endangered species within a cannibalistic society but represents in addition a recurrent source of mockery and threat to paternal authority. Through this figure, Mo Yan may well be locating his own ambivalent and compromised paternity vis-à-vis the younger Tiananmen generation.

Also written shortly after June 4 was Wang Shuo's *Please Don't Call Me Human* (*Qianwan bie ba wo dang ren*), originally serialized in a Nanjing literary journal from August to December of 1989, in the thick of the literary bans and cultural purge that descended on liberal writers (Barmé, *In the Red* 21). Opinions differ over why the novel succeeded in circumventing the censors: some speculate about the perpetual "stupidity" of napping officials, while others hypothesize that Wang's reputation, and deliberately crafted self-image, as a profit-seeking author of popular hooligan fiction gave him some immunity from watchdogs targeting more "serious" writers (Barmé, *In the Red* 95). Regardless, the novel is universally recognized as a caustic lampoon, satirizing everything from China's governmental bureaucracy and state security system to Chinese jingoism and masculine heroics. The protagonist, initially a Beijing pedicab driver with a fantastic lineage in the Boxer Rebellion and the apocryphal heir to its martial arts tradition, gets recruited to serve as China's sports hero in the next international Sapporo Games (a thin disguise for the Olympics). In the process of his training, and in the name of redeeming China's national pride and the yellow man's dignity from Western imperialism, he is not only brainwashed and commodified but also feminized and eventually castrated. In a final feat televised across the world, he smilingly and victoriously cuts away his own face, "a human mask," to reveal a "hideous, bloody mess" beneath (287). This grotesque parable of the emasculation, disfiguration, and dehumanization of the ordinary man has moments that provocatively if obliquely gesture toward Tiananmen. In one scene, for instance, in a rather brazen allusion to the Tank Man, the protagonist stands in front of a "column of enemy tanks" as they "rumbled toward him at a snail's pace, forming a wall of steel directly ahead, like a firing squad in front of a condemned man" (170). This historical mis-en-scène quickly dissolves, however, first into a cartoonish video-game-like battle sequence, then a media circus with screaming adolescent fans mobbing the hero, and lastly a police raid in which, in another telltale detail, "the masses in the square hit the ground like toppled grain stalks" (179). In Wang Shuo's irreverent and dystopic world, even a popular uprising against social injustice and political oppression crumbles into farce, and the novel ends with a vision of a hyperreal China and a post-apocalyptic Beijing as a desert city with "not a sign of humanity" (288).

Yet another intriguing work in this context is Zhu Wen's novella *Didi de yanzou* (Little brother's performance) (1996). Part of the "New Generation" of writers who began publishing after 1989, Zhu shot to literary acclaim inside the country with *I Love Dollars* (*Wo ai meiyuan*) (1994), a portrait of 1990s capitalist China that immerses itself with gusto in the milieu's seedily sex-obsessed and unabashedly cynical, if also self-consciously hollow, zeitgeist. This debut work may seem to give credence to an oft-remarked-on trend in post-Tiananmen mainland literature in which writers settle into tacit cooperation with the government by trading creative freedom for political silence. But as one critic argues, Zhu Wen's "unremittingly negative vision of China today and, by logical extension, of the political architects of this society" stands as a scathing criticism of "the political status quo" that is "ubiquitously implicit" (Lovell, Translator's 239). Likewise with *Didi de yanzou*, though in this later piece, implicitness takes the form of an event substitution. Despite the title's raunchy pun and the plot's surface focus on the "spermatic journey" of its cast of "sex-questing males," the story can be read as one of the most ingenious fictions on Tiananmen—in the words of the same critic, "a serious novella masquerading as a scurrilous burlesque" (Lovell, "Filthy"). As the author himself claims in interview, "I wanted to write about 4 June, about the atmosphere surrounding the demonstrations, but I couldn't," so he ends up writing about a radically different student protest movement: the 1988 anti-African demonstrations by university students in Nanjing. By diverting the historical setting from 1989 Beijing spring to this much-eclipsed earlier episode, Zhu also dramatically revises the image of the student protestors from political idealists and noble martyrs to libido-driven, hysteria-prone, and casually racist undergraduates. Tiananmen thereby degenerates from a political performance into what he impishly calls "adolescent carnivalesque," and the 1980s period of upheaval concludes for him with neither a bang nor a whimper but a "premature ejaculation" (qtd. in Lovell, "Filthy").

One other instructive example, fortuitously published in the same year as Zhu's novella but offering a much more somber approach to Tiananmen, is Beijing-based avant-garde writer Chen Ran's semi-autobiographical *A Private Life* (*Siren shenghuo*) (1996). In this intensely introspective novel, the narrator recalls, among the vicissitudes of her college years, falling passionately in love with a fellow student poet who became involved in the pro-democracy movement, then living through the difficult time after their aborted romance when he was forced into exile, and most tellingly, herself being hit by a stray bullet in the left calf one day that early summer. Contrary to the frequent and overt references to Tiananmen in the English translation, however, the Chinese original never names Tiananmen Square, June 4, or even Beijing (Schaffer and Song, "Narrative" 162). Instead, it repeatedly makes vague but charged reference to "the square," "the significant incident," and "that tragic period," and crucially, the whole narrative is structured as one of trauma (Schaffer and Song, "Writing" 6). Due to these elusive maneuvers, Chen's book has never gone out of print on the mainland and was even reissued in a new illustrated edition by a Beijing publisher in 2004 (Schaffer and Song, "Writing" 3–4).

Without a doubt, then, there exists a body of fictions within the PRC that attempt to write Tiananmen, whether earnestly, derisively, or traumatically, via metaphor or metonymy, catachresis or ellipses. These works are well worth probing in full, but they require a different set of identificatory procedures and interpretive skills, and ultimately, a separate conceptual argument than the one advanced in this study. To my mind, that other project must above all theorize a hermeneutics of evasion, one that provides a critical framework for not just the array of aesthetic tactics adopted by PRC writers but also these tactics' specific deployment in relation to shifting political exigencies. So, while there is obvious and significant continuity between mainland and diaspora in terms of authorial commitment to and political appraisal of Tiananmen's history, the two sites and their respective fictions seem to occupy polar ends on the spectrum of formal strategies. Where the latter *in-vade*, the former *e-vade*: as diasporic texts strive to access the 1989 Square by lapsing their distance from it, mainland ones evoke the same imagined space-time by skirting along its contours. Both lie "outside" the symbolic Square in this sense, and their mutual outside-ness can be understood as a structural relation to absolute state power, defined by a sliding scale of proximity, rather than any firm opposition of belief or desire.

Similar observations can be made about the fields of visual culture. On-screen, for example, Tiananmen crops up in films by mainland directors as well as those by diasporic ones, though in the case of Hong Kong cinema, the aesthetic of circuity appears with noticeable prevalence post-1997. The aforementioned *Lan Yu* by Stanley Kwan, for instance, departs from Bei-jing Comrade's original text by never directly mentioning the June 4 kill-ings, evoking them instead in one brief eerie scene of a flurry of bicyclists rushing by the distraught protagonist in a dark alleyway. Nonetheless, the "immediate legibility of this shorthand," along with the movie's explicit treatment of homosexuality, contributes to its ban on the mainland, where even black-market copies of its DVD have the Tiananmen scene expunged (Andrew Chan). By contrast, Sixth Generation filmmaker Lou Ye's *Sum-mer Palace* (*Yiheyuan*) (2006) includes extensive sequences as well as actual news footage on the massacre. Daringly marketing itself in international venues as the first mainland production to depict June 4, the movie was briskly banned by the PRC authorities and Lou Ye himself barred from filmmaking for five years.[6]

Despite this climate of prohibition and punishment, many mainland artists continue to commemorate Tiananmen through a range of means and styles. In the vibrant realm of visual arts, one well-known example is Yue Minjun's *Execution* (1995), which made worldwide headlines in 2007 when it auctioned for nearly $6 million and became the most expensive piece of contemporary Chinese art up until that point. Inspired by June 4, the painting hybridizes Francisco Goya's *The Third of May 1808* and Edouard Manet's *The Execution of Maximilian* to summon up parallel scenes of political violence, but in the artist's signature style of "cynical realism," the row of doomed men now stand against a red wall in their underpants, identical exaggerated smiles frozen on their faces. The color red also features prominently in the works of Sheng Qi, the artist notori-ous for having cut off his own little finger and buried it in a flowerpot as a personal act of defiance in 1989. Since returning to China after living abroad for nearly a decade, he has continued to paint quietly sinister por-traits of Beijing and Tiananmen Square. In works such as *Parade* (2007), *Red floor or clean square* (2008), and *Under the shadow* (2009), the Square is a site perpetually overcast with storm clouds and streaked with rain, and invariably awash in ominous swaths of grey and crimson.[7] Other artists resort to more experimental or ephemeral modes such as performance, combining it with photography to at once reenact and retain memories of 1989. The Tianjin-based artist Mo Yi, for example, staged a performance in Tiananmen Square on the tenth anniversary of June 4 by shaving his hair, eyebrows, and beard. He then took two photographs of himself but dated them 89-6-4, with the second one bordered in blood-red and his self-image cut in half (Wu Hung 220–21). Another poignant performance is Song Dong's *Breathing* (1996), also enacted in Tiananmen Square but on a subzero winter night, with the artist lying inert on the ground for forty minutes, breathing into one spot on the pavement and forming a thin sheet of ice there that vanished by morning. The disappearance of this trace of his breath conjures the government cover-up of the massacre while the accompanying photograph, taken by Song Dong's wife, recalls the living moment of the 1989 protests (Wu Hung 228–29).

In recent years, the Internet has come to endow Tiananmen with yet another mode of artistic remembrance and representational afterlife, as more and more artists within the PRC learn to take advantage of this technology. H. N. (Hsiang-ning) Han, a China-born and Taiwan-educated artist who worked in New York City for more than three decades before repatriating to the mainland in 2000, had painted an acrylic series on June 3–4 in 1989.[8] On Han's current Chinese weblog, while he is careful to omit his Tiananmen series and to avoid labeling any piece of art as Tiananmen-related, hints to the episode are surprisingly abundant and obvious. In 2008, for instance, in the days surrounding June 4, he uploaded a series of black-and-white sketches, magnified close-ups of his own drawings, under such innocuous subject lines as "a little bit of caring" (*yidian yidian de guanhuai*), "a little bit of pain" (*yidian yidian de chuangtong*), "a little bit of history" (*yidian yidian de lishi*), and last, "incident" (*shijian*). As the days progressed, the sketches he posted, at first blurry and context-generic, became increasingly identifiable as iconic images of Tiananmen—headbanded young men gathering atop vehicles, crowds raising fists and hands waving victory signs in the air, speeding bicycles and prostrate bodies, all against the silhouette of the Forbidden City. With even greater boldness two years later in 2010, in a blog entry called "old photographs and sketchbook" (*lao zhaopian huagao*) posted just one second before June 4—at 2010–06–03 23:59:59—Han revisited the Tiananmen theme by intercutting his own drawings with unmistakable photographic stills of the Beijing movement. Prefacing these visuals is a thinly veiled parable of punished children pleading to their mother to redress their grievance, to say to them now as the whole world watches, "Children! You've done no wrong!" ("Lao").

Finally, one other figure is of central importance for the development of Tiananmen art: the PLA soldier–turned-artist Chen Guang. A seventeen-year-old new recruit in 1989 when he served in the unit that was ordered to evacuate the Square, Chen left the army soon after, eventually enrolling in Beijing's Central Academy of Fine Arts to study oil painting. By the late 1990s, he had earned a reputation for his sexually explicit performance art and photographic self-portraits, but it was not until the past few years, almost two decades after the massacre, that he was able to reclaim Tiananmen as an aesthetic subject, with oil and canvas again his medium. Retrieving photographs he himself took for the army during the Square's clearing and cleanup, Chen brought to Tiananmen art—and June 4's historical memory—the unprecedented perspective of the former PLA soldier. His Tiananmen series comprises twenty-four works divided into eight themes: "Soldier," "Breakage," "Site," "Souvenir," "Remains," "Secrets," "Exploration," and "Wind" (Shu). To my mind, the most haunting pieces are those that combine a chilling photorealism with touches of expressionism. In the foreground, piles of paper and cloth drape over vaguely humanoid shapes as uniformed soldiers mill about and rifle through the debris; in the background, columns of smoke rise from the still-burning square. In the two pieces entitled *Breakage* (*Duan*), a group of soldiers look on, curious but nonchalant, as the toppled statue of the Goddess of Democracy is replaced by the larger-than-life body of a young man, presumably that of the artist, severed at the torso and sprawling across a square's broken beams. For Chen now, art is essentially ethical and human, and when he speaks of Tiananmen, his vista is planetary, species-embracing: "Art is not only about art, and artists need to work in the level of social morals. We often go to extremes when we talk about the incident in 1989 nowadays. We need to look at it in a more humane perspective. A lot of things, both domestic and international, happened during that period of time. Like the pull-down of the Berlin Wall, the collapse of the Soviet Union, the death of Ceausescu in Romania, and also the 1989 incident and the short-lived Modern Art Exhibition. When you consider the citizens, the students and the soldiers as a whole in the incident, you will understand how the individuals, the country and the power ruined their prospects in the waves of history" ("Interview"). At the same time, Tiananmen remains deeply personal for him. When asked by Ma Jian in 2009 why he decided to resurrect the past after all this time, Chen replied: "It's the 20th anniversary this year. I think it's about time. Anyway, I can't hold these nightmares inside me any longer" (qtd. in Ma J., "Great"). Along with this artistic output comes a new vocalness, to Chinese as much as Western audiences. As Chen comments in various interviews with foreign reporters: "For 20 years I tried to bury this episode, but the older you get the more these things float to the surface. I think it's time for my experiences, my truth, to be shared with the rest of the world" (qtd. in Jacobs). Elsewhere, he insists with particular urgency on the need for historical acknowledgment and personal integrity now, in the period of China's economic growth: "I'm still in touch with about a dozen [men] from my old military unit. None meditates about the past the way I do. Some are policemen today, or officials. They've got good jobs, and they owe that to what happened back in '89" (qtd. in Harmsen). Yet the path to speech and recognition remains ridden with danger. Three days after Chen mounted his Tiananmen paintings in the online exhibition *Impulsion to Extremeness* (*Dui jiduan de chongdong*) (2008), the website was shut down by the communist censors. As of now, his work travels mainly via the overseas Internet.

Tiananmen's Languages

One last but crucial facet of this story involves language use. Just as the geographical site of Tiananmen's cultural production has been dispersed across the globe, so its linguistic medium has been dislodged from Chinese into a multiplicity of languages. I concentrate on the interlingual exchanges between Chinese and English writings of Tiananmen because these are the languages I work with, and because of the dominance of English in the current international publishing industry.[9] One direct if unexpected repercussion of the PRC's ban on June 4 is that English has emerged as a major linguistic platform for the global discourse on Tiananmen in almost all genres. This is not a self-important proclamation about the necessity or privileged status of English as *the* language of Tiananmen; any such claim would rightly meet with quick skepticism. Rather, it is an observation about English's visibility as the linguistic route through which much Tiananmen writing passes or gets materialized in the post-1989 world. Of course, a copious amount has been written on the subject in Chinese itself, some even within the PRC despite the censorship there, as noted above. Yet the Tiananmen content of these works can attain full public scope and lifespan only outside of the mainland, many through translation—for better and for worse. To be sure, translation entails negotiation between not just words and meanings but also unequal power relations embedded within languages and cultures, so that even as a locally prohibited topic such as June 4 is brought into the open via an English translation, there can be a simultaneous "loss of ambiguity, difference and incommensurability," and even a pigeonholing of a writer's specific vision into the "universalizing pressures of western modernity" (Schaffer and Song, "Writing" 17–18). English hence operates as a key if also double-edged diasporic language of Tiananmen.

The famous case of *The Tiananmen Papers* starkly illustrates this phenomenon. As a compilation of hundreds of secret and internal documents shedding light on the decision-making processes of top CCP leaders in that fateful spring—documents supposedly smuggled out of the country by a midlevel cadre and then leaked to Columbia University political scientist Andrew Nathan—this massive volume was first published in English in January 2001, with the even more colossal Chinese edition following only several months later in April. Thus, the English translation of some of the most close-up and edifying primary records of Tiananmen preceded their originals in public appearance. According to Nathan, the book's contents were widely discussed and excerpted in the intervening months by Chinese Internet users in the PRC, who "back-translated" from English into Chinese based on the American edition ("Preface" xviii). Furthermore, as another index of this inversion of linguistic chronology, since the Chinese publisher came second to the Western one, successive foreign translations of the volume have been prepared, not on the Chinese text, but on the English-language one (Nathan, "Introduction" xli). However, partly due to this linguistic detour, the authenticity of the documents has since been called into question by not just PRC authorities but also some China scholars in the West (Baum 130–32; Alfred Chan 190–205), resulting in yet another international controversy on Tiananmen that remains unsettled. Regardless of the collection's authenticity, though, we cannot deny the tremendously far-reaching and defining power of English in the global circulation of Tiananmen discourse, in this case occurring a dozen years after June 4.

This commotion surrounding *The Tiananmen Papers* is by now a familiar tale, so let me offer a more literary example: Liao Yiwu's long poem "Datusha" (Massacre). Composed in the dawn hours of June 4 in Liao's home province of Sichuan, the poem is akin to a frenzied outcry, alternating between fragmented images of butchery and fierce exclamations of outrage. Its publication history is a revealing case of the priority of translation and the importance of English for Tiananmen literature. Knowing that it would not see print within mainland China anytime soon, Liao made an audiotape of his oral recitation of the poem, complete with "ritualistic chanting and howling to invoke the spirit of the dead," and then distributed the tape "via underground channels" (W. Huang ix). Partly due to this tape, Liao was arrested in 1990 and jailed for four years (Jiang 78; W. Huang x). While the poem remains unpublished in the PRC to this day (though it continues to spread in Taiwan and Hong Kong as well as the Chinese Internet), it has long ago been smuggled out of the country by Liao's friends. Its first print publication was in English translation, anonymous and retitled "The Howl" in the 1992 anthology *New Ghosts, Old Dreams*. So, what is by now one of the most celebrated Chinese-language poems on Tiananmen in fact first appeared in print via a linguistic detour into English, under a name that does not back-translate.

Alongside the theoretical arc outlined above, then, my book also contains a linguistic arc. Superficially, my ordering of texts may seem to have two Chinese-language works (*Taowang, Beijing Coma*) neatly bookend two English-language ones (*The Crazed, Lili*). Over this static concentric design, however, lies a turning spiral, or more aptly, a series of rotating squares. In the first chapter, I work with the original Chinese text of Gao Xingjian's play because this was its most widely distributed version even years after his Nobel award.[10] By the early 2000s, though, both Ha Jin and Annie Wang were writing in English, so that Englishness became no longer a derivative or auxiliary feature of Tiananmen fictions but an original language of their composition, even among emigrant authors whose first language was Chinese. Finally, near the end of this millennial decade, we observe the latest twist in Tiananmen's interlingual afterlife with Ma Jian's novel. As I will discuss in my conclusion, Ma wrote his magnum opus in Chinese and first conceived of it under the title *Routu*, literally "flesh earth" or "meat soil," evoking a host of visceral biopolitical images. The English translation, done by Ma's partner, Flora Drew, was released as *Beijing Coma* in mid-2008. The Chinese original, however, had to wait over a year to appear in print, in a reversal of publication chronology similar to that of *The Tiananmen Papers* and "Datusha." What's more, Ma's original title may be destined for the literary critic's footnote, for the press that now publishes the Chinese edition has elected to market the novel under the back-translated title of *Beijing zhiwuren*—literally a "Beijing comatose person"—and Chinese reviewers almost unanimously refer to the work by this name. So, ironically, even as Ma tries to restore the centrality of the Chinese students in his narrative of the Square, the milieu in which he writes behooves him to execute this restoration first and foremost in translation, in English. In our current phase of globalization, the works of the Chinese literary diaspora have become deeply intertwined with the modes and languages of commercial production in the West, leading to disjunctures and reversals like those we behold with *Routu/Beijing Coma/Beijing zhiwuren*. It awaits to be seen how the PRC's ascension as a global power today will impact this diaspora's future. What seems undeniable is that diasporic literature now reaches beyond the spheres circumscribed by the Sinoscript and the Sinophone (S. Kong, "Diaspora" 546; Shih 28–37), in a latter-day variation of the types of transnational and translational Chinese cosmopolitanism once seen in semicolonial Shanghai's Anglophone print culture that likewise had their "afterlife" through migration (Shen 135–60).

By way of a conclusion, let me describe my own modest route to this project. Like Annie Wang, I belong to the post-Tiananmen generation, in the sense that I am several years younger than those college students in the Square in 1989. But unlike her, I am not a Beijing native who was well-placed by history to be so near the scene of history's unfolding. And unlike Gao, Jin, and Ma, I was neither old enough to appreciate the symbolism and momentousness of the protest movement nor invested enough in the Chinese nation to feel the raw emotional tug of those television images of throngs and tanks. In my own ten years' dwelling with this project, I have come to share some of these writers' emotions and identifications, even if intellectualized, and if much belated. But in June 1989, Tiananmen was remote. It was a word with little resonance for a teenager from Hong Kong in Miami who felt out of tune with Chineseness as much as world politics, and who was prone to find refuge as much as escapism in reading novels. Fiction brought my attention back, after long lapse, to the Square. Even then, it took me five years to realize that the texts I was drawn to somehow converged, as if by accident, at this point, and five years more to see the shape of this imaginary rendezvous and sort out my sense of it. In its way, this book bears homage too to the de-alienating capacity of literature and the circuitous path of some diasporic arrivals.

1 / The Existentialist Square: Gao Xingjian's *Taowang*

Of the four writers in this book, Gao Xingjian is not only the oldest and the longest established but also the one with the most complicated reception history. Born in 1940, he is the only author here to have grown up in pre-communist China, in an environment where his early interests in Western literature, art, and music were safely encouraged. This childhood knowledge of an alternative sociopolitical reality perhaps made more acute his later experiences during the Cultural Revolution, when he, in a notorious gesture, burned a suitcase full of manuscripts to avoid persecution, and yet could not resist continuing to compose in secret in a reeducation camp for years afterward. Much of this biographical history would be literary lore to only a handful of scholars were it not for the 2000 Nobel Prize in Literature. In its landmark one-hundredth anniversary year, the Prize was awarded to Gao, propelling him into international fame. At the same time, it spawned mythologies of his life and work that shed light, above all, on the cultural-political dynamics of the post-1989 world. The millennial Nobel and its attendant cultural politics will therefore serve as my study's first nodal point for the post-Tiananmen literary diaspora's global significance. From this discussion of contexts I will tunnel backward, first to Gao's own essays from the 1990s in which he lays out his aesthetic philosophy, then to his 1989 Tiananmen play *Taowang*, with its dual portraits of state power and gendered violence. As I will argue through the arc of this chapter, what has been crucially obscured in the post-Nobel discourse on Gao is Tiananmen's cardinal role in shaping his theories of writerly individualism and existential flight—and this political relation must be retrieved if we are to counteract his conceptual erasure of totalitarianism and a possible world amnesia about the massacre and its implications for human responsibility.

Part I. The Prize and the Polis

NOBEL POLITICS

In 2001, the French journalist Jean-Luc Douin conducted an interview with Gao Xingjian, the newly crowned 2000 Nobel Laureate in Literature, the transcription of which was then published in *Label France*, a news magazine distributed officially by the French Ministry of Foreign Affairs. The preface to this interview, after naming Gao as the first Chinese writer to be awarded the Literature Prize, goes on to introduce him thus: "A victim of the Cultural Revolution in China, this dissident of the Tiananmen generation, a political refugee in France since 1988, became a naturalized French citizen in 1998" (Gao, "Literature"). Conspicuously, this biographical blurb constructs Gao's writerly persona from a primarily political perspective, and the signposts it establishes prepare the reader for an excursion into, not one writer's aesthetics, but one citizen's complex struggles with national politics. This deft interweaving of personal and national history divides Gao's life into three phases: first, that of "victim," implying involuntary subjection to and unjust suffering at the hands of state power; then, that of "dissident," indicating active resistance to a tyrannical government; and finally, that of "refugee," signaling failed resistance and forced flight from the homeland.

That Gao, like thousands of others, in fact fell victim to events of the Cultural Revolution is not to be denied. His second novel, *One Man's Bible*, a semi-autobiographical account of his Cultural Revolution experiences, amply testifies to this. What is debatable, though, is the description of him as a "dissident of the Tiananmen generation." The implication of this phrase is ambiguous on several counts. For one, Tiananmen has symbolically spawned multiple generations in twentieth-century Chinese history, from the May Fourth movement of 1919 and the lesser-known March Eighteenth Incident of 1926 to the April Fifth movement of 1976 and, most recently, the pro-democracy movement of 1989. The historical referent here is most likely the last. Yet Gao, who was already forty-nine years old by that time, can be considered "of this generation" only if one expands the category to include not solely the student protesters at Tiananmen Square but any participant in one of the numerous demonstrations around China that spring, whether in Beijing or elsewhere. Along this expanded interpretation, we can also note that the biography withholds two significant points: first, that Gao's final departure from the PRC in 1987 predates the

1989 Tiananmen protests by almost two years, and second, that this departure was precipitated not by any immediate danger to his person but by an invitation from the Morat Institute for him to lecture in Germany, whence he went on to settle in France (Yip 320). Although Gao had indeed been the target of several publication and performance bans inside China up until this point, most notably during the 1983 anti–spiritual pollution campaign (Yan xvi–xviii), his decision to leave the country was entirely voluntary, made out of consideration for the future of his writings. The by now widely publicized detail that he was declared a persona non grata by the PRC government did not occur until more than a year after his relocation to Paris. Opposed to this actual chronology, the interview profile misleadingly reconstructs a much more engagé narrative. By inverting the sequence of the politically charged signifiers "Tiananmen" and "refugee," it imparts the impression of Gao *fleeing* China in the wake of the massacre *as a result of* personal involvement with the democracy movement.

I begin with this scrutiny of a rather minor cultural document not to quibble with the news media, and not simply for the sake of historical accuracy. What requires investigation here is the larger issue of an international cultural politics that goes into the manufacturing of Gao's literary identity via his political one. In particular, we encounter in this episode of fame-making a process by which the identity marker "dissident" comes to intimate concrete ideological content, namely, that of pro-democracy activism. The problem is twofold. First, the word "dissident," when used by the West in reference to PRC contexts, has become a label ascribed very loosely to anyone from the mainland with some misgivings about the communist regime, regardless of his or her degree of political involvement or the substance of his or her arguments. The implicit assumption is that mere disagreement with the Chinese Communist Party (CCP) line constitutes sufficient criterion for dissident status, and the stripe of dissidence in individual cases is oftentimes not specified or taken to need specification. This discursive vagueness has two further repercussions. On the one hand, it promotes a reductive and binary image of the Chinese population as comprising either complacent communists or dissatisfied dissidents. On the other, it conflates the actual views and conduct of a diverse group of people, facilitating a conceptual slide whereby the range and compass of political dissent is contracted into a distinctly liberal-friendly brand of anticommunist, pro-democracy activism. In this framework, dissidence is typically followed by failed resistance and culminates in flight and exile. This narrative arc affirms at once the heroic efforts of the dissident (who tries but fails against overwhelming odds), the despotism of the communist state (which shows itself incapable once again of addressing grievances from within), and the benevolence of the West (which demonstrates its moral and political superiority by welcoming the forlorn exiles with open arms). The motif of distress-and-rescue no longer surreptitiously brackets but actively misattributes political positions to many on the dissent spectrum, effectively effacing difference in the name of dissidence.

Such, however, is also the most common narrative told of Gao Xingjian by the Western media. Indeed, in the past decade, Gao has come to fulfill the myth of heroic dissidence for the world like no other Chinese intellectual (until the emergence of Liu Xiaobo in 2010, as I will discuss in the next chapter), despite his own repeated rejection of the dissident label. The casting of Gao as *écrivain engagé*, so innocuously embedded into one interview's preface, is actually symptomatic of a much wider trend in international reportage on him. Especially on the heels of the Nobel announcement in October 2000—the press release of which reverentially described Gao's work as the site where "literature is born anew from the struggle of the individual to survive the history of the masses" (Swedish)—Western journalists, duly taking their cue, overnight turned him into a cultural celebrity and global icon. Their language was strikingly dominated by terms of dissidence and exile, and they invariably played up dramatic accounts of his trials, tribulations, and ultimate endurance within communist China.[1] By March 2001, the BBC would outright pronounce him "one of China's best known dissidents" (Chen L.). Tellingly, these news reports never said of Gao that he was a member of China's democracy movement or that he personally took part in the 1989 Beijing protests. They signified not by explicit misinformation but by tacit insinuation and selective reportage or nonreportage. The interpretive possibilities they created, both individually and collectively, oscillated between a valorization of dissidence in general and a more distinct suggestion of Gao's politics as kindred to Western liberal ideals.

This ideologically freighted reception may point to the dual political classifications of "dissidence" and "exile" as the primary cultural capital by which Gao captured his newfound international fame. Indeed, this was the very charge advanced by the PRC government—that politics, not art, was the main impetus behind the Nobel committee's decision. After the Nobel announcement, CCP officials were quick to denounce the Prize as politically motivated, and a leading spokesperson from the Chinese Writers' Association was prompted to give a public statement condemning the award as an illegitimate tool being used for political purposes ("Zhongguozuo"). The *People's Daily*, the official state newspaper, also ran a special report entitled "Nobel Literature Prize is Not Without Political Flavor." Overturning the Swedish Academy's praise of Gao for his "oeuvre of universal validity, bitter insights, and linguistic ingenuity, which has opened new paths for the Chinese novel and drama," the article asserted instead that, purely on artistic grounds, "there are many contemporary Chinese writers whose literary achievements far surpass Gao Xingjian's," and that "were Gao Xingjian not anti-PRC but a supporter of the communist party, his chances for winning would be equal to nil" ("Xianggang").

The case of Gao and his 2000 Nobel thus presents a significant moment of ideological confrontation between the PRC and the West in the post-Tiananmen period. More than this, it highlights the emerging pivotal place of the Chinese diaspora writer in the new millennium's global cultural politics. It is indeed not by accident, or aesthetic considerations alone, that Gao became the first Chinese writer to be awarded the Nobel Prize in Literature. In the post–June 4 world, as Chinese diaspora literature itself becomes a key site of competing international claims, whether in the form of accolades and awards or denunciation and censure, Chinese diaspora writers, particularly those who emigrated around 1989, are often caught in the political fray between the PRC and the liberal West. Within this milieu, the extent to which a writer is able to determine his or her own identity becomes a complicated matter.

As Gregory Lee argues in his essay on the poet Duo Duo—who did, in fact, flee the PRC on the day after the massacre and was subsequently thrown, if much more briefly, into the international limelight—the central predicament facing Chinese exilic writers today is one of identity formation. The question, according to Lee, is not so much whether these writers can write what they want, but whether they are able to define their own literary identity: "Certainly, the alternative to such cultural producers defining and determining their own identity will be having their identity determined by the Western Modernist establishment, concerned with commodification and packaging of the writer/artist, and the whole commercial circus that surrounds literary activity which reaches its whirligig crescendo when sanctioned, and sanitized, by the Nobel Prize for Literature" ("Contemporary" 61). Lee's argument, made in reference to Duo Duo several years before the 2000 Nobel, seems in retrospect to be even more germane to the post-Prize Gao. Certainly, the latter's sudden and dramatic catapult into worldwide fame lends credence to Lee's trenchant critique of the Western commodification of Chinese exilic literature. For Gao as for Duo Duo, "isolation and alienation were at the root of his impulse to write, but suddenly for a brief media moment, what his poetry *said* . . . did not as such matter." Gao's work, too, became "but a commodity, a sign of dissidence that the Western media could neatly, tidily read alongside Soviet and East European dissidents/dissidence." As Lee acerbically concludes: "In China it was the Chinese Communist Party and its organs of literary control which suffocated literary creativity. In the West it is the commercial exploitation, and the tunnel-visioned greed, and need, of the culture industry that attempts to consume [the Chinese exilic writer] and his production" (71–72).

While Lee provides a useful way of reading the Western capitalist co-optation of Chinese diaspora writers, there are two important differences between Duo Duo and Gao. First, unlike the former, Gao was not actually involved in—and did not even approve of, as we will see—any political activity in the PRC, so his "dissidence" was not simply packaged into a commodity but wholly fabricated by an external discourse. Second, unlike the exilic poet, who on Lee's description was "devoured by a brief orgy of a rapacious consumption" but then tragically abandoned after media interest in Tiananmen waned (70), Gao's reputation shows every sign of having thrived on the media invention of his politics. Before the Nobel, his published writing outside of the Sinophone and Francophone world was relatively scarce. Certainly, many of his works had been translated into French, and he himself had begun writing in his adopted language, mostly by translating his own Chinese plays. In English, on the other hand, most of his works were available only in scattered form, embedded in scholarly anthologies on post-Mao theater or in specialized academic journals, not as independent volumes circulating on the commercial mass market or even academic ones.[2] And although his first novel, the epic semi-autobiographical *Soul Mountain* (*Lingshan*), had been translated into Swedish and French in the 1990s, its English translator had trouble finding a publisher for it, especially in the United States and the United Kingdom, procuring a contract for the book's rights only in Australia and New Zealand (M. Lee, "Of Writers" 5–6). Since the Nobel, however, English-language publications of and on Gao have proceeded at a furious pace, and almost every year sees the appearance of a new book-length translation, retranslation, collection, or critical study of his work.[3] Furthermore, post-Nobel, he has been inducted into various literary canons, via college textbooks as much as scholarly publications and academic conferences. Aside from his popular role as the exemplary dissident writer, Gao has emerged in the past decade as a paragon of "world literature," "transnational literature," and "global Chinese literature."[4] His name now lies at the hub of intersecting discourses of tradition and modernity, cosmopolitanism and Chineseness, globalization and transculturalism.

This explosion of critical interest in Gao's oeuvre is understandable in light of the Prize, but the ensuing scholarly discourse on him is not entirely immune to hagiography and can at times replicate the ideological slant of the mainstream media. In particular, a prominent strand of scholarship has tended to bolster rather than debunk the heroic mythologies surrounding the Nobel laureate. For instance, the premier English translator of Gao's fiction and essays, University of Sydney professor Mabel Lee, has been instrumental in introducing his nondramatic work to Anglophone audiences. At the same time, although she would be the first to point out Gao's repeated and vehement objections to any kind of political branding, her evaluations of his writing often reinforce an image of him as valiant dissident. In one typical passage, for example, she writes:

> As a creative writer, Gao Xingjian sees only one option, to abscond. Against power politics, public opinion, ethical preachings, the benefit of the party and the collective, in order to preserve personal worth, personal integrity, and intellectual independence, i.e. freedom, the individual has no option but to flee. It is only by fleeing that one can preserve one's self integrity and autonomy. The alternative is either to rot in gaol, to be crushed by the criticism of the masses, to drown and be swept along by the flow of traditional practice, or to be tortured to the end of one's days by empty glory, oblivious to what the self is all about. ("Walking" 108)

In rather alarming language, Lee depicts existence in the PRC as so many forms of death—death by rotting, crushing, drowning, and continual torture, with none-too-subtle accents of Caesar's cowards. Against such a horrific backdrop, the alternative of individual flight to "freedom" cannot but be cast in exultant terms. This nesting of Gao's life within the moral configuration of an either/or—either cowardly submission to or coura-geous escape from oppression—bespeaks a deeply dichotomous worldview of Chinese tyranny versus Western emancipation, the very triumphalist framework that undergirded Western media reportage on the Nobel.[5] Nor is Lee unique in this scholarly apotheosis of Gao. Another critic who contributes to it is Kwok-kan Tam, the editor of a scholarly anthology on Gao's work. For Tam, Gao represents the paradigmatic "transcultural" writer of our time, "a globalized/dislocated cultural identity that poses a challenge to people who still cling to the idea of national identity at the end of the twentieth century" (Preface vii). Examining the "politics of recognition" behind the Prize, he acknowledges that politics entered into the Nobel committee's decision, but he interprets the episode as simply the international community's attempt to "challenge China's non-recognition of Gao . . . which hits hard on the complex of Chinese nationalism," when Gao's "achievements have long been recognized by scholars, literary critics, and theatre professionals" elsewhere ("Introduction" 4, 15). The implication here is that Gao, an accomplished and daring writer, can be granted the recognition he deserves only by enlightened institutions outside the PRC. The issue of Gao's own political views, or of how the international community "recognizes" him only by misrecognizing and fabricating his political identity, is left largely untouched. As Gregory Lee and Noel

Dutrait shrewdly note in this regard, Gao's posture toward his Nobel is itself not apolitical: "After all, was Gao's acceptance of the award not just as political an act as Jean-Paul Sartre's refusing it?" (748).

Ironically, as numerous scholars look to Gao for models of postnational, transcultural, or cosmopolitan identity, other cultural authorities have focused instead on his "Chineseness"—a term that operates simultaneously on ethnic, cultural, and national registers, and that comes to be commodified no less than his "dissidence." Without exception, Western media coverage on the Nobel foregrounded Gao's ethnic identity and national origin, marking him as a "*Chinese* novelist and playwright," a "*Chinese* dissident," a "*Chinese* exile," a "*Chinese*-born writer," and so forth. Again, the media might have been taking their cue from the Nobel Committee itself, which, despite its description of Gao's work as "universal," never failed to emphasize his Chineseness. As Julia Lovell points out, the Swedish Academy's 2000 Nobel press release curiously ignored most of Gao's drama, his most obviously existentialist and "universal" work, and concentrated instead on his two semi-autobiographical novels set largely in China and his one atypically "political" play on the Tiananmen massacre. Lovell hence wryly comments: "Is it perhaps the case that, despite the Swedish Academy's progressive and multicultural welcoming of Gao, as the first Chinese-born winner of the Nobel Prize, into the global fold of universal literary modernity, the Academy has dressed up the traditionalist Western view of Chinese literature as 'obsession with China' with praise of his 'universal validity' (a plaudit that is, arguably, far more obviously applicable to his drama)? Do Gao's novels depict an acceptably dissident Chinese 'imagined community' that the judges of world literature perhaps find absent in his drama?" ("Gao" 20). She answers these questions in the affirmative, concluding that the Swedish Academy fundamentally maintained an "age-old link between Chinese literature and (one version of) obsession with China, and the two-tier treatment of Western and non-Western literatures in world literature" (26).

Significantly, this ethnic-national reification of Gao by the Western establishment occurred at precisely the same time when voices within the PRC were vigorously repudiating his Chineseness. In stark contrast to the Sinicizing language of the West, a report issued by the official news agency Xinhua pointedly identified Gao as a "Chinese-*French*" writer. The report underscored the incidentalness of Gao's Chinese birth and the deliberateness of his national abdication by stressing that he was born in China but "went abroad in 1987 and became a French national afterwards" ("Nobel"). The message was clear: in the eyes of the communist authorities, Gao was no longer Chinese, was perhaps never authentically Chinese in the first place. This cultural repudiation of Gao is not limited to the government.

As Lovell elaborates, even mainland writers and intellectuals who approve of Gao's Nobel have faltered over his Chineseness, identifying him not as one of their own but as a "Chinese writer in inverted commas," "foreign literature worker," or "French writer." The more disgruntled among them complain about Gao's sophomoric Chinese, noting that the language in his post-exile novel is "that of a high school student . . . washed and simplified by French," or else they bemoan his literary deficiencies, frustrated at the world for thinking "he represents China" when "he's not good enough" as a writer tout court (qtd. in Lovell, "Gao" 28, 34, 30).[6] Of importance here is not the accuracy of these intellectuals' criticisms of Gao but the fact that so many of them express their reactions to his Nobel by appraising his Chineseness—and by performing their own ability to validate, discredit, or exceed it.

With keen prescience, Jo Riley and Michael Gissenwehrer already recognized Gao's susceptibility to being mythologized a decade before the 2000 Nobel. They distinguished "two kinds of myth" around Gao in the late 1980s: on the one hand, in China as much as the West, among academics and theater professionals, he was said to be the "most avant-garde, creative and stimulating playwright" of Chinese theater; on the other, among some European commentators, he was seen as a playwright working squarely within the modern European dramatic lineage of Ibsen, Beckett, Artaud, and Grotowski (111). The modernity versus tradition binary was thus already in place. Yet, the Nobel Prize and the subsequent media war over Gao's identity have substantially transformed this pair of myths. In its stead, a newer and much more overtly political phenomenon of the two Gaos has been inaugurated. On one side, there is the Gao Xingjian constructed by official PRC forums, at best a deviant and hyphenated Chinese whose work is not only mediocre but insufficiently authentic because adulterated by Western influences. On the other, there is the Gao Xingjian fashioned by the international media and literary establishment, lionized as a dissident and exilic Chinese writer who has valiantly synthesized Eastern and Western artistic traditions despite tremendous political pressures. Remarkably, then, in the very instant when Gao's Chineseness is repudiated within his original context of writing—and partly by the language in which he still writes—it receives insistent reaffirmation and reauthentication by translating cultural authorities almost everywhere else, even as these incorporate him into a larger discourse of globalism and commodify him as a latter-day citizen of the world.

Remarkable, too, are the multiple assumptions about identity and difference that underpin these two seemingly polarized discourses. While the PRC authorities, out of ideological interest, adopt a model of identity that is teasingly deconstructive, in which Chineseness can be dispersed along a gradient (with Gao measuring a deficit), the international media remain within the bounds of essentialism as they cling tenaciously to Gao's unshakable Chineseness of being. This contest over identity, though, belies the not so diametrically opposed invocations of "difference" on both sides. Where the PRC expels Gao from its ranks by an appeal to his difference, under the sign of political and cultural deviation, the West embraces him by a comparable appeal to his difference, but redefined under the sign of ethnic and cultural otherness. In this latter process of inclusion through continual exclusion, the West welcomes Gao into its fold only to expel him once again by constantly recalling his foreign origins. Ultimately, the institutional structures determining the horizon of Gao's identity reflect the shifting cultural politics of a post-Tiananmen world. Academic attempts to resituate him as a transnational or postnational subject have yet to fully account for the commodifying, exoticizing, and misidentifying forces within the very mechanisms producing his "global" identity.

INDIVIDUALISM AND NONCOMMITMENT

In the case of Gao Xingjian and his Nobel Prize, then, we find Gregory Lee's anxiety over the Chinese diaspora writer's identity formation played out in a most spectacular way. Gao himself, writing several years before his award, likewise deplores the dehumanizing effects of consumerist culture: "The objectification or commodification of people is precisely the end of human beings. If a person cannot say no to objects and preserve a bit of pride, can he or she still be considered human?" (Zixu 7).[7] And yet, this very commodity culture in the West has provided the means for Gao to gain and secure not just recognition but also a continued artistic career—and by extension, it has afforded readers and critics greater opportunity to delve into his oeuvre, as more and more of his writings become available in print and in translation. So, despite Lee's despairing diagnosis of Duo Duo, Gao presents a somewhat different scenario of the post-Tiananmen literary diaspora, one in which the writer acquires considerable and long-term agency to define, refine, and revise his own identity in light of external discourses. Indeed, Gao is a prolific essayist, especially in the decade before his Nobel, when he regularly wrote about his own creative work and aesthetic philosophy at large. This rich corpus will be instrumental in bridging the previous discussion of global cultural politics with my next section's targeted analysis of Gao's Tiananmen play. In particular, I will focus here on his theories of writerly individualism and political noncommitment.

Of Gao's many essays, about two dozen have been collected in the signature volume *Meiyou zhuyi* (Without isms) (1996). Here, Gao articulates a position that consistently resists two things: first, the ossification of thought and writing into dogma, or what he calls an "ism" (*zhuyi*); and second, the intrusion of societal will or collective politics into the realm of literature. From this, he charts a wider theory of *meiyou zhuyi*, variously translated as "without isms," "none-ism," and "no-ism"—in thought, the negation of any kind of dogma, and in literature, the lack of belonging to or belief in any one school of writing. It is with such a bid for artistic autonomy, for example, that he begins the original title piece, "Without Isms," often read as his literary manifesto: "Realism, romanticism, modernism and isms with labels such as new or old, critical or revolutionary, social or national or classist were applied to literature, and this heavy burden made it hard for China's fledgling modern literature to breathe" (64).[8] It will be highly instructive to track Gao's conceptual moves in this essay. As we can see, his opening statements have very specific referents. He initially stakes his thesis about "isms" not as an abstract universal principle but in relation to the history of twentieth-century China, via a contemporary debate about Western imports into Chinese literature. Before he ever explicates his personal aesthetic, all the signposts he invokes are grounded in modern Chinese contexts. Along this vein, he goes on to offer a brief account of his personal experience with political branding in the 1980s, when his works were successively labeled "modernist," "absurdist," and "reactionary." This autobiographical sketch, too, is made meaningful through key references to figures in the post-Mao period such as Wang Meng and Hu Yaobang. From here, he stages a larger claim about modern Chinese literature: "The disaster for Chinese literature is that there must always be judgments to enable the formulation of policies, directions, guidelines, principles, patterns and models, and to determine what is right or wrong, mainstream or non-mainstream. By failing to conform, one is consigned to the ranks of those to be criticized, banned, exterminated, purged, killed or destroyed" (65–66). And a bit later, with more specific temporal markers:

My experience of mass movements and mass tastes has taught me that these, like the so-called self, need not be worshipped and certainly cannot be superstitiously believed in. . . . However, when this social aspect is narrowly confined within the parameters of political function or ethical rules, and literature is turned into political propaganda and moral teachings, or even into an instrument of war for political factions, it is a terrible misfortune for literature. China's literature has not completely freed itself from this. Modern Chinese literature was worn out by political struggles lasting from the end of the previous century to the end of this century. (67)

Thus far, Gao has cast himself squarely within the bounds of national history, as a subject embedded in and heir to national events, and a writer responding to specific national historical crises. Against such an explicitly historicizing frame, however, he culminates his essay by outlining a theory of literature in the most ahistorical of terms:

> Literature is essentially an affair for the individual. It can be treated as an individual's profession, but it can also simply express his feelings and dispel his emotions, or it can feign madness so that he can say whatever he wants to gratify his own ego, and of course it can also intervene in current politics. What is important is that it is not forced upon others, and naturally it will not tolerate having restrictions imposed upon itself either, whether it be for the sake of the nation or the party, the race or the people. Endowing the will of these abstract collectives with authority can only strangle literature.
>
> For a frail individual, a writer, to confront society alone and utter words in his own voice is, in my view, the essential character of literature, which has changed little from ancient times to the present, whether it be in China or abroad, in the East or in the West. (67)

What is noteworthy, and exemplary, in the above passages is Gao's conceptual movement from the specific to the universal, and from history to metaphysics. This movement defines the larger organizational structure of his argument. He starts with context-specific claims about twentieth-century Chinese literature but then leaps to universal, context-independent claims about literature in general—"from ancient times to the present, whether it be in China or abroad, in the East or in the West." In one conceptual step, all qualifiers of time and place, history and geography, disappear, and only the sign of "literature," now devoid of context, remains. In his defense of artistic autonomy from the encroachment of political agendas and moral dogmas, Gao seems to use his own experiences and China's national history as supreme evidence. His argument thus adopts a logic of exemplarity: although literature's tragic fate at the hands of coercive politics has been epitomized in the country of his birth, this antagonistic relationship between literature and politics, for him, is nonetheless not unique to twentieth-century China. On the contrary, it is an essential, ontological conflict.

Tellingly, in this passage as in many of his essays, the most frequently deployed term is *geren*—the individual. Literature, as a property of the individual, is an index of each human being's existential confrontation with society and politics. Gao's recourse to the individual is so fundamental, so total, that we can call it a philosophy of individualism. Of course, he takes pains to eschew this term, since it, too, is an "ism." In his preface to the collection, he attempts to differentiate his theory of *meiyou zhuyi* from the idea of *gerenzhuyi* (individualism), stating that "without isms is not the same as isms that take the individual as its axis or philosophies that have this as their beginning point." Unlike individualism, without isms presumably "does not take the individual's judgments as its sole coordinate, since every individual is an other to other people, and an individual's experiences and judgments can only have relative meaning, not absolute value" (Zixu 3–4). His objection to individualism has less to do with its definition of the individual than its alleged epistemological classification of the individual as the transcendental basis of "absolute value" or knowledge. His own invocations of the individual, he maintains, are temporary and contingent. Still, he himself constantly attributes to the individual all the functions it would possess within a formal theory of individualism, such as its role as the "starting point" of experience and judgment, the "validating source" of "value and behavior," and even the ground of ethical "choice" and "human nature" (2–4). He may proclaim his refusal of teleological "conclusions" (*jielun*) and "ends" (*jieguo*) as well as any system of epistemological "verification" (*lunzheng*) along both a priori and a posteriori lines (*xianyan*), but his essays time and again take the individual as an axiomatic principle for all matters social and secular. He may hence be read as formulating a theory not of transcendental but of sociopolitical individualism.

In fact, beneath the universalist and existentialist veneer of Gao's theory, we can discern preoccupations of a distinctly communist Chinese stripe, which lend his defense of artistic autonomy greater urgency than it would otherwise receive in more capitalist or postmodern contexts. In particular, we detect a continuing anxiety over the issue of *nalaizhuyi*—"bring-it-in-ism" or "borrowism"[9]—an anxiety about artistic license over cultural imports and the limits of the properly or rightfully usable. Without doubt, this issue has been one of perennial concern for mainland writers from the Cultural Revolution onward. Gao enters this debate, not via a theory of cultural nativism or one of modernist hybridity, but with a catholic appeal to the individual writer as the ultimate justification for all cultural usage. We can perceive a parallel here between individualism and nativism, for both are attempts to provide a rationale for cultural handling. Where nativism sanctions the use of all things native by the native, individualism permits the use of all things human by the individual. The former postulates a collective nativity as the supreme source of legitimation for cultural appropriation, while the latter calls upon the singular unit of the individual for the same purpose. One justifies cultural use by appeal to an ownership bequeathed by national birth and cultural belonging, the other to an ownership bequeathed by species identity and creative originality. This last capacity is paramount for Gao, who insists on the transformative power of the writer to turn other people's cultural possessions into his or her own: "Some isms inevitably will be imported, but once writers transform these into things of their own, the original isms will have been considerably distorted" ("Without" 64). The figure of the individual, then, serves to enlarge the compass of the properly usable to its maximal limits for the writer. Like a protective ancestral spirit, it dispels every anxiety, every potential criticism of cultural appropriation.

Such a generous dose of license granted the individualist writer is not without its share of problematic assumptions and implications. First, we note the binarism in Gao's deployment of the term "ism." Early in "Without Isms," he posits: "Literary creation has always amounted to the surging of blood in the writer's own heart, and has nothing to do with any ism. If a work sets out to expound some ism it will certainly die prematurely" (65). This passage is symptomatic of Gao's overarching thesis on literature. On his formulation, literature either "expounds" doctrine or else "has nothing to do with" it. This either/or logic fails to differentiate between terms of indoctrination and terms of thought or analysis. Nowhere in the corpus of his essays do we find a discussion of literature benefiting from pre-ossified thinking, via a reflective adoption of the components of an "ism"—i.e., ideas, concepts, analytic terms—prior to their rigidification into doctrine. The potentially complex and dialectical relationship between writing and thinking, whereby the two mutually influence and deepen at the same time they probe and critique each other, is flattened into a simple antagonism. Indeed, there is a sense that, in Gao's extreme wariness toward doctrinairism, ideas are always already ossified, always already imperatives, so that even their first moment of contemplation requires suspicion. As soon as a term is taken up, it must be held at a distance, doubted, disowned. Hence his remark that he has "only doubts, and even doubt[s] all notions of value" (76).

Gao denies being a philosophical skeptic, stating that he does not "turn doubt into an ism or treat it as an absolute." In this regard, the individual stands as his axiomatic alibi once more, in that "value judgments and ethical standards arise from the individual's personal experiences and not other people's proof" (Zixu 2). To further distance himself from postmodernism, Gao takes an unexpected turn toward what he calls "the real world" (zhenshi shijie): "For the past twenty years Western literature has been undergoing a crisis because it has become lost in linguistic form. Literature loses its life if nonstop changes in form result in a loss of connection with the real world. I attach importance to form, but I attach more importance to reality. This is not limited to external reality, but exists even more vividly in the perceptions of humans living within that external reality." He is quite deliberate in criticizing Western literature's tendency to focus on language play, and this trend, he contends, has put contemporary literature "within its own demon walls," from which it must return to "the real world" if it is to be revivified ("Without" 71). By opposing language to "life" (*shengming*) and "reality" (*zhenshi*), Gao seems to invoke a structuralist distinction between sign and referent, signifying systems and the objective world, and his gesture toward Nietzsche's notion of the prison-house of language further summons up contemporary theoretical debates about formalism's social and political limits. He may therefore be read as critiquing Saussurian attempts to understand language through a complete bracketing of the social world. Surprisingly, in this contest between formalist and sociological literature, he takes the side of the latter. What's more, contrary to both mainland Chinese and Western perceptions of him as the radical avant-garde writer, he is actually rather conservative in his views toward both linguistic experimentation and cultural appropriation for Sinophone literature. This conservatism is already hinted at in his brief comment on Lu Xun at the outset of "Without Isms," when he calls Lu Xun's mode of borrowism "somewhat excessive" (64). More explicitly later in the essay, he laments that, given the history of Western imports into the Chinese language since the May Fourth period, the "Europeanisation of the Chinese language is so rampant that at times it is unreadable." He continues: "I do not totally oppose the use of Western languages to enrich modern Chinese; I am talking about respecting the language. I try to accord with the linguistic structures that have always existed in the language and not write Chinese that is unintelligible when read aloud. Even when playing with the language to convey content that cannot be expressed in normal sentence structures, I demand of myself that it be pure modern Chinese" (69–70). Mabel Lee's English translation of this passage is perhaps slightly stronger than what Gao's original would suggest, but it effectively captures the duality he erects between an authentic and a hybridized Chinese. Against the foreignizing forces that leave the Chinese language garbled and mangled, Gao expresses a preference for more traditional syntax, or sentence structures "intrinsic" (*guyou*) to Chinese, which is also for him a "genuine" or "pure" (*chunzheng*) modern Chinese. Exactly how Chinese can be "enriched" rather than corrupted by European linguistic influences is not clear. More importantly, what he fails to address here is the social dimension of language and syntax—a consideration at the heart of the May Fourth movement's egalitarian efforts to revolutionize Chinese from a classical, syntactically dense, and sociopolitically elitist language (*wenyan wen*) into one of greater vernacular simplicity and accessibility (*baihua wen*). In Gao's aesthetic philosophy, though, language and literature remain ever aloof from the concrete sociopolitical power relations of "the real world."

This tension between literature and reality corresponds to an analogous one between the social and the real. Despite his endorsement of a literature grounded in "the real world," this reality is never given determinant content. No sooner is "reality" conjured than it vanishes again into the private realm of the individual's "lived experience." And once the figure of the individual appears, it is inevitably pitted against the collective, and every conceptual venture into the social ends in refusal. Gao's essays waver between these two poles of a solipsistic self and a nebulous reality. We might say his is a kind of subjectivism rocked by socialist anxieties, an individualism compelled to uphold some social unit as a point of orientation. Gilbert Fong makes a similar point and notes that Gao's ambivalent "love-hate attitude" toward society, "his reluctance to totally cut himself off from humanitarianism in an effort to save the human soul," is "characteristic of the modern Chinese intellectual who rebels against his own Chineseness and yet rejects a Western individualism which pays no heed to society" (xvi–xvii). Ultimately, though, Gao returns to a theory of literature as pure expression, devoid of responsibility to anything beyond the individual writer. In his ideal scenario, a "writer who is devoted to writing and has responsibility only for his own written language will strive to absorb and reproduce in his own creations all that interests him in the cultures of humankind, from ancient times to the present" (73). He himself is exemplary, as he admits with a mix of unabashed egotism and fatalistic humility: "It is for myself, not to please others, that I write. And I do not write to change the world or other people, because I cannot even manage to change myself" (76). In the preface, he enunciates this fatalism more forcefully in relation to society: "Without isms does not dream of any imaginary society or social ideal. Besides, reality has broken every one of this kind of utopias, so there is no need to invent yet another lie about tomorrow" (Zixu 4). On a macro view, we can understand these tensions and contradictions in Gao's essays as symptoms of his diasporic position. The very terms and movement of his thought show him to be caught between the PRC's and the West's competing political discourses, between the ideological rhetoric of communism and liberalism, socialism and capitalism. Gao himself seems to believe this in-between role to be simply one of individual choice. As he avows in the concluding paragraph of "Without Isms": "As a writer I strive to position myself between the East and the West, and as an individual I seek to live at the margins of society" (77). Yet, given his severance of literature from politics, this avowal can at most signify on an aesthetic level, whereas his condition of in-betweenness is just as fundamentally ideological, saturating the language he wields and the languages in which he is caught up.

Gao's declaration of self-imposed marginality may bear a certain resemblance to Edward Said's thesis on the modern intellectual—a willful exile who prefers to "remain outside the mainstream, unaccommodated, uncoopted, resistant . . . tending to avoid and even dislike the trappings of accommodation and national well-being" (*Representations* 52–53). Gao, as a voluntary exile from the country of his birth, fits the bill. His theory of without isms and his wide-reaching skepticism also accord well with Said's ideal of the intellectual—as someone whose mission it is "to confront orthodoxy and dogma (rather than to produce them)" (11), to be "involved in a lifelong dispute with all the guardians of sacred vision and text" (89), and "to keep a space in the mind open for doubt and for the part of an alert, skeptical irony" (120). Beneath these superficial similarities, however, Gao differs from Said in one vital aspect: the *public* function of the intellectual. This is an uncompromising point for Said, for whom the intellectual must have "a specific public role in society." Said's intellectual is "an individual" too, but one "endowed with a faculty for representing, embodying, articulating a message, a view, an attitude, philosophy or opinion to, as well as for, a public" (11). For Said, the modern intellectual's primary task is "to speak truth to power." This task is a "special duty" (98) and a unique "obligation," not a matter of personal inclination. And it pertains to not just the intellectual's own culture and people but humankind: "To this terribly important task of representing the collective suffering of your own people . . . there must be added something else, which only an intellectual, I believe, has the obligation to fulfill. . . . For the intellectual the task, I believe, is explicitly to universalize the crisis, to give greater human scope to whatever a particular race or nation suffered, to associate that experience with the sufferings of others" (44). Insofar as a redress of these sufferings entails an engagement with "constituted and authorized powers," Said defines a properly *political* responsibility of the intellectual toward global realities, with the implicit ideal-end of a universal human polity where divisions of race and nation recede into the backdrop.

It is precisely this principle of an obligatory responsibility on the part of the individual to the collective—first of one's own nation and race, then of the global polis—that Gao negates. Not that literature should always refrain from touching on politics; on this score, Gao concedes that political intervention is one possible pursuit of literature. As he emphasizes, "Without isms is not politics and does not follow politics, but it does not oppose others from participating in politics." Yet one of Gao's most basic premises is the severance of any *necessary* relation between the individual and a polity of any scale. This relation exists only contingently for him, as a matter of personal choice rather than the writer's vocational duty. In marked contrast to Said, he rejects "abstract collective names such as 'the people,' 'the race,' or 'the nation,'" which for him can only weigh on the individual as a "forceful imposition" (Zixu 4). Gao will go on to reiterate these sentiments in his Nobel Lecture. This piece is worth quoting at length, for ironically, in this moment when his voice gains the widest international audience under clearly political circumstances, he insists all the more vigorously on the apoliticalness, powerlessness, and "frailty" of the writer:

> A writer is a normal person—though perhaps a person who is more sensitive than normal, and people who are highly sensitive are often more frail. A writer does not speak as the spokesperson of the people or as the embodiment of righteousness. His voice is inevitably weak, but it is this weak voice that is the most authentic.
>
> What I want to say here is that literature can only be the voice of an individual, and that this has always been so. Once literature is contrived as the hymn of a nation, the flag of a race, the mouthpiece of a political party or the voice of a class or a group, it can be employed as a mighty and all-engulfing tool of propaganda. Such literature loses what is inherent in literature, ceases to be literature, and becomes a substitute for power and profit. . . .
>
> In order that literature safeguard the reason for its own existence and not become the tool of politics, it must return to the voice of the individual, for literature is primarily derived from the feelings of the individual: one has feelings and articulates them. ("Case" 32–33)

We repeatedly encounter these themes in Gao's other essays. For instance, in "I Advocate a Cold Literature": "Originally, literature has no relation to politics. It is purely a matter for the individual, a kind of observation, a looking back on experiences, a bit of speculation and feeling, the expression of one's attitudes, and the satisfaction of reflective thought. . . . Hence, literature has no obligation to the masses or to society" ("Wo" 15–16). The shunning of writerly responsibility is even stronger in "Paris Jottings": "The writer is not the conscience of society, just as literature is not a mirror of society. He simply flees to the social margins, an outsider, an observer who looks on with cool detachment, with a pair of cold eyes. . . . He has responsibility only to himself" ("Bali" 22). This point is restated with some mockery later in the essay: "Responsibility is a strange word, a tight filet clamped down on the writer's head in order to drag him here and there like a sheep. All the more should the writer not be stupid and put it on his own head. To bear responsibility to oneself is to derive personal satisfaction from the process. It is enough if one finds oneself interesting" (27). Finally, in a 1998 interview, Gao will speak most bluntly about his relationship to the PRC and its people: "The future of the Chinese who live on mainland China is their business. There's no shortage of prophets willing to predict China's future. I am not prepared to assume the role of spokesperson for the Chinese, nor for the Chinese people" (Lee and Dutrait 747).

Crucially, Gao consolidated this aesthetic philosophy of writerly individualism and political nonresponsibility only after his departure from
China—and in the few years after June 4, when he penned most of his
seminal essays. In this respect, Tiananmen is arguably the decisive event
for Gao's critical self-definition, and also a crux moment for the congeal-
ing of his diasporic intellectual identity.[10] While his growing disengage-
ment from the social and political spheres can be explained partly by his
bitter experiences with mainland criticisms in the mid-1980s, it is telling
that his philosophical synthesis occurred shortly after the Beijing massacre. Rather than sustaining attention at the remote crisis, however, Gao's
diasporic eye has turned intensely inward. It is thus difficult to reconcile
his isolationism of the self with Said's demand that the intellectual stand
"between loneliness and alignment" (22). Indeed, what Gao outlines in his
essays may be deemed a theory of *noncommitment*—not social or political irresponsibility, as some mainland critics have accused him of, but the
negation of responsibility as a good-in-itself. Collectivities, regardless of
magnitude, duration, or ideological stance, unfailingly denote for him the
antagonistic other of the individual. They invariably stifle, distort, or crush
personal identity, never foster or empower. Only in contexts unfettered by
tugs of duty to a collective can the writer achieve full expression. Against
the tugs of the political community especially, Gao articulates a double
refusal—to belong to a polity, and to act as a citizen. Instead of the metaphorically agentive space of the margins, which designates for Said as for
other theorists a potent site of political dissent, Gao in fact favors flight
from the polity altogether.

This tenet of flight surfaces prominently in Gao's essays from the early
1990s onward. He writes in one: "If literary creation is to 'intervene' in politics or society, I believe it's even more fitting for it to 'flee,' so that one can
resist social pressures and spiritually purge oneself" ("Wo" 17). In another,
perhaps with an allusion to June 4, he pronounces: "Modern society has
not become any more civilized but continues to massacre people as ever
before, and in ever more ways. . . . The only thing left to those who refuse
slaughter and suicide is flight. Flight is in fact the sole method for ancient
and modern man alike to save himself" ("Bali" 20). From social resistance
to spiritual purging to self-salvation, fleeing fulfills ever more escalated
functions for Gao, even as it becomes ever more singular as a means of human survival. It is at once a psychological attitude, a sociopolitical posture,
and a metaphysical ideal. That Gao's most commonly used word for flight
or escape—*taowang*—derives from the title of his Tiananmen play is of
central significance, as I will explicate below. For now, let me underscore
that this thesis on flight is not merely social or political but existential,
that he advances it not just for writers and artists but for all men, and in

relation to not just specific forms of oppressive government but all human existence, from ancient to modern times. So, contrary to the international media's valorization of his dissidence, he never in fact endorses democracy as a political institution, for his theories of without isms and existential escape apply to communist as much as democratic societies. Indeed, in Cornelius Castoriadis's resonant phrase, Gao may be said to exemplify the writer who has "wriggled out of the city."[11]

Yet the city—in the Greek sense of the polis, the original site of political life and citizenship—cannot be made to vanish purely through an act of will or writing. While it has seldom gone unremarked that Gao arrives at his views out of a desire for artistic freedom, it remains dubious whether this conception of the individualist writer endowed with maximal autonomy, who writes only for himself and is responsible only to his own language, can be made compatible with a model of the writer as socially responsive fringe critic. When commentators examine Gao's philosophical outlook, their focus often rests on his perception of political structures, when the flip side of the question is perhaps even more fundamental. After all, the argument for autonomy is necessarily an argument for *conditions* that enable autonomy, that allow the writer or artist to create without directives and threat of persecution, that make possible the expression of viewpoints other than those of official power. This aspect of the polis as a potential guarantor of artistic freedom is never adequately dealt with in Gao's writing. He may at times anchor his ideas in the historical situation of twentieth-century China, but instead of analyzing the elements specific to this context that have led to what he sees as the suffocation of modern Chinese literature, he inflates this national history into a universal thesis on all polities. He may indeed be "universalizing the crisis," as Said proposes, but he does so not in order to promote a politics of dissent against unjust governments but to withdraw into solitary art, fleeing even from the subjugated groups that may seek his voice. Most of all, the history of totalitarianism and the suppression of artistic autonomy under its reign, a subject that Gao is perfectly placed to confront, gets taken up in his essays only to be leveled straightaway with all other modes of politics, and only to culminate once again in his affirmation of the individual. "Dictatorship must be opposed," he acknowledges, "under whatever flag it hoists, whether it be fascism, communism, nationalism, racism, or religious fundamentalism," but the purpose of this opposition is always to "win the freedom of without isms" (Zixu 5). His interpretation of Western fascism is also telling in its brisk conflation of totalitarian repression, exilic literature, and his own notions of individualism and artistic autonomy: "Under fascist rule in Germany and Spain, and under communist totalitarianism in the USSR, writers had no choice but to flee into exile. This served to escalate the globalisation of trends in modern Western literary thinking. Released from nation-state consciousness, the writer confronted the world as an individual with responsibility only to the language he used for writing" ("Without" 67–68). The political condition that arguably underpins Gao's entire philosophical worldview—totalitarianism—is all but conceptually erased.

This is not a narrow appeal to the historicist imperative, nor should Gao's views be invalidated on the basis of his attempt at metaphysics. Indeed, the enterprise of thinking the polis in transcendental terms is an indispensable one, and Gao's value to this study lies precisely in his locating of Tiananmen within the philosophical discourses of exile and displacement, the human and the polis. We can hence engage him on his desired conceptual plane by tracing briefly here an alternative genealogy of political thought, one that threads together universal notions of human life and human responsibility, so as to bring into sharper relief the core problems in his philosophy and the possibility of conceiving the polis otherwise. Given, too, his aesthetic penchant to interweave Eastern and Western traditions, antiquity and modernity, we can constellate for an instant two disparate thinkers: Mencius and Hannah Arendt.

"The whole teaching of Mencius," Arthur Waley tells us, "centres round the word Goodness [jen]. Different schools of Confucianism meant different things by this term. But to Mencius, Goodness meant compassion; it meant not being able to bear that others should suffer." Waley then calls attention to Mencius's two exemplars: "[Goodness] meant a feeling of responsibility for the sufferings of others, such as was felt by the legendary Yu, subduer of the primeval Flood: 'If anyone were drowned, Yu felt as though it were he himself that had drowned him.' Or such as was felt (so it was said) in ancient times by the counsellor I Yin to whom if he knew that a single man or woman anywhere under Heaven were not enjoying the benefits of wise rule, 'it was as though he had pushed them into a ditch with his own hand; so heavy was the responsibility that he put upon himself for everything that happened under Heaven'" (83). What is extraordinary in this description of Yu and I Yin is not so much their embodiment of goodness and compassion, as Waley emphasizes, as their having gathered upon themselves a supernumerary measure of responsibility. In both examples, we are given an account of an individual's sense of beholdenness toward those around him, a feeling contingent neither on bonds of kinship or friendship nor on contracts of service, yet of a magnitude far greater than what is culturally sufficient or expected. In both, this sense of responsibility works as though it were the most essential feature of social being. The second example moreover makes explicit what is implied in the first: this feeling of responsibility takes place in the province of the political and characterizes the relation between an individual and a political community. That the individuals in both cases are figures of power—Yu being the legendary founder and sage-king of the Xia dynasty, I Yin the minister of King Tang of the succeeding Shang Dynasty—is of course important for our reading of Mencius. His text, after all, is a tract on enlightened rulership, a document of monarchical times. Its definition of goodness, as a supreme gathering of responsibility for others onto oneself, is intended as a mode of imperial governance. To modern skeptics, Mencius's ostensible subordination of power to virtue can be read as a justification of benevolent despotism, of the sovereign's right to rule through a divinely bestowed moral superiority. Yet the argument here can also be read less cynically, as a philosophical precursor to a humanist ethics and politics for our time. In ethical terms, it means that every human being is capable of feeling and acting with the utmost benevolence toward another, any other, and in political terms, it imagines a human polity of all "under Heaven." The contemporary relevance of Mencius lies in his effort to reclaim the idea of responsibility from the sphere of the contractual and the proper, from coded hierarchies of formal conduct, and return it to the provenance of communal being. An individual is thus responsible not so much for other individuals as to human life itself. This, at least, seems to be the interpretation by which Waley made his translator's passageway into the *Mencius*, and this, conversely, is the suggestively anti-Confucianist formulation of Confucian ethics that cropped its way into English in 1939.[12]

We can call this model *bare responsibility* and distinguish it from *obligatory responsibility*, which operates within strictly delimited systems of interpersonal relations. Kinship bonds, for example, circumscribe parental and filial pieties not exacted of those outside the family. Similarly, national bonds oblige citizens of a country to treat each other according to a mutual set of laws in exchange for unique rights of residence in and protection by the state. Bare responsibility, by contrast, posits as its common denominator the life of the species: every instance of its practice emanates from an excess of provincial identities and aims to stretch the boundaries of the polis to include the whole of humankind. We can link this concept of bare responsibility to a number of current theories on cosmopolitanism and what we might call new humanism. In the past two decades, concomitant with the rise of globalization studies, there has been a resurgence of effort among intellectuals of myriad stripes to theorize cosmopolitanism and humanism anew, beyond the Enlightenment's political legacies of colonialism, imperialism, racism, and so on. Edward Said is again instructive in this context. Drawing on Frantz Fanon and especially the latter's reference to a "[real] humanism," Said argues forcefully against "identitarian" or nationalist politics and advocates instead a "global, contrapuntal analysis," one that is based not on a "symphony" or falsely harmonious view of world cultures but on an "atonal ensemble" that acknowledges the "complex and uneven topography" of worldly institutions (*Culture* 318). Not unlike Mencius, Said connects the perception of another's suffering with a sense of global responsibility as the basis of a humanist politics and ethics. This connection is again established by Paul Gilroy, who introduces the concept of "conviviality" to replace multiculturalism as a new model of planetary cohabitation (*Postcolonial* xv). Tracing his argument through the specific genealogy of black intellectual thought but exhibiting a certain debt to Said as well, Gilroy too promotes a "planetary humanism capable of comprehending the universality of our elemental vulnerability to the wrongs we visit upon each other" (*Postcolonial* 4). Likewise, Kwame Anthony Appiah outlines his ethics of cosmopolitanism by intertwining a commitment to pluralism with an ideal of "universal concern" or "obligations to others" (xv). Even Jacques Derrida, in his exploration of refugee and asylum rights, adopts the language of cosmopolitanism to propose an "ethic of hospitality," a notion, he points out, that is tautological, since *"ethics is hospitality"* (16–17)—a comment that cannot be made without an understanding of a species ethos. From the vanguards of postcolonialism and race studies as much as deconstruction, then—those schools of thought hitherto concerned most prominently with systems of difference—we now hear consistent and robust invocations of the human as the premise of a new global politics and ethics.

Behind these recent revivals of humanism, I would suggest, is the key figure of Hannah Arendt. Her lifelong project of thinking the human, and thinking of a paradigm of human rights beyond mere metaphysics, is arguably the philosophical point of origin for much contemporary discourse on ethical and political cosmopolitanism. Of particular influence has been her methodological approach to the human via negative routes, by way of pinpointing nodes in history that throw the idea of humanity into crisis. We can say she affirms a politics of the human exactly through those cataclysmic events that withhold or negate the principle of bare responsibility. One prime example is her well-known formulation of the banality of evil, which provides a powerful argument against models of responsibility premised solely on obligatory action. Her portrait of the Nazi soldier as a cog in the "mass-murder machine" is also the portrait of a paragon of obligatory responsibility: far from being a moral monster or perverse sadist, the average Nazi soldier who carried out daily execution orders saw himself simply as an honest jobholder and good family man, a model *paterfamilias* who felt he was shouldering the greatest share of responsibility for his family, his race, and his country by permitting himself to be mobilized by the state's call to arms: "When his occupation forces him to murder people he does not regard himself as a murderer because he has not done it out of inclination but in his professional capacity. Out of sheer passion he would never do harm to a fly" ("Organized" 130). What he asked exoneration from was responsibility to all communities beyond local ones. To such a psyche, the charge of crime against humanity would be incomprehensible, for he was above all a human being whose defining trait was the renunciation of bare responsibility.

Against race-based theories that try to explain the phenomenon of the Nazi through the German national character, Arendt insists it is the political environment of totalitarianism that has produced this modern type of the "mob man." "The totalitarian policy," she writes, "has completely destroyed the neutral zone in which the daily life of human beings is ordinarily lived" ("Organized" 124). The peculiar paradox of the totalitarian citizen is that the state obligates him to participate in acts of atrocity as a criterion of citizenship even as it absolves him of culpability toward communities beyond the nation-state. Under this polis, the "neutral zone" where people ordinarily live out the ethics of neighborly conduct, treating others not solely as compatriots but also as fellow human beings, guided not by duty and obedience but recognition of a shared humanity, becomes wholly incorporated into, and effaced by, state directives. This insight is partly what leads Arendt to a conviction that the most potent corrective for totalitarianism is a reclamation of the sphere of the human. Yet this reclamation, she realizes, must reach beyond the Enlightenment's idolatrous "enchantment" with and "reckless optimism" regarding mankind's innate nobility ("Karl" 84, 131). Especially with the development of nuclear technology and the prospect of species annihilation, the post–World War II world necessitates a reformulation of humanism along more pessimistic lines, where human beings must come to acknowledge with open eyes their shared responsibility for each other's good as well as "evil potentialities": "For the idea of humanity, when purged of all sentimentality, has the very serious consequence that in one form or another men must assume responsibility for all crimes committed by men and that all nations share the onus of evil committed by all others. Shame at being a human being is the purely individual and still non-political expression of this insight" ("Organized" 131).[13] In retrospect, we can see the idea of the human following a course of drastic reversal. The optimism in *Mencius*, which seeks to unite human beings in a common inherent proclivity for goodness, has evaporated in the postwar world, giving way to Arendt's vision of a humanity locked together in negative potential for species holocaust.

Arendt's argument for universal responsibility is anchored in another major aspect of her work: the dilemma of refugees and stateless peoples. The figure of the refugee lays bare for her the central paradox in the concept of human rights, for if the Enlightenment declared the Rights of Man to be inalienable, independent of all governments and innate to all human beings, then theoretically the dislocation of stateless peoples should manifest these rights in the starkest and most unobstructed light possible. But the decisive point for Arendt is that history proved the opposite true: "It turned out that the moment human beings lacked their own government and had to fall back upon their minimum rights, no authority was left to protect them and no institution was willing to guarantee them.... The Rights of Man, supposedly inalienable, proved to be unenforceable—even in the countries whose constitutions were based upon them—whenever people appeared who were no longer citizens of any sovereign state" (*Origins* 292–93). What the "calamity of the rightless" reveals above all is the vital link between human rights and the political community. Before a human being's right to live is ever challenged, there has to be "a right to have rights," which is also "a right to belong to some kind of organized community." Only a polity can guarantee human beings' right to life, and "only the loss of a polity itself expels [a human being] from humanity" (*Origins* 295–97). In direct antithesis to Gao's conception of the individual's flight from the polis as the epitome of human dignity, Arendt argues that "the instant when a person becomes a human being in general . . . *and* different in general, representing nothing but his own absolutely unique individuality," this individuality itself "loses all significance" (*Origins* 302). To be "a human being in general," stripped of all communal ties, is to exist in a condition of rightlessness.

Arendt gives this notion of generic humanness two additional names: "the abstract nakedness of being human," and the "mere existence" or "mere givenness" of human life, both recurrent phrases in her writing. Even more than the postwar refugees, the figures who most fully embodied this condition of naked humanity for her were the extermination camp survivors. In reference to them, she notes the nonsanctity of human beings' bare state: "The conception of human rights, based upon the assumed existence of a human being as such, broke down at the very moment when those who professed to believe in it were for the first time confronted with people who had indeed lost all other qualities and specific relationships—except that they were still human. The world found nothing sacred in the abstract nakedness of being human." When human beings are dispossessed of their political community, what they have left is only this nakedness or "dark background of mere givenness" (*Origins* 300–301). These passages from Arendt echo a phrase from Walter Benjamin's "Critique of Violence," in which he, too, speaks of the nonsacredness of human beings' "mere life": "Man cannot, at any price, be said to coincide with the mere life in him, any more than it can be said to coincide with any other of his conditions and qualities, including even the uniqueness of his bodily person. However sacred man is . . . there is no sacredness in his condition, in his bodily life vulnerable to injury by his fellow men." Indeed, Benjamin calls this belief in life's sacredness a "dogma," "the last mistaken attempt of the weakened Western tradition to seek the saint it has lost in cosmological impenetrability" (251). In light of Arendt's role as an editor of Benjamin's work, she may well have in mind his term when she writes of naked humanity and mere existence. After her, this terminology will be picked up again by Giorgio Agamben, in his by now well-known formulation of "bare life"—"the life of *homo sacer* (sacred man), who *may be killed and yet not sacrificed*" (*Homo* 8). Taking an enigmatic figure in archaic Roman law as his point of departure, Agamben elaborates a theory of modern biopolitics on which the space of the camp, where the state of exception becomes the rule, is now the "new biopolitical *nomos* of the planet" (*Homo* 176). Agamben's focus on the politicized bodies of modern *homo sacer* will be pertinent to my discussion of Ma Jian's *Beijing Coma*, especially in relation to Ma's critique of PRC totalitarian biopower. For now, it suffices to conclude that, from Mencius to Arendt to a host of contemporary theorists, there can be traced a philosophical lineage which persistently connects human life to a universal polity. Vis-à-vis this other genealogy, Gao's metaphysical severing of the individual from the polis appears profoundly solipsistic. More disturbing is that his retreat into the self has led him to quietistic positions on national and gender politics—as we will see in the Tiananmen play *Taowang*.

Part II. Fleeing Tiananmen

EXILE AND FLIGHT

Let us for a moment recast Gao Xingjian's diasporic condition in Arendtian terms. While his eschewal of politics is entirely understandable in light of the thorough politicization of art in PRC history and his own experience with harsh political criticisms in the 1980s, for more than two decades now, he has found a comfortable place in a new polity that not only protects his existence but prizes his writing. Even if this new context carries its own brand of consumerist tendencies, it is nevertheless a polity that affirms his right to belong and safeguards his artistic autonomy. Despite these political benefits, Gao has yet to rethink his theory of the polis. If anything, his denial of the writer's responsibility has taken ever-deeper and more recalcitrant root, and to ever-louder cheers of his role as the political exile par excellence. This cheerleading may stem in part from popular notions of the exilic writer as a melancholy rebel, nostalgic for his homeland but determined to rise above the fray of his country's politics. On this view, it seems perfectly right and proper that a writer in exile from an authoritarian regime should insist on the apoliticalness of art and find some solace in holding onto this belief. This romantic image is frequently projected onto Chinese émigré writers, sometimes by the writers themselves. Of Duo Duo, for instance, Gregory Lee recalls Chen Maiping's poignant metaphor of the exilic poet as "living in a valley between east and west," a valley that threatens to flood but offers no exit (Introduction iv). Less metaphorical, though, and more concretely precarious is the in-between situation of another group of Chinese "exilic writers" in history—those Angel Island detainees who in the early twentieth century also turned to literature, by carving or brushing poetry on prison walls, to air their grievances against America. The figure of the detainee, whose political identity is put in a state of indefinite suspension and who possesses no legal recourse to a guardian authority, has dramatically resurfaced on the global radar after 9/11 with Abu Ghraib and Guantanamo Bay, in our latter-day reincarnations of the camp that Agamben diagnoses as a space of exception. Following Arendt, we might call this category of suspended life *bare exile*.

The mode of exile Gao now occupies, however, is not bare but merely geographic. The fact that he has settled into a new polity that accords him citizenship and protection, and a community that encourages his writing and awards him fame and prestige, should signal a state of inclusion that is anything but exilic. Indeed, it can be argued that, when a subject attains this level of security, even when he or she remains geographically outside the country of birth, the word "exile" loses its political meaning. Gao, while still living in China and composing works of ideological danger such as *Bus Stop*, could be said to have fulfilled the role of a Saidian intellectual as well as what Leo Ou-fan Lee calls an "internal exile," someone who does not necessarily suffer "physical banishment to the peripheries of the country" but who chooses to "turn inward—the construction of a sanctuary of the soul that stands in a peripheral position vis-à-vis the omnipotent center" (234). In the PRC, he was an eminently political writer in this sense, for his deliberate detachment from and resistance to cooptation by the center marked his intellectual marginality. Once in actual physical exile, though, and especially after being naturalized as a French citizen and awarded the Nobel by the European community, he can no longer be deemed a political exile in any meaningful way. Instead, he now exists entirely within the folds of the polis. It is also this newly acquired political stability that allows him, with complete impunity, to plead the primacy of artistic integrity and the irrelevance of political responsibility. From this angle, Gao now exemplifies the very opposite of the exile—the luminary, the idol at the center of cultural authority, perhaps with shades of the sovereign who allocates to himself an exceptional power to use and appropriate other people's cultural goods.

Gao himself, tellingly, does not repudiate the name of exile. On the contrary, he embraces it as a positive and "completely normal" circumstance for the writer. He is wholly unsentimental on this score, and more than once has he spoken about the practical advantages of exile, and about the need to dispel the quixotic idea that exilic writers are tragically doomed to an "exceptional environment that leaves [them] unable to create" (Lee and Dutrait 743). As he states in his Nobel Lecture, exile represents the "inevitable fate of the poet and the writer who continues to seek to preserve his own voice" (595). Moreover, his affirmation of exile is much broader in scope, for he finds the condition not only creatively enabling for the writer but existentially necessary for the individual. In effect, he brings together the two distinct structures of exilic existence and existential exile. In one quintessential interview, he comments:

> What we're faced with now is not just a question of fleeing political oppression and the Chinese environment; there is also the flight from the Other, flight from other people. It was Sartre who said Hell is other people. But it's not enough to flee the Other, there's also the need to flee oneself. . . . I think the Self is like a black hole capable of sucking everything in. It's terrifying. So it's very important for an exile writer to flee the Self, that's the only way he can establish the lightness and calm he needs to write. So I feel that in addition to fleeing present political circumstances, there is also a perpetual flight. (Lee and Dutrait 743)

In his essays, Gao calls this notion of existential exile *taowang*, "flight" or "fleeing." By his axiom, every human being is always originally in antagony with both others and him or herself. In his aesthetic corpus, this theory of existential flight finds its fullest articulation in *Taowang*.

Taowang is a play whose reputation precedes it. While few critics analyze the text in any sustained way, most make a point of citing the circumstances surrounding its creation. Gao himself has been unusually vocal on this topic. In a 1991 speech at the Royal Dramatic Theatre of Sweden in Stockholm, where the play premiered, he described its genesis thus:

> In June 1989 after the Tiananmen Incident, a friend asked me if I could write a play for an American theater company. The play should be about China and, of course, related to reality. I agreed. In August the first batch of exiles from Beijing arrived in Paris and among them were a few of my old friends. At the end of September, I started

to write the play and finished it a month later. The theater company read the English translation and requested revision. I refused and had my friend pass on my words: Even the Communist Party could not coerce me into making changes to my manuscripts when I was in China, let alone an American theater company. ("About" 69)

In "Without Isms," Gao will reiterate this story with undiminished indignation: "The Americans wanted me to make changes, so I withdrew the manuscript and paid for the translation myself. When I write I have my own things to say and I will not make compromises to please the tastes of others" (74). The scholars most active in disseminating Gao's work have been quick to propagate this real-life drama around the play. Mabel Lee, for one, hails the episode as yet another illustration of Gao's "search for total freedom of artistic expression" and his rejection of "any compromise of the artistic self in literature" ("Gao Xingjian" 30). Reading the play as "an artistic exploration of some of the uncomfortable implications of group thinking and action" ("Gao Xingjian's" 285), she applauds Gao for not being one to "sacrifice his writing for a political cause" ("Pronouns" 253). Whatever the real extent of disagreement between the playwright and the American theater company that commissioned the play, this breach has been magnified into a bona fide controversy within the canonized lore of Gao scholarship. Aside from Lee, Gilbert Fong also remarks melodramatically that *Taowang* put Gao "at odds with" not just one particular American theater group but "the Chinese Overseas Democracy Movement" itself. Fong further insinuates that the movement was rather petty and self-interested, finding fault with the play out of wounded vanity because one of its own is portrayed badly, as "susceptible to doubt and emotional vacillations" (xiv). Sy Ren Quah also writes approvingly of Gao that "his intellectual consciousness has prevented him from producing a blind eulogy of the student demonstrators" (180), implying that those who would wish to see the script altered can only be motivated by extreme naiveté or ideological bias.

On the other shore of this uproar was the vehement condemnation of the play by PRC authorities, a matter cast histrionically by Fong as Gao's having "brought down the wrath of the Chinese government" in his unrelenting quest to "give full rein to his imagination" (xiv). Less talked about in this regard is the ironic fact that *Taowang*, though leading to the banning of Gao's work on all mainland stages, also happens to be his only play to be published in full in the PRC after 1986. As Henry Zhao explains, communist hard-liners were so enraged by the play that they reprinted and distributed it widely in 1990 in a special edition entitled *The "Elite" in Escape*. This booklet was prefaced by a vitriolic review denouncing the play "as 'a total lie' and accusing the author of 'having taken the criminal path of spreading rumours, mongering vilification and libel'" (95). In short, the mainland edition used *Taowang* to discredit the democracy movement and deny the massacre. Zhao helpfully records this incident but leaves unexplored the deeper question of why the play would so easily lend itself to antidemocracy propaganda, concluding simply that "the play, in a word, did not please anyone" (96). The Nobel Committee will go on to reproduce this slogan in its 2000 press release, promoting the play as a work that "irritated the democracy movement just as much as those in power" (Swedish). Undoubtedly, in the global cultural discourse, *Taowang*'s inception has served as a tantalizing biographical tidbit that buttresses the image of Gao as courageous and uncompromising artist.

Beyond the hullabaloo, I would argue that *Taowang* in fact typifies Gao's political quietism and exposes the risks of an aesthetic that universalizes totalitarian violence. Despite the ubiquitous citations of the play, critics have consistently and conspicuously failed to tackle its most troubling aspects—namely, its representations of the Tiananmen student and of the woman, and by extension, its implications for national and gender politics. Perhaps the relative unavailability of the play in English up until quite recently, as with many of Gao's essays, has contributed to this critical lapse, though European audiences became familiar with it early on, as it was translated into both French and German in 1992 and staged variously in Sweden, Germany, France, and Poland prior to the 2000 Nobel.[14] The retranslation and republication of the play in English in 2007 may well lay the groundwork for a future reassessment of Gao's oeuvre.

UNIVERSALIZING TOTALITARIANISM

The play is set in the ruins of an unnamed city in an unnamed country, and the action unfolds from the early morning hours to daybreak of one unspecified day.[15] Act 1 opens with the "rumbling sound of tanks on tar road" and the "continuous crackling of machine guns and submachine guns" in the background (*Escape* 3). Two twentysomethings, Young Man and Girl, have escaped from the shootings in an unidentified square and are hiding out in what looks to be a dilapidated warehouse. Soon after, they are joined by Middle-aged Man, who lives in a nearby apartment building but has run away from his home after witnessing a harmless old neighbor shot to death. The three strangers thus become fellow fugitives sharing a common predicament and place of temporary refuge.

As they discuss the military crackdown, the word "Tiananmen" is never mentioned. Indeed, throughout the play, Gao suppresses all specific geographical and historical markers, so that the connection to China and June

4 is only metatextual or paratextual. Audiences attending the play are assumed to already know its Tiananmen reference, and readers approaching the text are duly briefed by a scholarly introduction and then again by Gao's commentary afterward. Yet, as Gao goes on to emphasize in this latter piece: "*Escape* is not a socialist realist play. I believe that being alive means always on the run, either away from political persecution or from other people. One still has to run away from one's self, which, once awakened, is precisely what one can never run away from—This is the tragedy of modern man" ("About" 70). In his performance notes to the play, too, he stresses the primacy of its existentialist dimension: "Since ancient times, human existence has been an unending tragedy. Our play is an attempt to express modern man's dilemma in the classical tragedy form. . . . *Escape* is about the psychology of political philosophy [or more exactly: it is a politico-philosophical and psychological play]. It should not be made into a play of socialist realism, which seeks only to mirror contemporary political incidents" (67). Certainly, the stage set encourages such an existentialist interpretation. The vacant warehouse, the predawn darkness, the isolation from the crowds—these features combine to create a zone of social suspension where the three characters can act simply as individual human beings apart from collective identities. At the same time, since the warehouse is symbolically situated at the threshold of state violence and the characters are uniformly threatened with imminent death, they can be read as united in a basic human condition of confronting mortality, which presses upon them with ever-greater urgency the task of affirming their individual existence.

All the critics who have written on *Taowang* interpret it along these lines, which is to say, they read very much along the grain of Gao's own commentary and treat the play as fundamentally an existentialist drama about human nature and the human psyche. Citing Gao's essays, Henry Zhao, for one, avers: "To escape from Tian'anmen Square in the play is only a more dramatic example of the universal necessity of escape. . . . We can go a step further to argue that this is not a political play but an exploration into the primal instincts when the individual person is faced with the prospect of death" (98). Similarly, Mabel Lee contends that the play aims not to "wallow in the tragedy" but to put "under scrutiny . . . the human psyche and human behavior in the context of extreme terror and confrontation with death" ("Nobel" 7). She further suggests that the form of classical tragedy recommended by Gao "is aimed at inducing a psychological distance that will allow members of the audience to dissociate themselves from the emotional trauma of the specific events of June 4" so they can better engage in "critical thinking and reflection on those events," but that ultimately the philosophical thrust of the play "reinforce[s] the fact that the specific tragedy under scrutiny is not unique in human existence" (6). Sy Ren Quah falls into rank when he too maintains that *Taowang* "is not essentially a play about the demonstrators of the Tiananmen Incident. Metaphorically, it reveals a psychological predicament deeply rooted in human nature. It is also a personal manifestation of the playwright's need to flee" (182). Without exception, critics replicate Gao's logic by subordinating the particularity of Tiananmen to the universality of a human condition.

There is a striking doublethink here, however. While critics unanimously raise the sign of "Tiananmen" so as to designate the play as a political one—thereby bolstering the impression of Gao as at heart a writer of social conscience—they withdraw the pertinence of this sign as soon as Gao faces potential criticism on political grounds or heads down an awkward political path. Rather than confront the challenge of positioning Gao *both* philosophically and politically, they follow his lead by equating politics with mere heroics. So, following the authorial claim that *Taowang* is a "political philosophy play without any heroes" ("Without" 74), Zhao notes that "the three characters in the play . . . are hardly heroes" (95), Quah asserts that "a heroic figure [is] absent among the characters" (177), and Lee declares that "Gao knew he could not distort the truth by portraying [the students] as heroes" ("Nobel" 6). If, as Gao avows, *Taowang* is intended to be a "political philosophy play," then the political part of the equation has surely received much shorter shrift. Those mainland critics who vilified Gao for "spreading rumors" may well be accused of failing to read philosophically, but sympathetic scholars may equally be seen as failing to read politically.

In fact, the play is political through and through. Although all three characters are identified only generically by their gender and age, intimating an emptying out of collective identities, no sooner do they rendezvous than they assume the roles of spokespersons for various social groups or ideological causes—the Young Man for pro-democracy activism, the Young Woman for female autonomy, and the Middle-aged Man for individualism and noncommitment. They act and speak mostly as tokens rather than truly individualized personalities. In this sense, the play is more a political than an existentialist allegory, with each character representing a type—student, woman, writer—and its corresponding outlook on politics rather than the species category of the human. In particular, as we will see, the Middle-aged Man bears an unmistakable resemblance to the playwright himself, for many of this character's lines will reemerge almost verbatim in Gao's essays in the next decade. This fictional surrogate of the author cannot be straightforwardly read as the most representatively human character in the play unless we, too, indulge in a circular logic whereby Gao's theories are elevated into universal truths. Finally, this is

THE EXISTENTIALIST SQUARE / 67

a play driven more by dialogue than by action, more by the verbal contest of ideas and beliefs than by the mechanisms of an unfolding plot. Its principal moments of dramatic tension therefore lie in the characters' heated exchanges, especially those in which the Middle-aged Man gets provoked into debating the merits and demerits of sundry political topics with the Young Man or the Girl.

A prime example is the running dispute between the two men on the value of the democracy movement, a subject that constitutes the dialogical focal point of act 1. The Girl's shocked disbelief at the massacre and her frantic exclamations of "Bloodbath!" conveniently set the stage for the men's first political wrangle:

GIRL: No one could have expected something like that to happen.
MIDDLE-AGED MAN: They should have.
YOUNG MAN: And you?
MIDDLE-AGED MAN: They were worse than I'd expected.
YOUNG MAN: That's really something.
MIDDLE-AGED MAN: When you were mobilizing people you should have thought of ways to retreat.
YOUNG MAN: Did you?
MIDDLE-AGED MAN: I should have. . . .
YOUNG MAN: You already knew the ending, did you? So why did you let yourself get drawn into it?
MIDDLE-AGED MAN: (*Laughs bitterly.*) I couldn't help it. I hated this sort of dirty politics right from the start. (11–12)

We can pause here to note that, according to what are now the most reliable eyewitness accounts of June 4, it was not due to the student demonstrators' lack of an organized retreat that the massacre occurred. I will explore in greater depth in chapter 4 the circumstances of the evacuation, but I raise the issue of history now, not in order to accuse Gao of historical inaccuracy—he would, after all, refute this charge on the grounds that he is not writing a realist play that "mirrors" the Tiananmen incident—but to elucidate the Middle-aged Man's stance toward the democracy movement. On a purely emotional level, his attitude toward the student activists may be described as condescending and sanctimonious. Steeped in moral didacticism, he goes on to lecture the Young Man on the more correct, and more enlightened, understanding of the term "the people" (*renmin*):

MIDDLE-AGED MAN: Son, you don't have a monopoly on moral indignation. Everybody's entitled to it, otherwise there wouldn't have been so many people on the

YOUNG MAN: streets demonstrating and supporting you and your friends, and thousands of people wouldn't have had to be slaughtered!

YOUNG MAN: So do you think the people's struggle for democracy and freedom is totally meaningless?

MIDDLE-AGED MAN: (*At once getting agitated.*) Don't talk to me about "the people." They're just the millions of people living in this city, unarmed except for soft drink bottles and bricks. But bricks are no match for machine guns and tanks! It was so obvious. What they did was no more than a heroic way to commit suicide, but suicide just the same. People are so naïve, they can't help making fools of themselves [literally, stupid: *yuchun*]. (12)

Beyond the emotions, the Middle-aged Man's high-minded remonstrances clearly carry a political judgment as well. It is strongly implied in these passages that he foresaw the bloodshed, that he "already knew the ending" before it happened, that the outcome was "so obvious" to him. This suggestion of foreknowledge coincides with what Gao will later say of himself in an interview, that he "was able to predict the suppression of the demonstration a few days before June 4, 1989" (Quah 180). What the Middle-aged Man—and presumably Gao—express here is the political opinion that the Tiananmen movement was doomed to failure from the start. According to this widespread and rather hackneyed view, the massacre was inevitable, and since civilians were no match for the communist government and its tanks, the students who led the protests should take the blame for their foolishness, recklessness, and immaturity, having sacrificed not just their own lives but those of innocent supporters. It is within the framework of such a political condemnation that the Middle-aged Man embeds his remark about the student leaders' lack of a planned retreat. This indictment resurfaces a bit later in more severe terms:

YOUNG MAN: Your philosophy isn't worth a fart. It can't save anybody.

MIDDLE-AGED MAN: And your rashness? Who can that save?

YOUNG MAN: Are you saying that we shouldn't have started the democracy movement?

MIDDLE-AGED MAN: If a massacre is all it leads to, then it's better not to have any.

YOUNG MAN: (*Stands up and approaches menacingly.*) What exactly do you mean by that?

MIDDLE-AGED MAN: What I mean is: if you only care about starting something without considering how it might end, and if you only go on the attack without organizing a retreat, then you shouldn't be in politics. You'll just become a sacrificial lamb in this game. You're really too green to be playing with politics, son. (26)

Incidentally, the Middle-aged Man's relentless chastising of the Young Man provides the most concrete illustration of how Gao's theories of political noncommitment and existential flight shape up in the face of actual political crises. His is a classic formulation of the bystander's supposed perspicacity, mixed with the proverbial wisdom of hindsight. Instead of trying to delve into the complexities of the event to gain some historical understanding that one can take into the present and future, the Middle-aged Man blames the victims for the tragedy and absolves himself of the need to comprehend or take partial responsibility. Instead of analyzing the specific situation at hand, he makes philosophical proclamations about the futility of collective politics in general. He then moves decisively into the existentialist realm with his thoughts on escape: "Escape! Escape is what we have to face now! It's destiny, yours and mine. To live is to escape, to run for your life all the time!" (14). And a bit later to the Girl: "It's our destiny, yours, mine, even his. It's in a man's destiny to escape, to run for his life" (27). And finally to the Young Man again:

MIDDLE-AGED MAN: Just because I don't want to be a playing card in someone else's hand, I've got to have my own will, my own independent and immovable will. So I've no choice but to run away!

YOUNG MAN: (*Becomes calm and hostile.*) I see. Then are you running away from us as well? Running away from the democracy movement?

MIDDLE-AGED MAN: I run away from everything related to the so-called collective will.

YOUNG MAN: If everyone were like you, there'd be no hope for this country.

MIDDLE-AGED MAN: What's a country? Whose country? Has it taken any responsibility for you and me? Why should I be held responsible for it? I'm only responsible for myself.

YOUNG MAN: And you'd just watch and let our nation perish?

MIDDLE-AGED MAN: I'm only interested in saving myself. If one day our nation is going to perish, then it deserves to perish! . . . Let me tell you, I don't subscribe

> to any ism, I don't need to. I'm a living human
> being. I'm not going to put up with being mas-
> sacred, or being dragged away and forced to kill
> myself. (28–29)

The Middle-aged Man's existentialism is not Sartre's but more aptly deemed a kind of fatalism, since for him no human action is adequate to changing or improving the social lot. In his speeches, the human condition and death itself become argumentative tools against the Young Man's pleas for political action: "Son, you have to stand it even if you can't. You have to stand defeat. Your blind enthusiasm is futile in the face of death" (13). If it is the human condition to suffer oppression, from oneself as much as others, then to oppose such oppression is inherently, existentially futile.

Since the Middle-aged Man's invocations of existential escape (*taowang*) and without isms (*meiyou zhuyi*) will reappear almost verbatim in Gao's essays, we are hard-pressed not to read this character as the authorial persona. We are moreover led to conclude that, in Gao's eyes, June 4 is chiefly a vehicle to paint in large strokes the oppressive capacities, not just of China's communist government or of authoritarian or ultranationalist regimes in general, but of *all* polities. The city in the play's backdrop, set afire by the military and filled with billowing smoke (8), is symbolically every city, every polis. This political allegory in turn functions to justify the necessity of existential flight, since every citizen, every human being who lives in a polis is thereby transformed into a refugee or fugitive. Along a metaphysical analysis, this movement from particular to universal can validly be entertained. Along a political one, however, this move problematically reduces and even normalizes totalitarianism into a species condition. As in Gao's essays, the particular political formation that leads to state-sanctioned bloodshed is conceptually erased and then metaphorically universalized. More specific to this play, the political context of Tiananmen—the flight of democracy activists from a state-orchestrated massacre—is summoned as a prototype only to be dismissed as a concrete reality for its participants. As a result, even a remote and detached spectator such as himself can now creatively appropriate the political fugitives' plight as an analogue to his own exile, for on Gao's logic, he too is an existential escapee. His aesthetic philosophy of the writer's universal license serves him well here, for the Tiananmen episode becomes eminently appropriatable without his jeopardizing either his repudiation of the PRC or his self-image as the cosmopolitan writer. This is the way in which *Taowang* existentializes the Square—and the way by which Gao inadvertently normalizes and legitimates totalitarian power.

But if there is one significant difference between Gao and the Middle-aged Man, it is surely their degree of distance from the massacre itself. This difference of location, I would argue, matters essentially. As much as Gao fashions the Middle-aged Man in his own image, it is patently not the case that he at any point lived on the threshold of Tiananmen's violence. His first knowledge of and access to the horrors of June 4, like much of the world's, occurred from afar and was mediated by television images and newspaper reports. Gao's diasporic location in 1989 coincides with Ha Jin's, and as I will discuss in the next chapter, the consciousness of diasporic distance pervades Jin's *The Crazed*, structuring almost every aspect of the novel's representation of the Square. By contrast, despite his overt cynicism and censure of the student activists, Gao produces a text that displays a subtle yearning for origin's violence, a nostalgia for being on-site at the place and time of China's greatest recent national trauma. He cannot directly experience such an event in the diaspora, but he can imaginatively and vicariously come into ownership of it via his double in the play. In this respect, we may speculate that the conflation of Gao with the Middle-aged Man, far from being an interpretive blunder, is actually a move meticulously plotted and promoted by the playwright himself, who takes pains to render this character recognizable as his fictional counterpart. If anything, given that *Taowang* precedes Gao's many essayistic formulations of existential flight and political noncommitment in the 1990s, we can say he has gone on in the post-Tiananmen decade to compulsively write and rewrite himself back into the play, in the exact image of his protagonist.

In this light, we might be tempted to interpret *Taowang* as an instance of traumatic writing. Gang Gary Xu, for one, reads Gao's two novels through precisely this lens, arguing that "the real traumatic core of Gao's writings" is the dilemma that "he writes in order to remember only to find writing requires the forgetting of what he desperately tries to remember" (126). Xu's reading converts Gao into a prototypical trauma victim of national crises, especially the Cultural Revolution, but such a reading falters when applied to *Taowang*. Since Gao did not personally live through June 4, any attempt to read this play via trauma theory must first establish the diasporic and appropriative perimeters of his artistic claiming of the massacre, an issue on which I will elaborate in the next chapter. What is striking about *Taowang* is Gao's aesthetic contraction of his diasporic distance. Despite his espousals of political detachment and intellectual aloofness, he pointedly projects his surrogate self onto origin's scene of violence. Indeed, as the play proceeds, the Middle-aged Man's symbolic marginality in relation to the Square becomes remapped, so that he edges ever-closer to the center of the killings. Ultimately, Gao's fictional locating of his authorial persona at the site of trauma serves less as a dramatic device for bearing historical witness than as circumstantial warrant for leveling criticism at the student movement.

Were Gao one to take a serious interest in the analysis of history, he would have found an abundance of published material in the last two decades to disabuse him of some of his initial reactions to the democracy movement. It is not my purpose here to provide an authoritative account of Tiananmen as a corrective to Gao's political opinions; such a task is beyond my ability, in any case. In chapter 4, I will explore in greater depth the controversy around the actual details of the massacre, but for now I will briefly mention a few relevant works that have shed invaluable light on the issue of the CCP leadership's decision to deploy force. Crucially, these works dispel a popular sentiment, endorsed by Gao and expressed complacently by his Middle-aged Man, that the protest movement was fated for a bloody end right from the outset—a sentiment that all too often serves as moral artillery against the students themselves. If the victims are partly to blame, then why follow in their footsteps by continuing their fight against tyranny? Bystanders can henceforth rest assured in conscience and mind, their sense of responsibility and feelings of revulsion assuaged. Among the earliest commentators to refute this view, however, was Ruan Ming, who wrote in no uncertain terms just two months after the massacre: "It is not true that the 1989 Democracy movement was doomed to failure" (Liu, Ruan, and Xu 108). Ruan maintains that "the real reason why the Democracy movement of 1989 failed is that the reformers within the Party were too indecisive, waiting and looking on, wavering and backing up. They, not the students, lost the opportunity"—and they, more than the students, were the ones "not united or organized" (104, 108). An erstwhile midlevel Party official in Hu Yaobang's pro-reform camp, Ruan has since left the PRC and gone on to write a study of Party politics in Deng Xiaoping's era, arguing that, ultimately, it was Deng's pragmatic succumbing to the antireform hard-liners that led to the carnage of June 4 (Ruan).

Ruan's argument has received some validation with the publication of *The Tiananmen Papers*. This massive compilation of government documents—including state security bureau reports and secret Politburo meeting minutes, all smuggled out of the PRC by a Party official with the pseudonym Zhang Liang—chronicles the CCP leadership's shifting viewpoints and internal power struggles during that Beijing spring. The documents reveal that the Politburo was not only intensely divided at the top but actually had a three-man majority in favor of dialogue with the students rather than martial law. As Andrew Nathan comments in the introduction to the volume, had this majority faction carried through on their vote and opened dialogue with the students, it "would have tipped the balance toward political reform, and China today might well be an open society or even an electoral democracy, possibly under the rule of a reformed Communist Party" (xviii). On Nathan's assessment, the students and the reformers "shared many goals and much common language," but "through miscommunication and misjudgment, they pushed one another into positions in which options for compromise became less and less available. . . . The slide to calamity seemed slow at first but then accelerated as divisions deepened on both sides. Knowing the outcome, we read the story with the sense of horror that we receive from true tragedy" (lv). Zhang Liang himself writes in the preface that, although the Tiananmen movement's failure was "inevitable," this failure stemmed from "the weakness of the reform faction at [the] highest levels of Party leadership" as much as the "divisions among the demonstrators and their lack of a tight organization or program" (xxxi–ii). He will later modify this statement in an interview by clarifying that "bloodshed was completely avoidable," that "it was not necessary to have killings" ("Tiananmen").

Together, these perspectives offer a compelling case against the notion that the democracy movement was doomed from the start. They do not deliver a "blind eulogy" that romanticizes the students as heroic martyrs, but they do attempt to uncover and evaluate the multifaceted reasons behind the movement's tragic outcome. In the process, these works broaden our understanding of the communist leadership and afford us a look, at once hopeful and heartrending, into the inner workings of a totalitarian government that nonetheless came extremely close to reforming itself from within. In short, in direct antithesis to *Taowang*, these works demystify totalitarian power. Craig Calhoun puts it most judiciously: "The democracy movement of 1989 was creative, vital, and full of possibilities. It did not succeed, over the short run, in achieving many of its participants' goals. Yet to say it was foreordained to fail is not realism but cynicism. Sometimes social movements do succeed against all the odds; fate speaks only after the fact in human life. For the Chinese people, and for the world, the events of spring 1989 have value as an inspiration, not just as a cautionary tale" (x). That Gao does not take into consideration any of this published material is a matter of authorial choice, of course, but his disregard adds neither wisdom nor perspicacity to his portrayal—and his audiences' comprehension—of Tiananmen.

What Gao gives us instead are simplistic and polarized images of 1989. In the play, the democracy movement is represented by the hotheaded student on one end and the wise writer-intellectual on the other. We have already explored how the Middle-aged Man hosts many of Gao's personal views. In addition, this character embodies the voice of worldly experience and shrewd insight in the play, and he is invariably given the most eloquent lines and intricate arguments. From the first, he is depicted as a paragon of grace under pressure. When he first enters the warehouse, the Young Man asks with hostility, "What do you want?" to which he answers with urbane composure, "Just looking for a place to hide, to smoke a cigarette" (7). Evidently, he is capable of cool-headedness and sarcastic humor even in the face of flying bullets. Though wishing to be a detached observer, he, too, as he soon discloses, was reluctantly drawn into the movement when he was asked to sign a petition. "How could I say no?" he says wryly. "Sometimes the signatures weren't even mine. People called you up and said your name had to be there. How could you refuse?" (24). The Middle-aged Man is thus presented as an intellectual who maintains dignity and calm even when crushed between the pressures of competing political groups.

The Young Man, on the other hand, is repeatedly shown to be crude, impetuous, and zealous to the point of hysteria. A mere mob child, he lacks individuality and substance of thought, and when matched against the older man, he cannot sustain a rational debate about the merits of the very political causes he champions. For every cynical and jaded rebuke by the Middle-aged Man, he counters with empty bravadoes, stock phrases, and ideological platitudes, such as "The people's struggle for freedom will triumph sooner or later, even if it has to be won with blood!" (13), or "call for a general strike by the workers and students! A civil war will soon break out!" (28). When he fails to convince the older man of the value of collective action, he alternately gets angry and aggressive, hollers, and at last dissolves into sobs and sinks into a sulky silence. His final, sputtering words on the topic of the protest movement are "All that bloodshed for nothing? But history, history will remember this day! This blood-stained day! This victorious day—" (30). It is therefore entirely in keeping with his character when, at the end of act 1, he impatiently scrambles to be the first to leave the warehouse and is thought to be killed by gunfire outside. The Middle-aged Man then passes this verdict: "He wanted to be a hero. The fool, he killed himself" (53). And a fool he is. Indeed, what is noticeably absent from the play is an interlocutor who can speak intelligently for the student movement and adequately engage the Middle-aged Man in political dialogue.

THE GIRL AND THE SPECTATOR

This denouement to the masculine debate about national politics conveniently sets the stage for the play's gendered drama in its second half. At this pivotal point, the Young Man's presumed death sends the Girl into immediate hysterics: "They've killed him!" she screams several times. The Middle-aged Man is thus prompted to take control of the situation. "Stop being hysterical!" he barks and, irritated, slaps her in the face. He then gruffly offers to sacrifice himself in order to protect her: "Go to the back and wait! Don't shout if they come looking for us. Don't utter a sound! Go and hide at the back, didn't you hear me?" (47). This display of paternalistic machismo has the effect of propelling the Girl into the older man's tender embrace. "Don't leave me on my own," she pleads, taking his hand. "Don't smoke, I'm scared of fire and light, I'm scared of everything." At her urging, and out of sheer pity, he starts to kiss her, as she "stands on her toes, enraptured." She soon becomes aroused and throws herself passionately on him, and after a brief initial protest, he yields to her "wild" and "wanton" womanhood (48–49). This scene of sexual consummation at the end of act 1 already foreshadows the play's climactic conclusion.

Midway through act 2, the Young Man is revealed to have survived his temporary exit and returns to the warehouse, only to discover with much embarrassment and resentment what he has missed in the meantime. At the beginning of the play, he had been the one to act as the strong manly protector to the Girl's damsel in distress. Indeed, throughout much of the first act, the two youngsters perform to a T stereotypical gender roles of masculine fortitude and feminine frailty. Their first scenes together, for example, repeatedly highlight the Girl's agitation and terror on the one hand and the Young Man's calmness and gallantry on the other. As she variously moans and weeps about the blood splattered on her dress, her sense of suffocation, and the imagined wounds on her body—"Where did this blood come from? . . . All over, I've got blood all over me! . . . My chest. I can't breathe. I'm going to die . . . I don't want to be a cripple! . . . I feel sick . . . I'm going to puke . . . I can't stand the smell of blood. . . . I really feel like crying"—he tries to soothe and steady her: "Calm down! It's only on your dress. Other people's blood. . . . Don't be silly. . . . You're perfectly all right. . . . Of course you're alive. We both are. We've managed to escape from the Square. . . . I'm right here beside you" (4–6). Tellingly, this scene occurs prior to the Middle-aged Man's stage entrance. The implication seems to be that the student activist breaks down into irrational tantrums only in the face of the wiser intellectual, and conversely, that it is only in the face of female weakness that he appears heroic and stalwart.

If the Young Man is discreet enough to step aside while the Girl takes off her blood-splattered dress in this initial moment, he will exhibit his masculine strength again with greater sexual prowess later in act 1, perhaps as a form of displaced aggression at being bested by the Middle-aged Man in political argument. Here the Girl relapses into a nervous hallucinatory trance: "I really can't take it any more! . . . My nerves are going to snap any minute! . . . I've got no feelings left, not even a little bit, my whole body's as stiff as a corpse. I wish somebody'd just shoot me and finish me off . . . I can't hear anything. Where am I? Don't leave me, I'm dying . . . floating,

floating on a river full of dead bodies . . ." In response, the Young Man tries once more to reassure her: "Close your eyes. . . . Just relax. Lean on me . . . You're good, alive and well . . . I'll protect you, I'll be with you all the time." This time, however, he delivers more than his share of chivalry as he exacts tribute in the form of fondling and kissing: "Your whole body is talking . . . Don't worry. I'm here . . . to caress you . . . so warm and soft." This physical intimacy between them comes to an abrupt conclusion when he, incited to sudden heights of desire by the obscene sound of passersby urinating outside the warehouse, frantically embraces and kisses her, even though she struggles to push him away (17–19).

The sexual interruption is only temporary, however, for this is the very scene the Young Man will resume at the play's end—on much more menacing terms. Upon his return to the warehouse, he spies the Girl's naked body and quickly infers what has happened between her and the older man. Dumbfounded and hurt, he threatens to leave, but she cajoles him into staying, and he collapses, sobbing, into her arms. He then begins to kiss her forcibly, over her shoves and protests. "How come you let him?" he demands, indicating the Middle-aged Man. "I wanted to," she answers coldly. "I'll do it with anybody I want! As long as I feel like it." "Anybody? Anybody who happens to pass by?" he asks, stunned at her indiscriminate promiscuity. "Even an asshole? Some horny philandering asshole! . . . You sure know how to put on an act! Whore—" (56). At this insult she slaps him, then kneels down and starts to cry. Without fail, her familiar display of female vulnerability halts him. Momentarily recalled to his chivalric code, he apologizes with much contrition. This detour into civility, though, does not last long, for the Girl proves herself to be his equal in the ways of verbal provocation and mockery. Refusing to play the forgiving woman this time around, she snarls bitterly: "'Sorry, sorry.' Always the same old 'sorry.' Just this one word is enough for a man to hurt a woman." She then reproves him in language oddly reminiscent of the Middle-aged Man's: "Nobody can save me. Nobody can save anybody. We're all passers-by. Don't think that just because you pulled me away and saved my life, I should be your woman, and I'll have to sleep with you. . . . You think that women are cheap, right? That they can't live without men? You're just a little boy, but you've got such a filthy mind" (57). Her vindication of the worth of women, and her diatribe against the "filthy" offenses of men, waxes even more vehement at the older man's show of sarcasm: "But you men are all the same inside. You think that women are all bad, but it's you who are the dirty ones. You only feel good after you've made women dirty, but in actual fact you've only managed to make yourselves dirty" (60). Finally, targeting both men, she explodes into a long speech on behalf of all women:

You're all depressed [or suffocated: *biemen*]. When you've dumped your troubles onto women, every one of you is a hero. You can't stand loneliness, but you demand that women be alone. You can't face yourselves, and the only thing you can do is prove that you're a man, a real man in front of women, but you won't allow a woman to prove herself, that she's a woman, a woman with integrity, dignity, and desires! (*Stands up. Proudly.*) You only allow yourselves to have desires, but you won't allow a woman, someone you possess, someone you claim to love, to have desires for anything but you. You only allow yourselves to have your so-called freedom, spirit, and will, but you won't allow other people to have them. You just pass on your pain to others—Every one of you is selfish, ugly, and wretched, and dying to show off your ego. (*Laughs to herself.*) You're only real when you're in front of women, the naked bodies of women, and when you're naked as well. (64)

After this clearly feminist speech, the Middle-aged Man suddenly takes her in his arms and kisses her; she—inexplicably—reciprocates, nestling into his embrace. It is in this instant that the Young Man, jealous, enraged, but feeling licensed to transgress at last, dashes over and wrestles her onto the ground. In the rape scene that follows, the two "roll around in the muddy water" as the Girl first "moans, then howls loudly like a wounded animal." In a perverse kind of narrative fulfillment, her recent anxieties over "filth" and her invectives against men's "dirtiness" are exteriorized in the plot and revisited on her own body. Gao's stage directions here dictate that the rape be prolonged, lyricized, almost ritualized: "Everything happens slowly and solemnly, accompanied by the continuous sound of dripping water." The Middle-aged Man has enough presence of mind to break away, but the Young Man appears not even cognizant of his own assault when he utters his last lines in the play a moment later, in panic and fright over the Girl's unconscious body: "What's wrong with you? Wake up! Wake up! She—?" (65).

So, in an alarming and rather bizarre turn of events, the student activist regresses into not only a mob child but, more damningly, a rapist, and an oblivious one at that. In an inversion of the student-government power dynamic that forms the play's backdrop, Gao casts his sole representative of the student movement in the role—not of victim, whether in part or in full—but of sexual aggressor, one of infantile and unthinking brutality. But the Girl, too, Gao implies, is a guilty victim. Just as the Middle-aged Man reprimands the Young Man early on for being "too green to be playing with politics" (*ni wan zhengzhi tai nen*) (26), so he says to the Girl after her feminist tirade that she is "playing with fire" (*ni zai wan huo*) (64). In both these grim warnings, he uses the word "play" (*wan*), at once compar-ing the two young people to children and invoking a rhetorical equivalence between the Young Man's national politics and the Girl's gender politics. Through the voice of the Middle-aged Man, Gao seems to suggest that the Girl is an overly reckless proponent of women's freedom, that by making speeches—like the Tiananmen students—in front of the wrong audience, she too is foolishly courting a destructive end. Indeed, the Girl's rape in the immediate wake of her fierce critique of patriarchy suggests a logic of punishment—for her insolent transgression into the masculine realm of politics, for her foolhardy demands for sexual freedom, and in the end, for playing the feminist.

In this conclusion to *Taowang*, we detect a correlation between Gao's unsympathetic critique of Tiananmen activism and his more sympathetic but nonetheless misogynistic critique of feminism. By aligning the mas-sacre of the students with the rape of the Girl, he maintains the conser-vative viewpoint that the disempowered of a society should not petition for their rights and freedoms too vigorously, since forcing the issue with the powers-that-be will only result in a wreaking of sovereign violence on their own persons. The disenfranchised and the powerless should flee from the polis and from every incarnation of power. To band together and form a collective movement is at best futile; at worst, it leads to further violence and possibly self-destruction. No doubt this is the implication of *Taowang*'s finale: the two young champions of the politics of freedom, hav-ing escaped the scene of a large-scale massacre, in the end cannot avoid a microcosmic reenactment of the use of force with each other. This is, after all, Gao's core criticism of all modes of collective politics. And this, finally, is the sinister way in which his theories of existential flight and political noncommitment become compatible with a kind of quietism, one that resigns itself to and perhaps even inadvertently validates every existing system of repressive power.

Significantly, the concerns raised by these two vectors of the play—the politics of gender and that of national governance—while interrelated, are not utterly interchangeable. I would suggest that it is precisely through a scrutiny of gender disparity in *Taowang*, a play ostensibly premised on national politics, that we can uncover a larger problem in Gao's writing, namely, his contradictory handling of the concept of otherness. As al-ready noted, critics of *Taowang* have consistently avoided tackling its most unsettling elements, particularly its representation of gender. As far as I know, in English-language sources at least, no critic has even mentioned the rape scene. This omission allows Henry Zhao, for instance, to declare with startling confidence that *Taowang* showcases Gao's "intense social-commitment," "social consciousness and sense of responsibility" (98). Sy

Ren Quah, in a more balanced analysis, nevertheless skirts the scene by focusing on the more gender-neutral denouement afterward, which enables him to conclude, in an existentialist vein friendly to Gao, that "by fleeing the collective, the individual will need only deal with problems of his or her own self" (184). Most curious of all, Mabel Lee, in her discussion of the play, focuses on the theme of sexuality at length and even summarizes in detail the physical flirting between the characters, only to abruptly switch to an exegesis of *One Man's Bible* just when she would have been obliged to address the Girl's rape. In place of that scene of sexual violation, Lee distills several narrative moments from Gao's novel that involve women voluntarily and enthusiastically offering their bodies to the autobiographical protagonist, moments that facilitate her feel-good thesis about Gao's portrayal of "sexual lust" as "an affirmation of life, a lust for life, in situations of extreme terror" ("Nobel" 8). By ignoring the play's representation of sexual violence, however, these critics end up giving subtle ideological consent to it.

Claire Conceison is therefore quite right in exhorting that issues of gender need to be "subjected to more self-conscious and deliberate feminist analyses" by Gao's critics. As she points out, his "disturbing gender hierarchies and depictions of the female . . . beg for immediate feminist critique or at least more serious analytical engagement" (752). A number of critics have heeded Conceison's call, most notably the contributors to a 2002 issue of *Modern Chinese Literature and Culture* devoted entirely to Gao's work. In the lead article, for example, Julia Lovell provides an instructive reading of Gao's two novels as largely a masculinist enterprise aimed at "recenter[ing] the marginal male intellectual" in post-Mao China ("Gao" 22). She situates him within the generation of post–Cultural Revolution male writers who feel a "deep sense of male anguish at their recollections of impotence while suffering political repression," and who consequently turn to quasi-autobiographical narratives of sexual fantasies and exploits in order "to reassert their freedom, strength, and masculinity" ("Gao" 25). Gang Gary Xu extends this gender analysis in a more positive direction when he reads Gao's novels as metatexts exposing the "symbolic constructedness" of gender itself, especially gender as constructed through traumatic events. Xu is, however, perhaps a bit too eager to acquit Gao of misogyny when he feeds the latter's "equation between political violence and sexual violence" into a psychoanalytic theory of masochism on which the emphasis shifts from gendered corporeality to the psychic economy of theatricality (119–25).

It is this equivalence between political and sexual violence that Carlos Rojas, in the same issue, firmly rejects, arguing that the female constitutes an "axis of alterity" in Gao's fiction. Of Gao's critics, Rojas is the one who most takes the Nobel laureate to task for his representations of gender. Where others credit Gao with cleverly transcending or self-consciously deconstructing gender differences, Rojas proposes that feminism constitutes a central ideological blind spot in Gao's writing, in which claims of feminism persistently get suppressed, erased, or denied (199–202). It is with biting irony, then, that Rojas titles his piece "Without [Femin]ism." None of these critics address Gao's drama at any length, if at all, and none deal with *Taowang*, but Rojas's critique can be aptly transferred to Gao's Tiananmen play. While an aesthetic of alterity is certainly not a necessary evil in the realm of literary representation (and theorists from Gayatri Spivak to Jean Baudrillard have usefully mobilized a notion of radical alterity in the service of postcolonial subaltern politics as much as critiques of contemporary mass media), I would nonetheless agree with Rojas and go further to propose that attention to the tendency toward ideological suppression in Gao's work will be valuable for pinpointing not just his gender politics but also his very conception of citizenship. Bringing these two aspects into interpretive alignment will clarify his problematic position of ideological complicity along multiple axes of alterity.

Returning to *Taowang*, then, we recognize how Gao's unequal gender politics is already apparent from the outset with his naming of the characters. Whereas the two men are referred to by gender-neutral terms distinguished only by their relative age, the female character is referred to as *Guniang*, which Gilbert Fong literally and fittingly translates as "Girl," even though she is several years older than the Young Man. The name conspicuously not chosen is "Young Woman," since the word for "woman" (*nüren*) connotes someone with sexual experience. All the same, the Girl's sexual identity is a point of debate in the play in a way not applicable to the men. In act 1, for example, the Middle-aged Man constantly calls her a "girl" while she repeatedly corrects him with "Stop saying 'girl' this and 'girl' that" (24) and "I'm a woman!" (48). Gender is hence mobilized as a determining factor only when the character is female, and then the relevant shades of difference become entirely a matter of sexual knowledge. Even the Girl's two aspirations—to become a wife and mother, and to be a successful actress—are highly feminized, dreamed of solely in relation to men, and emphatically tied to the sexualized body (21–23). Gao attempts to naturalize this link between woman and the sexual body by having the Girl herself, as we saw above in her definitive feminist speech, equate "reality" with "the naked bodies of women" (64). Although her criticism of the Middle-aged Man's philosophical posturing may be read as an intriguing instant of Gao's dramatic self-irony, we cannot but observe, too, that Gao stages this self-critique chauvinistically, by making the Girl ventriloquize his own gender biases and represent herself as wholly sexuality and body, in stark opposition to the men as mind and politics. In addition, in spite of her participation in the student demonstrations, the play defines her in terms of not national politics—a masculine realm consigned to the Young Man—but womanhood and corporeality. The only route by which she can enter the political domain is via gender, i.e., feminism. Yet even in this respect the Middle-aged Man will not grant her political authority, as evident in his crabbed remark to the Young Man: "It's real fun to listen to a woman talking philosophy like this" (61).

Gao's reduction of women into sexual bodies has the effect of essentializing them as bare life. Recalling Agamben's thesis, we can say that the rape scene at the end of *Taowang* posits women as the existential *homo sacer* to male sovereign aggression, an interpretation enhanced by the play's allegorical atmosphere. On this reading, the play seems to intimate that, even in circumstances of shared vulnerability to state power, even in the warehouse's suspended zone of relative protection, a woman will never acquire complete safety in the presence of men, and so she must live cautiously, moderately, modestly. By extension, the license permitted men to take part in affairs of the world, to enter into the polity, can never be fully accorded women by virtue of their greater and dual exposure to bodily violence. What the Girl brings upon herself may seem to be a gendered version of suicide, corresponding to what the Middle-aged Man calls the heroic mass suicide of the student activists (12), but the salient difference is that, while both the Girl and the Young Man successfully escape the carnage in the Square, at least temporarily, she alone cannot escape the more fundamental condition of womanhood, even in the symbolic space of common humanity and existential refuge. This is a point Gao drives home by having the absent scene of violence in the Square re-created exclusively, exceptionally on the female body. In effect, political violence—which Gao theorizes as universal violence—is uniquely displaced onto and inflicted upon the woman. In the play's existentialist calculus, not all "others" are equal, for some bear the brunt of actual suffering more than others. From this perspective, the closing scene that comes after the rape—where heavy pounding at the door signals the three characters' discovery by the troops and portends their eventual death together (66)—gives the impression of a dramatic cop-out. If the three share a common fate as victims to external power, if all distinctions of otherness are again erased among them as they face the same existential death, then it is pointless to hold anyone accountable for his or her actions in this life. The Young Man as much as the playwright can thus safely escape from specific responsibility to the burning polis as much as the violated woman.

Gao, however, plays a double game with the theme of escape. On the one hand, he promotes fleeing as the only mode of being that can preserve an individual's humanity and dignity. On the other, he advocates a kind of marginal spectatorship for the writer. In his essays, he often presents himself as a writer of "cold literature" who stands "at the social margins so he can better observe with stillness and self-reflect" ("Wo" 17), "an outsider and an observer who looks on with a pair of cold eyes [*yishuang lengde yanjing*]" ("Bali" 22). His notion of "looking" (*guancha*), unlike more current theories of historical witnessing, is not tied to any sort of social or political mission and is more properly regarded as a form of detached spectatorship. Its sole function is to satisfy the individual's personal desires and interests. In *Taowang*, this translates into the Middle-aged Man's contradictory stance toward violence. No "hero" by his own admission, he is as quick to flee the killings around the Square as anyone, and he justifies this as an unavoidable existential condition. Yet he also describes himself rather archly as a "bystander" or "passer-by" (*luren*) (26), someone who cannot help but watch events unfold from the sidelines even though he has no wish or intention to become a direct participant.[16] With this self-portrait as an isolated observer of national drama, he insinuates that he is after all a man of conscience with psychic investments in the country's well-being. When this role of the aloof spectator is transferred to a scene of sexual violence, however, it becomes suddenly much more chilling. Having warned both young people of their imprudent behaviors, the Middle-aged Man stays true to his self-description as a nonactivist and noninterventionist when he merely stands by and stares at the spectacle of the rape, "looking very sad" but unmoved to action even when the Girl keeps crying out, "No!" (65). He is implicitly credited with objectivity of mind for extricating himself from the two's rolling bodies, but paradoxically, and contrary to both his earlier reaction to the military crackdown and his advocacy of flight from every situation of power and force, he fails to absent himself from this scene of gendered violence, remaining not only anchored to the site of the woman's ravaging but transfixed by the sight of it. In effect, he comes to occupy the role of voyeur—complicitous in a guilty pleasure that no amount of "looking very sad" can nullify. Indeed, were he to live up to his own philosophy of escape or execute his role as passerby more fully, he would flee the scene of this latter crime as swiftly as he had that of the political massacre. Once more, then, we see an asymmetry in the way Gao portrays cool spectatorship vis-à-vis the gendered other versus the political other.

This brings us to the issue of Gao's own complicity in representational violence. Despite his self-proclaimed "fragility" and powerlessness as an individual and a writer, *Taowang* divulges his unconscious and incongruous positioning of himself in relation to power and lack. Ultimately, he lacks neither authorial agency nor complicitous desires when he grants himself the artistic license to re-present the Tiananmen massacre as the rape of the Girl, and then to project himself as spectator and voyeur at the scenes of both crimes. This collusion is in turn dramatically erased through his appeal to the theory of existential escape, by which he appropriates the plight of Tiananmen activists and of violated women alike as parallels to his own geographical exile and supposed intellectual marginality. At the same time, by existentializing the Square, he erases both gender inequality and totalitarianism as specific, nonuniversal structures of oppressive power, as well as his own possible complicity in them.

Most ironic of all, contrary to his self-presentation as first and foremost an individualist writer whose views and beliefs arise purely from his autonomous self, Gao's entire worldview is actually and vitally grounded in the Tiananmen episode. As noted, *Taowang* in fact precedes the 1990s essays in which he lays out his many theories of without isms, existential flight, political noncommitment, and detached spectatorship. His aesthetic philosophy, far from being an intellectual system that springs independently and wholesale from the chambers of a solitary mind, can in fact be traced back to his historically specific response to the PRC's use of force on June 4. Although he is in the habit of citing Henri Laborit's *Eloge de la fuite* (In praise of flight) as a book kindred to his own philosophical outlook, he himself admits that he discovered Laborit only after he finished writing *Taowang* (Lee and Dutrait 743). Gao, of course, is not one to attribute his own ideas to political history, but it will be his translators and critics who, in their canonization of him, decisively reverse the historical chronology and obscure the political debt. And so Mabel Lee, for one, after pointing out that Gao's theory of fleeing is galvanized after he wrote *Taowang*, goes on to explicate Laborit's thesis as Gao's philosophical "starting point" ("Nobel" 5). By contrast, we can say Tiananmen is the historical starting point of Gao Xingjian the individualist existentialist writer, and also the ideological origin of Gao Xingjian the Nobel winner. That is to say, possibly unbeknownst to himself, Gao is an eminently Tiananmen-inflected writer, and the international authorities in charge of literary canonization have aided in burying the trail of the massacre.

Gao's relation to Tiananmen is not simply one of moderate sympathy for the student activists, and certainly not one of political support for the movement, but essentially one of exilic nostalgia for the scene of origin's violence and ideological complicity with the power that wielded that violence. The nonrecognition of the specific nature of his link to Tiananmen has led the international media to rebrand his nostalgia and complicity as "dissidence." This raises the question of what needs and desires Gao satiates for the West. The answer can only be speculative, but on one level, perhaps his erasure of totalitarianism, from the writing of *Taowang* to his later essays, facilitates a kind of global amnesia about the massacre. This amnesia does not entail an utter forgetting of the event itself, for the memory of Tiananmen is resurrected frequently, if misleadingly, enough by the West, the media coverage on the 2000 Nobel being a good index. Rather, perhaps, this amnesia entails a forgetting of responsibility and complicity, of the memory of the world's position as spectators and voyeurs—much like Gao himself, psychically projected onto the conveniently proximate figure of the Middle-aged Man—enrapt by the scenes of atrocity brought close to home by technology, literally into the space of one's home via television, but not close to home enough to compel political or ethical intervention, either in personal or collective form. What Gao facilitates is this mode of empty memory, where the event becomes mediatized as a spectacle, imagistically globalized and diasporized but evacuated of all political and ethical urgency. At the same time, worldly spectators can be exonerated for their spectatorship when ensconced in Gao's soft humanism. With China's meteoric rise as an economic and political force on the international stage today, the task of reexamining Tiananmen's imprint on our current global cultural politics becomes ever more pressing. The task of reversing Gao's aesthetic of amnesia will fall to the most recent diaspora writer of Tiananmen, Ma Jian, in his 2008 novel *Beijing Coma*, which most fully reconnects June 4 as a cultural memory to the longer history of PRC totalitarian politics that both predates and postdates the massacre.

Finally, given Gao's harsh but timely critique of nationalism, we may be tempted to construe his determined attempts at existentializing space itself as symptomatic of a certain yearning for denationalization, a global map devoid of national boundaries. His prominence as a diaspora writer who combines Asian and Western aesthetic traditions contributes to this popular understanding of him as someone who strives to carve out for himself a new mode of inhabiting globalization by deterritorializing the imagination. Indeed, he frequently refers to himself as a "citizen of the world" in just this sense. Yet this effort is not unique to Gao, nor can it override the enduring significance of space and the power effects of national and governmental boundaries. The resurrected desire for humanism in our time, in order to distinguish itself from its Enlightenment precursors, must resolutely tie the politics of the human to a continual awareness of historical legacies of sovereign power. Gao, however, erases real differences in the world's unequal modes of political being, particularly the difference between his location now in a territory of political privilege and others' location in one of political repression. This theme of the persistence of location, nationality, and power will get taken up by Annie Wang in *Lili*, a text that situates Tiananmen within a larger international dynamics of global capital and contemporary orientalism. Before Wang's novel, though, we will first take an intermediate step toward globalization in Ha Jin's *The Crazed*, for which Tiananmen is conceived not existentially but diasporically, not as a universal species condition but an inaugural point for the Chinese diaspora.

2 / The Aporetic Square: Ha Jin's *The Crazed*

Ha Jin, the pen name of Jin Xuefei, is perhaps best known today for his numerous prestigious awards in the U.S. literary arena over the past dozen years. He is popularly thought of as an émigré Chinese writer who has "made it" in America, someone who came to the vocation of creative writing relatively late in life but nonetheless succeeded in establishing himself as a preeminent author in English, an adopted language that he, as is often noted, still speaks with a thick accent. For many, Jin serves as the poster child of immigrant success and the herald of a new breed of global literature, holding out the promise of cultural rebirth through transnational crossings and bilingual imaginings. Yet Jin's work can usefully be read in counterpoint to this image of writerly accomplishment. We can begin by situating his Tiananmen novel, *The Crazed* (2002), against the backdrop of two Nobel Prizes that bookend the decade of its publication, and in particular, against the worldwide representations of the Chinese intellectual that these prizes have promulgated. As in the previous chapter, I open here with a brief discussion of contemporary global discourses of the Chinese dissident, but then I turn to the novel itself to isolate two key themes, the student-intellectual relation and (im)perception, so as to elucidate Jin's changing self-image as a diaspora writer. The chapter's second half will focus on the text's portrayal of the massacre and the Square in order to bring to light what prevailing culturalist views of Jin do not—that he is above all a writer of political rather than cultural Chineseness and a critic of totalitarian power, but one whose vision is saturated with an aesthetic of diasporic witnessing and trauma. The final section, which explores Jin's reception on both sides of the Pacific, will help to locate him more specifically in a 1990s global critical terrain and to reveal Tiananmen's ongoing impact on Chinese diaspora discourse at large.

Part I. The Scholar and the Student

NOBEL POLITICS, ANOTHER DECADE LATER

Nobel awarders seem to mark their relationship to Chineseness in intervals of ten years. Where the 2000 Prize in Literature turned Gao Xingjian overnight into one of the most prominent global Chinese writers of our time, the 2010 Peace Prize, in an uncannily similar manner, bestowed instant international fame to Liu Xiaobo. Yet, unlike Gao, and long before either Nobel award, Liu had already made a name for himself inside China. In the mid-1980s, he had gained notoriety in academic circles for his bold and vociferous attacks on the post-Mao literary establishment. A mere Ph.D. student in his early thirties at the time, he had scathingly upbraided his professional superiors and cultural patriarchs for what he saw as their reactionary return to "roots." His iconoclastic outlook combined with his confrontational and brassy personality made him an outcast, albeit an illustrious one, in the years leading up to 1989, when he was regarded as more "the enfant terrible of Chinese literary critics" than a serious political activist (Calhoun 118). As Geremie Barmé expounds: "Liu's extreme and outspoken attitudes had made him generally unpopular with his peers on the Mainland. Notorious in Beijing as an abrasive and even ill-mannered figure, Liu was found intolerable by some people more used to less brusque (although not less demanding) cultural figures. In Beijing, his coarse, stuttering harangues during academic meetings, public lectures or even at sedate dinner parties in which he would assault every aspect of conventional wisdom left few people, either Chinese or foreign, kindly disposed to the fiery critic" ("Confession" 57).

Liu, however, thrived in his ostracism and turned isolation into a philosophical credo. Several years before Gao solidified his formulations on individualism and one year before the Tiananmen uprising, Liu published an essay entitled "On Solitude." In it, he condemned the Confucian tradition of the literati as servants to the state and called instead for a revolution in the idea of the Chinese intellectual:

> It's become fashionable for intellectuals to talk about self-negation. . . . To my mind the question at the heart of this intellectual self-negation and self-examination, which is also the self-negation of Chinese traditional culture itself, is the need for the individual to extricate himself from the collective consciousness and break free of all external bonds so as to enter a liberating state of solitude. . . .

Solitude implies independence, self-reliance; it means not following the crowd. . . . While many intellectuals, especially undergraduate and postgraduate university students, like to put on the mask of
nonconformist isolation, they are in fact united by their collective
consciousness. . . . For Chinese intellectuals, solitude must start with
a complete negation of the self, because throughout our long feudal
history, Chinese intellectuals were never independent thinkers, they
were but "court literati." The establishment of the imperial examination system assured the rulers of a means of depriving intellectuals of their independence. People studied not to become independent
thinkers but to win a career in the bureaucracy, in the hope of serving an enlightened ruler. This predetermined political goal restricted
the development of the personality and limited range, depth, and
perspective of knowledge. By the Ming and Qing dynasties there was
virtually no school of thought apart from Confucianism. (207–8)

Of himself he would declare: "I am myself, nothing more. I worship no one
and am no one's lackey; I'm a perpetual loner. This [creed] is the basis of
true pluralism. . . . In feudal society, people believed their fate depended
on a savior, an emperor; what we need in China today is the attitude that
whether you go to heaven or hell is all up to you" (208–9). Liu's assertion
of the intellectual's necessary independence and self-reliance, his supposed antipathy for collective thinking, and his self-description as simply a "perpetual loner" and "nothing more" clearly anticipate many of the
themes in Gao's essays. Liu's style, though, is decidedly brasher, cruder,
the voice of the irreverent young rebel rather than that of the elderly sage-
philosopher (recall here the discontented but authoritatively chiding voice
of the Middle-aged Man in *Taowang*). Apart from tone, Liu differs from
Gao in another crucial respect: his attitude toward politics. As the passage
above suggests, Liu sees intellectual individualism as the "basis of true pluralism." In contrast to Gao, then, who opposes the individual to the polis
as such, Liu defines the intellectual not in terms of a categorical refusal of
politics but as the very foundation of a democratic society.

This key difference between the two Nobel laureates is displayed with
remarkable starkness in their opposite conduct vis-à-vis Tiananmen. Although both men were safely abroad in the spring of 1989—Gao had been
residing in France since 1987 while Liu had left China in 1988 as a visiting scholar, first at the University of Oslo, then the University of Hawai'i
and finally Columbia University—the former decided to stay on in France
while the latter flew back from New York to Beijing in April, at the start
of the student protests, with the express intent of joining the democracy

movement. Barmé is again instructive in explicating Liu's distinction among overseas Chinese intellectuals during this period:

> Liu certainly was frustrated by the empty talk of Chinese émigrés in America and inspired by the student protests. Chen Jun also talks of the moral pressure Liu had felt at work on him following the burgeoning of the student demonstrations. While other Chinese intellectuals pontificated on the origins, significance and direction of the student movement from the Olympian heights of the West, Liu had the courage of his convictions. Chen quotes Liu as saying: "Either you go back and take part in the student movement; otherwise you should stop talking about it." He was critical of Fang Lizhi's reluctance to participate so that the movement could maintain its "purity." Liu felt it was important for people who had been part of the democracy movement in China in the past or those who had studied it now to come out and direct it. ("Confession" 59)

According to Barmé, Liu's aggrandized self-image as a man of action who follows through on his word despite potential danger, an image modeled after his romantic idols of Rousseau and Nietzsche, may have contributed to his decision to return to China ("Confession" 60). An equally romantic belief in the unavoidable suffering that comes with moral courage may further shed light on Liu's almost "suicidal" behavior after June 4, when he resisted going into hiding or seeking asylum abroad—like most student leaders and intellectuals involved in the protests at the time—and instead appeared to "court disaster" by openly riding around Beijing on a bicycle, as though to complete the final scene in a long-standing "tragedy of individualistic and heroic Chinese intellectuals of the last century: to travel a course from self-liberation to self-immolation" ("Confession" 53). This apparent martyr syndrome notwithstanding, there is heaven and earth between Liu's deliberate return to the Square during the actual state of emergency and Gao's belated and elaborately justified self-distancing from it. Liu would go on to help launch a four-man hunger strike in the Square beginning on June 2 (along with the Taiwanese rock star Hou Dejian, the reformist think-tank head Zhou Duo, and the former chief editor of Beijing Normal University's weekly Gao Xin), and though this hunger strike was meant to last only seventy-two hours, as a symbolic gesture of the intellectuals' solidarity with the students under conditions of martial law, its fateful timing placed the four men inside the Square on the eve of its evacuation. Thus did Liu and his cohort become vital agents of history, negotiating with army officers for the safe passage of the last group of students from the Square in the early hours of June 4.

With the 2010 Peace Prize, Liu's reputation comes full circle, from iconoclastic critic to iconic dissident, but the circle itself has become globalized. As in the case of Gao, Liu's role as the consummate Chinese intellectual of our time has been largely determined by those outside the PRC—even if Liu himself remains in prison inside the country. Once again, the individualist thinker and pro-democracy advocate is held up by the world as the epitome of Chinese intellectual integrity. The difference is that, with Liu, there is no need to fabricate his political involvement in Tiananmen or his ensuing persecution by the communist government. Liu Xiaobo's life lives up to its mythology. Despite several jail terms after June 4, he continued to risk his personal freedom by forwarding the campaign for democracy from within the PRC from the 1990s onward, most recently by co-drafting Charter 08. He fulfills superbly Edward Said's paradigm of the intellectual as a public figure who speaks truth to power, who symbolically occupies the margins of a polis so as to better critique its regime's excesses. Indeed, Liu has solidly supplanted Gao as the new global face of the Chinese intellectual. What persists from the millennial Nobel to this latest one, or perhaps what gets revived, is the underlying geopolitics of recognition, whereby the liberal West plays enlightened defender once more to the incorrigible Oriental despot. With Liu as with Gao, this global geopolitics with regard to Chineseness is profoundly tied to Tiananmen. As I argued in the previous chapter, contrary to the international media's anachronistic narrative of Gao as a writer whose dissident politics led to his exilic status, an inverted and linearized chronology along which identity and belief precede event, Gao in fact arrived at his philosophy of existential flight only after—and precisely in light of—June 4. In reality, then, not only has Tiananmen produced a new generation of refugees post-1989, but more fundamentally, it has galvanized subsequent world discourses about China around the figure of the Chinese intellectual-dissident-exile, shaping the very conceptual languages and frameworks through which Chineseness is written, comprehended, and sometimes rewarded. Liu Xiaobo represents the latest incarnation of this ongoing phenomenon of Tiananmen's global discursive effects.

Significantly, this contemporary worldwide representation of the Chinese intellectual as the quintessential *écrivain engagé* is wholly dissolved in the fictional work that most closely connects Tiananmen to 1980s intellectual culture, Ha Jin's *The Crazed*. No stranger to prizes himself, Jin can be considered the American counterpart to Europe's Gao. Since winning the 1999 National Book Award for his debut novel, *Waiting*, Jin has gone on to become one of if not the most prolific and widely read contemporary American writer of life under communist China. Up until a recent novel (*A Free Life*) and short-story collection (*A Good Fall*), Jin's fiction has dealt exclusively with PRC national history, from the Korean War (*War Trash*) to the Cultural Revolution (*Under the Red Flag, Ocean of Words, Waiting*) and the post-Mao era (*In the Pond, The Bridegroom*) to the 1989 Tiananmen episode (*The Crazed*). And most recently, instead of moving forward chronologically into the present, his latest novel (*Nanjing Requiem*), released just days ago even as I write, rewinds to an earlier period of national crisis by focusing on the Second Sino-Japanese War and the Nanjing Massacre. Along the way, Jin has garnered an impressive array of awards, winning three Pushcarts, a Flannery O'Connor, a PEN/Hemingway, two PEN/Faulkners, and a Guggenheim. Additionally, unlike Gao, Jin composes exclusively in English (setting aside for the moment his self-translation into Chinese), which facilitates his standing in the United States as a domestic rather than foreign writer. His entry into the American literary mainstream is further signaled by the enthusiastic reception of his work by such highbrow institutions as the *New Yorker*, which has favorably reviewed almost all his books and recently published one of his short stories.[1] Jin's literary rise in the United States thus parallels Gao's across the Atlantic, and in a roughly contemporaneous time frame.

As we saw with Gao, this institutional appropriation of the contemporary Chinese diaspora writer by the West does not necessarily reflect a writer's aesthetics or politics in any nuanced way. Rather, it is symptomatic of the broad cultural-political conditions by which the Chinese diaspora writer's work now comes to be circulated and read outside of the PRC. To be sure, a writer's willingness to criticize the communist government can help smooth his or her path into the Western liberal establishment, and Jin too makes himself amenable in this regard. Indeed, perhaps the most basic point of convergence between Jin and Gao is their decision to represent Tiananmen at all. Not only does this choice of subject matter allow both authors to brand themselves as unequivocal opponents to totalitarian state power, but the very act of writing Tiananmen in the West becomes performative, at once a defiant rebuke of the communist regime's censorship and an implicit validation of the expressive freedoms afforded by Western democracies. On the issue of the geopolitics of artistic autonomy, Gao and Jin are in total agreement.

Jin, however, is no existentialist writer. Although he professes to be a humanist, commenting forthrightly in an interview that, "unlike most academics, I do believe in universals and that there is truth that transcends borders and times" (qtd. in Zhou 274), his humanism never eviscerates human experience of its geographical coordinates but is always grounded in specific historical spaces and times. In antithesis to Gao's, Jin's universalism does not oppose the timeless to history, the human to the polis. As he puts it in another interview: "I've never intended my writing to be political, but my characters exist in the fabric of politics. That is to say, it is impossible to avoid politics, especially in China" ("Art"). The polis as such matters in his fiction, as do the particularities of communism and the forms of life it yields. He will not be one to erase political distinctions and generalize the totalitarian state as a planetary paradigm or June 4 as the culmination of all collective politics. With almost stubborn tenacity, his writing retains the PRC's historical and political specificity and resists abstracting it into simply any modern nation-state. In this respect, Jin's diasporic aesthetic is much more kindred to Ma Jian's than to Gao's.

Of the imagined geographies of his fiction, Jin is perhaps best known for his portrayal of Cultural Revolution China. Although *The Crazed* depicts the decade after, the liberalization era under Deng Xiaoping, Jin intimates that the Cultural Revolution's legacy continues to be felt in everyday social life into the late 1980s. The novel focuses on the sphere of academe and presents a deeply pessimistic portrait of the disintegration and death of intellectualism in the post-Mao period. On the surface, the novel seems to be only incidentally about Tiananmen. The bulk of the story, in classic bildungsroman style, follows the personal and academic travails of a graduate student of comparative literature in the wake of his mentor's stroke. Much of the novel is set in a hospital room, as the protagonist overhears and then tries to unravel the mysteries of his teacher's ravings. While this narrative appears modest in scope, dwelling mostly on private relationships and professional rivalries in a provincial university town, its temporal setting in the spring of 1989 and its spatial climax in the blood-splattered streets of Beijing render the novel an important instance of Tiananmen fiction. Through the titular metaphor, Jin anchors his Tiananmen plot in the key figure of the crazed scholar-intellectual. The novel's concluding address of the massacre must therefore be read not apart from but in direct relation to its central narrative of small-town academic life, which is also Jin's retrospective meditation on the myriad ways the intellectual as social ideal becomes defeated and destroyed—not after June 4, but already in the decade preceding it.

Ultimately, Jin's dystopic appraisal of the pre-Tiananmen intellectual realm can be understood in terms of his own diasporic position in 1989. Of the four writers examined in this book, Jin was the one located farthest from Beijing, and also the one with the longest absence from China, at the time of the military crackdown. He is also the writer with the most heightened sense of his own diasporic removal from the events of June 4, returning time and again in interviews to this historical moment as the inauguration of his immigrant life. This acute self-consciousness of the link between Tiananmen and his own diasporic condition manifests structurally in *The Crazed* via what I will call the lost Square—a site gestured at by the novel as the heart of China's national struggle, yet simultaneously a site of failed arrival for the novel's narrator and hence a conspicuous narrative lacuna for Jin as much as the reader. Where Gao's Square is existential, Jin's is aporetic. This vanishing of the Square, I would suggest, epitomizes Jin's diasporic aesthetic and the diasporic melancholia that saturates his corpus.

INTELLECTUAL RUPTURES

As we saw with Gao's *Taowang* and as I will elaborate in chapter 4 concerning the diasporic image wars on Tiananmen, discussions of 1989 often draw attention to the volatile relationship, alternately collaborative and contentious, between intellectuals and students during that Beijing spring. If one of the main dramatic tensions of Gao's play lies in the ideological sparring between the Middle-aged Man and the Young Man, this scene of political discord along generational lines and its attendant social types have become all too familiar in Tiananmen discourse by the mid-1990s. Global commentators on Tiananmen frequently marshal these two stock figures—the young, idealistic, hotheaded student protester versus the older, more cautious and world-weary but much wiser intellectual—as explanatory synecdoches for what went wrong with the democracy movement. Many of these accounts tend to posit the student-intellectual relationship as an oppositional one, casting the two groups as utterly discrete social categories. Gao's play, in fact, is one of the earliest articulations of this relation as ossified, perhaps hyperbolically, difference. These approaches tend to shift the focus of analysis away from the political clash between democracy and totalitarianism and displace the principal line of conflict from the people versus the state to students versus intellectuals, radicals versus moderates. In doing so, they have had the damaging effect of polarizing debates about Tiananmen and, worse, escalating disagreements about political method into accusations of moral blame.

Ha Jin's *The Crazed*, by contrast, takes as its starting point an originally idealized continuum between student and intellectual, but one that is thrown into crisis at exactly this watershed moment of the days leading up to June 4. The novel's first line already associates Tiananmen with the central motif of intellectual rupture: "Everybody was surprised when Professor Yang suffered a stroke in the spring of 1989" (3). Shenmin Yang, the most apparent though not the only possible referent of the titular "crazed," had seemed the model intellectual before his stroke: an energetic and dedicated teacher and an erudite and respected scholar of comparative literature, he was the envy of his colleagues and a paragon for his students at Shanning University. The novel's protagonist and narrator, Jian Wan, is at once Yang's chief pupil and son-in-law to be, engaged to his daughter, Meimei. Of these two relationships, the one of greater priority for Jian is undoubtedly that with the father. Not only does Jian's tutelage under Yang predate his acquaintance with Meimei, but the story of the couple's ostensible courtship, narrated through a flashback, revolves entirely around the younger man gaining the older one's approval about career choice. Three months prior to his first meeting her, Jian had received a lucrative job offer from a Hong Kong trading company but had ultimately declined it, heeding Yang's advice to forego materialism so as to continue his study of poetry, to enrich his "heart" and become a spiritual "aristocrat" instead. The announcement of his engagement to Meimei comes at the end of this backstory, as a one-line capstone to the larger masculine narrative of quasi-filial obedience and vocational inheritance. Tellingly, Meimei is referred to in this last line not by name but merely as "[Yang's] daughter" (67), the patriarch's prize to the protégé for faithfully following in his footsteps.

The novel, of course, opens with the decisive disruption of this projected plot of Confucian patronage and elite social continuance via Yang's stroke, which in turn coincides with the eruption of pro-democracy protests in Beijing. The dimension of the national allegory is plainly evident: Yang is not just a prototype of the Chinese intellectual but simultaneously an emblem of China itself in 1989. His cerebral "blood clot" and "blockage" at the beginning of the novel (13–14) find numerous objective correlatives in the "blocked" streets of Beijing later in the text (300–301), and his eventual fatal brain hemorrhage (257) prefigures the scene of a student being shot in the head (303) and the carnage at large in the capital toward the novel's end. More horrifically, the gradual enfeebling and putrefaction of Yang's body, wrenched out of his control and reduced to a spectacle of slow living death, offers a potent dual metaphor of the decay of the intelligentsia as well as that of the national polity. With macabre fastidiousness does Jin dwell on the details of the professor's corporal rot, from the "festering boil below his left shoulder blade" and its draining pus to his "diseased gums . . . ulcerated in places and bleeding" and his "heavily furred" tongue (59), from his "fingers reddish and swollen, with fungus-infested cuticles" (123) and his molding head where dead hairs amass to the "whiff of decay escap[ing] from his insides" (60). Yang's stroke, then, does not simply represent the country's mental breakdown but functions as the premise on which Jin allegorizes late-1980s China as a grotesque body rotting inside and out.[2] As we will see, the paralytic and putrid near-cadaver as a symbol of the national body politic will resurface in Ma Jian's *Beijing Coma*, with even greater imagistic force and argumentative scope. This deployment of the single decrepit body as a trope for post-Mao China evinces a powerful strain of the gothic in Tiananmen fictions. Conversely, we could say that

Tiananmen marks one route by which Chinese diasporic literature finds its way to a gothic aesthetic and then repeatedly, hauntingly returns to it.

At the same time, the device of allegory allows Jin to amplify the resonances of Yang's sometimes lucid, sometimes rambling voice, which, under auspices of madness, is ultimately the only one that can speak truth to power. Yang, in other words, gives both body and voice to the country's decomposition. In his post-stroke speeches, he constantly spews forth cynical conceits of China, likening it to a "chopping board" at one point (220) and a "pickle vat" at another (206), and the Chinese to pieces of meat or marinated vegetables. "In such a pickle vat," he tells Jian, "even a stone can be marinated and lose its original color and begin to stink" (206). In his more inspired moments, Yang spins out one sinister parable after another of life under authoritarian rule, and it is not by accident that his thematic accent falls consistently on the suffocation of the mind.

The novel opens, for instance, with his revisionist version of Genesis. The moral of the story, Yang tells Jian, is that "Man's life cannot but be alienated from itself," that after living out his first twenty years as a carefree monkey and the next twenty as a laborious donkey, the life of the human intellect begins only when Man's "body is worn out, his limbs are feeble and heavy, and . . . his brain . . . has begun deteriorating too." Nonetheless, Man continues to cramp his brain with knowledge until one day it "becomes too full and cannot but burst . . . like a pressure cooker which is so full that the safety valve is blocked up, but the fire continues heating its bottom." The result, with none too subtle echoes of Yang's own stroke and the concurrent Beijing protests, is that "the only way out is to explode" (12). This retelling of species origins, in which biblical themes of human creation are recouched in Marxist language of self-alienation, may be read as a parody of communism's prioritizing of physical over intellectual labor, and perhaps even as a camouflaged diagnosis of the psychopolitical causes behind Tiananmen. Whether Yang himself is fully aware of the interpretive reverberations of his story does not matter so much as the fact that his life exemplifies the cerebral failure he outlines. Yang's equation of humanity with the intellect reflects his elitism, to be sure, but also a deep disappointment in his own failure to live up to the ideals of his youth.

A few pages later, Yang offers another bleak parable, this time with more overt cues to 1980s China:

> All the time he has been thinking how to end everything, to be done with his clerical work, done with his senile, exacting parents, done with his nagging wife and spoiled children, done with his mistress Chilla, who is no longer a "little swallow" with a slender waist but is obsessed with how to lose weight and reduce the size of her massive

backside, done with the endless worry and misery of everyday life, done with the nightmares in broad daylight—in short, to terminate himself so that he can quit this world. . . .

But he lives in a room without a door or a window and without any furniture inside. Confined in such a cell, he faces the insurmountable difficulty of how to end his life. On the rubber floor spreads a thick pallet, beside which sits an incomplete dinner set. The walls are covered with green rubber too. He cannot smash his head on any spot in this room. He wears a leather belt, which he sometimes takes off, thinking how to garrote himself with it. Some people he knew committed suicide in that way twenty years ago, because they couldn't endure the torture inflicted by the revolutionary masses anymore. They looped a belt around their necks, secured its loose end to a hook or a nail on a window ledge, then forcefully they sat down on the floor. But in this room there's not a single fixed object, so his belt cannot serve that purpose. Sometimes he lets it lie across his lap and observes it absentmindedly. The belt looks like a dead snake in the greenish light. What's worse, he cannot figure out where the room is, whether it's in a city or in the countryside, and whether it's in a house or underground. In such a condition he is preserved to live.

. . . He's thus doomed to live on, caged in an indestructible cocoon like a worm. (16–18)

The implicit tenor of this figurative "cell" and "indestructible cocoon" is undoubtedly China, but one that is no longer marked with the telltale signs of the Maoist state from "twenty years ago," with its public denunciations and mass persecutions. In the politically relaxed climate of the late 1980s, the man in the story can have a job as a clerk, the means to support his parents and spoil his children, even a mistress with a Western name (a detail Jian picks up on and mulls over at length) and a leather belt to boot. By all external measures, the man leads a bourgeois life and leads it unharassed. Yet, from Yang's perspective, this contemporary milieu is even more insidiously disempowering than the Cultural Revolution, when people at least had the ability to commit suicide in their prisons. In his new situation, the man is cushioned all around, utterly protected from self-harm but also utterly deprived of self-determination. There is no longer any detectable difference between life in the city and life in the countryside: that formerly all-important geographical distinction has disappeared from view in the uniformity of the current era. All is made comfortable, and all are merely "preserved to live." Akin to Yang's body, the cocoon-cell carries multiple connotations. While it allegorizes the nation on a macro level, it simultaneously conjures up the novel's environment of the provincial town, hovering between rural and urban. More specifically, it captures Yang's private hospital room, where he is ostensibly cared for by the state and preserved as a future "national treasure" (7) but is in reality left to degenerate "in broad daylight." Yang makes the self-reference explicit in one of his last cogent moments, in a desperate cry to Jian: "Oh, how can I get out of this suffocating room, this indestructible cocoon, this absolute coffin? How can I liberate my soul? I don't want to die like a worm" (203).

The intertextual allusion here that renders Jin's national allegory unmistakable is Lu Xun's famous metaphor of China as an iron house without windows. In his preface to *Call to Arms*, Lu Xun recounts the episode that first prompted him to turn to fiction writing: "In S— Hostel there were three rooms where it was said a woman had lived who hanged herself on the locust tree in the courtyard. Although the tree had grown so tall that its branches could no longer be reached, the rooms remained deserted." This setting of the enclosed courtyard, where the instrument of suicide has now grown out of reach, quickly brings to mind the cocoon room and prison cell of Yang's story. And like the pre-stroke Yang, the patient scholar who devotes himself to the transcendent study of poetry, Lu Xun depicts his younger self here as a humble scribe content with "copying ancient inscriptions" and letting his life "slip quietly away" had it not been for the fateful visit of a friend one day. "What is the use of copying these?" his friend demands, and then asks Lu Xun to contribute to the revolutionary magazine he is editing (4). Their next exchange is Chinese literary lore:

> However I said:
> "Imagine an iron house without windows, absolutely indestructible, with many people fast asleep inside who will soon die of suffocation. But you know since they will die in their sleep, they will not feel the pain of death. Now if you cry aloud to wake a few of the lighter sleepers, making those unfortunate few suffer the agony of irrevocable death, do you think you are doing them a good turn?"
> "But if a few awake, you can't say there is no hope of destroying the iron house." (5)

Republican-period China, liberated from imperial rule but still shackled by the ideologies of feudalism and imperialism, is for Lu Xun an iron house forever shrouded in darkness, "absolutely indestructible," and a place of inescapable psychic suffocation. Nonetheless, at his friend's urging, he turns to fiction as a means of "destroying the iron house," thus demonstrating a basic faith in the efficacy of intellectual and literary labor, and not solely in itself but in the interests of national salvation. As Jin puts it in his introduction to a recent edition of Lu Xun's short stories: "Clearly from the very beginning [Lu Xun] saw himself as a spiritual doctor, a Nietzschean superman in a sense, who would try to diagnose and cure the disease in the soul of China, the Sick Man of Asia. His medicine was literature, which he believed could stir and wake up the Chinese" ("Introduction" ix).

Like many contemporary Chinese writers, Ha Jin is at once indebted to and rebellious against this canonized father of modern Chinese literature. On Jin's assessment, Lu Xun became the perfect tool for the communists precisely because of his conscious subordination of literature to politics. Lu Xun's "conception of literature is founded on utilitarianism," Jin observes; "for him, literature must serve a purpose and contribute to the liberation of the Chinese from their feudalistic culture and capitalist oppression. As a result, every piece of writing must be useful in the struggle, like a dagger or a javelin." Moreover, Lu Xun "subsumed literature and arts under politics; this coincides with the communist theory of the function of literature and arts, which must form a part of the revolutionary apparatus" ("Introduction" xiv). Jin's evaluation echoes Gao Xingjian's lament that "it was a misfortune for literature that the writer Lu Xun was crushed to death by the politician Lu Xun" ("Bali" 15). In Jin's as much as Gao's eyes, Lu Xun represents not a paragon but a cautionary tale. For them both, one of the primary lessons of communist history is that literature can never be made subservient to politics, whether for the party-state or an oppositional collective. On the necessity of art's independence from external pressures, Jin and Gao sound a similar chord.

As Jin maintains in his essay "The Spokesman and the Tribe," "genuine" literature "must be predicated on [its] autonomy and integrity": "The writer should enter history mainly through the avenue of his art. If he serves a cause or a group or even a country, such a service must be a self-choice and not imposed by society. He must serve on his own terms, in the manner and at the time and place of his own choosing. Whatever role he plays, he must keep in mind that his success or failure as a writer will be determined only on the page. That is the space where he should strive to exist" (30). Like Gao, Jin does not prohibit writers from serving a larger cause, even a nationalist one, but this service must never take priority over art for its own sake. Indeed, Jin recounts in this essay how his own career trajectory and self-image have been revised along exactly these lines. When he first began to write in the United States, he admits, he saw himself as a "spokesman for the unfortunate Chinese" back home, partly because of the education he had received in China, and partly because, like many émigré writers from less-developed countries, he felt guilty for "emigrating to the materially privileged West." Over time, though, he found this claim to be "groundless," especially when he discovered that "a country can take a writer to task and even accuse him of misdeeds, betrayal, or other crimes against the people" (4). In his most recent phase, Jin tends to see himself as a "migrant" writer, but he is now more cynical about the efficacy of writers at large: "I could agree with Gordimer wholeheartedly that a writer must be 'more than a writer' and must be responsible to the well-being of his fellow citizens. . . . However, as I continued writing, the issue of the writer's essential gesture as a social being grew more complicated to me. Writers do not make good generals, and today literature is ineffective at social change. All the writer can strive for is a personal voice. . . . There is no argument that the writer must take a moral stand and speak against oppression, prejudice, and injustice, but such a gesture must be secondary, and he should be aware of the limits of his art as social struggle" (29). So, although Jin affirms the need for writers to confront social and political ills much more strongly than does Gao, he too ultimately concludes on a note of individualism, on the private ends of literature. Renouncing the prototype of the tribal spokesman, he now avows: "I must learn to stand alone, as a writer" (28)—an echo, as it turns out, of Liu Xiaobo's manifesto on intellectual "solitude." Still, Jin recognizes that the stance of individualism is not itself apolitical within the PRC, for "the Chinese authorities are afraid of truthful stories told from an individual's point of view" ("Art").

In *The Crazed*, the extent to which Jin rejects Lu Xun's example of politicized art can be gauged by his pointed rewriting of the iron house conceit. In a scene that parallels the one above where Lu Xun's friend visits him at Shaoxing Hostel, Jin dramatizes a pivotal conversation, one that Jian fortuitously overhears, when one of Yang's colleagues pays him a visit at Shanning Hospital. As the colleague attempts to reassure Yang that his work has been appropriately reallocated during his absence, Yang dismisses his academic duties as futile "clerical work" and goes on to proclaim the utter impossibility of true intellectualism in China:

> "Who is an intellectual in China? Ridiculous, anyone with a college education is called an intellectual. The truth is that all people in the humanities are clerks and all people in the sciences are technicians. Tell me, who is a really independent intellectual, has original ideas and speaks the truth? None that I know of. We're all dumb laborers kept by the state—a retrograde species."
>
> "So you're not a scholar?"
>
> "I told you, I'm just a clerk, a screw in the machine of the revolution. You're the same, neither worse nor better. We are of the same ilk and have the same fate, all having relapsed into savagery and cowardice. Now this screw is worn out and has to be replaced, so write me off as a loss." (153)

other professor suggests that the younger generation of scholars ιn will "make improvements" and "learn from [the older men's] and losses," Yang sneeringly retorts, "At most he'll become a se-ι." And then, in the novel's most direct allusion to Lu Xun, Yang concludes of Jian: "He'd better leave this iron house soon so that he won't end up a mere scribe here. In our country no scholars can live a life differ-ent from a clerk's. We're all automatons without a soul" (154). Jin's implica-tion is clear: Lu Xun, despite his lofty ambitions, was a "mere scribe" even to the end of his career, a "screw in the machine of the revolution," and Yang is his fictional successor. The trappings of intellectual labor may have changed, the revolutionary may have turned academic, but the intellec-tual's essential function as a "dumb laborer kept by the state" remains the same. This is just the vision of the post-Mao intellectual that Liu Xiaobo criticizes. But instead of a call to arms, the iron house here provokes a de-sire for immigration. There is an epiphany here for Jian as for Lu Xun, but not one that affirms the value of intellectual work for the national good. For the first time, Jian realizes that his mentor has never fully validated his efforts at acquiring a Ph.D. This realization sets in motion a process of self-doubt that will dramatically change the course of Jian's life in the remain-der of the novel: "The former vision of myself as one who must study hard to become an eminent literary scholar had vanished, replaced by the image of a feckless clerk who was already senile but wouldn't quit scribbling" (158–59). Jian is akin to one of the light sleepers in Lu Xun's iron house who has woken up to the cry of alarm, but rather than demolishing the house so as to emancipate his compatriots from their unwitting yet gruesome fate, he is led down a different path by Ha Jin—one that leads close to but ultimately backfires away from the center stage of national politics.

But even before Jian rouses to this epiphany, he has been gradually made privy to the crumbling of Yang's façade. Sitting beside the professor's hospital bed for weeks on end and somewhat grudgingly acting the part of the filial caretaker, Jian becomes the accidental eavesdropper to the lat-ter's unleashed unconscious. The teacher's mind, he notes, "now resembled a broken safe—all the valuables stored in it were scattered helter-skelter" (179). As he learns in these weeks, Yang's past is a tragic one, if not uncom-monly so. Branded a "Demon-Monster" during the Cultural Revolution for having translated foreign poetry (73), Yang was publicly denounced and then sent to the countryside for reeducation, separated for years from his wife and infant daughter. Yet he never loved his wife as much as a woman from his youth who had scorned him for his poverty, and in recent years he has begun a secret love affair with a female graduate student, a woman of his daughter's age. Although outwardly unrepentant about the vocation he has chosen and ever self-righteous about the spiritual nobility of poetic studies, Yang poststroke oscillates between leveling audacious if veiled criticisms at the state and, more shockingly and disappointingly for Jian, singing sycophantic hymns to the Communist Party while verbally acting out self-aggrandizing fantasies of power. His last words, whispered into Jian's ears alone, testify to the accumulated bitterness of his life: "Remember, avenge me and . . . don't forgive any one of them. K-kill them all!" (260). Far from being the contented scholar and model family man, Yang is in fact fiercely haunted by his past, never having resolved his rage and hatred for those who wield power, yet deeply self-loathing about the impotence of the intellectual in both domestic and professional life. As Jian belatedly realizes, his mentor, "driven to despair . . . must have thought of officialdom as the only possible way to live a life different from a futile intellectual's" (275). Ha Jin intimates that Yang's failure is not moral or individual but sociohistorical and structural: it stems from his generation's inability to overcome the ravages of China's politics and live up to the elevated, perhaps impossible, ideal of pure intellect. The vision of the scholar-intellectual projected by Yang at his most dignified—a person who rises above political interests and material gain to dedicate himself wholeheartedly to the study of literature—is one that Gao proposes in very similar terms. But in Jin's novel, communist history has effectively eroded not just the body but the spirit behind this ideal, leaving behind a husk of a man, and of a nation, that fatally implodes on itself.

It is noteworthy that Jin's portrait of the spiritual malaise of institutionalized pursuit of knowledge in this milieu diametrically opposes prevailing accounts of PRC intellectual life in the 1980s. More often than not, this decade has been characterized as one of nationalist ferment and fervor, the era of reform that nurtured, if unevenly so, the grand hopes and dreams of intellectuals emerging from the long shadow of the Cultural Revolution. Especially in hindsight, the 1980s can appear the period when elite utopianism attained its height before June 4 brought it crashing down and Deng Xiaoping maneuvered China irrevocably down the road of 1990s hypercapitalism. Jing Wang, for one, provides a vivid sketch of this decade's cultural atmosphere: "Future historians will remember the 1980s in China as a period of utopian vision on the one hand and an era of emergent crisis on the other. Euphoria and great expectation swept over the nation as the Party's economic reform completed its first initiative of promoting household-based agriculture. . . . At the juncture of 1985, the metaphor of consummation could well have captured the apex of national jubilance" (1). The mid-1980s in particular "witnessed a symphony of unmitigated optimism. As the state's modernization program steered the country into imagined prosperity, the intellectuals not only collaborated with the Party in its reconstruction of the socialist utopia, but busily proliferated their own discourse on thought enlightenment" (37). As Wang points out, even into the seemingly dystopic mood of the late 1980s, when the general sense of national cultural crisis culminated in the TV series *Heshang*, intellectuals remained unshaken in their haughty but thoroughly earnest self-perception as "architects of Chinese modernity," a privileged elite endowed with the capacity and entrusted with the moral mission to search out the right "paradigms that would steer China into a tantalizing future" (39). The specter of Yang as the monstrous body of a tragically repressed and schizophrenic scholar, outwardly sedate but inwardly seething and dying, rarely rears its head in this fundamentally optimistic picture.

Perhaps the device of allegory renders the causality of events ambiguous. Is the collapse of the intellectual as social ideal in 1980s China that which propels the students into the Square, or is the mass protest movement's ghastly denouement that which sounds the death knell for the post-Tiananmen intellectual? Both scenarios seem operative in *The Crazed*. Jian heads to Beijing only after being disillusioned with the example of his teacher, but Yang's brain hemorrhage mirrors the Tiananmen bloodshed too evocatively for him not to be read as a metaphorical victim of state violence as well. Indeed, along Jin's variety of allegory, there is little difference between the two readings. His representation of the intellectual is not so much anachronistic as archetypal: he is less invested in meticulously chronicling the shifting identity and function of the PRC intellectual than in advancing a macrohistorical critique of the impossibility of intellectual life in twentieth-century China. This critique encompasses the Republican period of Lu Xun's time with the rise of communism and its aesthetic imperatives as much as the millennial moment of the novel's publication. In Jin's long view of Chinese history, the social outburst of 1989's Tiananmen is but one indicator of a whole century's worth of accumulated stresses on the national psyche, just as Yang's stroke is but one belated symptom of a whole lifetime's worth of suffering.

In this sense, *The Crazed* has almost nothing to offer in terms of an event-specific analysis of 1989's Tiananmen, except to embed it as yet another instance of crisis within a broader history of national ruptures. Thus, after returning to Shanning from the capital, Jian has an extraordinarily generic reaction to the massacre:

> Ever since I boarded the train back, a terrible vision had tormented me. I saw China in the form of an old hag so decrepit and brainsick that she would devour her children to sustain herself. Insatiable, she had eaten many tender lives before, was gobbling new flesh and blood now, and would surely swallow more. Unable to suppress the horrible vision, all day I said to myself, "China is an old bitch that eats her

own puppies!" How my head throbbed, and how my heart writhed and shuddered! With the commotion of two nights ago still in my ears, I feared I was going to lose my mind. (315)

The haunting voice of Lu Xun is heard once again in this passage. Cannibalism, made famous by Lu Xun in "A Madman's Diary" as a metaphor for the self-predation of precommunist feudal China, is aptly mobilized by Jin and superimposed onto the June 4 crackdown. At the same time, perhaps Jin is alluding also to James Joyce's trope of Ireland as "the old sow that eats her farrow" (206), which would partly account for the gender shift in national allegory from Lu Xun's masculine cannibal to Jian's vision of the "old hag" and "old bitch." Whether meant ironically or not, the Chinese nation at its most "horrible" comes to be personified now only via some species of the aged female. As we will explore in the next chapter, Jian's and perhaps Jin's casual misogyny here is typical of the masculinism of much Tiananmen discourse, a subject that Annie Wang trenchantly satirizes in *Lili*. Furthermore, as we will see in chapter 4, Ma Jian, too, resurrects the cannibal in relation to Tiananmen in *Beijing Coma*, though he will carry this motif to its most grotesquely literal end.

Joyce is germane here in another crucial respect—as a model of the exilic writer for Ha Jin. In this closing moment of *The Crazed*, as Jian has his epiphanic vision of cannibalistic China and pronounces his decision to leave the country for good, Jin, in a parallel metatextual gesture, strongly flags his own departure from Lu Xun's mold of the nationalist writer by summoning an alternative and non-Chinese icon of the exile-embracing artist: Stephen Dedalus, who in effect becomes Jian Wan's modernist predecessor. Like Gao in *Taowang* before him, Jin takes refuge in a narrative closure of flight. If Jin is a more historical (if not historicist) writer than Gao, he nonetheless intimates a similar conclusion that individual freedom and intellectual integrity cannot survive in China, that these qualities can only be achieved abroad. As Yang advises Jian early on in the novel, "You can live a real intellectual's life [in the United States] after you earn a Ph.D. from an American university," for "scholars in the West lived more like intellectuals" (104–5). By the novel's end, Jian will pursue a comparable route. His most triumphant epiphany—that he "acted like a counterrevolutionary . . . a free man capable of choice . . . [who] defied a prescribed fate like [his] teacher's" (321)—is followed by his resolution to escape China once and for all, to leave first for Hong Kong and then possibly "Canada, or the United States, or Australia, or some place in Southeast Asia where Chinese is widely used" (322). In the narrative arc of *The Crazed*, then, the Tiananmen incident has value only insofar as it ascertains an insight that should have been obvious to Jian long ago, and insofar as it finally and successfully catapults the hitherto self-absorbed hero into a journey to enlightenment—overseas.

This recourse in flight and exile as the inevitable finale of June 4 is not unique to Jin but constitutes a dominant paradigm for diasporic fictions on Tiananmen. It might even be deemed a kind of imaginative impasse, one freighted with ideological assumptions about the PRC and the West that diaspora writers are not always ready to examine or question. On this point, Annie Wang and Ma Jian will both depart from Gao and Jin. While the latter two share the conviction that art should exist purely for itself and that the communist regime, by stifling the human soul, disables any meaningful form of creativity, Wang and Ma suggest otherwise, the former through her transnational career path post-2000 and the latter through the mainland setting of his protagonist's cerebral revivification. From this perspective, Jin as much as Gao could be called writers of a romantic elite tradition, and it is not by accident that both conjure Lu Xun as an iconic forebear, a literary patriarch to be superseded in Oedipal fashion, and that both spotlight the intellectual-student relation over any other in their Tiananmen fictions. At the end of *The Crazed*, we could almost hear Jian's implicit hymn to exilic freedom, but one that ultimately returns to an intellectual ethos of ethnic-national spokesmanship, as if he too will at last go forth "to forge in the smithy of [his] soul the uncreated conscience of [his] race" (Joyce 253).

Still, an important difference between Gao and Jin is that the latter highlights, not a reified distinction between student and intellectual, but the broken trajectory between the two. We may therefore read *The Crazed* as a work that, rather than taking at face value the moral and political antagonism between Tiananmen students and intellectuals, by contrast charts the lingering course by which the student-intellectual continuum becomes irreversibly severed. If Yang occupies the role of the crippled intellectual along this spectrum, Jian embodies neither pole but is instead an in-between figure of suspended development. Neither scholar nor student, intellectual-advisor nor activist-protester, he too, like Yang, represents a Tiananmen plot indexed by failure, a failure not of political struggle but of sociohistorical continuity. The intellectual ruptures of national history yield his narrative of disrupted bildungsroman. This involves the stalling out of progress as much as regress, for while Jian never inherits the mantle of the teacher, neither does he fall back into the part of the impetuous undergraduate. Hence, unlike Gao's undisguised censure of the Tiananmen students via the allegorical figure of the Young Man in *Taowang*, Jin's focus on Jian does not amount to a wholesale commentary on the student movement.

On the contrary, Jin is emphatic about marking his protagonist's distance, both geographical and ideological, from the students in the Square.

From the outset, Jian endorses Yang's belief in political detachment, and time and again he expresses approval of Meimei's shunning of the demonstrations in Beijing, calling her "smart and coolheaded" to "never entangle herself in politics" (55). After abandoning academe, he briefly aspires to enter the Policy Office with the high-minded goal of eradicating systemic corruption from within, but his efforts at playing the savior are briskly thwarted by the local Party secretary. His eventual decision to go to the capital and join the democracy activists has less to do with political commitment, the coming into consciousness of his political identity in relation to the nation, than with personal "desperation, anger, madness, and stupidity." Taking over the titular metaphor from Yang, Jian confesses: "I was crazed, unable to think logically, and was possessed by an intense desire to prove that I was a man capable of action and choice. So I set out for the capital with a feverish head" (295). This theme of Jian's psychic stasis, where the very concept of an authentic awakening into full sociopolitical subjectivity is continually withheld from him, is manifested repeatedly as a failure to see.

Instances of Jian's imperception pervade the novel. Most relevant to the Tiananmen plot, Jian is portrayed as a self-centered myopic graduate student who concentrates solely on his studies and exams while doggedly ignoring all signs of political and social upheaval around him. Jin pointedly includes references to radio broadcasts of the Beijing movement via the Voice of America throughout the novel, but he just as pointedly underscores Jian's persistent passivity. Though initially astonished at the Tiananmen news, Jian for the most part takes it in with neutral noncomment, as though the protests were transpiring on another planet (57). This insularity filters down to Jian's everyday life. Despite being installed at the professor's bedside as a primary caregiver, he watches over Yang's body without ever noticing its spectacular deterioration, and it takes Meimei's return from Beijing for this to come embarrassingly to his attention. And though engaged to Meimei for years, Jian never clues in to the possibility that she may have courters at her university in the capital until she jilts him in a letter and shows up unexpectedly at a dance party escorted by the local Party secretary's nephew. Finally, it is only by eavesdropping on Yang's rants as well as others' conversations in the hospital room that Jian discovers the many secret relationships and machinations that have occurred on his own university campus for years, from Yang's adulterous affair to the Party secretary's blackmailing of Yang with this knowledge. Even after learning of the Party secretary's recurring tactics, Jian continues to act the classic fall guy by carrying out an errand for her in a remote village while she sabotages his job application for the Policy Office. Like Yang, Jian's character can be read in the context of the system that produced him. Just as the older man saw himself as a cog in the revolutionary machine, so the younger man's careerism and pragmatism, tunnel vision and obtuseness are all traits fostered by the corrupt environment of the university campus, where power politics crisscrosses the daily life of professors as much as of students. As the perpetual navel-gazer and gullible target of others' secret schemes, Jian functions more as a social type than a unique subject within the novel's survey of the post-Mao intellectual milieu.

This theme of failed discernment can be encapsulated by one particular scene midway through the novel. In a rare moment of distress one morning, Jian decides to deviate from his normal routine and takes a break from his study regimen by visiting a gallery. En route, he bicycles past some police vehicles and notes to himself that the heightened security must be in response to rumors of a demonstration, planned by a local teachers' college, later that afternoon. Giving no further thought to these external events, he is swiftly absorbed again by his personal drama and goes on to describe in detail each piece at the art exhibit. One painting that catches his eye is entitled *A Poet: No, Not in the Presence of Others*. Jian muses that, from a distance, the figure resembles "a scarlet rooster," but up close it presents a terrifying phantasm:

> The piece was vertically long and presented a tall, emaciated man in a tattered cloak, the end of which flapped in the breeze. . . . With his neck stretched, the poet seemed to be yearning to chant something, but unable to bring it out. A huge earring hung from his earlobe, casting on his throat an elongated shadow, which reminded me of a noose. A half-transparent mask almost shielded his nose and mouth. His shifty eyes and hollowed cheeks suggested a fearful ghost rather than a man. This painting made me wonder whether there had been an oversight on the part of the authorities that had allowed it to be included. Quickly I turned away. (95)

This scene captures an instant of failed self-recognition. As Jian reveals earlier in the novel, he is by nature an "absentminded man and often neglected small things," so people nickname him "the Poet" even though he has never written a poem (59). Such absentmindedness is plainly displayed when he confronts this stylized self-image without recognizing it as a potential gothic double. The painting's depiction of the poet as a withered phantom, yearning but voiceless and half-faceless, is all too evocative of what Yang fears he has become and what Jian would be. What is more intriguing here, however, is the suggestion that the poet throttles himself with his own ornament, which perhaps hints at the complicity between the poet and the state, or else the inadequate and ultimately self-strangulating methods of contemporary writing. Either way, despite detecting the work's transgressive edge, Jian quickly turns away from it, as though unable or unwilling to sustain his view of such compromised and defeated defiance—an ocular move that crucially anticipates how Jin will stage his protagonist's relation to Tiananmen Square.

Indeed, it may be that this idea of imperception is already encoded in Jian's name. For Ha Jin, one of the advantages and pleasures of writing Chinese names in English transliteration is surely the ability to stage interlingual puns. So, "Jian" brings into auditory play the most common Chinese word for that pinyin, "to see" (*jian*). Although the Chinese edition of this novel uses another *jian* for the protagonist's name—the character for "firm" or "resolute"—the linguistic echo nonetheless amplifies the novel's running theme of sight. In his short fiction, Jin shows himself to be not averse to such puns, often with ironic overtones, and often to parody norms of masculine behavior. In "A Tiger-Fighter Is Hard to Find," for example, the title character, Wang Huping, whose given name might mean "the tiger subduer" or "tiger suppresser" in Chinese, gains much fame and female adulation for his manly prowess in wrestling a fake tiger but suffers a mental breakdown in the face of a real one. Similarly in "Man to Be," the protagonist, Nan, whose name is a homophone of the Chinese word for "man" (*nan*), is the only one in a party of rapists who turns suddenly impotent at the bark of a dog. Most recently, Jin revives the name Nan for his quasi-autobiographical protagonist in *A Free Life*, where a post-Tiananmen Chinese immigrant in the United States struggles with his poetry as much as his now racialized masculinity. This technique of ironic reverse naming may likewise apply to Jian, the ever-flawed seer. At the same time, "Jian Wan" may signal a kind of belated vision, in the multiple ways that Jian arrives belatedly (*wan*) at his decisions and insights. In the context of this novel's address of June 4 especially, the issue of witnessing becomes paramount, and Jian's everyday myopia can be tied to two other related forms of failure: his abortive journey to the Square, and his remote witnessing of national history at the imagined site of its greatest clash and crisis.

Part II. The Lost Square

REMOTE AND BELATED WITNESSING

Whereas the structural movement of Gao Xingjian's *Taowang* in relation to the Square is literally centrifugal, center-fleeing, that in Ha Jin's *The Crazed*, after much stasis, is centripetal and then centrifugal, marked by a much-deferred voyage toward the Square before a violent expulsion away from it.[3] In the latter's penultimate chapter, Jian arrives in Beijing by train at 8:00 p.m. on June 3. He arrives in time for the massacre, almost punctually so. This timeliness, though, is offset by a slight spatial dislocation. As Jian and his fellow students discover, they have no means of getting to the Square itself, since all public transport in the city has been halted. The subway is closed, and all the buses have been mobilized by the people to barricade the streets against the army's advance. Fortuitously, the students notice a minivan taxi, whose driver takes some of them, Jian included, past several roadblocks to within a ten-minute walk of the Square. Once on foot, the Shanning group proceeds about a hundred yards before being scattered by a surging crowd.

This is the spot where the novel's crux scene of historical witnessing occurs for Jian, and it is the closest he ever gets to the Square. Elbowing his way halfway through the crowd, Jian watches as what looks to be a college student tries to talk to the troops inside a personnel carrier, "lecturing" them that "they had been deceived by the government, and that the city was in good order and didn't need them here." People in the crowd, assuming that this army unit will retreat like those in preceding days, boldly declare that they will blockade the street and protect the Square with their lives. This scene of youthful idealism and communal high spirit, even bravado, recalls much documentary footage of the historical Tiananmen. What transpires immediately afterward in the novel, however, is where fiction splits from documentary, as Jin unfolds for us an instant of traumatic witnessing, first-person and close-up. As Jian pushes forward to get a better look, a jeep pulls up and a colonel descends. Ever the reader of surfaces, Jian is initially "impressed by the officer's handsome looks," but the officer's next move flouts all his expectations: "Without a word [the colonel] pulled out his pistol and shot the student in the head, who dropped to the ground kicking his legs, then stopped moving and breathing. Bits of his brain were splattered like crushed tofu on the asphalt. Steam was rising from his smashed skull" (302–3). The troops then open fire with real bullets, and Jian flees with the throng before finding shelter in an alley for the night. No extant documentary footage gives us this proximate a view of the actual massacre.

The macabre image of the student's smashed skull, summoned by Jin as a visual synecdoche of the imagined carnage inside the Square, can be read as the culmination of the novel's ongoing dramatization of intellectual death in post-Mao China. If Jian is the stunted intellectual-to-be, the embryonic scholar who never matures into one, this other anonymous student's death suggests an end to all youthful intellect, idealism, and activism. It is noteworthy that the manner of student death here—a bullet to the head—parallels the premise with which Ma Jian will begin his Tiananmen novel, in which the protagonist-narrator is likewise shot in the head on the night of the massacre. The theme, and fear, of intellectual demise obviously looms large in the imagination of Tiananmen authors. Where the two fictions depart, though, is in their imagined afterlife for this symbolic cerebral wound. For Jin's Jian, this encounter signals the decisive cessation of intellectual life and oppositional politics for China, dispelling any illusion he may still have held for figures of authority and propelling him out of the country for sheer survival. For Ma's Dai Wei, on the contrary, his head injury precipitates a new phase of clandestine if comatose mental life within post-1989 PRC. In antithesis to *Beijing Coma*, *The Crazed* constructs Tiananmen as an inaugural event for the diasporic subject.

Along the same vein, Jin links Tiananmen to diaspora by resolutely keeping his protagonist outside the Square at its moment of anticipated catastrophe. In the hours of the students' final exodus from the Square, against the backdrop of the iron house's burning, Jian is seen trapped in his alleyway, a lost corner on the larger map of the massacre—and ironically at this most crucial of junctures, he dozes off. The Square's clearing therefore happens textually offstage, literally in an interval of the narrator's unconscious. Yet it is after Jian wakes up from this historical slumber that he seems able for the first time to rise to the occasion of heroism. If he has hitherto failed to fulfill his fantasy of playing savior to the downtrodden, he now volunteers to carry a wounded boy to a nearby hospital, an act of courage that allows him to escape from the alley and eventually the capital.

On Jin's representational grid, then, Jian's approach to Tiananmen is a limited one: he gets close to the Square but never fully arrives there. The Square itself remains a spatial aporia, literally a place of impasse, in the text. In the overall scheme of things, Jian remains a partial witness at the edges of history, not a deliberate participant or consequential actor at the center of it. Through the accidental convergence of national and personal life, he stumbles onto one micro instance of state violence and gets caught up in it, but at its outer perimeters. He is akin to a man who, in a half-daze, staggers into a theater at the very moment the drama of his epoch reaches its climax, and although his view of the main stage remains obstructed, the bits of brutality he glimpses from the margins are enough to traumatize him for good, sending him reeling out of the theater, transfigured. The novel's concluding chapter finds Jian back in Shanning the next day, bedridden and feverish, capable only of muttering, with echoes of Yang, "They killed lots of people, lots" (313).

At most, Jian serves as a tardy witness, one who stumbles by chance onto the hideous spectacle of the massacre's aftermath. In the other major scene of historical witnessing in the novel, this time belated rather than remote, we find Jian wandering around a Beijing hospital in the early dawn hours of June 4: "I was astonished by the number of the wounded in the hospital. The corridors and the little front yard were crowded with stretchers loaded with people, some of whom held up IV bottles and tubes for themselves, waiting for treatment. A deranged young woman cried and laughed by turns, tearing at her hair and breasts, while her friends begged a nurse to give her an injection of sedatives." Jian then goes in search of the hospital morgue, where Jin continues to underscore the language of the ocular and Jian's role as a witness: "I went there to have a look. The tiny morgue happened to adjoin the garage, and three nurses were in there, busy listing the bodies and gathering information about the dead. An old couple were wailing, as they had just found their son lying among the corpses. Most of the dead were shot in the head or chest. I saw that a young man had three bayonet wounds in the belly and a knife gash in the hand. His mouth was wide open as though still striving to snap at something" (309). This image of the open-mouthed young man evokes the painting of the poet in the art gallery—"yearning to chant something, but unable to bring it out" (95)—suggesting yet another metaphorical double but also foil to our hero. Finally, coming upon the hospital's backyard garage, Jian discovers that it has been converted into a makeshift morgue for storing overflow corpses. The piles of mangled carcasses he beholds there is one of the eeriest sights in the novel, and significantly, it is a delayed sight of the evidence and not of the event itself: "But the garage was an entirely different scene, where about twenty bodies, male and female, were piled together like slaughtered pigs. Several limbs stuck out from the heap; a red rubber band was still wrapped around the wrist of a teenage girl; a pair of eyes on a swollen face were still open, as though gazing at the unplastered wall. A few steps away from the mass of corpses lay a gray-haired woman on her side, a gaping hole in her back ringed with clots of blood" (309–10).

Jin surely has in mind here those gruesome images of Tiananmen victims that circulated in the world media after June 4 and that continue to circulate on the Internet today.[4] We can, moreover, detect a strong quality of visual belatedness in this passage, an impulse on Jin's part to bear witness to the atrocity after the fact via a graphic and quasi-photographic narrative reproduction of the bodies as evidence. These densely descriptive passages work to generate, not a reality effect via the surplus of details, but an attestive or authenticating effect hinging on the evidential force of corpses. What mutilated corpses in particular testify to is not the individual lives they once led but the fact of horrific death, the fact of their having been grotesquely killed, and the certainty of it. Roland Barthes ascribes this potency of irrefutable authentication to photographs: "The photograph does not call up the past (nothing Proustian in a photograph). The effect it produces upon me is not to restore what has been abolished (by time, by distance) but to attest that what I see has indeed existed" (82). Every photograph is "a certificate of presence," "an emanation of *past reality*: a *magic*, not an art," and as such "possesses an evidential force": "From a phenomenological viewpoint, in the Photograph, the power of authentication exceeds the power of representation" (87–89). Writing, by contrast for Barthes, can yield no such certainty, for it is the "misfortune (but also perhaps the voluptuous pleasure) of language not to be able to authenticate itself" (85). Barthes's musings predate technologies of photo-editing and might sound outmoded in our time, but perhaps it is precisely in an age when even photographs lose their incontrovertible "evidential force" that writing must in turn be summoned to complement and bolster photographs' residual veridical power. While language remains intractably representational rather than verificatory, in the case of a disputed and officially erased atrocity such as June 4, a fictional thick description of mangled bodies does not assume evidential force in relation to reality or the past per se, but it does attest to a writer's belated psychic impulse to annex history and provide a kind of proof—through not memory but projection, as not a return but a first arrival, and not to remember what one has done in actual life but to imagine what one would have done in a parallel life had one been there with the photographer. In this sense, Ha Jin's narrative wallowing in the details of corpses points to a desire to approach the Square via not art but what Barthes would call magic, with Jian as his magical proxy seer.

As Jin remarks in passing in one essay, "to preserve is the key function of literature . . . to combat historical amnesia" ("Spokesman" 30). The more complicated question of how to preserve history in fiction, however, is not one he tackles explicitly. From *The Crazed*, we can extrapolate that his mode of combating amnesia is emphatically neither mimetic nor speculative, neither testimonial nor ulterior. He does not submit a first-person eyewitness account of mass killings that purports to give creative truth to history, as if he could adequately reconstruct the whole massacre simply by exerting his powers of sympathetic imagination. Yet neither does he refrain from writing any scene of state violence altogether out of strict fidelity to autobiography, or else a theoretical belief in the episode's absolute alterity from the realm of representation. Instead, the method by which Jin memorializes Tiananmen is a compromise between these two paths. He offers a first-person narrative that bears historical witness to June 3–4, but via a narrator whose imperfect and peripheral vision, at best remote and belated, is repeatedly emphasized. His narrator's failure to arrive in the Square as the central place of national struggle indicates a sense of loss of entry into the emblematic space of state power as well as of collective rebellion, a loss that the text accentuates. By the end of the day, Jian fails to have perceptual access to either the realm of the party-state or that of the protesters. Crucially, this textual self-marking of structural and perceptual distance from the Square is not a feature of Jin's historical realism, a nod to the real "geography of the killing" that Robin Munro, for one, insists on (811). As I will explore at length in chapter 4, most scholarly accounts of Tiananmen now agree that there was in fact no mass slaughter inside the Square on June 4, and that most of the killings occurred on the streets outside the Square on the eve of its evacuation. As George Black and Robin Munro contend, reports of vicious butchery in the Square, though by now "enshrined in myth," are but "pure fabrication" (236). Ma Jian will be the writer to chronicle this history with meticulous topographical exactness in his realist epic. Ha Jin, by contrast, does not present Jian's tale as a corrective. If anything, the denouement of *The Crazed* keeps intact the popular myth of a massacre inside the Square. One of the novel's last references to the Square, full of foreboding, comes from a woman in the alley who cries out in despair (again with echoes of Lu Xun's "A Madman's Diary"): "Lord of Heaven, please save those kids in Tiananmen Square!" (305). Insofar as the reader's knowledge of June 4 is filtered entirely through Jian, and insofar as Jian himself remains ignorant to the end about the students' fate, the novel leaves the Square an ominously blank space where anything could have unfolded. In this situation of crisis, nothing is so powerful, as Black and Munro note, as when "the screen goes blank" (246). Their comment refers to television, but the analogy to the suggestive power of fiction and its aporias seems equally valid. In Jin's novel, the massacre transpires in the gaps of Jian's narration, literally between the lines.

DIASPORIC TRAUMA AND POSTMEMORY

Ultimately, this narrative gap in *The Crazed* can be understood within the context of Ha Jin's own diasporic relation to Tiananmen. Of the four writers in my study, he is the one with the greatest distance from the historical massacre. Although none of the other writers were inside the Square on June 4 itself, both Ma Jian and Annie Wang were in Beijing that spring, and both personally witnessed the demonstrations in the streets and went to support the students in the Square. Gao Xingjian had been lecturing in Europe since 1987, but Ha Jin had been abroad even longer, having left China in 1985 for a Ph.D. program at Brandeis. Hence, by the time of Tiananmen, he was already four years removed from PRC cultural and political developments. This temporal lapse may account for the asynchrony we noted above between his gloomy rendition of 1980s intellectual life in *The Crazed* and the more jubilant one given by scholars such as Jing Wang, as well as his narrator's ironic but apt descent into sleep and blindness at the historic hours of the Square's clearing. Spatially, too, Jin riddles his text with signs of remoteness, and we can read the theme of Jian's myopia, his never quite correctly adjusted vision, within this framework.

Aside from biographical trajectory, Jin is also the fiction writer here most acutely self-conscious of his diasporic distance from, and the one most mindful of his own mediated access to, the historical Tiananmen. In interviews, Wang and Ma are prone to emphasize their personal exposure to and participation in the mass protests of that spring, perhaps as a self-authenticating gesture. As for Gao, when he speaks of Tiananmen, he rarely details the means by which he first learned of June 4, usually focusing instead on his moral stance afterward. By contrast, Jin is often careful, even adamant, about foregrounding the television as his primary medium of knowledge about the massacre—and thereby locating himself as a diasporic viewer in the United States at the time. In one typical interview, he states: "I was devastated watching the Tiananmen massacre on television. I knew it would be impossible to go back to China and write and teach honestly. . . . My whole image of China was changed" (qtd. in Rightmyer). Few interviewers have failed to pick up on Jin's insistent self-location in relation to Tiananmen, and it is by now de rigueur for author profiles on him to mention that he watched televised coverage of the massacre and subsequently decided to remain in the United States. In another typical interview:

> [Interviewer]: How hard was it to make the decision to stay in the United States after viewing on television the events in Tiananmen Square? If that hadn't happened, how would your life and your writing have changed?
>
> Ha Jin: . . . Without the massacre, I would have returned to China and wouldn't have become a creative writer. Probably I would have been a university professor. (Interview)

What is worth highlighting is that Jin himself has cast his relation to Tiananmen all along as one of long-distance perception, an act of what I will call *diasporic witnessing*. The language of trauma also figures prominently in his self-accounting: "It was very traumatic for me. It's such a brutal government. I was very angry, and I decided not to return to China" (qtd. in J. Thomas). And more recently: "But after the Tiananmen Square massacre, I was lost for some time. I was going through a lot of psychological torment. I was very sick. I was in a fevered state for several months. . . . Yes, after Tiananmen Square I realized it was impossible for me to return because I would have had to serve the state. I might've become an academic, but every school in China was owned by the state. I just couldn't do it. The massacre made me feel the country was a kind of manifestation of violent apparitions. It was monstrous" ("Art"). The rhetorical echoes with *The*

Crazed are unmistakable, especially the final chapter's passage describing Jian's post-Beijing delirium. It is also revealing that, for Jian as for Jin, news of the massacre arrives via the media. Where the author watched televised images of the crackdown from the United States, his fictional hero hears reports of it from Shanning over the radio:

> Back in the dormitory, I dozed away in bed again. Whenever awake, I would listen to my shortwave radio, and tears welled up in my eyes from time to time. On the BBC a reporter said plaintively that an estimated five thousand people had been killed, that many students were crushed by the tanks and armoured personnel carriers, that a civil war might break out anytime since more field armies were heading for Beijing, that forty million dollars had just been transferred to a Swiss bank by someone connected with the top national leaders, and that an airliner was reserved for them in case they needed to flee China. However, another reporter, a woman from Hong Kong, told a different story. She said composedly that at most about a thousand civilians had been killed, that the government was in firm control of the situation, that the police were rounding up the student leaders, and that dozens of intellectuals had been detained. The foreign reporters on the radio tended to contradict one another, whereas no mainland Chinese, except for the government's spokesman, Mu Yuan, and a lieutenant colonel in charge of clearing Tiananmen Square, dared to comment on the event. The officer repeatedly stressed that the People's Liberation Army had successfully quelled the counterrevolutionary uprising without killing a single civilian. I listened and dozed off by turns. (314–15)

The medium by which news of the massacre travels differs for Jian and Jin, but the fact of mediated and partial knowledge is the same. The many consequences of government censorship—discrepancy among reports, uncertainty about exact casualty counts, the suspicion of a massive cover-up by the regime—structure Jin's as much as Jian's remote and traumatic reception of the event. Above all, fears of the worst, of five thousand people murdered and numerous students crushed by tanks in the Square, remain intact. Tiananmen, for Jin as for his near namesake, is a "monstrous" drama that has been glimpsed from afar, one that can be replayed in the feverish mind's eye but never utterly rid of its dark spots. And for both, it is decisive in inaugurating a diasporic existence. Without Tiananmen, Jin would have finished his Ph.D. degree and gone back to China to become a university professor of literature, in a fulfillment of the student-intellectual continuum, just as Jian would have followed in Yang's footsteps to become a scholar of comparative poetry and a nominal "clerk" for the state. Both teacher and student are fictional counterparts of what the author envisages he himself would have been, along the tracks of his original life plan. Tiananmen is the history that intervened, arresting him in an instant of accidental diasporic witnessing. Henceforth, he could not bring himself to return to his country of origin, which has been irrevocably transformed into a site of trauma.

Jin's unusual form of nonpersonal and far-flung trauma can be explicated in the terms of trauma theory. Both his repeated biographical accounts and fictional re-creation of June 4 suggest a psychic relation to Tiananmen that fits the mode of intersubjective trauma as theorized by Marianne Hirsch. Hirsch is centrally concerned with the transgenerational memory of Holocaust survivors' children, which she expounds through the idea of *postmemory*, "the relationship of children of survivors of cultural or collective trauma to the experiences of their parents, experiences that they 'remember' only as the narratives and images with which they grew up, but that are so powerful, so monumental, as to constitute memories in their own right." At the same time, looking beyond the context of the Jewish Holocaust, Hirsch acknowledges that her model "can be more broadly available" and "need not be restricted to the family, or even to a group that shares an ethnic or national identity marking" ("Surviving" 9–10). This notion of intersubjective and transgenerational trauma, of a profound existential shock triggered not by direct personal experience but by remote and mediated cognition, is particularly useful for elucidating Jin's psychic affiliation to Tiananmen. In Jin's case, postmemory may be operative through an ironic generational reversal. Instead of inheriting monumental parental memories that overshadow his private ones, he has been stunned in his life's tracks by images of death of the next student generation, students who might well have been his own a few years down the road in an alternate history. After that moment of visual exposure, he could not resume his singular life apart from the next generation's trauma, one that has become powerfully, monumentally intergenerational and even diasporic in scope. In addition, his emotional and psychological reactions mirror those of the postmemorial child upon first encountering a Holocaust photograph: a sense of "ultimate horror" and a "kind of revelation," a "negative epiphany," a feeling that "something broke"; a sense of "rupture" and a "radical interruption through seeing"; and most strikingly, a tendency toward "compulsive and traumatic repetition" (Hirsch, "Surviving" 5, 6, 8). For Jin, the urge to compulsively repeat seems to have taken the form of recounting over and over again to willing interviewers the same moment of his traumatic sighting, of watching televised coverage of the massacre. In *The Crazed*, this compulsion can be traced in his containment and condensation of the massacre via a handful of iconic images of mutilated bodies, images that keep haunting Jian in a way reminiscent of Holocaust postgenerational trauma. As Hirsch notes, the latter often manifests itself through a "striking repetition of the same very few images, used over and over again iconically and emblematically to signal this event," rather than a "multiplication and escalation of imagery" ("Surviving" 7). Jin's description of his composition process for this novel likewise intimates a dimension of authorial trauma, of repetition rather than proliferation: "But I couldn't finish [the manuscript]—I didn't even mean to finish it, I just couldn't get the story out of my head, and I had to write to calm myself down. . . . That book was a long struggle. I didn't have the ability I needed to write it so I put it aside and returned to it again and again and again. I had started writing it in 1988, but I didn't finish it until 2002. It became my eighth book" ("Art"). Lastly, Jin's repeated personal testimonies about his diasporic position on June 4 and his aporetic configuration of the Square in *The Crazed* resonate all too well with Hirsch's exposition of the displaced, vicarious, belated, and mediated qualities of postmemory: "The term 'postmemory' is meant to convey its temporal and qualitative difference from survivor memory, its secondary, or second-generation memory quality, its basis in displacement, its vicariousness and belatedness. Postmemory is a powerful form of memory precisely because its connection to its object or source is mediated not through recollection but through representation, projection, and creation—often based on silence rather than speech, on the invisible rather than the visible" ("Surviving" 9). Following Hirsch, we can call Jin's fiction an example of *diasporic postmemory*, a form of remembering origin's trauma via its dispersed and scattered afterimages. In this light, the lost Square can be read as the supreme aesthetic expression of Jin's diasporic postmemory vis-à-vis Tiananmen.

One other biographical element is noteworthy here: Tiananmen provided the means by which Jin completed his first book manuscript and could thus be deemed a vital factor in his becoming a novelist. As he reveals in interviews, *The Crazed* was actually his "first book," begun in the United States over a year before Tiananmen ("Art"; Kellman 82). The original story revolved solely around the academic plot and the student-mentor relationship. Chronologically, then, the initial composition of this book preceded that of *Waiting* and *In the Pond*, both set during periods of PRC history that Jin himself had lived through, both written later but completed earlier. At first, Jin thought of *The Crazed* as an "excursion," since he believed he would go on to write in Chinese once back in the PRC. Tiananmen was the turning point in his linguistic identification: after 1989, he decided not just to immigrate but "to write in English exclusively" (Kellman 82). From one angle, this timeline explains the apparent incongruity between the novel's main focus on academic bureaucracy and intrigue and its abrupt climactic crescendo in the theater of national politics and organized violence. But from another perspective, it is telling that, of all the rough drafts of his fiction, Jin would fasten onto this one as the basis of his Tiananmen vision, as though his thoughts on contemporary Chinese intellectual life could not be rounded out and given shape until Tiananmen happened, and conversely, as though Tiananmen brought into relief his running meditation on the post-Mao intellectual. June 4 gave the novel its new life and eventual closure, both as a narrative and an act of writing. Insofar as it concludes with the very episode that made him a voluntary immigrant and eventual creative writer, *The Crazed* marks the inception point of Ha Jin as a diasporic author as well as the historical endpoint of his China saga. After this, he will not go on to write a full-length novel set entirely in post-1989 PRC, only short stories. It is as though Tiananmen demarcates some temporal limit in Jin's imagined homecomings, the fictional frontier that, once hazarded, at last allows him to "leave contemporary China in [his] writing" for good. Perhaps the diasporic trauma precipitated by Tiananmen has at last been put to rest, and we do see Jin moving forward in his writing, if not in the novel immediately following *The Crazed*, then certainly in the more recent *A Free Life* and *A Good Fall*, both of which are largely located in the United States and address more classically Asian American themes of immigrant struggle and cross-cultural confusion. Jin himself may attribute this authorial turn to his changing self-perception as a writer, to his ability to at last "negate the role of . . . spokesmanship" and "to stand alone" ("Spokesman" 28), but this perceptual shift seems uniquely tied to Tiananmen as the historical origin of his writerly identity, the epochal threshold of his existential relation to China.

Indeed, Jin himself may not have been fully aware of the extent to which his whole oeuvre, up until the most recent pieces, has been psychically bound up with the rupture of 1989. Of course, he has often been asked about the persistent China focus of his writing, his habit hitherto of staying exclusively within the confines of PRC national history, so he must have been very cognizant of the fixity of his backward gaze. Yet what may elude conscious reflection is that this nostalgic intransigence has been determined not simply by the circumference of his knowledge but by the psychic circuit around the homeland that was first put into motion by June 4. For Jin, after Tiananmen, China cannot but be saturated with a sense of violent cruelty and irreversible loss, but by the same token, the emotional recompense attainable through imaginary homecomings—peaceful and entirely on his own terms—becomes incalculable. His continual attempts to recollect the lost homeland by fictionalizing a plethora of parallel lives in different periods, lives that are also frequently wrecked by brutality but are nonetheless revivable via their textual brethrens (and Jin is nothing if not astoundingly prolific, a writer of great resurrection speed), recall Julia Kristeva's portrait of the melancholic exile:

> Melancholy lover of a vanished space, he cannot, in fact, get over his having abandoned a period of time. The lost paradise is mirage of the past that he will never be able to recover. He knows it with a distressed knowledge that turns his rage involving others (for there is always an other, miserable cause of my exile) against himself: "How could I have abandoned them? I have abandoned myself." . . . For in the intervening period of nostalgia, saturated with fragrances and sounds to which he no longer belongs and which, because of that, wound him less than those of the here and now, the foreigner is a dreamer making love with absence, one exquisitely depressed. Happy? (9–10)

To be sure, Jin is not as luxuriously self-indulgent or uncritically home-affirming as Kristeva's dreamer, but his compulsion to write and rewrite various episodes of Chinese historical trauma does bespeak a melancholic attachment to the homeland as "vanished space," and also an oblique pleasure derived from the performative repetition of these narrative returns. More than any other writer in my study, Jin epitomizes a mode of diasporic melancholia toward China. And of all his works, *The Crazed* with its lost Square best captures this psychic structure of impossible yearning for a lost origin that is at once magnetic and repulsive, replete with hope and terror.

It is therefore with a certain amount of irony, though perhaps not completely unforeseeable given the logic of extremes and reversals, that Jin in his latest phase has come to renounce his nostalgia for China along with his previous self-perceived role as the tribal spokesperson. More precisely, rather than admitting to his former nostalgia and announcing a timely break from it, he has lately begun to advance a broader philosophical argument against nostalgia as a mode of writing for emigrant authors. In the essay "The Spokesman and the Tribe," Jin refers not to his personal evolution but to diasporic attitudes in general when he writes: "As a matter of fact, in our time the intense attachment to one's native land is often viewed as an unnecessary and anachronic feeling that tends to debilitate migrants. I would even argue that, for many displaced people, nostalgia is also blended with fear—the fear of uncertainty and of facing the challenges posed by the larger world and the fear of the absence of clarity and confidence provided by the past. In essence, nostalgia is associated mostly with the experience of a particular type of migrants, namely, exiles." Citing Salman Rushdie's *Shame*, he continues: "The debunking of the tree metaphor makes it clear that human beings are different from trees and should be rootless and entirely mobile" (22). Against the "exile," Jin posits the "migrant" as the proper modality for the diaspora writer. In an interesting conceptual move in another essay entitled "An Individual's Homeland," he redefines the idea of "homeland" by dissociating it from nativity: "The dichotomy inherent in the word 'homeland' is more significant now than it was in the past. Its meaning can no longer be separated from home, which is something the migrant should be able to build away from this native land. Therefore, it is logical to say that your homeland is where you build your home" (84). Emphasizing travel over nativity, "arrival more than return," the search and the reconstruction more than repossession or the destination, Jin concludes his essay volume, again with echoes of Rushdie, by proclaiming that "we should also imagine how to arrange the landscapes of our envisioned homelands" (86). This manifesto for aesthetic rootlessness and mobility, for detachment from the native land and an end to nostalgia, harmonizes well with his commitment to universal humanism, but it is surely a far cry from his own writing trajectory. Perhaps it is a hard-won outlook, achieved only after his long melancholic journey through an envisioned lost China via three books of poetry, three collections of short stories, three novels, and one novella. Yet, in light of his own authorial path, the origin-negating position is not one that adequately or accurately describes his oeuvre up until this point, and most certainly not one that he launched into at the onset of his diasporic career. That he has finally formulated a credo of migrancy does signal a step beyond his former melancholia, though the lack of an explicit recognition of his former state may hint at some residual repression yet.

As of now, most of Jin's writing lies before that forward step, and it is this prior corpus that fits neatly within a dominant paradigm in current scholarship on twentieth-century Chinese literature, one constructed around the critical nexus between historical violence and national trauma. The burgeoning of trauma studies in the mid-1990s first constellated around reexaminations of the Holocaust, but the field and its lines of inquiry have since been absorbed into other disciplines, above all literary and cultural studies. Since the early 2000s, the notion of trauma, especially trauma on a national scale, has become influential in scholarship on modern Chinese literature and film, though in a somewhat loose fashion, and often not through a strictly psychoanalytic framework but as a general set of analytic categories.[5] Among this body of scholarship, what strikes me as most pertinent to a reading of Ha Jin is David Der-wei Wang's *The Monster That Is History*. Though at first glance a work that also falls within the paradigm of national trauma, Wang's study far exceeds the psychoanalytic perimeters of trauma theory, drawing as much from Benjamin and Foucault as from Freud. A rich and erudite investigation into twentieth-century Chinese fictions of the gothic and phantasmagoric, the book opens by invoking the familiar framework of national violence and the role that literature can play in filling the gaps of history. As Wang observes from the outset, "One can hardly read modern Chinese history without noticing a seemingly endless brutality totted up in dishearteningly large figures," but "fiction may be able to speak where history has fallen silent" (1–2). But when Wang speaks resoundingly of "the monster that is history," his conception of monstrosity is neither merely pejorative nor headily celebratory but stems from an ambivalent mythological figure in classical Chinese texts—*taowu*, a monster of "menacing origins" and associated with superlative evil, but also a creature known for its "divinatory powers," able to see into both past and future (6). Most importantly, because of this combination of ferocity and foresight, *taowu* eventually became identified with history itself in Chinese discourse, as Wang explicates: "Since history reveals both past and future, it is referred to as the *taowu*. . . . The metamorphosis of the *taowu* from monster to historical account, while indicative of the amorphous power of the ancient Chinese imaginary, points to one way in which Chinese history took form. . . . In other words, the monster is invoked as an objective correlative, so to speak, to the human account of past experience, registering what is immemorial and yet unforgettable in Chinese collective memory, and cautioning against any similar mishaps in the future" (7). Wang's vision of Chinese history is hence that of a polymorphous force that can maim and haunt but also foretell and enlighten, at once disturbing and safeguarding collective memory. It is this dual understanding of history that most illuminates Ha Jin's immemorial but unforgettable relation to June 4—the monster that is, for him, Tiananmen.

RECEPTIONS AND RECOVERIES

The foregoing framework of trauma and melancholia, of the haunting force of remote history and the reconstructive power of diasporic postmemory, has uses other than that of textual illumination. This theoretical framework can help substantially recast critical perceptions of Ha Jin as a diasporic writer. In particular, it can push our comprehension of his writing beyond the potentially constrictive terms of linguistic or cultural Chineseness. Of the four authors in this study, Jin is the one most frequently read in terms of language and culture, especially via such rubrics as bilingualism and transculturalism, whether in praise or disparagement. Yet this obstinate spotlight on his relation to Chineseness as a category of cultural or linguistic identity risks obscuring what I see as the most significant and powerful intervention of his oeuvre—namely, his critique of totalitarianism. Tiananmen is thus an especially instructive topic to recall in this context, for it allows us to foreground his engagement with Chineseness as first and foremost a function of political history rather than cultural identity, of state power rather than linguistic difference.

As an entry point into the complex and at times charged terrains of Jin's reception, let me begin this final section by returning to the chapter's opening subject of the prize and its international ramifications. For starters, let us note that Jin's shift in self-perception from "tribal spokesman" to "migrant writer" is not without its roots in personal anguish. When he laments in "The Spokesman and the Tribe" that, "at any moment, a country can take a writer to task and even accuse him of misdeeds, betrayal, or other crimes against the people" (4), he likely has in mind, among other things, the controversy surrounding his first major published work, *Waiting*. In 1999, news of this novel winning the American Book Award brought Jin to the attention of many Sinophone readers both inside and outside the PRC, but it also embroiled him the following summer, as the Nobel Prize did Gao Xingjian just a few months later, in the international politics of literary recognition. In a scathing book review entitled "Trading on Honesty," Beijing University professor Liu Yiqing accused Jin of "emphasizing China's backwardness" and "cursing his compatriots and becoming the American media's tool for defaming China": "Under Ha Jin's lying pen, the many good and honest ordinary people of China . . . have become a laughing stock for Americans. It is precisely because there are people like Ha Jin, who would not hesitate to sully their own fellow citizens for the sake of winning prizes, that the West, especially the U.S., has long failed to change its impression of the Chinese, formed from the early twentieth century, as cowardly and weak, ignorant and lazy, opium-smoking and foot-binding, and not daring to retaliate even when their pigtails are pulled." Liu's jingoism comes across loud and unapologetic. Fittingly if ironically (in light of Gao), she begins her piece by opining that the Nobel Prize might finally be within reach for Chinese authors. Her review reportedly led Jin's mainland publisher to retract its plans to publish the Chinese translation of *Waiting*—the only novel of his ever to have been published by a mainland press but one that is now out of print. What is unusual about this incident, though, lies not in the attack itself or the ensuing censorship. As Joseph Fewsmith comments: "Censorship and attacks on writers are nothing new in China . . . What was different, however, was that the person who denounced Ha Jin's novel was no hidebound Marxist ideologue—the sort who routinely criticized liberal writers a decade ago—but rather a Western-educated professor of literature at Beijing University, the font of liberal thinking in modern China" (1st ed. 1–2). Liu, in fact, holds a Ph.D. from the University of Chicago. Yet such upper-crust liberalism, as Rey Chow points out, is not exempt from "the politics of ethnicity in postcolonial modernity." Quite the contrary: "Suspicion and condemnation are but the flip side of an equally characteristic situation in which, for instance, the Nobel Prize in Literature has been coveted yearly among contemporary Chinese writers. . . . This is a situation in which, even as the West is rhetorically denounced for being imperialist and orientalist, knowledge of the West, access to the West, and recognition by the West remain the very criteria by which ethnics judge one another's existential value and social success in the postcolonial world" (*Protestant* 188–89). Not one to mince words, Chow calls this PRC psychodynamics "ethnic *ressentiment*" (189).

Although Liu Yiqing's chauvinistic assault may seem crude, it does encapsulate a recurring concern in criticism on Ha Jin, namely, his representation of Chineseness to cultural and linguistic others in a global frame. I will dwell at greater length on debates about diasporic autoethnography and orientalism in the next chapter, since Annie Wang overtly thematizes these issues in her novel *Lili*, to a degree that Jin has yet to do in his writing. Nonetheless, the charge of self-exoticism is one that plagues Jin as much as Wang, and, indeed, the vast majority of Chinese emigrant writers in the West. Given that Jin has canvassed almost every major traumatic episode of Chinese history in his fiction and rarely hesitates to censure communism's suffocating effects, and given that he writes primarily in English and predominantly for an American audience, he presents an all-too-easy target for cultural watchdogs on the lookout for "traitors" or "sell-outs."

Such vilification of Jin from the Sinophone literary world extends beyond the PRC. In 2007, the prominent Taiwanese author Zhu Tianwen, through the fictional persona of a local male reader in her novel *Wuyan*, mocks Jin for building his career in the West via cheap tricks, such as relying on "straight translation from Chinese to write his English-language novels." Zhu's protagonist fumes about how, when "translated back into Chinese, Ha Jin is like someone who had been flash frozen. When he woke up, he had no inkling as to the events that had transpired in mainland China in the 1980s. Earnestly and with excitement, he retells what other people have already narrated, except not as well" (qtd. in Tsu 103). In terms reminiscent of Liu Yiqing's, Zhu imputes to Jin self-exoticism and linguistic betrayal, insinuating that he dwells on bygone nightmares of the Cultural Revolution out of ignorance of contemporary China even as he capitalizes on his foreign background by creating a quirky pidgin English. However, as Jing Tsu rightly points out, Zhu's sneering dismissal of Jin's English writing as a "gimmick of translation" is itself underpinned by a problematic assumption about the priority of the original language to "hold a translation accountable." Tsu embeds this volatile exchange between "a monolingual Chinese writer and a Chinese Anglophone diasporic writer" within the larger cultural dynamics of "global literary governance" in modern Chinese literature, whereby "prestige in the international marketplace engenders local antagonisms, as writers judge one another—especially their closest peers—as rivals in what is often perceived as a zero-sum game." In effect echoing Chow's thesis on postcolonial ethnic resentment, Tsu observes that, far from harmonizing differences, globalization "further baits and divides" Chinese writers today (104). "The real battle," Tsu suggests, is not abroad in the West but "at home," and it is this homegrown battle over linguistic authority that most immediately prompts Jin to write his self-defense in *The Writer as Migrant* (105–6).

If Jin's Chineseness has been called into question by critics inside the PRC and Taiwan, many of those outside have risen to his defense. They often do so by rejecting "authenticity" as a premise and formulating instead some version of the alternative question: how does Jin transcend Chineseness, or else transform the literary sites he occupies from within or from their periphery? Regardless of the answer, the common impulse has been to tackle the matter of Jin's Chineseness in cultural rather than political terms, or more exactly, as a problem of reconceptualizing cultural identity rather than one of interrogating state power. Indeed, surprisingly, most critics are quick to pass over the anticommunist thrust of Jin's writing, and in lieu of political analyses, discussions of his cultural and linguistic identity abound.[6]

We can isolate three overlapping patterns of critical responses here. The first involves evoking a multiculturalist binary of universalism versus difference. On this reading, Jin is typically and approvingly characterized as a humanist, a writer of "the human heart" who "sacrifices cultural specificity" (Oh 421) and "Chinese cultural difference" (Zhou 275) in favor of depicting universal experiences. The terminology of "transcendence" and "emotion" predominates, as critics try to rescue Jin from his Sinophone detractors by diverting attention away from the China-specific aspects of his work toward its more humanistic or sentimental dimensions. Along this interpretive line, a diaspora writer's proper strategy for countering orientalism and exoticism is to reach for the universal and the human, not as a political ideal à la Arendt, but as an aesthetic emptied of cultural distinctiveness. This reading presupposes that Jin would be primarily preoccupied with undermining orientalism rather than totalitarianism, Western representational politics rather than communist party-state power. Cultural anxieties eclipse issues of political governance here. The second strand of critical responses, likewise prioritizing cultural politics over state power as the main axis of evaluation, concentrates in particular on Jin's Anglophonism, specifically his linguistic tactics for handling the disjunction between the English of his composition and the Chinese milieus of his stories and poems. On this score, critics diverge widely. Some view Jin as intentionally writing in a "transparently plain English" that panders to an American "multiculturalist ideal of providing privileged and total access to Chinese 'difference'" (Yao 140); others see his English as offering a "viable model for cultural translation" but no "new global literary language capable of reflecting multicultural sensibilities" (Oh 421, 426); and still others find his fiction a fertile source of "language innovations" full of "hybrid" and "bilingual creativity" (H. Zhang 307). Despite these contradictory assessments, however, critics along this second pattern of reading are united in their focus on Jin's diction as the basis of delineating his cultural identity. In one extreme case of this language-centered approach, Jin's work is lauded as making its "best contribution" purely on the "formal level," with its "content" completely bracketable (Lo 18); in effect, the significance of Jin's writing is reduced entirely to its language. Finally, along a third critical strain, attention is again directed away from Jin's many critiques of the communist regime, this time toward his impact on the conceptual boundaries of various canonical literatures. One critic includes Jin in a catalog of nonwhite Anglophone authors who, in the age of globalization, write new versions of "Janglish" and ring the "death knell" for the very concept of "national literature" (Hassan 279). Others lay claim to Jin as a "transformative force" for both American and Asian American literature (Zhou 276), or a key figure whose work "underscores the need to continue expanding the notion of 'Asian American' beyond the conceptual boundaries of national citizenship and the referential domain of the United States" (Yao 112). Still others argue for his instrumentality in redefining modern Chinese literature from a nation-bound and language-based model to one that is "transnational, translinguistic, and global" (Lo 14), and in "the future direction of a global Chinese literature that is not exclusive to one language" (Tsu 111). That Jin can be appropriated with equal facility by those endeavoring to expand or deconstruct the category of Chinese literature as by those with similar designs on American and Asian American literature clearly signals his multilateral utility for critics with an eye on the global.

These lines of reading bring into relief the complex cultural and linguistic entanglements of Jin's writing, and when read alongside each other, they usefully illuminate the many tensions in Jin's evolving aesthetics. Just on the topic of his employment of the English language, for example, there is clearly no critical consensus, not even about whether his diction is "plain" or "hybrid," straightforwardly monolingual or experimentally bilingual. Nonetheless, without acknowledging the persistent political impetus of Jin's work, culture-centric readings threaten not only to camouflage a crucial component of his aesthetics but also to perpetuate the erasure of totalitarian state power as an enduring force in today's world. Indeed, this omission enacts another instance of global amnesia about Tiananmen—not the fact of the massacre itself, but the potential meanings and prolonged repercussions of the massacre on diasporic subjects. In this circumstance, we must continue to keep in view the elements in Jin's corpus that resist deterritorialization and planetarization, that remain through and through polity-specific (rather than merely nation-specific). It matters that his target is a communist party-state and its sovereign exercise of brute force, and that he forwards this critique in the very historical moment of the PRC's ascending geopolitical and economic power.[7] If Gao Xingjian's political (in)difference was erased under the sign of a monolithic dissidence by the world media at the time of his Nobel award, Ha Jin's very real political dissidence has ironically been buried under the sign of his cultural difference. What sorely needs recuperation now is a notion of *political* difference, the yet pertinent distinction in our time between a totalitarian state with its authoritarian resilience and a democratic state with its attendant liberal biases—despite, or precisely because of, these political entities' ever more intertwined interests in the current global capitalist economy.

What accounts for this consistent deflecting of attention away from Chineseness as the identity of a political structure to Chineseness as the identity of a cultural other in the Anglophone critical reception of Jin's work? It is as if his critiques of PRC totalitarianism are too self-evident for exegesis, or else too familiar from all the media hype to require much elaboration. As Steven Yao speculates, "the depth and breadth of the mainstream acclaim [Jin] enjoys has apparently obviated any need for cultural advocacy or ideological recuperation" (112). More surprising still is that, in spite of Jin's high profile in the United States in the past dozen years, American literary scholarship on his work remains scant. On this scholarly neglect, Yao suggests that one influential factor might be the "basic simplicity of [Jin's] realist style," which seems to make "any extended historical or cultural explication . . . largely superfluous" (111–12). I would add that, given the repeated and acerbic castigations of Jin by Chinese critics on both sides of the Taiwan Straits, his Western defenders perhaps fear falling prey themselves to allegations of China bashing and China ignorance, of naively consuming, replicating, or exacerbating Jin's putative orientalism. As a preemptive maneuver, many avoid the theme of regime tyranny in preference for the more innocuous ones of cultural identity and language use. This fear may itself reflect the other side of Rey Chow's ethnic postcoloniality argument, for critics stationed in the West, notwithstanding being "ethnic" themselves, can feel all too vulnerable to accusations of neoimperialism from those in the non-West, not least those in the most autocratic of "postcolonial" regimes.

To reinvigorate political inquiries into Jin's work, we can situate him in relation to recent theories on the Chinese diaspora. Since the early 1990s, the theoretical alliance between deconstruction and postcolonialism in the works of such critics as Gayatri Spivak and Homi Bhabha has led to numerous conceptual models of diaspora that are deeply inflected with deconstructive and postcolonial tenets. A prevalent view in current diaspora discourse, for example, centers on the destabilizing and deparochializing potency of diaspora as a mode of alterity or difference, one that can powerfully dislodge all kinds of hegemonic authority. While the study of diasporas is certainly not new, the emergence of critical theories of diaspora as such in the past two decades, in literary and cultural studies as well as a host of social science disciplines, can be understood in this context. Indeed, "diaspora" has come to function as a utopian category for much current academic discourse.[8] By the turn of the millennium, this deconstructive and postcolonial paradigm has come to pervade—and proliferate—scholarly studies on the Chinese diaspora. In particular, we can discern a profound absorption of the deconstructive-postcolonial doctrine that diaspora presents a vitally disruptive force capable of unsettling identity, in all its facets, from the essentialisms of the nation-state. For Chinese scholars who are themselves located in the diaspora and who aim to denationalize the concept of Chineseness or wrangle it away from the political stronghold of the PRC, this critical blueprint has been remarkably fruitful.

The earliest and perhaps most famous, yet also most controversial, of these Sino-diasporic articulations is Tu Wei-ming's early-1990s model of "cultural China." Tu's principal argument is that the geopolitical centers of Chinese populations in Asia no longer have a monopoly over what it means to be Chinese today. Instead, the construction of Chineseness is now spread widely across what he calls three "symbolic universes: (1) mainland China, Taiwan, Hong Kong, and Singapore, (2) overseas Chinese communities throughout the world, and (3) the international communities of scholars, students, officials, journalists, and traders who provide a global forum for China-related matters." In Tu's resonant phrase, "the geopolitical periphery may have already become a new cultural center." While he does not employ a deconstructive vocabulary, we can construe his project as fundamentally a cultural deconstruction of China's geopolitical authority. He describes his goals thus: "To explore the fluidity of Chineseness as a layered and contested discourse, to open new possibilities and avenues of inquiry, and to challenge the claims of political leadership (in Beijing, Taipei, Hong Kong, or Singapore) to be the ultimate authority in a matter as significant as Chineseness" (Preface viii). An analysis of Ha Jin within this deconstructive geopolitical framework can do much to recover, and perhaps diffuse anxieties over, the political content and significance of his work in relation to PRC state power.

Within Tu's grid, the second symbolic universe of the Chinese diaspora has come under special fire. One contentious element here is his origin-recentering characterization of the diaspora. Unlike in the case of the Jewish diaspora, Tu contends that

> the state, or more precisely China as a civilization-state, features prominently in the Chinese diaspora. Because the Chinese diaspora has never lost its homeland, there is no functional equivalent of the cathartic yearning for Jerusalem. Actually the ubiquitous presence of the Chinese state—its awe-inspiring physical size, its long history, and the numerical weight of its population—continues to loom large in the psychocultural constructs of diaspora Chinese. . . . Few diaspora Chinese ever speculate about the possibility of China's disintegrating as a unified civilization-state. The advantage of being liberated from obsessive concern for China's well-being at the expense of their own livelihood is rarely entertained. The diaspora Chinese cherish the hope of returning to and being recognized by the homeland. ("Cultural" 18–19)

So, even as Tu purports to contest and challenge the hegemony of geopolitical centers in Asia, he ironically reinstates the centrality of "China," now abstracted from the communist state into a "civilization-state," which nonetheless essentially circumscribes the loyalty, mentality, and orientation of diasporic subjects. For this conservative cultural politics, he has been variously taken to task by subsequent Chinese diaspora critics, who disagree not so much with his core thesis as with his insufficient commitment to its theoretical and political potential. For example, Sharon Hom, in editing an anthology on Chinese diaspora women's writing, also adopts a deconstructive and postcolonial lexicon for her gloss of "diaspora" as a structure of "ambiguity" and "movement" with "transgressive" and "destabilizing" capacities (3–4). Although she cites Tu's cultural China as a theoretical starting point for her volume, she objects to his territorial anchoring in China, his prioritizing of ethnic identity, and his neglect of, among other things, class and gender (10). Likewise, in her deconstructive exploration of diasporic identity as a site of "hybridity . . . multiplicity, uncertainty and ambivalence" (2), Ien Ang validates Tu's attempt to "decentre the cultural authority of geopolitical China," which she sees as "critical insofar as it aims to break with static and rigid, stereotypical and conventional definitions of Chinese" (40–41), but she too questions his model's latent "desire for . . . another kind of centrism, this time along notionally cultural lines." As with Hom, what Ang disputes is not the underlying motivation of Tu's project but his "homogenization" of the diaspora and his deficiency in carrying out his own argument to its most "radical potential" (42–43). Yet another example is Olivia Khoo's study of Chinese diasporic femininity in contemporary visual and popular culture. She, too, articulates her theoretical position by refuting Tu's cultural China model, which she criticizes in more vehement tones than the others as a "hegemonic metanarrative" that "invokes the notion of roots and origins, and a return to an essential China" (14). Against Tu, Khoo claims for her own "ex-centric" model of Chineseness a radical transnationality that "cannot be mapped as a distinct geographical area," that does not try to "replace one centre with another," and that "eschews the place of origins (specifically, mainland China) as the ultimate signifier" as well as "Southeast Asia as other economic models have done" (15–16).

Several points are worth highlighting in these post-Tu formulations of the Chinese diaspora. First, they all share a largely celebratory view of the diaspora as a site of contestatory, interventionist, or deessentializing power. The rubric of diaspora, from these perspectives, is most useful when harnessed to a progressive politics of difference, whether along the axis of race, gender, sexuality, or class.[9] Second, while the later critics rightly expose the limits of Tu's vision so as to stretch the political reach of his diasporic critique, they all owe a certain theoretical debt to his notion of cultural China, which has been instrumental in launching the critical venture of looking to the diaspora as a key locus for deconstructing Chineseness. The deconstructive mandate to dislodge and debunk, however, can sometimes become monopolizing in itself, so much so that any diasporic longing for origin can come to be regarded with suspicion, as a sign of retrograde or complicitous centrism. Paradoxically, these two opposite dependencies on Tu's framework—as at once starting point and point of departure—underscore his seminal role as a negative origin for subsequent theorists. Finally, the origins-repudiating model of diasporic Chineseness, if totalized, can fail to make sense of the continual tug of origins for many diasporic subjects. One exemplary manifestation of this tug is the obvious "psychocultural" charge that China retains for many diaspora writers. To be sure, there is a gradient of homesickness and "China obsession," to recall C. T. Hsia's phrase, but the gravitational heart of much diasporic literature undoubtedly rests with the land left behind. Although not all diasporic subjects "cherish the hope of returning to and being recognized by the homeland," as Tu proposes ("Cultural" 19), the dynamics of remote trauma and melancholia can still impinge considerably on diasporic psyches—as with Jin and Tiananmen. Tu's model, though inadequate, may yet have its relevance. In this theoretical context, to recognize diasporic trauma and postmemory as key components in Jin's aesthetics can make salient the myriad ways origin lives out its afterlife in the diasporic imagination, not necessarily as naïve essentialism or nostalgic euphoria, but possibly as partial haunting and incomplete mourning, and equally importantly, as a counterpolitics and literary ethics.

Most importantly for this study, it merits remembering that Tu's efforts at decentering Chineseness were undertaken at a critical historical juncture: the one or two years immediately following June 4. In a quite substantial way, he was responding, like many diasporic intellectuals at the time, including his cohort of authors for *The Living Tree* anthology and budding writers such as Ha Jin, to the crisis of loyalty and self-definition that Tiananmen triggered. In fact, the shadow of June 4 looms large over Tu's pages, as he repeatedly grapples with the psychic and emotional fallout of the massacre from a self-consciously diasporic vantage point. As he admits in one passage: "The massive exodus of many of the most brilliant Chinese intellectuals from the mainland during the last decade clearly shows that the civilization-state has lost much of its grip on the Chinese intelligentsia, and the Tiananmen tragedy may have irreversibly severed the emotional attachment of the diaspora Chinese to the homeland. The meaning of being Chinese, an issue that has haunted Chinese intellectuals for at least three generations, has taken on entirely new dimensions" ("Cultural" 24). Undeniably, Tu's focus is elitist: his eye is firmly fixed on the intelligentsia, whether within the PRC or abroad, and June 4's legacy is registered mostly in terms of its "near-total alienation" of intellectuals from the governing regime ("Cultural" 26). Nevertheless, his ambitious enterprise of a large-scale redefinition of Chineseness, his sustained wrestling with the diaspora's relation to Chinese identity through a valorization of the periphery in opposition to the PRC in particular, has been formative for the scholarly groundswell in Chinese diaspora studies in the past two decades. We can therefore observe that, in a vital and long-term if noncausal manner, Tiananmen has played a pivotal role in shaping the orientation and substance of academic discourses on the "Chinese diaspora" as such.

To contextualize both Jin and Tu in another direction, we can remind ourselves here, strategically, of the theoretical forerunner whose model of diaspora underpins much of current diaspora discourse: namely, Stuart Hall's conception of diasporic identity, and more specifically, his acknowledgment of the enduring power of origin as a "great aporia." In an oft-cited essay, Hall outlines two ways of understanding cultural identity. What has become enshrined as an article of faith in many diaspora theories is his second, and decidedly more poststructuralist, definition:[10]

Cultural identity, in this second sense, is a matter of "becoming" as well as of "being." It belongs to the future as much as to the past. It is not something which already exists, transcending place, time, history, and culture. Cultural identities come from somewhere, have histories. But, like everything which is historical, they undergo constant transformation. Far from being eternally fixed in some essentialized past, they are subject to the continuous 'play' of history, culture, and power.... In this perspective, cultural identity is not a fixed essence at all, lying unchanged outside history and culture. It is not some universal and transcendental spirit inside us on which history has made no fundamental mark. It is not once-and-for-all. It is not a fixed origin to which we can make some final and absolute return.... Cultural identities are the points of identification, the unstable points of identification or suture, which are made, within the discourses of history and culture. Not an essence but a *positioning*. (225–26)

Hall himself leans toward this second conception of cultural identity, which he sees as better capturing the flux of historical experience for diasporic subjects, especially "the traumatic character of 'the colonial experience'" (225). Clearly writing from a host of poststructuralist positionings himself, Hall conjures the Heideggerian language of "becoming" as much as the Derridean one of "difference" and "play," joining Foucauldian vocabulary of the interplay of "history, culture, and power" and the "production and reproduction" of identities to the postcolonialist one of colonial "ruptures" and "traumas" as well as Bhabha's notion of "hybridity." In almost pedagogical fashion, he cites Derrida's *différance* and then explicates its double connotations of difference and deferral (229) before tying the concept back to a postcolonial politics of diasporic identity formation (235). What is often forgotten in theoretical citations of Hall, however, is his first definition of cultural identity—as "one, shared culture, a sort of collective 'one true self,' hiding inside the many other, more superficial or artificially imposed 'selves,' which people with a shared history and ancestry hold in common." This first sense of cultural identity seems to be a classic expression of essentialism, but Hall stresses that it has "played a critical role in all postcolonial struggles which have so profoundly reshaped our world" and "continues to be a very powerful and creative force in emergent forms of representation among hitherto marginalised peoples" (223). For Hall, this first model is not so much accurate as instrumental, a collective vision that allows dispossessed groups to re-create and reimagine their lost origins, even if these reimaginings are "not the rediscovery but the *production* of identity," "not an identity grounded in the archeology, but in the *retelling* of the past." What is decisive for diasporic peoples is the "experience of dispersal and fragmentation," which has irrevocably made of any origin "the great aporia" (224), but beyond this irreversible fragmentation, origin-as-aporia still retains a tremendous and tenacious power to structure diasporic desires and to "restore an imaginary fullness or plenitude set against the broken rubric of our past" (225). Rather than a wholesale rejection of nostalgia as recidivist metaphysics, then, and rather than a simplistic opposition of origins to displacement, Hall recommends thinking about diasporic identities as "'framed' by two axes or vectors, simultaneously operative: the vector of similarity and continuity; and the vector of difference and rupture" (226). Even if his accent falls on the latter, he takes care not to discard the former out of hand, paying homage instead to its postcolonial and diasporic political utility as well as its sociopsychic persistence. Diasporic identity, above all, is a dynamic movement defined simultaneously by deconstructive and reconstructive compulsions. Hall thus voices the disappearance of origins, not as a conceptual telos or an end-in-itself, but as a theoretical assumption about diasporic peoples' existential loss and imaginary gain. Given the fissures and dispersals of history, the homeland can only be reconstituted by diasporic subjects as a "great aporia," but one now invested with awesome interpellating and even unifying power.

Tu's origin-yearning model of cultural China instantiates just such an insight, and without question, Ha Jin's *The Crazed* resonates profoundly with this trope of origin as well. Indeed, Jin outlines a perfect spatial counterpart to Hall's sense of diasporic identity's doubleness—to wit, the lost Square as a site similarly "framed" by two "vectors," at once centripetal and centrifugal, at once intensely craved and deeply traumatic but also ultimately unfathomable and unrepresentable. Perhaps it is the historical timing of Jin's own diasporic arrival that has led to this unlikely rendezvous between the self-professed humanist writer and the poststructuralist critic. Coming to the United States in 1985 as a graduate student of English literature and continuing to study and teach in the American university system after Tiananmen, Jin was well-situated to witness, firsthand and close-up, the institutional emergence of diaspora theory as a poststructuralist-saturated field, and alongside it, that of trauma studies. These were the most proximate discourses circulating around him in the years leading up to and following 1989, exactly the years of *The Crazed*'s tortuous, stumbling, repetitive composition. These were the discourses that would undergird his later writerly self-identity—in his words, "unlike most academics"—as a believer in universal and transcendent truth. Thus, notwithstanding his self-assessment as a writer who alienates American academics on matters of the universal, his fiction can be read as epitomizing the very tenets of 1990s poststructuralism. *The Crazed* grows out of this very particular cultural and historical milieu, marking a unique point in the development of Tiananmen literature, one demarcated by Jin's postemigrant status in the 1990s U.S. academy. The vanished Square delimits an encounter, fortuitous but far from aporetic, between this elite institutional circumstance and an instant of diasporic traumatic witnessing. Yet, without appreciating the traumatic and melancholic undercurrents in Jin's writing, one can all too easily misread or deride his compulsive imaginary returns to China as gullible hubris or ideological misguidedness, or worse, multiculturalist collusion and calculated opportunism.

To anchor Jin's work more solidly in its historical and material contexts, two recent readings seem to me to have opened up another fruitful path. The first is Steven Yao's appraisal of Jin's poetry within the genealogy of Chinese American verse. Like many of Jin's Anglophone critics, Yao focuses on the latter's language, specifically the crux issue of how he bridges the English of his composition and the Chinese identities he lyricizes. Unlike most, however, Yao is deeply critical of Jin's linguistic choices. For Yao, Jin's trademark style of "plain English" and his "unwavering commitment to linguistic transparency" are only too "accommodationist" as an Asian American poetics, which fails to tax the average American reader in either diction or thought (140). What is particularly valuable about Yao's methodology is his deliberate grounding of Jin's work within its U.S. contexts. Yao instructively reminds us that, despite the near-absence of the United States as a narrative geography in Jin's writing, it remains his most immediate sociopolitical and geopolitical environment and must therefore be given due consideration in any address of his aesthetics and mainstream success. On Yao's argument, Jin's anticommunist stance serves a dual purpose for his American readers. On the one hand, his humanist poetics combined with his use of simple English function to render the foreign content of his writing "transparent" to American audiences, thereby appeasing the public's perennial appetite for multicultural narratives of otherness. On the other, his many portrayals of the recurrent persecutions and brutalities of the communist regime help to shore up a self-congratulatory attitude about the United States' political superiority. In Yao's view, Jin's writing conveniently feeds a post–Cold War mentality, one that lingers into the 1990s decade of his rise to literary fame, "immediately before radical Islam gained temporary ascendancy as the most pressing threat to global 'American interests' following the events of September 11, 2001" (111). At heart, Yao's censure of Jin is rooted in an Asian Americanist cultural politics, with its imperative to combat American racist stereotypes of Asia as the yellow peril and the Asian as a despotic or victimized other. Within this framework, the import of diasporic trauma and melancholia is largely subordinated to that of ethnic representation. Yao's reproach is not unwarranted, since Jin's fiction too evinces an at times facile idealization of America as the land of political freedom and economic opportunity, social intimacy and true friendship.[11] Juxtaposed against his many uncompromising portraits of the horrors of communist China, Jin's somewhat naïve pro-Americanism is indeed problematic and may partly explain why he has yet to be embraced by most Asian American scholars.

The other significant recent analysis of Jin unfolds in Jing Tsu's study on Sinophone "literary governance." In counterpoint to Yao, Tsu locates Jin squarely within a lineage of Chinese diasporic bilingual writers, one that extends back to Lin Yutang and Eileen Chang. Instead of exploring Jin's reception in America, then, Tsu's eye is fixed on Jin's reception in the Sinophone world. For her, Jin's numerous clashes with Sinophone cultural authorities are neither unique nor unprecedented but typify the pressures exerted by native (and nativist) critics and readers on overseas Chinese writers since the beginning of the twentieth century. Against Zhu Tianwen's cutting satire of Jin, Tsu maintains that there is, "in fact, no pure mother tongue in current Sinophone writing, even though claims of authenticity are still bandied about as ground for recrimination and betrayal" (105). Though stemming from an opposite disciplinary direction and ending with a contrary assessment of Jin's cultural politics, Tsu's reading nonetheless converges unexpectedly with Yao's on one point. In the midst of discussing another controversy around Jin, this time regarding *War Trash* and its putative plagiarism of a Chinese-language memoir, Tsu notes that Jin's novel actually speaks to multiple audiences, and that the surface narrative of the plight of Chinese POWs in an American military camp during the Korean War also "appropriately touched on the sensitive nerve of the then stirring controversy in the United States over the detainees at Guantanamo Bay." In line with Yao's U.S. grounding, Tsu here zeroes in on the American resonances of Jin's novel and the ways it "brought the question of historical accountability to bear on its English context" by turning "one historical experience into an allegory for another by using one language to speak for another" (110). Tsu's allegorical reading of Jin's bilingualism brings to light the multiple interlocutors of his fiction, revealing how his Chinese and American addresses are potentially overlapping rather than mutually exclusive. Finally, Tsu adds that, in response to the recurring charges of linguistic betrayal, Jin decided in early 2010 to translate *A Good Fall* back into Chinese himself, so as to declare "an open allegiance to the mother tongue in translation" (111). Whether this effort at self-translation succeeds in curbing nativist antagonism awaits to be seen. Yet it is telling that, even in Chinese, Jin now foregrounds his self-identification as a diasporic "migrant" writer through his translation of the collection's title: *Luodi*, not a literal back-translation of the English title but the first part of the Chinese idiom *luodi shenggen*—"to fall to the ground and take new root," a proverbial metaphor for the longtime emigrant—though, intriguingly, Jin also elides the second half of this expression, perhaps intimating that a good fall does not preclude him from continuing to move between new and old grounds.

By way of provisional closure, let me return to David Der-wei Wang's symbolic creature mentioned earlier: the *taowu*, at once monster and diviner, devourer and guardian of the past. Ultimately, this dual conception of history seems to me most apt in capturing not just *The Crazed* but, more generally, Tiananmen fictions in all their multifacetedness. The ghost of June 4 may indeed haunt many diaspora writers of the massacre, but the past is not a purely traumatic force that continually swallows all psychic energies in the present. The theoretical framework of trauma sheds much light on Ha Jin's writing from the past dozen years, and *The Crazed* is undoubtedly an exemplary work in this respect. Yet Jin embodies only one prototype, and perhaps an anomalous one, of the Tiananmen writer. While diaspora authors may share common subject matters and dwell on the same historical moments of national upheaval, he seems to have lived out to an exceptional degree a perpetual sense of hauntedness in his fictions. Not every diaspora writer, however, fits this mold of the melancholic remote witness, inexorably caught in the throes of writing and rewriting an originary scene of diasporic trauma. By extension, the genre of Tiananmen fictions is not merely a symptom. Already we have seen in the previous chapter that Gao Xingjian's *Taowang*, far from displaying the playwright's constant mournfulness toward or haunting by the Chinese nation, on the contrary universalizes June 4 as an existential condition. And as we will see in the next chapter, Annie Wang directs an even more trenchant and irreverent critique at the category of the nation as she attempts to debunk both "China" and "Tiananmen" along lines of gender and class. While also concentrating on an episode of historical violence, she will not be one to characterize its residual imprint as an unshakable phantom; if anything, the historical weight and emotional priority of the past will become transmogrified, updated and globalized, in her hands. So, even as Ha Jin emblematizes one model of the diaspora writer, the deconstructive and postcolonialist inflections of his lost Square mark one phase in the ongoing development of academic discourses about displacement and belonging, the diaspora and the human. The stage marked by Jin is preceded by Gao's late 1980s moment, when the conceptual nexus between dislocation and humanism was most often theorized in terms of exile, whereas both this and Jin's deconstructive diasporic aesthetics have since been superseded in the early years of the twenty-first century by the rubrics of globalization and capitalism that dominate Wang's novel. Indeed, in this latter-day phase, Jin himself has turned away from pre-Tiananmen China. In *A Free Life*, at last, we see him emerging from the 1989 threshold and venturing forth into the imagined geography of a post-Tiananmen PRC, not as the lost space of a native homeland, but as a now strangely foreign country. Beijing, previously the all-too-familiar site and sight of remote trauma, now becomes visually unhinged from its past images and is "hardly recognizable" (530). In this newly disjointed landscape, the patches of origin we glimpse through Jin's fiction are no longer fragmented ruins of a great aporia but commodified slices of an unlived future—a hypercapitalist China that far outpaces Jin's new protagonist's own suburban American life. This will be the global scape on which Annie Wang stages her anachronistic, hyperreal Tiananmen.

3 / The Globalized Square: Annie Wang's *Lili*

Among the authors examined in this book, Annie Wang is an anomaly. She is the only one who currently lives both inside and outside of mainland China: leaving in 1993 to study journalism at the University of California at Berkeley, she has since moved back, first to her native Beijing in 1999, then relocating to Shanghai in 2004, and now dividing her time between the two Pacific coasts. Concurrent with this geographical shuttling is a bilingual writing career. Moving with ease between languages, and comfortable with high and low cultural forums alike, she has built on her corpus of Chinese fictions with *Lili* (2001), her first novel in English, as well as an immensely popular column-turned-novel that is universally dubbed the Chinese *Sex and the City*. Wang thus belongs to a new generation that cannot be neatly categorized as either exilic or diasporic, embodying instead a model of the contemporary globe-trotting transnational subject. Her place in this study, however, is not only apropos but all the more valuable as a result, for she brings into relief a flight path of the post-Tiananmen literary diaspora that may well become the dominant one for younger writers to come. In this regard, *Lili* serves as a revealing index of the paradoxes of globalization. The novel registers many of the tensions of a transnational aesthetic, not just by explicitly thematizing a geopolitical difference between the PRC and the United States, but also in marking Wang's own equivocal stance toward global and bicultural capital, especially given her emphatic self-positioning as a Chinese woman writer. This chapter will hence proceed mainly from text to context, from an analysis of the novel's portrait of the Square as a paradigmatic site of capitalist flows and neocolonial desires to a discussion of Wang's authorial negotiations with

Chinese and American literary markets. But first, since she is above all a keen observer of how misogyny and gendered power can ally with neo-orientalism and geopolitical power, let us begin with a related cultural document, one that internationalizes the most iconic, and phallic, image of Tiananmen—the Tank Man.

Part I. Female Hooligans and Global Capital

THE TANK MAN, INTERNATIONALIZED

One of the most memorable scenes in Antony Thomas's documentary film *The Tank Man* (2006) shows four Beijing University students being presented with a photograph—that of a lone Chinese man, dressed casually in dark trousers and a plain white button-down shirt with sleeves rolled up partway, carrying what look to be ordinary plastic grocery bags in both hands and facing a column of tanks in the middle of a wide boulevard. To the American and British audiences at whom this film is directed, the photograph will quickly bring to mind the most prominent visual emblem of the 1989 Tiananmen movement: the Tank Man, that unidentified citizen who blocked the path of army tanks on Changan Avenue on June 5, since made famous by the international media as an icon of individual defiance against totalitarian power. In Thomas's film, however, the Beijing University students, all of whom appear to be about twenty years old and would have been at most three or four at the time of the massacre, pause in long silence before this picture. When asked whether it holds any meaning for them, they seem to fumble for answers. "Looks like some military ceremony," one woman whispers to her neighbor. Then more loudly to the interviewer: "Well, I can see four vehicles. I'm not sure about the context. It might be a parade or something. I really don't know. I'm just guessing." Another woman concurs: "I really can't tell anything from this picture. There's no context." Finally, the one young man in the group asks, "Is this a piece of artwork? Did you make this up?"

The documentary's point is clear. Since 1989, the PRC government has not only suppressed historical facts about the democracy movement and the military crackdown but also worked to impede the circulation of information—and the passing down of cultural memory—concerning the incident. Thomas's pedagogical voice-over in this key moment of the film drives this point home:

> Beida, the University of Beijing, and the most prestigious in all of China. In 1989, Beida was the nerve center of the student movement that would inspire a popular uprising. Today's undergraduates enjoy

all the benefits that have flowed into China A [the prosperous China of capitalist growth, versus China B, the social underbelly of China's capitalism]. Largely the children of the elite, they enjoy freedom of travel and a lifestyle many Western undergraduates might envy. But what do they know of their recent history? . . .

Whatever they [the four students] may have heard about 1989, it was clear that they had never seen the Tank Man picture. . . . The image was shown once, in 1989 on China Television, re-branded as an example of the army's restraint. But the picture was quickly withdrawn and never shown again. No one under 20 in China is likely to have seen it. (*"Tank Man* Transcript")

Thomas is noticeably careful not to overstate his case about China's historical amnesia. He acknowledges that, even if Tiananmen is an officially censored topic in the PRC educational system and state media, the students may well have heard about it from informal sources. Nonetheless, he insists that the Tank Man remains a wholly unknown and unremembered figure for the post-Tiananmen generations. As he notes in a post-production interview, there was, as always, a government minder monitoring the filming session that day, so "if any of those four [students] knew that they were looking at an infamous, banned picture, at the very least, there would have been a nervous sideways glance. But there's nothing" (*"Tank Man*: Making"). For Thomas, the Tank Man is nothing less than a flash point in the universal human struggle for freedom, and the Beijing University students' nonrecognition of this image epitomizes the enormity of the PRC's mind control and the post-Tiananmen generations' historical ignorance. The documentary performs its cultural authority on and participates in the knowledge production of Tiananmen precisely by dramatizing a stark division between its own knowledge possession and the Chinese subjects' lack thereof.

Still, some American viewers of the film remain skeptical of Thomas's claim, finding it hard to believe that an entire generation of Beijing college students would have no reference point whatsoever for the Tank Man. Some speculate that the four students might have been merely pretending not to recognize the photograph, perhaps out of fear of persecution for speaking to the foreign media about a Tiananmen-related topic. When this possibility was posed to Thomas in an online live chat the morning after the documentary first aired on PBS, he responded adamantly: "If they were pretending, they were actors worthy of Oscar awards. I studied their expressions very carefully and for many times during editing. There wasn't a glimmer of recognition from any of them. . . . No one in that room had any knowledge of the Tank Man's act of defiance." There is a certain irony to Thomas's response: even as the Beijing University students in this filmic encounter repeatedly invoke the necessity of context for photographic interpretation, expressing a persistent desire to restore image to history, Thomas in his metacommentary evinces an opposite desire to flatten history into image, to reduce the historical processes and lived experiences of generational memory or its erasure to (his own) purely individual visual analysis.

The question here hinges on how we are to interpret the students' "silence," if we take this term to include their professed nonrecognition of the picture. For Thomas, this silence can only signify bafflement and ignorance, a cultural "tragedy." For the skeptical viewer, though, his absolute refusal to entertain other interpretations smacks a bit of the cultural outsider's excessive self-assurance and may even imply a kind of colonialist attitude, one that, despite its lofty commitment to human rights advocacy, denies the Chinese students a deeper interiority, a more complex awareness of the volatile conflict of interests between domestic concealment of knowledge and foreign demands of exhibition. Indeed, even as Thomas indicates that he fully realized the Tank Man "experiment" to be "very dangerous" for him and his crew to conduct, that they risked having their tape confiscated at the time, he never goes on to address the greater potential danger of his actions for the Chinese students, or the way his experiment placed them within a tug of power between the nativist/nationalist regime of knowledge and his own Western liberal agenda. Instead, Thomas comments at length on taking pains to thwart the communist authorities by creating an impression that his film was nonpolitical. Not only did he not discuss the photograph with the students afterward, but he displayed the photograph only after talking to them "on all kinds of innocuous subjects for 20-plus minutes to relax them," then deliberately moved on to "another bunch of innocuous questions," so that the Tank Man would seem to be just one passing item among many (*"Tank Man*: Making"). These maneuvers probably helped to protect the students to some extent, but his emphasis throughout is on successfully producing his film rather than probing how the students might have navigated the cultural politics and probable perils of being interviewed by Western journalists on a censored topic.

The most complicating detail in this scene occurs when the young man in the group, prior to answering the interviewer, whispers to the puzzled woman beside him, "June 4." To his credit, Thomas keeps this footage in the film, but he later dismisses the young man's comment as ultimately unrevealing of the students' broader historical awareness. "My firm opinion," he says in an interview, "is that [the young man] was the only one who sensed that the photo had something to do with the events of 1989, but the Tank Man meant nothing to him" (*"Tank Man*: Making"). Yet this moment in the film clearly shows that the Tank Man image triggers a mental file for the young man, even if we can only guess at the true extent of his knowledge. Then again, in accordance with Thomas's description, it does appear that the young man's prompt fails to conjure deeper associations for the young woman next to him, whose smile remains a mixture of unguarded innocence, perplexity, and embarrassment. The other two women look uncomfortable but strangely expressionless; there is no obvious clue to their thoughts.

What the film captures here, I would submit, is a *spectrum* of ignorance and half-knowledge, and a tension between partial recognition and the self-censored display of such recognition. Even if we find no telltale sign from the students' facial expressions, no nervous sideways glance or overt gesture of simulated ignorance, the cultural amnesia suggested in this scene seems somewhat more uneven, and probably far more complicated in its inner negotiations of terror and guilt, ethnic pride and cultural self-loathing, than the film's exegesis would have it. Of course, these psychic negotiations are not incompatible with but exist along a continuum with the loss of historical knowledge that will inevitably result from more than a decade of official censorship. The intersection of these two mechanisms—the state's external suppression and the psyche's internal repression—may well define the post-Tiananmen generations' specific form of historical forgetfulness: not a uniformly blank slate, but in some instances, as with the young man's reaction to the Tank Man picture, a flash of recognition followed by a disavowal, a failure to acknowledge, identify with, or take public ownership of one's national history in the presence of others. Whether he would have spoken more freely in the absence of either foreign cameras or government monitors is open to debate. In any case, compared to the mental vacuum of complete oblivion posited by Thomas, this latter type of historical amnesia, in its implicit complicity with the communist apparatus of erasure, may constitute the more disquieting mode of cultural tragedy.

At a macro level, what *The Tank Man* raises in this episode is the problem of reconstructing historical memory of, and wielding knowledge about, Tiananmen in an international and cross-cultural context. Who possesses this knowledge and who does not? Who has the cultural power to convey this knowledge—or stage its ignorance—and for whose edification? A perusal of the documentary's production team and sources of authority will show that it consists mainly of Western journalists and scholars, with an impressive cast that includes Robin Munro, Orville Schell, Timothy Brook, Jonathan Mirsky, John Pomfret, Perry Link, and Nicholas Bequelin. A few Chinese dissidents are also briefly cited, including former student leaders Feng Congde and Xiao Qiang as well as activists Harry Wu and Han

Dongfang. Conspicuously absent are the most famous student leaders of the Tiananmen movement such as Chai Ling, Li Lu, and Wuer Kaixi, all of whom by 2006 had become the representative faces of Tiananmen to Western audiences via several earlier documentary films and numerous public appearances and newspaper reports. It may be that *The Tank Man* aims to present an alternative view of Tiananmen from the one previously tendered by those student leaders in exile (a topic I will explore more fully in the next chapter), hence its minimal reliance on their testimonies. In fact, the film's predominantly Western cast makes it a prime example of what Tu Wei-ming calls the third "symbolic universe" of "cultural China": "the international communities of scholars, students, officials, journalists, and traders who provide a global forum for China-related matters" (Preface viii). Moreover, by virtue of its academic distance, Thomas's film arguably offers a more balanced account of Tiananmen than does any prior documentary on the subject. But at the same time, by dramatizing somewhat too heavy-handedly the dichotomy between its own host of Western experts and the implied masses of ignorant Chinese youths today, the film risks falling into a colonialist representational position. The more severely it draws this binary between haves and have-nots, possession and deficiency, along a West-East axis, the more precariously it teeters on the edge of a neo-imperialist division of power/knowledge.

In the next chapter I will discuss how Ma Jian's *Beijing Coma* domesticates this issue of Tiananmen's memory/amnesia along a vertical, intergenerational axis within China itself. In this chapter, as an entry point into Annie Wang's *Lili*, I will begin by noting that Thomas's geopolitical partitioning of knowledge about Tiananmen converges with a gendered politics of knowledge subtly at work in the Beijing University interview. While the one Chinese male student in the group is presented as coming closest to the kind of historical consciousness possessed by the largely male film crew from the West, the three female Chinese students under scrutiny, by contrast, are narrated as retreating into a semiotic register of ambiguity and inscrutability. In this pivotal scene of the film, the young man mediates Western memory/knowledge and Chinese amnesia/ignorance even as the latter nexus is emphatically gendered female.

This hierarchy of power/knowledge about Tiananmen along intersecting lines of nationality, ethnicity, and gender establishes the central theme and core critique of Annie Wang's novel. Of the four Tiananmen works in this study, *Lili* is the one that most thoroughly internationalizes the representation of Tiananmen—and also the one that most explicitly engages with its own diasporicness as a text representing Tiananmen to Western readers. Wang's portrait of late 1980s Beijing as an international capitalist hub, though at times seemingly anachronistic, serves to resituate

Tiananmen discourse within a more current framework of China's globalization. This anachronism allows her to tackle concerns of a contemporary Chinese neocoloniality within a global capitalist order that has produced new relations of power between Westerners and Chinese as well as among Chinese themselves. If we adopt Wang's neocolonial perspective and scrutinize *The Tank Man* for nativist subversive tactics, we might detect a strange parallelism between Thomas's insistence on the students' ignorance and the students' emphasis on their own ignorance, between their repeated questions about the photograph's context and their remarks about their own lack of knowledge of this context—as if these students, like the shrewd and image-savvy hunger striker in *Lili*, are only too eager to perform the expected gaps in consciousness in front of foreign cameras. Thomas's film and Wang's novel therefore designate two opposite poles in the cross-cultural geopolitics of knowing Tiananmen. Both set out to represent the incident for Western audiences in the first years of the new millennium, but while *The Tank Man* implicitly defines the West as the site of historical understanding and world memory of Chinese trauma, *Lili* reclaims and rearticulates this memory by rendering the West's entry into post-Mao PRC, not in the liberal vocabulary of human rights advocacy or democratic education, but as a neo-imperialist penetration that opens up China only by wedding capital to orientalism.

Among diasporic fictions, Wang further charts a middle path in reconfiguring Tiananmen's relation to the nation. Where Gao Xingjian deterritorializes the episode altogether by setting his play in an unnamed country and existentializes the Square by emptying it of place and time, both Ha Jin and Ma Jian address the massacre through a strictly national frame anchored in the PRC, thereby perpetuating an intellectual tradition that C. T. Hsia has notoriously called the modern Chinese writer's "obsession with China." Wang, however, circumvents both the nation's erasure and its hegemony by plotting the transnational scope of global capital. Indeed, her novel may be read as at once transnationalizing and denationalizing the representation of Tiananmen. On the one hand, her depiction of 1980s Beijing as an allegorical neocolony exposes the porous boundaries of the new China, nowhere more evident than in the hybridized lives that congregate in that capital city. Yet money and goods flow decisively from West to East in her novel, and this one-way traffic is contingent on not just international circuits but also the inequality between nations and peoples. In short, the category of the nation remains meaningful for Wang in mapping subjects within the global coordinates of economic and cultural power.

At the same time, she supplements a criticism of America's global dominance with a trenchant demythologizing of "China" within the Tiananmen narrative. Unlike the other male writers of Tiananmen fictions,

Wang does not assume the voice of social, moral, or political authority in relation to China. To be sure, Gao's Middle-aged Man, Jin's Jian, and Ma's Dai Wei all consider themselves outsiders to power and thus marginal figures within the nation-state to some extent: the first is a self-described existential fugitive, the second an unwitting political pawn, the third a victim of government-sanctioned military violence. Nevertheless, each inhabits a privileged periphery and is put forward by his author as the representative voice of a proper counterdiscourse, whether in terms of a universal human condition or the particularities of PRC civil society or political governance. Wang's protagonist, by contrast, continually finds herself silenced by gender and class as much as ethnicity in debates about the nation. While Gao and Jin as well as Ma couch Tiananmen's meaning primarily in terms of an ideological struggle among different social elites (intellectuals, students, and the Communist Party leadership), Wang alone desacralizes Tiananmen by shifting attention away from these elite groups toward a figure at the fringes of national politics: the female hooligan. Her novel is relentless in uncovering the persistent inequalities internal to Chinese society itself, especially along axes of gender and class, which legitimate some claims to national identity while excluding others. *Lili* is thus at once a feminist critique of Chinese nationalism's patriarchy and a demythologizing of student elitism. Wang's fiction, we might say, analeptically occupies the symbolic space and time of Tiananmen in order to lay bare the unequal power relations between as well as within nations, the geopolitics as well as the social power reproductions of capitalist China. In this respect, *Lili* can be read against the ethnographic eye of Western documentaries such as Thomas's—not as a more authentic insider account of Tiananmen by a spokesperson of the native intellectual elite, but as a diasporic female autoethnography that probes China's globalization from the vantage point of a neocolonial subaltern, borrowing this voice to de-idealize "China" for both Western and Chinese audiences. This literary self-positioning carries its own advantages and pitfalls, of course, and as I will ultimately argue, *Lili* epitomizes exactly this equivocal capital of contemporary Chinese transnational literature.

ORIENTALIST CAPITAL

"I believe everyone has his Eastern and Western sides, just like yin and yang. That's how the universe becomes one. I'm here to find my Eastern side." So announces Roy, the novel's central male character, to Lili in their first meeting (32). Throughout the novel, Roy constantly—and unironically—broadcasts views that combine adulation of China's romanticized past with condemnation of China's material present. An ex-Berkeley hippie and anti–Vietnam War protestor turned liberal journalist and Sinophile spiritual seeker, and in the course of the novel, the well-intentioned but high-minded love interest of the titular heroine, Roy is readily identifiable as an updated caricature of the classic Western orientalist adventurer. In this first encounter with Lili in Inner Mongolia, he already gives voice to a host of clichés about "the East." When asked what constitutes his "Eastern side," he replies: "I'm not sure, really. Maybe it's something about achieving peace in my consciousness by emptying my mind and weakening my ambition. . . . To me, Chinese civilization forms the foundation of all East Asian cultures. There are just too many things to take in" (32–33). In his quest for mystical wisdom, he will later tour Taoist and Buddhist temples around Beijing, interview Lili's Buddhist-practicing grandmother in her hermit's retreat, and finally spend two months meditating with monks and reciting scriptures in a monastery. Despite his professed desire to "take in" Eastern thought, however, he exhibits an underlying unwillingness or resistance to truly incorporating the other's culture for self-transformation. So, at the end of his monastery sojourn, when asked by Lili whether he has converted to Buddhism, he is quick to reply, "No, I still consider myself Jewish," even as he goes on to lay simultaneous claim to Buddhism: "But Buddha is in my heart" (144). For Roy, "the East" is perfectly assimilatable as distilled civilizational remnants and abstracted philosophies of a distant past. It does not essentially disturb his sense of cultural self—as a subject of Western modernity. His detour into the monastery, like a brief layover for the cosmopolitan jet-setter, is also the last we hear of his religious pursuits.

Lili, whose first-person voice provides a running ironic commentary on Roy throughout the text, is already alert to his orientalism in their initial conversation. As she muses to herself: "In China I see everything but peace. People are wearing greed and impatience on their faces. . . . Maybe his East exists only in ancient China" (32). In this early observation by Lili, Wang briskly redirects our attention from China's tradition to its modernity. The transcendental "peace" sought by Roy resonates with particular irony when juxtaposed against the novel's eventual culmination in Beijing's mass protests. Fittingly, then, the next significant exchange between the two takes place against the backdrop of Tiananmen Square itself. On their way home from their first date, as they pass by the Square (in a scene occurring months before the start of the demonstrations), the sight of Mao's portrait instantly inflames Roy. "I can't understand how one person can so dominate this vast nation," he declares (45). He then launches into a speech on American versus Chinese national psychology, contrasting the former's independence of thought with the latter's predisposition toward mindless political worship: "We dare to *question* our leaders. We don't get in trouble if we criticize our president. How about here? Mao's policies have harmed so many innocent Chinese citizens, yet you still sing eulogies of him." When Lili remains quiet, Roy intuits that he has crossed a line and concedes: "I admit that we Americans still idolize our leaders—John F. Kennedy, for example." But he cannot help adding: "But God is God, and Satan is Satan" (46). Roy's reverence for Chinese antiquity goes hand in hand with a demonization of Chinese modernity; the Buddha and Mao personify his bipolar vision of China.

In this largely one-sided debate about China's national psyche and politics, Wang underscores—not the relative intellectual merits of the two interlocutors, as Gao does with the Middle-aged Man and the Young Man in *Taowang*—but the cultural power and political immunity necessary for someone to enter into this discourse in the first place. In fact, the thematic weight of this scene rests not in Roy's almost parodically orientalist avowals but Lili's perspicacious yet mostly unspoken self-reflections. Her first reaction to Roy's provocative statement about Mao, for instance, is defensiveness. "Ever the journalist!" she scoffs to herself. "He is digging for news even on a date" (45). Her wariness of the Western ethnographic eye, of being perceived as the native informant, intensifies as the conversation continues:

> I grow suspicious. I have heard that Western journalists often interview Chinese by treating them to lavish dinners and shows and then prying information out of them. Such Chinese "sources" usually get into big trouble afterward and are punished for "breaching national security."
>
> I don't want to get into trouble for talking about politics with a Western journalist. Only crazy Yuan would do a dumb thing like that. I don't want to meet any more prison guards. (46)

Lili is keenly conscious of the potential hazards of engaging in political discourse, a fact of which Wang reminds the reader at every opportunity. The narrator's interior monologue therefore serves as a vehicle for Wang to convey not simply her disdain for American orientalism but also the Chinese subject's canniness in confronting it.

This passage can usefully be read alongside the Beijing University interview from *The Tank Man*, since what Wang elaborates here is the missing "depth" behind the documentary's superficial profile of Chinese youths today. Through the interiorizing lens of Wang's novel, we may speculate that the female university students in Thomas's film might also have heard about Western journalists and their interviewing tactics, that they, too, might fear recrimination by communist authorities and so feign ignorance through silence. Absent government monitors, though, Lili is perhaps freer to point out the Westerner's cultural paternalism. As she quips:

"What else do you think the Chinese need or don't need? . . . Roy, maybe you *are* smarter than the Chinese, and maybe it's true that yours is the greatest country in the world, but we Chinese don't like Westerners' giving us orders." But even as she resorts to this ready-made position of national autonomy, she immediately acknowledges to herself, if not aloud to Roy, that she is "quoting clichés from the *People's Daily*" (47). In talks about China's politics, Lili knows that her own voice is far from autonomous, that she is caught between orientalist and communist truisms, silence and mimicry. She understands that, at its heart, the dispute about "China" involves power rather than "truth" or "justice": "I argue not because I wish to defend China; I am not a government lackey. I argue because Roy already has everything: money, education, respect from others, freedom to travel. And now he also wants to be right all the time. This is called *deli bu raogren*—meaning that once you have truth and justice on your side, you always want to have the upper hand. He would make a good Party member. I talk because it is the only way I know to save face" (47).

It is crucial to note that Wang presents orientalism as an unavoidable premise for contemporary Sino-American relations and not as a false consciousness to be overcome. The narrative invests very little energy in rescuing Roy from his cultural arrogance or bringing him to a less superior attitude toward modern China. Although Lili discerns and internally mocks Roy's orientalism from the outset, she does not dwell at length on or exert much effort in enlightening him. As the passages above imply, such pedagogical acts in turn presuppose a position of domestic power/ knowledge, a position Lili well knows she does not occupy. Instead, Wang stages several scenes in which Lili confronts just those sources of authority that aim at cleansing Chinese women of Western influences, in contexts highly tied to the state's disciplining of the female hooligan's body. The novel opens with one such scene. Arrested on charges of "corrupt lifestyle and hooliganism"—that is, for being unemployed and sexually promiscuous before marriage—Lili is sentenced without trial to three months of "rehabilitation through labor" (3). The prison guard incessantly berates the female inmates as "a pack of scumbags" (4), as "wanton" and "evil slut[s]," and in one instance publicly slaps one woman for wearing lipstick, denouncing it as a foreign pollutant and antirevolutionary "poison" (6). Already in this first chapter, Lili articulates her marginality—or more exactly, her criminality—within the nation-state via class as much as gender, identifying herself not merely as a Chinese woman but a "bad woman": "The Communist Party is very proud of its role in liberating Chinese women from . . . ancient customs. But a woman's private life is still not her own. Those who lose their virginity before marriage are still spat upon. The only difference between feudal times and our own is that back then 'bad women' were seen as amoral fox spirits, whereas now they are labeled corrupt bourgeois" (8). The indigenous label of the female hooligan, of "*shehui zhazi*, meaning the scrapings from the bottom of the social barrel" (24), completely demarcates Lili's place in this post–Cultural Revolution moment of PRC society; it is the way she comes to be seen, not just by agents of the law, but by her parents and neighbors as well.

Deviant female sexuality accrues extra meaning, however, within the framework of China's globalization. Toward the novel's end and during the Tiananmen protests, after Lili has been living with Roy for some months, she is visited by two men from the Ministry of National Security, undoubtedly the most repugnant characters in the novel. As they interrogate her about her relationship to the American journalist, they, too, like the prison warden, criminalize her sexuality, but this offense now takes on an additional layer of national betrayal. Exasperated by Lili's calm but impudent retorts, one of the men yells: "You disgusting bitch! How can you be so shameless? You like being fucked by foreign cocks, don't you? You think they are big, don't you? China is corrupted by foreigners' hookers like you" (273). The other man adopts a different approach, cajoling Lili to cooperate with them by appealing to her patriotism. Roy, he claims, "is a class enemy of our nation" who "has consistently and maliciously demonized and insulted the Chinese people and the Chinese government," and "beautiful young women like you are good targets for those vile foreigners" (274). In effect, the government agent mobilizes the rhetoric of anti-imperialism and anti-orientalism to conscript Lili into national obedience, even as he implicitly threatens her with sexual violence by massaging her shoulders and fondling her back. Both episodes highlight Lili's vulnerability within the state in terms of gender and class: before both the jail warden and the security police, the female hooligan can be made subject to verbal abuse and physical harassment, incarceration and molestation, with utter impunity. If Lili cannot enter into an equal dialogue about China with Roy, she is even more powerless to defy the domestic authorities in their disciplining or punishment of her body. And in both instances, the state exacts national and sexual compliance by masking its own coercive strategies as a protection against Western hegemony.

In anchoring itself in the female hooligan's perspective, Wang's novel proposes that orientalism may be the lesser evil next to the combination of China's inveterate sexism and communist authoritarianism. The plot hence concentrates on developing rather than debunking Lili's romance with Roy, on her gradual accommodation to rather than challenging of his worldview. Indeed, if orientalism is often theorized as a gendered structure of domination where the East is metaphorically feminized, Wang further suggests that, in the contemporary phase of China's globalization, it is precisely Chinese women who stand to gain cross-cultural agency within both the PRC and the global economy.

One episode amply illustrates this. Walking together one day in the posh neighborhood of Jianguomenwai, "Beijing's 'global village'" (50), Lili and Roy meet a beggar woman with three young children in tow, all dressed in rags. "We haven't eaten for three days," the woman wails. "I'm from the countryside and have no relatives or friends here. Please, soften your hearts and take pity on me" (53–54). Roy immediately hands her a ten-yuan bill; she lavishes Buddhist blessings on him before happily trooping off with her brood, but not before flashing Lili a knowing smile. An instant later, Lili recalls having met the woman several years ago at a Beijing party, looking like a "fashionable movie star" in a "chic short black dress." As she had confided to Lili on that occasion, her dream was to leave China and live abroad. Addressing Lili as a fellow hooligan, she had said with frankness:

> "It's no fun being Chinese. You know that, don't you? This place is doomed. It's dirty, poor, corrupted, and crammed with uneducated people. Nowadays everything is for sale, and everyone has green eyes out to get everyone else and is jealous of everyone else's wealth. Did you see on the news the other day where thugs from Henan killed seventeen people driving fancy cars in Shenzhen, using knives to cut their throats and genitals? It's crazy! To tell you the truth, I've had enough of this fucking place. . . . Don't shit me, girl. We're undesirable scum, with no diplomas, no high-ranking fathers, no good reputations or good jobs. The only chance we have is to get out." (54–55)

Capitalist China, on her description, is a killing field where Chinese prey on each other for material self-advancement. Those with neither money nor connections can thrive only by leaving the country, but to leave, they need money. The woman's solution to this catch-22 is a kind of entrepreneurial self-orientalization: she pays "country kids and retarded people to beg with her in different areas of Beijing," especially the wealthy sectors occupied by foreign tourists and businessmen (55). With her earnings she hopes to buy South American citizenship papers for herself and her boyfriend, immigrate to Panama or Columbia to open a Chinese restaurant, and eventually have a baby and put down roots in the United States. Meanwhile, instead of preying on other Chinese, she and her boyfriend have organized underground gangs that literally capitalize on foreign capital by acting out foreigners' expectations of mass rural poverty and then exploiting the latter's sense of self-righteous pity. Paradoxically, then, globalization enters into this post-Mao world as both mishap and blessing, producing intraethnic violence as much as interethnic exploitation, national disillusionment as much as expanded horizons of desire and fantasy. When Lili warns Roy of these "street hustlers" and he dismisses her warning, she comments sardonically: "Oh, I see what it is: you love to show off your superiority, don't you? It makes you feel good when these people beg from you, right? I guess you're the savior of the world here" (56–57). Significantly, Wang does not undercut the beggar woman's "profession" by calling its morality or social efficacy into question, nor does she attempt to portray the illegal syndicate as equally predatory toward the subaltern subjects it recruits, which would surely complicate the straightforward anti-orientalist critique of this scenario. On the contrary, Wang confirms the beggar woman's diagnosis of foreigners by having Lili call out Roy's cultural complacency and messiah complex. The novel thus intimates that, as Westerners appear ever more naïve and outdated in their interactions with the new China, a generation of urban Chinese women, by contrast, plays an increasingly pivotal role in the international flow of capital. In this specific cross-cultural encounter, money passes from American to Chinese hands as a direct result of the female hooligan's self-orientalizing performance. As we will see, this deployment of subterfuge as a tactic of power-gathering—what might be termed capitalist trickster politics—will resurface again in the novel's Tiananmen chapters.

For now, Wang shows Lili to be not wholly dishonest toward Roy but also not entirely unmanipulative in her reliance on his foreigner's status. After their argument about the beggars, for example, he takes her shopping at the International Trade Mall and pays for all her expensive purchases. As teenage clerks fawn over her, Lili thinks guiltily to herself: "To them I'm a Chinese woman with a 'white devil'; I can feel their subtle, unfriendly, nosy stares. It is their animal instinct. Female monkeys do the same to one another. . . . I blush and can't help feeling like a beggar accepting handouts from this rich Western man. But actually I'm worse than a beggar—I am like a concubine" (58). Comparing herself unfavorably to her chance acquaintance, who at least preserves sexual independence, Lili admits that her relationship with Roy is far from purely sentimental. It is only by attaching herself to a foreign man that she can at last enjoy the luxuries afforded by Deng Xiaoping's open-door policy: "hot water, marble floors, fragrant Zest soap, American-size towels. A life with privacy" (103). This socioeconomic self-advancement has its psychic toll, however, as she shamefacedly dubs herself a "monkey" and "concubine." The entry of Western capitalism into Deng-era China, Wang insinuates, has transformed Beijing into the consummate contact zone, and Beijing women into neocolonial beggars and mistresses. Even as these women gain greater control over their domestic situations by profiting from foreigners, they end up compromising their dignity and integrity.

Moreover for Lili, even as she gains greater mobility by traveling around Beijing with Roy on his ethnographic adventures, seeing "things that a normal Chinese woman would not otherwise see" (75), this newfound gendered mobility and its attendant lessons eventually separate her even farther from other Chinese female lives. Having early on repudiated her mother's example as a serious musician who spends her life teaching for a pittance, Lili goes on to reject every other mode of female life she comes across in the novel. One is that of the religious hermit as embodied by her maternal grandmother. Prompted by Roy's interest in Buddhism, Lili reconnects with her estranged Grandma, whom she admires as a tough trailblazer who lived and loved courageously, who survived with fortitude the deaths of husbands as well as successive campaigns of political persecution. Yet Lili finds herself unable to embrace the otherworldly detachment and emotional barrenness of her grandmother's current life, which seems to reduce life itself to "just six syllables—*Om mani padme hum*" (138).

In a similar vein, Lili refuses to take refuge in an idealized notion of the countryside as the site of pre-capitalist innocence. Her journey with Roy to the ironically named Up Village provides abundant reason for this. This section of the novel is narrated as a series of tableaus on peasant female misery. The first woman Lili meets, though only twenty-seven and hence one year younger than she, is so wrinkled that she looks older than Lili's mother (164). The second woman, "thirty-six and not bad-looking, but deaf and mentally retarded," is married by a matchmaker's arrangement to a man in his late fifties who "badly needed a woman to have sex and children with" (168). This woman's preteen daughter goes unnamed because her father did not want a girl, has a huge scar on her scalp because her father did not care enough to find her medicine after a childhood accident, and is crippled in both legs by polio because no treatment was available (169). The third woman, a cantankerous old widow, lives with her mentally handicapped son in a shack with no glass on the windows and no sheets on the clay bed (171). Facing these impoverished women, Lili feels self-disgust and shame, recognizing her urban privilege for the first time: "Here I am, towering over all of them, wearing a leather coat and high boots, coming into their home with my foreign boyfriend. Yes, I am a 'fake foreign devil'!" (164). She is at once shocked and embarrassed that, ensconced in the capital just two hundred kilometers away, she has "never imagined that such poverty could exist in a place so close to Beijing. The voices of these peasants are unheard, their image unseen in that neon city" (167). Even the relatively better-off women in the village, though materially provided for, are still treated by the men as servants, secreted away from company to cook in the kitchen per feudal custom (177). Wang thus stresses that the brunt of rural hardship is borne by women, since they must in addition endure the persistent misogyny and abuse of peasant men. As Lili bitterly thinks to herself, "Drinking spirits and beating their wives are the peasants' favorite pastime" (180). At the same time, Wang emphasizes Lili's voice here as that of a privileged outsider who is not without her own social hypocrisies and blanket judgments. If Roy is the ethnographer in China, Lili is an autoethnographer in the village. Tellingly, Wang does not absolve her heroine of partial responsibility when the couple's country voyage ends with the murder of a baby girl and the suicide of the girl's mother. Just as Roy's eternal cultural paternalism time and again brings misfortune to those Chinese he tries to help, so his attempt to play "savior" by adopting a poor girl infant—an enterprise about which Lili has misgivings but to which she basically consents—indirectly causes the deaths of two female peasants (210). In the end, witnessing what she construes as the hopeless poverty and inveterate sexism of the countryside leads Lili to reaffirm her choice of life: "To me poverty is the absence of opportunities. Roy and I can come to this place, observe the nudity of a retarded man, and listen to his mother's sad story, but they can't get out of this dead end of their lives. This is what all poverty is about. That's why I would rather be a rich foreigner's mistress than live an honest life here" (174). At the end of her travels, what Lili resolves is *not* to take flight, either in mind or body, from China's globalization but to inhabit it fully, within all its contradictory and compromising consequences. This entails living with Western capital, orientalist conceit and power inequities included. What outsiders and locals alike, and Lili herself, often condemn as opportunism and greed is here reframed as the sociopsychic by-products of a changing world order.

Within this cultural space, Wang further delineates two opposing modes of life for Chinese urbanites. On one extreme are former movie actresses who "marry out." Many of Roy's American friends, as Lili learns at their housewarming party, are married to China-born Chinese wives, a "new fad" among foreigners and local women alike. These unions are emotionally hollow, but the women flaunt them as a status symbol in the new China. "My husband knows enough Chinese only to say 'I want it' and 'I don't want it,' but the only thing he really ever says is 'I want it'; he's never said 'I don't want it,'" one woman boasts. "Meanwhile, the only Chinese I say to him is 'I don't want it!'" (104). As one of sundry social effects of Western capital/ists in China, interracial marriages are presented in the novel, not as a product of cross-cultural understanding, much less love, but as a means of mutual commodification. Within this system, young urban Chinese women are only too eager to take advantage of American men's Asian fetishism. Lili's relationship with Roy approximates these marriages, for Roy, too, has a history of falling for Asian women. The one individualizing detail he offers about his Japanese American college sweetheart, for instance, is that she played the koto "beautifully . . . filled with simple, plain tones" (36). Although Roy differs from the other American men in that he not only speaks Chinese fluently but possesses more knowledge about China than does Lili herself, casually citing a Confucian proverb that escapes her even in their first exchange (33), this difference serves to accentuate all the more the inequality of education and cultural authority between them, the distance between his Berkeley pedigree and her hooligan upbringing.

The other mode of living with Western capital is exemplified by the minor character Yao, whose name signifies a double, and double-edged, structure of lack/want (*yao*). As a figure of neocolonial desire, Yao embodies an ambivalent model of chauvinism and complicity. A former history major in college, he is now a private tour guide, one of many "*getihu*" or independent entrepreneurs who have started their own businesses under Deng's liberalization policy (150). As such, he can turn his knowledge of Chinese history into personal profit by driving foreign tourists to ancient sites in his private jeep. Yet the profession of tour guide, as innumerable postcolonial narratives have argued, is itself fraught with the ideological baggage of colonial history. Yao's case is no exception, but he, too, like the beggar woman, plays a subversive role on his own orientalist stage, albeit with less camouflage and more rancor. At one point, he shows Roy and Lili around the Imperial Summer Palace, that paradigmatic site of China's colonial trauma. With his usual ethnographic condescension, Roy remarks: "Why are there so many walls in China, anyway? I don't like walls; they block freedom and segregate people. Maybe it was better for the Chinese that the Western nations did invade. At least that helped break up the corrupt Manchu government." To this, Yao rejoins with a sound-bite lesson on the history of Western imperialism in China, replete with "opium, gunboats, and colonialism" (155–56). So, even as he lives off of Western capital in the present, Yao cannot refrain from attacking its past in highly jingoistic terms to his current benefactors. The result is a mixed psychology of self-contempt and race hatred. As he admits to Roy: "On the one hand, the past has taught us to hate Westerners; on the other I personally have to love them because I get only Westerners as customers, never locals. That's why I follow you like a dog. I'm not shy; I want to get ahead" (156). Yao's self-description as a "dog" echoes Lili's "monkey" one from earlier, testifying to a common cultural abjection on the part of those Chinese who "get ahead" by feeding on Western capital. Finally, at the trip's conclusion, a more heated altercation arises between the two men—precisely over the payment for Yao's services. When Roy hands him sixty yuan, the latter is furious and insists on being paid in U.S. dollars: "Are we Chinese so worthless in your eyes that you're willing to spend more money on dog food than on a hardworking Chinese tour guide, a college graduate?" (158). It would seem that the debilitating sense of being treated like a dog haunts Yao, even in the absence of intentional disrespect from the racial other. Wang here showcases the ambivalence of the native within the PRC's new global economy: divided between nationalist pride and capitalist yearning, collusion and vengeance, Yao refuses to be debased by international double standards and demands equal pay for his labor along a first-world currency, but his penultimate posture in the novel, caught by Lili in a backward glance, is ambiguously torn between "frustration and disgust," frozen between staring at the money and actually pocketing it (158).

Conspicuously, Lili remains silent throughout this whole episode. As she notes to herself: "I want to help Roy, but I know my participation would only add fuel to the fire: Yao would just ignore me or maybe even attack me for being a Chinese 'sellout'" (158). Once again Wang underlines the gendered imbalance of power in nationalist debates about China. Despite Lili's and Yao's shared cultural abjection, Wang none too subtly stresses a gendered difference between them when she has Yao confess to displacing his racial anger onto women. "I use the money I earn from you guys to go to nightclubs that have blonde Russian waitresses," Yao brags to Roy at one point. "We say that to screw white women is to get revenge on the intruders of the eight nations. . . . Why should I always serve Westerners; why not the other way around?" (156). By embedding Yao's sexism within a more fundamental wound in the national psyche, Wang invokes a familiar model of colonization as symbolic racial castration (Fanon; Eng). Indeed, Yao is as much a caricature as Roy, and his narrative function no less par for the course. As a prototype of China's neocolonial emasculation, he is necessarily blind to his own class and gender privileges, the educational background and masculine security that afford him a degree of mobility and fluency unattainable to the female hooligan. In line with this portrait is his naïve parroting of official propaganda. Unlike Lili, Yao does not evince any critical self-awareness vis-à-vis the communist regime's internal hegemony. When he parades the Imperial Summer Palace before Roy and lectures the American on the Opium Wars, what he suppresses is the communist state's own calculated appropriation and enshrining of this site—as evidence of national historical injury, hence an instrument for inciting continued antagonism against the West and a method of manufacturing political consent at home. What's more, Yao counters Roy by reiterating an imperialist script that is not even his own but the Communist Party's, justifying the state's ethnic repression as national self-rule: "To us," he tells Roy with unqualified assurance, "the Manchus are as Chinese as the Tibetans" (155).

Together, the exogamous movie actresses and the native informant/ nativist avenger outline two extreme paths of dwelling with, and within, orientalist capital. Both are declined by Lili. Yet it is only after tracing the contours of these myriad zones of life that Wang at last opens the curtain on the center stage of her novel: Tiananmen Square. That is to say, it is squarely on the messy and quite prosaic terrains of China's globalization—and emphatically not the lofty terms of a domestic strug- gle for political authority between intellectuals and the state, students and the Party—that Wang locates her Tiananmen drama. In doing so, she reimagines Tiananmen from a largely masculine and elite discourse to one that revolves around the politically fringe figure of the female hooli- gan, now resignified as the pivotal desired object as well as desirous agent of orientalist capital. In turn, she shifts Tiananmen's analytical context from the politics of governance to that of culture—in its late capitalist formation as a sphere of commodification and mass consumption. This constitutes the most distinctive implication of Wang's novel: the myth of Tiananmen as the grand clash between communism and democracy, totalitarianism and freedom, is to her much less adequate to explicating ordinary lives in contemporary PRC than the banalities of popular con- sumer culture. For Wang, globalization has meant that even political dis- sidence in communist China now at best takes the form of, and at worst becomes devoured by, capitalist consumption. Tiananmen symbolizes this new reality at its core, not its radical rupture. In this light, *Lili* is nothing short of a wholesale demythologizing of Tiananmen and a timely repackaging of it as cross-cultural capitalist theater—dramatized for the novel's Anglophone readers as a not so remote experience of globalization that includes them, precisely as readers.

ROCK AND ROLL SQUARE

Timely, I say, in the sense of a temporal updating that is also a histori- cal anachronism. Although *Lili* is ostensibly set in the mid- to late 1980s, its atmosphere of a ubiquitous commodity culture and its characters' so- phisticated familiarity with Western imports seem to index the hypercom- mercialization of the 1990s rather than the cautious liberalization of the previous decade, which has been characterized more modestly as a period of "marginalized capitalists" and "disguised capitalists" (Tsai 50–60). In the wake of Tiananmen, Deng Xiaoping faced the task of regaining politi- cal authority against Party conservatives who faulted his liberal reforms for the pro-democracy movement, and in a strategic but risky bid to re- build his prestige, Deng boldly called for even greater economic expan- sion for China in his 1992 southern tour (Fewsmith, 2nd ed. 21–79). The 1990s henceforth became the decade of accelerated capitalism that put the PRC on the track to becoming a global economic power. As the political economist Yasheng Huang asserts, "Globalization is the story of the 1990s, not of the 1980s" (54).[1] Perhaps it is de rigueur in the current intellectual climate to read a millennial cultural text such as Wang's through the theoretical lens of globalization with all its denationalizing potential, though I suspect that this interpretive maneuver, if made too swiftly, can obscure a vital historical link between Tiananmen and globalization itself. While Wang's anachronism serves to demystify Tiananmen within a nationalist narrative, it may also confuse cause and effect, obfuscating the direct role that the massacre played in pushing the PRC toward globalization. Indeed, it is not an exaggeration to say that our present stage of global capital, in which China now overtakes Japan as the world's second-largest economy and challenges the United States' place as economic world leader, is historically contingent on the fact of the Beijing massacre, on Deng's shrewd shifting of both domestic and international attention away from politics to economics, away from repressive measures to the opening of markets, in the post-Tiananmen years. Wang's thematic priorities can be viewed as one product of this historical legacy.

So, it is the globalizing Beijing of the 1990s that resonates in Wang's portrayal of that "crazy, distracted city," in all its material indulgence and decadence:

> Fancy hotels, supermarkets, discos, Kentucky Fried Chicken, construction sites, open-door policies, "socialism with Chinese characteristics," "spiritual pollution," export permits, handicapped role models, learning from the solider Lei Feng, t'ai chi, Sigmund Freud, existentialism, "the Four Basic Principles of China's socialism," the one-child policy, foreign-exchange currency, Japanese soap operas, pest-extermination campaigns, nepotism, young nannies, kung fu novels, the new rage for studying abroad, breakdancing and the "moonwalk," Wham and George Michael, getting rich quick, the notion that foreign moons are bigger and rounder, color TV sets, dishwashers, refrigerators, sewing machines, ESP, New Tide literature— Beijing is chaotic, overwhelming, waiting impatiently to change itself again and again. (40)

Wang's description of consumerist confidence in *Lili*'s Beijing, where characters from all walks of life behave with utter savoir-faire in the cultural landscape of late capital, is in sharp contrast to the 1980s China presented in both Ha Jin's *The Crazed* and Ma Jian's *Beijing Coma*. In the latter texts, pre-Tiananmen China exhibits all the growing pains of a socialist society making its faltering transition into capitalism. Where Lili casually catalogues dozens of eclectic commodities and trends by way of summing up her childhood city in the above passage—her very syntax replicating the modes of reification and rapid consumption that epitomize commodity culture—signs of capital are paused over with much greater marvel by Jin's protagonist. Jian takes special notice, for example, when a classmate cooks with a new electric stove "at least 1,500 watts strong" (31), and he recounts how Professor Yang's two-door refrigerator, bought in Canada during a conference trip, is nothing short of a campus legend among faculty and staff (43). If this rather crude excitement showcases the provincial setting of Jin's novel, the college students of Ma's Beijing are only slightly more urbane when it comes to capitalist goods. A key object in *Beijing Coma*, for example, is the camera. A commodity that Dai Wei at one point acquires through his Hong Kong girlfriend and then resells in Guangzhou for a profit of one thousand yuan, which covers a full year's rent for their room (75), the camera is far from a commonplace item in the novel even among those well-off university students who eventually assemble in Tiananmen Square, which explains their heavy reliance on foreign cameras to record the movement. Roy's presence in *Lili* therefore facilitates Wang's retroactive conjuring of a metropolis where the availability of Western commodities can be taken for granted even by a street hooligan.

On a biographical level, we can attribute this anachronism in the novel to Wang's place in history. Born in Beijing in 1972, she was only sixteen in 1989 and hence two academic generations behind the college students who initiated the protest movement. Unlike Gao and Jin, she was on-site to witness the demonstrations firsthand, visiting the Square every day ("Conversation"), though unlike Ma, she was fortuitously placed there by nativity and did not have to travel far. Most importantly, though a self-described "Deng Xiaoping kid" ("People's"), she came of age as a writer only in the post-Tiananmen phase of Deng's regime. So, she has perhaps backward superimposed the 1990s cultural environment onto the 1980s milieu of *Lili*. On a narratological level, however, and whether intended or not, this anachronism functions to dislocate the Tiananmen chapters from their real historical moment. Instead of historical realism, the generic codes of which typically mask the temporal lapse between the written event and the writing act, what Wang gives us is a novel that denaturalizes its Tiananmen references and reveals them as belated signifiers, retrospective constructions of a future time. This narrative effect is not incongruent with Wang's account of her own stylistic choices and thematic investments. As she comments in one interview: "People have called [*Lili*] documentary fiction, but I don't like the label because I'm less interested in the events and more in giving an insight into an individual's psyche" (qtd. in Stanford). She is also forthright in noting that *Lili* is not "a political book," that "it offers an emotional rather than a political history of Tiananmen." Most telling of all is the texture of her memories of the Square: "I went to

Tiananmen Square for the rock and roll atmosphere, not democracy. I was 16 and full of energy, not politics" (qtd. in Crampton).

And it is exactly this ambiance of rock and roll that saturates Wang's fictional reincarnation of Tiananmen Square in *Lili*. In contrast to Gao and Jin, Wang does not leave her Tiananmen fiction outside the Square. Yet her Square, unlike Ma's, is not fastidiously realistic but contains shades of the hyperreal. As the protest movement picks up momentum, Lili, hitherto aloof from and apathetic to mass politics, finds herself drawn to the Square every day: "It's magical and I am spellbound. I don't understand democracy or human rights. It feels like a rock concert, where sharing the excitement with others is more important than listening to the performer's lyrics" (236). The rhetoric of pathos rather than logos threads through these chapters. Repeatedly, Lili expresses her presence in the Square not as political self-education but as emotional enjoyment:

> I like to go [to the Square] simply because I enjoy being with others, seeing colorful banners and wild clothing. People come to make friends, listen to rumors, and share drinks, cigarettes, and the latest news. Some come to the square to feel powerful by breaking the rules, others to feel important by delivering speeches to an eager audience.
>
> Every day there are demonstrations and parades through the streets of Beijing. Some of the marchers obviously have no idea why they're marching; they're just joining in the excitement. . . .
>
> I don't participate in the activities; I am simply curious. I don't have the political consciousness of Yuan or the college students, nor do I have Roy's journalistic interest. I am just one of the millions of unsure Beijing citizens. (230–31)

The atmosphere is that of an enormous party, not a somber political rally. Unlike the conversations about "China" between Roy and Lili, here in the Square gossip supersedes debate. The language of feeling, of emotion, predominates over that of thought or reason. That crucial moment of epiphany, of the subaltern subject awakening to a sense of national self-consciousness, is entirely absent. Instead, Lili underscores her continued incomprehension of even the most basic political concepts. For instance, when an unnamed student leader, "a handsome northerner with curly hair . . . his voice husky but hypnotic" (237)—the obvious fictional counterpart of Wuer Kaixi— addresses the crowds, Lili is so moved by the general passion around her that she joins in the slogan shouting for the first time, even though she has no intellectual grasp on the content of her words:

> This eloquent young student leader is a good and powerful talker. His fervor inflames the audience. There is a thunderstorm of applause.

Many people have tears in their eyes. Strangers hug me, their tears dampening my cheeks and their hot breath tickling me. It is impossible for me to remain unmoved. I hug them back and feel a sense of camaraderie.

"Democracy now! Democracy now! Democracy now!" the audience chants. I chant with them. I don't know what democracy is, but it's a mantra. The physical vibration of the word can create positive energy. (239)

This scene is soon followed by a parallel one in which "the number-one student leader"—an unnamed Chai Ling—gives a long sentimental speech about "that sacred word *democracy*" (246–47). Once again the "crowd begins to chant with the girl," and once again Lili feels herself "deeply touched," not by the words' substance but by their solemnity and earnestness, so much so that she begins to march with the hunger strikers, physically becoming part of the protesting throng (248). By the third day of the hunger strike, Lili has been transformed into a volunteer nurse, working with the medical teams to help transport collapsed students to the hospital (257). Five days straight in the Square later, she still admits to not understanding democracy and not knowing what the students truly want, though she stays because she likes "this new feeling of being needed by and connected to people" (264).

Throughout these chapters, Wang withholds the names of the real student leaders who make cameo appearances so as to emphasize Lili's outsider status in the Square, even as her detachment converts into participation. Ironically, then, while Lili can rattle off with ease the names of foreign music stars such as Wham and George Michael, the most well-known student leaders in her hometown remain unknown to her. She recognizes that, even in the midst of a national democracy movement, a domestic class hierarchy persists between students and citizens: "College students are the pioneers of the movement, heroic and loved by everyone. Historically, students are the backbone of almost every major social movement in modern China. Now they are on hunger strike, in the limelight. Citizens like me are on the fringes: we merely watch, listen, applaud for them, support them, and admire them" (253). Finally arguing back against Roy in their discussions about China, she further gives voice to a class-conscious view of the hunger strike as an elitist political strategy: "The whole non-violent thing sounds too elite; I just can't understand it. All I know is that there are millions of poor people in China. All they want is to have enough to eat" (244). By aligning the antiheroic Lili with the anonymous millions who poured out in spectacular support of the movement that spring, Wang clearly aims to redirect "the limelight" from the students to the citizens, from the elite to the masses. This, too, can be read as part of her demythologizing of Tiananmen, a deflating of it from the elevated realm of political idealism to the mundane one of the populace's humble needs. Perhaps she is paying homage to the plebeian constituents of a movement that, after all, inspired even the thieves of Beijing to go on a sympathy strike (Black and Munro 365 n. 3). Implicit in this rewriting of Tiananmen is the idea of democracy itself: is not this magnified view of the Square and of Beijing, Wang seems to ask, much more democratic in spirit than the isolated focus on students and intellectuals versus Party leadership?

Wang's analogy of the rock concert is of course not strictly metaphorical. In the visual archive of Tiananmen, some of the most iconic images involve the rock stars Cui Jian and Hou Dejian singing such signature tunes as "Nothing to My Name" and "Descendants of the Dragon" to swaying hordes of students. In fact, popular music was an integral part of the culture of Tiananmen both before and during the demonstrations. As Hou Dejian observes: "Popular music, of course, came from the West. When young people try to express themselves, to sing about their own concerns, it is really a form of liberalization. That's why this music played a very important role during the movement. When someone takes part in a rock concert, that kind of crazy feeling is all about self-liberation and about self-expression" ("*Gate*"). Echoing this sentiment, Wuer Kaixi credits Cui Jian with capturing the spirit of his generation: "His song 'Nothing to My Name' expresses our feelings. Does our generation have anything? We don't have the goals our parents had. We don't have the fanatical idealism our older brothers and sisters once had. So what do we want? Nike shoes. Lots of free time to take our girlfriends to a bar. The freedom to discuss an issue with someone. And to get a little respect from society" ("*Gate*"). In these and other historical reflections on Tiananmen, the relation between political action and popular culture is always enunciated as a mutually reinforcing one, with the latter playing a supplementary role to the former. The songs "express" preexisting feelings; they do not determine the mood of political disenchantment and spiritual void. In reference to the protests, it is never in doubt that cultural "self-expression" is solidly harnessed to the political agenda of "liberation" and "freedom." Implicit here is a rather traditional literati assumption that the students act as masters of themselves, that no matter how "crazy" they get, they are ultimately in control of the forces of culture.

Wang, however, upends this politics-culture hierarchy when she proposes that, for the students as much as the ordinary citizens in the Square, Tiananmen is through and through a capitalist spectacle. Tiananmen in *Lili* is not a political movement embellished with the occasional rock concert. Quite the reverse: for Wang, the machinery of mass consumption has taken on such existential magnitude in capitalist China that it can now turn around and consume the masses themselves, swallowing up even rebellious voices of political resistance. Pop singers arrive to speechify on the importance of a free press, shouting slogans and being chased by female fans for autographs (231). Student leaders wave their hands like "movie star[s]" to swarms of admirers screaming, "I love you" (239). Groups of student demonstrators don different styles, some singing rock songs rather than the national anthem, others "dressed in the outfits of Beijing's punks," still others "wearing black sunglasses, mimicking the Mafia of Hong Kong" (226). The Square becomes a theater of free-floating mimicry, with protesting students imitating pop stars imitating political dissidents, all eager to perform for eager spectators. All, "in an eerie fashion," appear like "extras on a movie set" (250). Even street peddlers copy the celebrities by tantalizing audiences with "police-brutality stories," propelling themselves into "temporary star[dom]" (233). For their part, the crowds chant democratic slogans with as much gusto as they do the names of their favorite idols of the moment. In an impish quasi-fictional move, Wang transcribes the lyrics to Hou Dejian's "Descendants of the Dragon" but assigns the song to the invented character of Lili's U.S.-born rock star cousin, Johnny Cardiac. Hitherto indifferent to both China's politics and his mainland family, Johnny suddenly materializes in the Square, wearing "an outfit consisting of a potato sack, a pair of sunglasses, and a white headband marked with the words *Love* and *Freedom*—a hippie wanna-be," and makes a speech about Chinese pride. The people roar with approval, and he launches into two patriotic songs. Lili, though skeptical of his motives, makes explicit Wang's suggestion here about the formidable potential of consumer culture to mobilize the masses: "As Johnny sings, his eyes are closed, tears pouring down his cheeks. Maybe the student movement has changed him, or maybe he's just a good faker. But as a pop star, he has a power that most intellectuals lack. I have seen poets, scholars, and professors give speeches in the square, but Johnny unites and mobilizes people—educated and not, young and old—like no one else" (261). Capital may be materially absent in this free concert, but the infrastructure of capitalist commodification and consumption is everywhere visible in these sketches of the Square.

In the context of Wang's novel, this revaluation of Tiananmen from elitist politics to capitalist consumption is not necessarily progressive or retrograde. On the one hand, Lili feels bound to a greater collective for the first time in her life; on the other, this emotional connection is problematically characterized by an unremitting ignorance. She gains unprecedented access to a national arena through the student movement, but she never comes to an understanding of "democracy," and her actions are more self-alienating than self-actualizing. "The chant makes me not me anymore," she narrates at one point. "I have become a stranger to myself" (248–49). The import of this cliché is ambivalent. Is the female hooligan's transformation into a Tiananmen participant a model of political citizenship or of mindless mob following? Is her sense of fulfillment a genuine mode of democratic empowerment or the late capitalist revival of false consciousness? Both possibilities are evoked by Wang. As with Johnny Cardiac, there lingers an indeterminacy around Lili. The significance of Wang's text, however, does not lie in settling these questions decisively. Rather, it lies in what the questions themselves make salient: the need to rethink political agency in globalizing China and to reframe the concept as inexorably embedded within the dynamics of capitalist consumption. This is not a quietist refutation of agency altogether, à la Gao's argument for existential flight. As with the everyday politics of dwelling with and within orientalist capital, Wang offers two opposing examples on the spectrum of political agency as enacted in the Square.

At one point during her visits to the Square, Lili is invited to live in a tent with three female students who have joined the hunger strike. With this move, Wang opens a narrative window onto the inner space of student life. No longer a physical outsider, Lili now provides the reader with an insider's look at a segment of student activism. What she finds surprises her: more so than the throngs outside the tent, these women are revealed to be shallow consumers of popular culture, using their radio-cassette recorder not to get updates from the Voice of America or the BBC but to listen to love songs by Johnny Cardiac all day. To pass the time, they smoke and gossip on trivial topics: "Smoking distracts them from their hunger pains. They talk about boyfriends, generation gaps, young mistresses kept by rich old men, hometowns, dorm stories, pop singers, perfume, and ways of cheating on tests. None of their conversation is about the movement, except when they argue about which student leader is cutest. They giggle a lot. They are happy" (251–52). They chatter about heartthrobs, Chanel perfume, Reeboks, and movie actresses—everything but democracy. To Lili, their statements are "so girlish, so unpolitical, so unheroic" that she has a hard time reconciling their shallowness with the student leaders' solemn rhetoric outside the tents: "They seem so carefree and so obsessed with beauty—they're even more superficial than I am. But they are also college students fasting for some kind of ideal that I don't understand" (252). Wang makes no attempt to develop or deepen these women, nor does she detract from their commitment to the cause. As the hunger strike drags on, Lili watches as they "become weaker and weaker, far less talkative," their lips paling, their hair "tangled and unkempt," their bodies reeking— "but still they refuse to leave" (256). For Wang, these women embody one set of contradictions of political agency in the capitalist Square.

The other emblematic figure in the novel's Tiananmen chapters is a male hunger striker who goes by the name of Jackson. When asked by Lili why he uses an English name, he replies: "My Chinese name doesn't sound good. Michael Jackson is my idol, so I named myself Jackson." Unlike the three female hunger strikers, though, Jackson is not just another worshipful consumer of popular culture and Western goods, nor is he a naïve idealist about the radical measures adopted by the movement. While he wears a board that histrionically announces, "I Love Life, I Need Food, but I'd Rather Die Than Live Without Democracy," he confides in Lili that he has squirreled away a stash of candy in his pocket (244–45). The sign, he explains, is "only a gesture": "The government isn't honest with us. Why do we have to be honest with it and risk our lives? We aren't stupid like our fathers, are we? We want to embarrass the government, not die trying." Nonetheless, he urges Lili to protect his secret, since he knows the students need to "win the sympathy of the citizens" for the hunger strike to succeed (246). Savvy to the ways of antigovernment protest, Jackson exemplifies a breed of domestic trickster politics, one that pragmatically resorts to subversive tactics to navigate between state and citizen power in the interests of larger political ends. Similar to the beggar woman in the face of orientalist capital, he is not averse to self-commodification and deceitful manipulation of others' goodwill. Above all, like his namesake, he fully grasps the capacity of the iconic image and the public spectacle to mobilize the masses in the culture of late capital. In role-playing the persona of a heroic and self-sacrificing patriotic youth, he taps into a familiar cultural mythology in twentieth-century China but updates it for a contemporary audience whose short-lived attention can only be sustained by easily consumable and commoditized images. Neither Gao Xingjian's hotheaded ideologue nor Ha Jin's self-absorbed individualist, Jackson is Wang's much more flattering portrait of the Tiananmen student as a shrewd and purposeful political agent in the age of China's globalization.

Relevant here is Joseph Esherick and Jeffrey Wasserstrom's concept of "political theater." In their study of the Tiananmen students, Esherick and Wasserstrom argue that it would be imprecise to characterize the protest movement as a truly pro-democracy one if the term *minzhu* is taken to mean a Western-style plural-party system. Most participants in the movement sought to reform socialist society, not to overthrow the Chinese Communist Party, and few students at the time had any deep knowledge of democratic governance. What's more, Esherick and Wasserstrom point out that many students consistently displayed an "elitist reading of *minzhu*" and a "distrust of the *laobaixing* or untutored masses" as well as a "lack of concern for the needs of workers and peasants" (31). In a parallel vein, Elizabeth Perry postulates that the Tiananmen movement failed ultimately because of the limits of the students themselves, who acted with an elitist blend of "intellectual traditionalism" and "Confucian morality" that excluded the participation of the rank-and-file, especially of entrepreneurs and workers: "The shared assumptions of rulers and rebels served to reinforce preexisting authority relations, ensuring that China's protest movement did not become its revolution of 1989" (147). On this issue, Wang does not go so far as to depict the students as uncaring or callous toward the citizenry, but she does use Lili to voice a commoner's sense of alienation from the students' elitism. What reverberates strikingly with Wang's theme of theatricality, however, is Esherick and Wasserstrom's contention that Tiananmen was less a philosophically coherent political movement than an instance of Chinese political theater—a "cultural performance before a mass audience ... that expresses beliefs about the proper distribution and disposition of power ... and other scarce resources" (39). By marching through the city streets, occupying Tiananmen Square, and embarking on a hunger strike, the students were acting out the symbolic components in a familiar script of public protest in China drawn from "a historically established 'repertoire' of collective action ... emerging out of traditions of remonstrance and petition" (32–33). The students' performance was therefore "designed to impress and move an audience, not a lecture designed to inform" (40).

Consonant with Esherick and Wasserstrom's argument, all the Tiananmen students in *Lili*, from the unnamed leaders with their movie-star mimicry and pathos-soaked oratory to the diverse hunger strikers, all aim to impress and move, not inform. Wang has no qualms, however, about ironizing and postmodernizing the notion of political theater, which in her novel is far from a somber reenactment of Confucian rituals but is instead the frenzied culmination of contemporary China's commodity fetishism. In this sense, she banalizes the students to some extent, peeling back their self-orchestrated image as extraordinary political heroes. Yet she does so not to castigate the students as bad-faith actors but to embed them within the continuum of a consumerist mentality that they share with ordinary citizens like Lili. Akin to Esherick and Wasserstrom, too, Wang accentuates an indigenous lineage of plebeian protest when she has her various anonymous student leaders repeatedly summon May Fourth as "the first step in the patriotic democracy movement of Chinese students" (238). Most telling in this respect is the conspicuous absence in her novel of the Goddess of Democracy, that giant papier-mâché statue built by undergraduates at the Central Academy of Fine Arts and erected in the Square just days before the massacre. This sculpture was partly modeled on the U.S. Statue of Liberty, and few Western chronicles of Tiananmen have failed to mention it, often with the subtle insinuation that Chinese dissenters must rely on Western idols for inspiration—even though, as the art historian Wu Hung emphasizes, the Goddess of Democracy was "a borrowed symbol . . . modified into an indigenous image" and was certainly "not a copy" (43–45). Wang's eliding of this key "theatrical" detail, particularly noteworthy against her backdrop of pervasive mimicry in the Square, suggests a modicum of nativist loyalty yet. Overall, the theory of political theater provides a constructive supplemental context for reading Wang's representation of the Square as a spectacle—not least because it, too, like her examination of global capital, helps to situate Tiananmen within an analytical framework focused on historical changes in social power relations, a framework that goes beyond mere moral or cultural censure.

Part II. Equivocal Transnationalism

BILINGUALISM AS DIASPORIC FEMININITY

By the 1990s, with five books already successfully published in Chinese and a solid fan base within mainland China, Wang could easily, and much more comfortably, have elected to write *Lili* in her native language. The Tiananmen novel, however, will serve as her linguistic rite of passage into English. Intriguingly, when asked in interviews about her language choice for this work, Wang consistently foregrounds issues of gender rather than political censorship:

> The reason I chose writing it in English is because I couldn't write the "bad girl" *Lili* in Chinese. It's interesting that words are always associated with their cultural context. Some attractive concepts become undesirable in Chinese. For example, privacy refers to something that one doesn't want others to know about, something almost evil. Individualism means selfishness. The direct translation of ambition is a wild heart, again a negative expression in China. These negative connotations of words contradicted what I believed, blocking the free flow of my thoughts. Moreover, I wanted to explore subjects like female sexuality and class differences, which were taboo in China. Lili is a disaffected girl who lives a life of violence, sex, betrayal, distrust, self-loathing, shamelessness and cynicism. Her character was too much for the Chinese principle of sobriety and decorum, especially in early 1990s. ("Conversation")

For Wang, the Chinese language is deeply rooted in conservative moral values of "sobriety and decorum," especially regarding female sexuality. While she acknowledges that political pressure is a real concern for Sinophone writers, she invariably puts greater emphasis on the cultural expectations and perceptual limits imposed by the language itself. English, by contrast, enables her "to write without self-censorship and worries about cultural land mines" ("New"). Wang is, of course, well aware of the state censorship around June 4, firsthand evidence of which is the much-abridged Chinese translation and mainland edition of *Lili*, with most references to Tiananmen expunged (Stanford). Yet she rarely explicates her linguistic switch to English in terms of political suppression. Instead, she repeatedly evokes the voice of female impropriety that English affords her: "When people write in Chinese, they worry they will get punished. When I write in English, I don't want to worry. I can use profanity, street language, bad girls" (qtd. in Weisenhaus).

Wang is not alone in linking English to a specifically female sense of writerly authority and autonomy. Her broad-stroked account of the Chinese language's demonization of "privacy" and "individualism" may smack a bit of Western stereotypes, but it is precisely via the perceived freedom of English that many Chinese diaspora women writers likewise find release from the psychological inhibitions of their first language. Yiyun Li, for example, speaks similarly of the ability to escape self-censorship as a reason for writing in English: "I can't write in Chinese at all. I think it's more like self-censoring, than other people censoring me. I don't know—I just feel so much more comfortable writing in English" (Y. Li). Liu Hong too refers to the mentally liberating effect of English: "Writing in English, I can be free. It's not just political, it's personal. I feel I can be almost a different kind of personality. I'm more open, more able to express myself. I'm less worried about what other people or my family might think" (qtd. in Angel). A common thread running through these remarks is a feeling of personal comfort and expressiveness in English, as opposed to a debilitating self-consciousness of the judgments of imagined readers in Chinese. In short, English is one of the main pleasures of diaspora for these women authors. While language choice does not cut strictly across gender lines in diaspora literature, it is telling that Wang, in an essay canvassing contemporary "Chinese émigré authors," aligns herself much more readily with Geling Yan and Anchee Min—both of whom write in English (though Yan also writes in Chinese)—than with Ma Jian. The latter she characterizes as "stubbornly defend[ing] his unwillingness to read or write in English" and whom she quotes as averring rather smugly: "I'm a genius. I write because of my talents and inspiration. I don't need another language" ("New"). In this context, then, we can read Wang's oft-cited metaphor of her English infancy as the supreme articulation of her feminist perspective: "The 26 English letters make me a child again, naïve, bold, fearless, primal. I could profane, question, and break the stranglehold of traditional Chinese culture. *Lili* is the manifesto of my youthful revolt" ("Conversation"). In a literary tradition where patriarchal authority is habitually allegorized as age, her invocation of childhood may signal not just generational icono-clasm but a distinctly female self-positioning.

Notably, Wang is the only writer in this study to command a sizeable readership in the PRC—and hence the one, from the perspective of recep-tion and consumption, most wide-reachingly bilingual and transnational. Ha Jin composes solely in English and is an established figure in the U.S. literary scene, and though he is actively involved in the Chinese trans-lations of his own work for Taiwan and Hong Kong publishers, he must rely on these translations to reach a mainland readership. The explicitly anticommunist stance of his novels also ensures his marginality there; as he indicates in one interview: "It's not possible for some writers to get pub-lished in China. They are able to publish their own books, but they can't be economically independent or reach a large audience. All my books have been translated into Chinese, but you can't find them on mainland China, and no official Chinese paper would ever review them" (Rightmyer). By contrast, Ma Jian writes solely in Chinese, but as I will clarify, the circula-tion of his recent work in its original language of composition is so lim-ited that it must pass through the route of translation into English before it becomes known for the first time to most Sinophone readers. Finally, although Gao Xingjian writes in both Chinese and French and is widely recognized in Europe as a bilingual author, the censorship of his work by the communist government, combined with the avant-garde nature of his post-exile writing, has kept his mainland readership minuscule. Wang herself comments on this point in her essay: "Four years after U.S.-based Ha Jin won a National Book Award and three years after France-based Gao Xingjian was honored with the Nobel Prize in Literature, the work of these two internationally hailed Chinese authors is still largely unseen inside China. Sadly, the China-born authors now emerging on the world's literary stage remain largely unknown inside their native country. Some are still banned" ("New"). Of the four writers here, only Wang succeeds in galvanizing a broad audience in the PRC by tapping into popular genres of fiction as well as making use of mass media forms such as the newspa-per column and the weblog. And she is the only one to have returned to reside part-time in the PRC since her departure in 1993, moving back to Beijing in 1999 and relocating to Shanghai in 2004 to run a fashion maga-zine (Wang, *PostGlobal*). She now divides her time between Shanghai and California—a trajectory that, as one critic points out, "is not unique but instead emerging as a typical career path for a number of young writers who are currently catching transnational attention" (Ommundsen 337).

These brief biographical details suffice to highlight the vast distance separating Wang's female subject position from Lili's. In the novel, Lili does not know any foreign languages and is acutely aware of her marginal status within China's new global economy, where English is the language of power and Americans the people of money. Wang, by contrast, can speak of her own bilingualism with the glibness of a cosmopolitan consumer. When asked online by her Chinese readers whether she would continue to compose fiction in Chinese, she answers: "I think I will. Just like I eat burgers as well as rice, listening to rock and roll as well as meditative Chinese music I live with both Chinese and English" ("Conversation"). This statement is a far cry from Lili's constant reminder to the reader that multilingualism remains a form of precious cultural capital withheld from her. Wang, of course, belongs to a much more privileged class background than her eponymous heroine. Her father was a senior editor at the official PRC newspaper *People's Daily*, and she grew up in an environment of relatively liberal education both at home and in the larger cultural scene of 1980s Beijing. In fact, Annie (whose Chinese name is Wang Rui) and her two older sisters, Charlotte (Wang Wei) and Emily (Wang Fei), are minor cultural luminaries in China, collectively known as the Wang Sisters and sometimes the Chinese Brontës. This is a family mythology the sisters have partially self-created through their coauthored 1997 autobiography, *Three Wang Sisters' Skies and Dreams*, as well as their mother's recent bestselling multimedia memoir of them, *The Story of the Chinese Bronte Sisters* (Bates 55). As Wang admits, she and her sisters are hardly oppressed Chinese women or hooligans jaded by their destitute past. They can more properly be branded as a new species of post-Mao urban "intellectuals" who have risen to prominence in the post-Tiananmen era. As she elucidates in one interview: "The Wang Sisters represent the group of Chinese intellectuals (I cannot think of a better word) who love high culture and non-commercial art. We're like the American version of PBS-viewers. We grew up in the 1980s Beijing cultural circle. Materially speaking, we were not wealthy, but concerts, classic music, poetry, painting, art exhibitions, ballet, and salon style get-togethers where we discussed art and politics were an important part of life" ("Beijing's"). Elsewhere, Wang describes herself as a "bobo, a bourgeois bohemian": "I have a house in California, I have a house in China. I own a car there. I wear several brands, but I'm not rich" ("People's"). The sensation of Annie Wang the bilingual transnational female writer, then, is a product of multiple advantages in both family and historical circumstance. Her casual equation of languages to food and music symptomizes a feature of her class of post-Tiananmen yuppies, for whom cultural identity is constructed via individual consumption choices more than shared ancestry or social codes and beliefs. Even the label "bourgeois bohemian" is expounded in terms of personal material ownership and transnational mobility. In this framework, languages take on the characteristics and functions of commodities: as goods to shop for and acquire, as markers of cosmopolitanism and status within a globalizing China. Wang's self-assured attitude toward her bilingualism is an index of her generational gap from an older writer such as Ha Jin, for whom English, as he never tires of pointing out, comes with painstaking slowness and was initially a means of "survival" in America (*Migrant* 32).

Lili, on the other hand, falls into an in-between generation that follows Jin's but precedes Wang's, a generation comprised of runaway kids whose parents were subjects of the reeducation policy but who themselves were too young to be incorporated into Mao's ideological machinery during the Cultural Revolution. As Lili recalls of her gang of hooligan friends: "Our generation just missed becoming Red Guards—and also missed the disgrace that came later. After our parents and older siblings were sent to the countryside, some of us were left alone, while others were looked after by relatives who often gave their young charges a hard time. We hung out on the streets, lived for kicks and sex" (61). If the Red Guards were symbolically Mao's children, those just a few years younger effectively became generational orphans—not old enough to be the Party's instruments or enemies, but just old enough to take their lives into their own hands, run away from the countryside and their families there, and piece together an alternative commune in the city. Wang is, of course, not the first to diagnose the phenomenon of hooliganism as a direct consequence of the Cultural Revolution, nor is she unique in linking it to the dilemmas of China's new market economy. Her heroine represents to some degree the hooligans' collective victimization by a socialist past and ambiguous fate in a capitalist present, surviving though not truly thriving on the pursuit of material wealth in a social system that despises them as deviant elements. Significantly, Wang's scrutiny of the social present via the national past is carried out via a narrative appropriation of the hooligan figure along axes of class and generationality. One might thus read *Lili* as itself a work of diasporic intellectual nostalgia for hooliganism. The question then becomes: Why?

For one answer, we might turn to the metamorphoses of PRC literature across the very generational chasm dividing the hooligan Lili from the "bobo" Annie—to wit, the pre- vs. post-Tiananmen rift. The transition of Deng's China from the modest liberalization of the 1980s to the accelerated capitalism of the 1990s has meant a withering of the intelligentsia's cultural authority. In the new landscape of commodity fetishism dominated by rock concerts, movie stars, and brand-name fashion, Chinese intellectuals find their high-minded concerns about national politics and social conscience ever more peripheral. Furthermore, the types of highbrow literature that writers such as Gao Xingjian, Ha Jin, and Ma Jian strive for, each with his own aesthetic preferences, to be sure, but all united in the ambition to pen elite literature, become increasingly outdated for post-Tiananmen mass readers and consumers. Avant-garde absurdist theater, nineteenth-century-style realism, the epic national allegory—these are the aesthetic forms of choice of our three male Tiananmen authors, but they are seldom successful as literary genres in post-1989 China, not because they are censored, but because they don't sell. It may be an ironic result of globalization's disjunctures, to use Arjun Appadurai's word, that these writers have earned renown, not in the capitalizing terrains back home, but in the international publishing venues that capitalize on their exilic or anticommunist stances. The diaspora, then, may open up an afterlife for Chinese writing in more ways than one: as a political safety zone for Tiananmen fictions, certainly, but also as an evacuation site for obsolete cultural and aesthetic modes. Appadurai would call this dimension of diaspora a "mediascape," itself a product of globalization and not without its ideological and financial aspects, which constructs "imagined worlds" of the place of origin through "image-centered, narrative-based accounts of strips of reality" (9). The rub here, of course, lies in the traditionalist and elitist forms of these Chinese diasporic narratives, their aesthetic self-distancing from the electronic mass media that typify their very epoch.

The 1990s for the PRC, in Jing Wang's apt phrase, were a "desublimated era" (268). If the "zeitgeist of the 1980s" was characterized by a nationalist and elitist optimism—"a decade designated as 'the new era,' reigned over by intellectuals, and marked by unrelieved humanistic sentiment and the will to de-alienate" (262)—the 1990s were "the Golden Age of Entertainment" (266) as well as "an age of Attitude" (263): "The age of innocence is gone.... Mockeries reverberate. Verbal spews are street theater. It has become a national knack to satirize a society gone mad with consumerism while quietly going along with the greed" (261, 263). The defining face of this new decade was Wang Shuo, best-selling author of hooligan fiction, champion of ordinary folks, "spurner of elite culture" (269), and most crucially, "the first specimen of a 'marketized' literature that promotes 'bestseller consciousness' (*changxiao yishi*) above all else" (262). Many of the trademarks of Wang Shuo's novels can be spotted in *Lili*: a cynical hooligan protagonist, a mockery of intellectuals and a deconstruction of elite discourse, an elevation of the riffraff and miscreants of China's new capitalist economy, and a reveling in the material and carnal desires of consumer culture. Additionally, as Jing Wang points out, despite the supposed antagonism between the hooligan and the intellectual, Wang Shuo himself depends on the educated elite for his readership as well as popularity and thus has a semiotic relationship with them: "His is a parasitic persona whose rise (and perhaps future downfall) is closely intertwined with the destiny of the intellectuals whose literary taste he commands and at times reproduces" (284). So it is not surprising that the hooligan narrator would get co-opted by Annie Wang the self-confessed bourgeois intellectual. Even her nostalgia for the hooligan as a rather romantic icon of national trauma and spiritual hollowness can be read as a second-order and belated reiteration of the melancholic wistfulness of Wang Shuo's antiheroes. As Yibing Huang observes, underneath the ennui and insolence of Wang Shuo's characters in fact pulses an intense sentimentality, "a nostalgia and yearning for the world in which [the hooligan] grew up and which now has almost entirely evaporated" (72). And like Wang Shuo, Annie Wang is absolutely in step with the forces of the literary market.

Of course, Annie Wang cannot be wholly reduced to a late-coming replica of Wang Shuo. We would be remiss to ignore, for one, the gendered perspective she insistently imports into the hooligan narrative, especially the damning portrayal she presents of hooligan culture as buttressed by masculine egotism and a denigration of women. One exemplary passage drives this point home. Lili, while the girlfriend of a gang leader, was regularly asked to offer herself sexually to his buddies, "the same way he shared food and cigarettes with them," and she would comply in order to survive: "I became a trophy, a 'comfort woman' in his gang. The other members became more loyal to him because their big brother was so generous that he didn't even get jealous when they slept with his woman" (95). This hard-hitting moment in the novel may not be standard fare for 1990s hooligan fiction, but it is readily recognizable within another pertinent context— that of Chinese diasporic women's writing.

Indeed, Wang's gender exposé of hooligan society is best read, not as a direct feminist challenge of Wang Shuo or hooligan literature per se, but as a marker of her novel's diasporicity. *Lili*, after all, is first and foremost an English-language text, and its audience-conscious author surely knows that the theme of Chinese women being brutalized by a sexist society and a ruthless regime is one of the narrative staples of diasporic female literature—a genre that has likewise become phenomenally popular during the decade of *Lili*'s composition, but in the West.[2] Primarily autobiographical, this genre typically focuses on the public and private ordeals of women throughout twentieth-century China. Most critics cite Jung Chung's *Wild Swans* (1991) as the inaugural text, though Nien Cheng's *Life and Death in Shanghai* (1987) remains a notable forerunner, and their numerous successors include Anchee Min's *Red Azalea* (1993), Ji-li Jiang's *Red Scarf Girl* (1997), Hong Ying's *Daughter of the River* (1998), Adeline Yen Mah's *Falling Leaves* (1998), Ting-xing Ye's *A Leaf in the Bitter Wind* (1999), Gao Anhua's *To the Edge of the Sky* (2000), and Aiping Mu's *Vermilion Gate* (2000). If it is difficult to imagine Wang Shuo taking up the subject of June 4 with gravity, Annie Wang's salient adoption of this event as the backdrop of her novel is thoroughly in tune with the strident invocations of China's tumultuous history by other diasporic women writers before her. So, when she incorporates into this Tiananmen narrative a gruesome and seemingly gratuitous episode of Lili's childhood rape—"Three times in one night" (29)—by a Communist Party secretary during the Cultural Revolution, we may not be injudicious to read it as another fictional appropriation on her part, this time along the grains of Chinese diasporic women's writing.

So, it would be accurate to say that Wang is not simply a critical observer and sometimes satirist of capitalist China but also an exceedingly market-savvy diaspora writer. The capitalist fever that permeates *Lili* also defines the milieu in which Wang sees herself as embedded as a writer, a milieu she embraces and from which she derives financial success even as she parodies it from both sides of the Pacific. She is not one to don the robes of the old-fashioned intellectual who sneers at pop culture and market trends. On the contrary, as a bilingual author writing for both Chinese and Western audiences, she is highly mindful of and quite pragmatic about capitalizing on literary vogues in both China and the West. This means more than a general awareness or casual acceptance of market pressures on literary production. In her essay on Chinese diaspora novelists, Wang puts her journalistic research skills to good use and shows her firm grasp on the concrete ins and outs of international publishing as well as the profit differentials between Chinese and American markets. "Each year," she writes, "China publishes almost 180,000 titles, half of which are textbooks. (The U.S., by contrast, publishes about 60,000 new titles annually.) The publishing industry is China's third-largest taxpayer, behind the tobacco and liquor industries. Because of the huge potential of China's book market, international publishing groups like Bertelsmann are waiting to pounce." It is perhaps not fortuitous that this discussion of the Chinese literary market occurs in the midst of Wang's interview with Wang Shuo, who is cited as "one of the rare Chinese authors who has made his fortune by writing for the domestic Chinese market" but who nevertheless has "mixed feelings" about Chinese publishers. "They're all profit-seeking," Wang Shuo is quoted as saying with a tinge of lament. "They use me and I use them. Most of the time, they care only about making big money. They have a huge first print run of my book. Afterwards, they don't bother printing 10,000 copies per year because it's small money. That's why you can hardly buy my previous books now" ("New").

In this transnational circuit, the figure of the female hooligan does double duty for Annie Wang. On the PRC side, the hooligan is a fictional persona Wang can annex for its cultural cachet in the post-Tiananmen era. Unlike Wang Shuo, she does not belong to the generation that grew up in the cracks of the Cultural Revolution, nor did she live the hooligan lifestyle of unemployment, aimless drifting, and petty criminality in the post-Mao years. Lili is not a thin disguise for her youthful rebellious self, however much she promotes the "bad girl" authorial image. Most of all, hooliganism for her is not an ethos bred by personal experience and staked as an anti-establishment cultural aesthetic during a period of national transition. By the time she started composing *Lili* in the early 1990s, the "Wang Shuo phenomenon" had already swept over China, with "swarms of discontented youths" in Beijing flaunting "cultural T-shirts" scribbled with his signature pet phrases (J. Wang 262). At the same time, on the Western side, the ill-treated Chinese woman is a fictional persona Wang can expediently assume, since she already has the ethnic and gender alibis. Yet, unlike Jung Chung, Nien Cheng, Anchee Min, Hong Ying, and the other Chinese diasporic women writers of an earlier generation, Wang herself did not endure social upheavals or historical tragedies. Lili's trajectory of hardship, deprivation, and orphaning is not Wang's, nor are the female hooligan's class-inflected experiences of gender abuse and violence. Absent these autobiographical anchors, *Lili* is at its core a hybrid work of ambidextrous assimilations.

FLEXIBLE ETHNOGRAPHIES

This bilateral cultural capital enjoyed by Wang entails its own ambivalences, however. For one thing, the immense commercial success in the West of Chinese diasporic female literature has led to some stern responses on the part of critics. The prevailing concern is that of self-orientalism. On the milder end, Helena Grice, grouping diasporic female texts under the rubric of "Chinese American/British narratives" that "write Red China," proposes that their "critical reception . . . may be symptomatic of a cultural resurgence of orientalism" (104). By locating orientalism in these texts' reception rather than authorship, Grice gives herself room to foreground the feminist work they perform in bringing to light "previously obscured or suppressed perspectives" and inserting "a range of female voices into the cultural discourse revisiting China's twentieth century history" (125). Harsher in their assessment of the genre are Xueping Zhong, Wang Zheng, and Bai Di. Concentrating specifically on Cultural Revolution memoirs, Zhong et al. deplore the "all-too-familiar lenses of persecution, violence, victimization, sexual repression, and so forth" dramatized by these female narratives (xiii). What they contest is not so much the individual authenticity of each memoir as the genre's collective exoticization of Maoist China. In the United States particularly, they claim, "stories exposing the tragedy of the communist rule found a huge market among Americans, ranging from liberals crusading for human rights to anticommunist conservatives. . . . The collective imagination of the Mao era in America, in turn, becomes heavily shaped by these dark age narratives" (xx–xxi). This "dark age" tendency notwithstanding, Zhong et al. fundamentally affirm the potency of diasporic female writing when they advocate for their own autobiographical "counternarrative" of the Mao era (xxvii). In contrast, Lingchei Letty Chen denounces the entire corpus of "expatriate" Cultural Revolution memoirs. She is the critic most unsparing in indicting Chinese diaspora writers, male and female alike, for self-orientalism: "Two common mnemonic practices among Chinese diasporic writers are self-victimization (capitalizing on the authenticity of the suffering 'I') and self-exoticization (emphasizing on abjection to create an eternal incomprehensibility that characterizes the exotic Orient). Together they form a new discourse of self-Orientalization" ("Translating" 30). On Chen's verdict, expatriate memoirists deliberately exploit orientalist stereotypes and Cold War anxieties about communist China in order to leverage moral authority and cultural capital, all in the pursuit of commercial gain. Her primary target is Jung Chung's *Wild Swans*.

These criticisms are mainly directed at Cultural Revolution memoirs, but Tiananmen fictions are no less susceptible, since they are similarly written by diasporic authors for global readers and center on an equally notorious episode of communist brutality. Moreover, since the allegation of self-orientalism hounds female writers with particular ferocity, Annie Wang is perhaps more vulnerable to attack than the male writers of Tiananmen. Above all, she too, if on a smaller scale than some of the other female writers, has successfully tapped into the demands of an international publishing market. Sooner or later, then, and notwithstanding its overt treatment of capitalist self-orientalization as a trickster tactic, *Lili* will be caught up in the critical maelstrom.

Actually, the self-orientalism conundrum is not new for Chinese cultural producers who aspire for global visibility. For a cognate discussion, we can turn to the slightly earlier controversy that surrounded Fifth Generation filmmakers such as Zhang Yimou and Chen Kaige. Their films about feudal and rural China achieved international acclaim in the mid-1980s and 1990s but were at the same time widely castigated by Chinese viewers and reviewers for primitivizing China and pandering to foreign audiences. As Jane Ying Zha comments: "All my American friends love Zhang's movies, all my Chinese friends hate them. . . . Why? What offended the Chinese in these movies? . . . It could be summed up in one thing: selling oriental exoticism to a Western audience" (qtd. in Chow, *Primitive* 176). (This is, of course, prior to Zhang's recent reclamation by the PRC government as its chief propaganda director, most notably in the opening ceremony of the 2008 Beijing Olympics.) Rey Chow has tackled this issue at great length, ultimately arguing in favor of the filmmakers as executing "a kind of postmodern *self*-writing or *auto*ethnography . . . also a form of *intercultural* translation in the postcolonial age" (*Primitive* xi). As a premise, Chow theorizes twentieth-century Chineseness in terms of a dual-layered visuality. "To be Chinese" in the modern world, she contends, has meant not simply to come into possession of the gaze via technologies such as film, but more intricately, to inhabit this subject position of the gazer while retaining traces of having formerly been gazed at as the objectified colonized other. Vision itself "bears the origins of ethnographic inequality," so that "in the vision of the formerly ethnographized . . . what are 'subjective' origins now include a memory of past *objecthood*—the experience of being looked at—which lives on in the subjective act of ethnographizing like an other, an optical unconscious" (*Primitive* 180). This invocation of an "optical unconscious," a term Chow derives from Walter Benjamin, ensures for her argument that no act of visual self-representation by a Chinese filmmaker to a foreign audience can be free of its colonial lineage. She is then able to appeal to this "irrevocably" auto-ized mode of ethnography to defend Zhang Yimou and his cohort from accusations of self-orientalism. Contemporary Chinese cinema, she posits, is not neo-orientalist; it is "a new ethnography," "the Oriental's orientalism":

> It would hence be imprecise, though not erroneous, to say that directors such as Zhang are producing a new kind of orientalism. For if orientalism, understood in the sense Said uses it, is in part a form of voyeuristic aggression, then what Zhang is producing is rather an exhibitionist self-display that contains, in its very excessive modes, a critique of the voyeurism of orientalism itself. (Mis)construed by many as mere self-display (in the spirit of airing one's dirty laundry in public), this exhibitionism—what we may call the Oriental's orientalism—does not make its critique moralistically or resentfully. Instead, it turns the remnants of orientalism into elements of a new ethnography. Like a Judou turning around, citing herself as fetishized woman and displaying to her voyeur the scars and wounds she bears, this ethnography accepts the historical fact of orientalism and performs a critique (i.e., evaluation) of it by staging and parodying orientalism's politics of visuality. In its self-subalternizing, self-exoticizing visual gestures, the Oriental's orientalism is first and foremost a demonstration—the display of a tactic. (*Primitive* 171)

To be sure, Chow puts a great deal of conceptual weight on the inescapability—in the form of unconscious remnants or memory traces undergirding visuality itself—of China's colonial past and ethnographized status. While she deftly avoids and rightly rebukes the position of "defensive nativism," we might be tempted to question her convenient labeling of the Fifth Generation directors as "postcolonial" and her interpretation of their aesthetics as "parodic" (*Primitive* 178, 171, 202). Still, we can usefully read Annie Wang's entwined motifs of self-orientalism and spectacularity as a latter-day extension of Chow's thesis. That is, we can read *Lili* as an autoethnographic staging and parodying of China—and more specifically, of Beijing and Tiananmen Square—as sites of a neocolonial spectacle for and within global capitalism. Antony Thomas's *The Tank Man* is only one specimen within this configuration. Certainly, compared to Zhang Yimou, Wang wears her parody much more on her sleeves, not to mention her pointed satire of the Western ethnographic eye and her intentional hailing of a Western audience via language choice. The paradigm of autoethnography resonates especially with Lili's remark that, in the Square, "everybody is both an observer and a participant"—a metatextual allusion to the discourse of cultural anthropology, and also an implicit counterpoint to Roy's euphoric self-description as "a witness to history" (236). The Square, Wang intimates, is not an innocent theater where any passerby immediately assumes the role of historical witness. Instead, it is a power-infused arena where ethnography is enacted, by Chinese and Westerners alike, vis-à-vis the imagined object of "China." Chow's theoretical maneuvers can help elucidate some of these complexities in Wang's novel and deflect overly general charges of self-orientalism.

Of late, this ameliorated notion of autoethnography has been transferred to a context even more closely tied to Wang's, that of Chinese diasporic femininity. Sharon Hom, in her introduction to a collection of memoirs, essays, and poetry by "Chinese women traversing diaspora," designate these female narratives as precisely "a type of auto-ethnographies, field reports written by native informants from/to reconfiguring fields" (5). Olivia Khoo further innovates on this model of diasporic female auto-ethnography by formulating the idea of a "Chinese exotic." Just as Chow differentiates between old-fashioned colonial orientalism and contemporary "Oriental's Orientalism," so Khoo suggests that, unlike old hegemonic species of colonial exoticism, the Chinese exotic is a "new mode of representation"—produced not inside the PRC but within sprouting Chinese diasporic spaces (2). Khoo argues that contemporary China, no longer seen as the primitive other as along Chow's analysis, now enters into a phase of "capitalist development of diasporic . . . modernities," and accordingly, "spectacularised images of Chinese femininity" undergo a shift (5). "The Chinese exotic," she maintains, "is also differentiated from colonialist or imperialist exoticism in that it conceives of women and femininity, not as the oppressed, but as forming part of the new visibility of Asia, connected with the region's economic rise and emergent modernities.

What is exotic now is no longer the old (primitive) China within Asia, but the idea of a new Asia (Asia the cosmopolitan, the rich, the modern, and the technological). Similarly, what is exoticised about new images of Chinese femininity are precisely these things" (12). Insofar as these fresh exotic images of Chinese femininity reflect the economic rise of Asia and the emergence of Asians as capitalist agents, they "can be negotiated so as to create the possibility of positive agency for its subjects" (170). In other words, Khoo too attempts to redeem self-orientalism as a powerful and potentially self-empowering representational mode for Chinese cultural producers in the era of global Asian capital.

Khoo's theory of new Chinese diasporic modernities offers another valuable framework for understanding, not so much *Lili* on a textual level, but Wang's place within the macro cross-cultural politics around Chinese diaspora literature today. In fact, insofar as Lili stays fairly true to the prototype of the oppressed Chinese woman along an older genre of diasporic women's writing, Khoo's Chinese exotic fits this novel less well than Wang's next work in English, *The People's Republic of Desire* (2006). In the past decade, Wang has become much better known internationally for this latter novel, which originally ran as a weekly fiction column in Hong Kong's *South China Morning Post* from 2001 to 2004. Enormously trendy and popular, this column—often dubbed the Chinese *Sex and the City*—acquired a huge fan base, in print and eventually online.[3] No longer just "Beijing's Badgirl," Wang's persona has been updated to that of a "fumchi" ("female, upwardly mobile Chinese international") (Riminton). This is the very image Wang promotes of her latest heroines: four young urban professionals, successful and sophisticated, whose foremost desires are sex and money. "They are very intelligent, capable, beautiful, but they can't find husbands," Wang sums up ("People's"). Analogous to the author herself, the narrator is a Berkeley-educated returnee from America who works for an English news agency in early 2000s Beijing, where she and her friends are utterly steeped in a "Westernized" lifestyle of consumer goods and casual sex. The atmosphere of rampant commodification from *Lili* gets a postmillennial upgrade as Wang sheds both hooligan disguise and historical anachronism. If *Lili* encapsulates an internal incongruity between Wang's post-Tiananmen, hypercapitalist, transnational moment of writing and Lili's pre-Tiananmen, neocolonial, not-yet-globe-trotting moment of narration, the protagonists in *The People's Republic of Desire* at last catch up with their creator as their fictional and her real-life epochs converge. Clearly, the "comfort woman" reference from the earlier novel constitutes only one identificatory posture in Wang's larger corpus, as she shows herself to be quite nimble in staging a range of Chinese female subject positions within the capacious, and ever-evolving, field of diasporic women's literature. Hers, we might say, is a flexible feminism.

Even this brief overview of *The People's Republic of Desire* will quickly summon up another genre relevant to Wang: that of contemporary "chick lit." As Wenche Ommundsen notes, chick lit is associated with a host of pejorative connotations such as "formulaic, market-driven plot," an "obsession with consumerism," and "politically regressive portrayal of young women," so that as a whole it is frequently derided as the "cultural equivalent of junk food" (329). Yet Ommundsen also persuasively argues that the genre is not simply a shallow and opportunistic by-product of the market economy but can be better understood within intersecting contexts of postfeminist writing, global capitalism, and multiculturalism. Given its "capacity to accommodate cultural difference and produce local variants which speak directly to the pressing concerns of women in a wide variety of circumstances," chick lit makes for "an ideal site for the study of globalization." So: "To regard chick lit as merely the complicit product of the new cultural norm of individualism defined by consumption, or even as one of its main instruments of propaganda, would be to ignore the genre's capacity for ambivalence, variation and cultural mutability. From frivolous and facile to complex and sophisticated, from complacent to politically astute, from formulaic to genre-bending, chick lit both reinforces and critiques dominant trends in contemporary culture" (333). Within this continuum, Ommundsen regards *The People's Republic of Desire* as a particularly complex if ambiguous case. On the one hand, the novel can be "best described as social commentary masquerading as chick lit" (335), reporting on contemporary China's rapidly changing social landscape while poking fun—so says Wang herself—at Chinese yuppies' obsession with brands and fads, at its most ambitious exposing the "soullessness and chaos" of the times. On the other hand, the novel serves up that which it ostensibly parodies with so much fidelity and gusto that it has ironically been used, as Wang herself indicates, as a "fashion guide among some yuppies and yuppie wannabes in China" (qtd. in Chhibber). The novel's message is thus "difficult to pin down," since it can be construed as simultaneously "chick lit or a parody of chick lit," a "straight reportage of social customs in China" or a caricature of them (Ommundsen 337). In the end, though, Ommundsen contends that "Chinese chick lit in English ... signals the demise of diaspora literature as we have known it, and the beginning of a more truly transnational and transcultural era" (333–34). Like Khoo, she stresses these diasporic female texts' contemporariness, since the vision of China they deliver consists of a two-way migration between equally global and modern settings, not "between China as the past and the West as present and future" (342). Despite recurrent disparagements of the genre, then, she affirms chick lit authors for having the "saving grace of honesty," for offering an "accurate diagnosis not only of their own dilemmas, but of the numerous paradoxes of the contemporary world" (339).

Ommundsen's explication of chick lit as a self-conscious index of globalization that explodes older conceptions of diaspora literature perfectly suits *The People's Republic of Desire*. It is slightly *too* contemporary, however, for *Lili*. There, Wang's engagement with Tiananmen elevates the novel above the chick lit label and into a more highbrow category. It is this Tiananmen focus that compels Kay Schaffer and Sidonie Smith, for instance, to situate *Lili* within the framework of human rights fictional discourse, as "a novel of transformation and faith in the possibilities for China's political future, including enhanced rights, dignity, and justice for its citizens." Schaffer and Smith embed Wang within a larger matrix of contemporary diasporic narratives, which they view as performing the crucial function of circulating human rights issues globally in our time, "extend[ing] the regime of human rights into China and back to the West again in telling stories" (218). This earnest treatment of *Lili*, though, fails to take into account Wang's acerbic satire of Roy's liberalism, and intertwined with it, the facile wielding of human rights discourse by Westerners in Chinese contexts. Indeed, as we will see in the next chapter, Schaffer and Smith's appraisal can be applied much more fittingly to Ma Jian and *Beijing Coma*. For now, let us conclude by underscoring these contradictory evaluations that orbit Wang as a diasporic female writer of popular global fiction. Her Tiananmen novel in particular epitomizes the equivocal capital—linguistic, cultural, financial, political—afforded by contemporary transnationalism. As literature becomes progressively captured into the mechanisms of an international publishing industry, works amenable to human rights advocacy such as Tiananmen fictions may actually be more, not less, susceptible to commodification. In this light, we can say that capitalist self-commodification is at once content and form of Wang's oeuvre, that she co-opts marketable trends as briskly as she gets co-opted back into trendy markets both East and West. Yet, precisely because of its ambidexterity, *Lili* is an exemplary text for disentangling the emergent contradictions of globalization.

The theoretical paradigm that best articulates *Lili*'s diasporic logic, I think, is Donald Nonini and Aihwa Ong's "Chinese transnationalism," or what Ong later terms "flexible citizenship." "There is nothing intrinsically liberating about diasporic cultures," Nonini and Ong justly point out (325), since diasporas, "like any cultural formations, are grounded in internal hegemonies and systems of inequalities" (324). As we saw in the previous chapter, diaspora can be, and has often been since the early 1990s, theorized as a potent configuration that displaces and/or expands on provincial boundaries of cultural identity (Hall; Gilroy, *Black*; Clifford), and this deconstructive blueprint has been variously transferred by scholars to investigations of Chineseness in the last few years (Hom; Ang; L. L. Chen, *Writing*; Ng and Holden). *Lili* too deconstructs essentialist notions of Chineseness along lines of gender and class, but the theme of orientalist capital and the related element of Wang's own ambidextrous assimilationism entail that no exploration of the novel or its author would be complete without a scrupulous address of China's globalization. In this context, Nonini and Ong sketch out an indispensible model for retheorizing contemporary Chineseness, which they claim "can be understood only in terms of the multiplicity of ways in which 'being Chinese' is an inscribed relation of persons and groups to forces and processes associated with global capitalism and its modernities" (4). In other words, "to be Chinese" today is not to possess a preexisting cultural identity with the additional capacity of being influenced, enhanced, or corrupted by global capital, but rather to already and necessarily be shaped within its dynamics. The distinguishing modes of subjectivity in this milieu are "mobility," "flexibility," and "accumulation"—"wild and dangerously innovative powers" that can also become harnessed by and "incorporated into the open-ended logics of flexible capitalism itself" (20). Chinese transnationalists can now break out of old molds of identity and identification but can also "be disciplined either to support hegemonic views of regimes of truth . . . or to undermine them" (26). As for the quandary of ethnography, Ong, too, perceives self-orientalism as a flexible tactic that may be deployed complicitously or agentively: "In a world of Western hegemony, Asian voices are unavoidably inflected by Orientalist essentialisms that infiltrate all kinds of public exchanges about culture. I use the term *self-orientalization* in recognition not just of such predicaments but also of the agency to maneuver and manipulate meanings within different power domains" ("Chinese" 195). Adapting Ong's term, we might call Annie Wang a supremely flexible literary citizen, whether apropos femininity or generationality, language use or generic material, shuttling with adroitness between Western and Chinese markets, suavely accumulating their respective literary trends and converting them into both cultural and financial capital. Lastly, as Ong asserts, this "flexible citizenship is shaped within the mutually reinforcing dynamics of discipline and escape" (*Flexible* 19)—a condition that circumscribes satiric critiques as much as capitalist collusions. And Wang, undeniably, does both.

GLOBALIZATION'S "SOMEWHERE"

Let us end by returning to *Lili*, on the note of its own denouement. As the Tiananmen movement draws near its bloody closure, the novel's final few chapters throw up a series of hastily and chaotically unfolding plotlines: the reunification of the hitherto fragmented Chinese family; the metaphorical resurrection and remasculinization of the Chinese father-qua-intellectual; the sudden reappearance of Lili's ex-boyfriend gang leader and their tearful reunion, before his no less abrupt melodramatic death in the massacre; Roy's deportation back to the United States by communist authorities; and Lili's discovery of her pregnancy with Roy's baby and the anticipated but unnarrated birth of their biracial child. This frenzied finale puts into play a host of paradoxical narrative desires, including a fantasy of restoration of the traditional family structure, a redemption of the patriarchal intellectual for the Chinese family and nation, a laying to rest of Cultural Revolution traumas such as the hooligan legacy, a severing of the vexed romance with the Western orientalist, and a promise of female independence in post-Tiananmen China, albeit with an ethnically hybridized afterlife. These desires, however, are all left unresolved.

The novel's final paragraph is especially cheeky in flaunting its ambiguity. After telling the reader that she survives the crackdown, Lili adds: "The Lili of Beijing died that night, but a new Lili was born somewhere else. Somewhere where freedom and respect bloom" (307). Wang undoubtedly wants the reader to ask, where is this "somewhere"? She teasingly hints at the possibility of a diasporic, perhaps even American, rebirth for her heroine, but she just as coyly withholds the exact location of this future. Were we to decipher this last line biographically, the answer would be straightforward. Wang, as she has repeatedly stated in interviews, was "so disappointed by Tiananmen and the death of idealism in China" that she eventually went abroad to study at UC Berkeley in 1993, and instead of "sink[ing] under the weight of history," she decided to "have fun with [her] writing": "China needs some humour. We all need humour in our lives" (qtd. in Chhibber). We know that "fun" and "humour" led to *The People's Republic of Desire*. But we also know, given all the points of disconnection between Wang's and Lili's lives, not to take easy recourse in the author's biography.

Rather than pinpoint this "somewhere," it is perhaps more illuminating to unpack the meaning of the word's very indeterminacy, to comprehend this textual ending's eluding of place as the very sign of the novel's contemporary situation. That is to say, the spatial vagueness of "somewhere" may itself signal the sense of deterritorialization that characterizes globalization's geographic imaginary—of the world as composed not of discrete national units with policed boundaries but transnational flows and networks and virtual spaces. Appadurai would call these spaces the "scapes" of globalization: "The new global cultural economy has to be seen as a complex, overlapping, disjunctive order, which cannot any longer be understood in terms of existing center-periphery models.... The suffix -scape allows us to point to the fluid, irregular shapes of these landscapes, shapes which characterize international capital as deeply as they do international clothing styles." Appadurai names five such scapes—ethnoscapes, mediascapes, technoscapes, finanscapes, and ideoscapes—which together form "the building blocks of... *imagined worlds*" (6–7). Wang's cosmopolitan lifestyle, globe-trotting between Beijing and Berkeley, Hong Kong and Shanghai, happens within this same global cultural economy. The utopian timbre of Lili's future "somewhere" hence evokes at once an implied "nowhere" as well as the "imagined world" of a Chinese transnationalism that is already the case for her creator. Similarly from this perspective, the novel's delineation of a neocolonial center-periphery model is already outdated, not just an anachronism but an archaic remnant outstripped by Wang's reality.

Two additional points remain to be made about *Lili*'s final emptying out of national geography. First, read against the conclusions of Gao's *Taowang* and Jin's *The Crazed*, the unspecified site of Lili's projected destination can also connote a gendered ambivalence about diaspora. For Gao, political flight is only one strand of the universal imperative of existential flight, without which there is only death, while for Jin, escape from the PRC to the democratic West represents the sole path of survival for the intellectual-scholar. For both, self-exile is an autonomous act of the masculine individual who stands independent of all kinship structures and social ties. In *Lili*, however, emigration is a difficult process, and Wang's resolute focus on women further highlights the unequal gender dynamics surrounding the matter. As seen above, "going diaspora" can carry the undertone of not just cultural-ethnic betrayal but sexual prostitution. As Lili bemoans with exasperation at one point, "Why is it patriotic for a Chinese man to sleep with a foreign woman and unpatriotic for a Chinese woman to sleep with a foreign man?" (273). And yet, as the novel makes plain, one of the few routes by which nonaffluent Chinese women can leave China is to "marry out"—an option that Wang holds out for Lili via Roy. The spatial ambiguity of Lili's future "somewhere," though, marks Wang's hesitancy in concretizing this option. As a result, the novel ends on a note of marital uncertainty, with the "new Lili" suspended between domesticity and flight, homeland and diaspora, single mother and orientalized wife.

Second, and in tension with the aforementioned gender reading, the figurative deterritorialization at *Lili*'s closure is related to Wang's bisection of China in the rest of the text. Although there is no question that the narrative unfolds in the PRC, the novel's national geography is partitioned somewhat simplistically into Beijing and Up Village, the city of global capital and the countryside of abject poverty. Except for a short opening detour into the dreamlike Inner Mongolia, there is no in-between zone of life, no middle space in the jagged terrains of China's globalization. This imagined geographical dichotomy is advantageous for Wang's narrative, for it makes more clear-cut Lili's decision to embrace capitalism and socially advance herself as a "rich foreigner's mistress," since the alternative would be, on the binary terms of the novel, a life of rural misery. *Lili's* national imaginary, then, is scarcely nuanced even from the outset. This feature of the novel may in turn account for the salient absence of a group of people who are arguably of central importance to any examination of Chinese lower-class women within global capital: namely, the millions of migrant female workers whose cheap labor oils the engine of the PRC's present-day economic boom. The stories of "factory girls" so movingly detailed by Leslie Chang, for instance, are wholly passed over in *Lili*, and this critical blind spot contributes to the ongoing invisibility of these women as the world's new subalterns. Indeed, if all the desired commodities in Wang's oeuvre are labeled "Western," then local labor can be conveniently hidden, along with all its associated social problems—and this is not yet to confront the more familiar and current phenomenon in which even "Western" brands now ubiquitously bear the "made in China" label. Wang's Beijing upbringing and multiple metropolitan residences in adulthood may ultimately shield her from a great deal of transformation in the hinterlands of her native country.[4]

In the final analysis, though, we can recontextualize *Lili* within the history of Tiananmen discourse and interpret Wang's inattention to urban laborers as a refusal to *re*direct attention to workers as the alternative nexus of the movement. Not only were workers the second-largest and thus a highly visible group of Tiananmen participants in 1989, but their identity as a class of underdogs and the chief victims of the massacre has been so valorized by intellectuals both Chinese and Western post-Tiananmen that Wang has perhaps deliberately refrained from writing in the voice of their defender. This intellectual tendency to champion workers is partly evidenced above by Perry's as much as Esherick and Wasserstrom's arguments, but I will illustrate it at greater length in the next chapter. By contrast, much less discussed are issues of gender and sexuality in relation to Tiananmen, and Wang pointedly begins her novel within this analytical gap. As Lee Feigon notes, there were "very few women leaders of the Chinese struggle for democracy in 1989" (167)—and this applies not only to the students but also, as academic advocates of a non-gender-specified rubric of "workers" rarely mention, to the laboring classes as well. This general dearth in female leadership can explain the lack of gender studies of Tiananmen, but by the same token, the stark imbalance in gender power should compel a more sustained look at the gender dynamics of protest politics. In this regard, Feigon rightly points out that, since "males still dominated the upper levels of the movement, both in composition and tone" and that "women were relegated for the most part to traditional kinds of supporting roles," Tiananmen definitely "did not mark a radical new chapter for gender relations in China" (167–68). Furthermore, as we will see in the next chapter, although one of the most prominent leaders in the student movement was a woman—the self-declared Commander in Chief of the Square, Chai Ling—she has since the mid-1990s come under fire from PRC intellectuals, diaspora scholars, and Western critics alike, becoming one of the most intensely vilified figures in the worldwide discourse on Tiananmen today. Wang alludes to this furor when she has the trickster hunger striker Jackson tell Lili that "the number one student leader . . . has many followers, though some students don't like her because they think she's selfish and manipulative." "But me," Jackson adds, "I like her. She's a good speaker, really powerful" (246). Yet Wang also hints that a truly feminist inquiry into contemporary China cannot settle for a simple reclamation of this lone female icon. In fact, as Feigon clarifies, Chai herself was hardly the paragon of progressive gender politics in 1989, at times "appear[ing] to see herself as simply a stand-in for the men who should have been in her position," at other times "pander[ing] to an image of herself as a mother figure" (171–72), and at bottom no less elitist than her male counterparts in her approach to matters of gender discrimination, willingly subordinating the feminist agenda to "more pressing problems" of national politics (168). And after all, Wang is too skeptical of self-made national heroes, and too canny about the ephemerality of media culture and stardom, to attempt to resanctify a fallen political leader, female or otherwise. No one so far, however, has protested the neglect of female hooligans in the grand chronicle of Tiananmen, and it is from this empty space of world memory that she gives life to *Lili*.

4 /   The Biopolitical Square: Ma Jian's *Beijing Coma*

With Ma Jian's *Beijing Coma* (2008), Tiananmen receives its fullest treatment in literature to date—as at once history and myth. Of all extant Tiananmen fictions, this is the work that stays closest to social history, minutely tracking the rise and fall of the student pro-democracy movement; at the same time, it is the work that most powerfully distills Tiananmen's political significance, epically charting the macro history of the communist state but insistently foregrounding 1989's enduring legacy within it. As the most recently published book among those examined in this study but also the densest one textually, *Beijing Coma* merits its own route of engagement. Hence, in direct reversal from my first chapter on Gao Xingjian, for whom authorial reception and discursive context were thickest, here I will tunnel backward from the novel itself to the earlier, wider, and still abiding debates around Tiananmen. In the first part, I focus on the novel's central themes of intergenerational memory and its severance, biopolitical and capitalist cannibalism, and most crucially for Ma, the continuous regime of sovereign biopower in the long span of communist history. In the chapter's second half, I will use the novel as a prism through which to recall and reexamine Tiananmen's fraught historiography, from the initial mythologies surrounding the June 3–4 massacre itself to the subsequent diasporic image wars over the "radicalizing" of student leadership. Fiercely intervening on these debates, Ma fictionally retraces the students' steps out of the Square to the site of their deaths but symbolically overlaps this scene with our current moment of China's economic ascendance—so as to herald a national as much as global future for which Tiananmen will again be a crux point, forking down the paths of either a lingering comatose life or a reactivation of the utopian polity.

Part I. Tiananmen Cannibals and Biopower

THE TIANANMEN MOTHERS
AND INTERGENERATIONAL MEMORY

I began the previous chapter by discussing the international and cross-cultural politics of historical memory and knowledge production about Tiananmen via Antony Thomas's documentary *The Tank Man*. What this film (or Annie Wang's *Lili*) does not bring to light is the split within China itself between pre- and post-Tiananmen generations—and the rupture in historical consciousness along not a geographical horizon of East-West but the vertical relation of parents to children. This intergenerational understanding of China's historical amnesia can serve to return the locus of agency, and that of responsibility, for collective memory back to the Chinese themselves. It is therefore no accident that the trope of parentage, with all its connotations of an endemic bond and endogenous transmission, comes to be precisely the one deployed by democracy activists within the PRC who continue to labor for Tiananmen's official recognition and memory.

Most well-known in this context is the Tiananmen Mothers organization. Founded by Ding Zilin, a retired philosophy professor whose teenage son and only child was shot and killed on June 4, this group actively campaigns to disseminate information and educate the public about the massacre both within and outside of the PRC. Despite its name, the Tiananmen Mothers comprises not just mothers but also fathers, relatives, and friends of Tiananmen victims. The nominal emphasis on parenthood, however, and maternity in particular, is not so much a misnomer as a symbolic invocation highlighting the intense sense of familial loss, generational severance, and reproductive breakage caused by the massacre.

It is with similar overtones that the writer Liao Yiwu records an interview with a "Tiananmen Father" in his recent collection of oral histories, *The Corpse Walker*. In this interview, Wu Dingfu narrates how he learned of the Beijing massacre and his son's death in it only days after June 4, through fragmentary briefings by Party officials in his provincial hometown. "Xinjing is a small town," he tells Liao. "The Communist Party did a good job of blocking news. We didn't know anything about the killings." As Liao bitterly comments: "The whole world saw the tapes of the bloody crackdown. The Chinese were the last ones to learn the truth" (223). In this instance, the failure of intergenerational knowledge runs in a reverse direction, with the father being denied information about the circumstances of his son's death. Yet Liao also suggests it is the bereaved parents like Wu who ultimately act as the most powerful narrators and cultural memorialists of Tiananmen, who most directly safeguard and transmit the massacre's memory for China's succeeding generations. In this light, the stories of Tiananmen parents and the work of the Tiananmen Mothers organization perform not only a personal task of mourning but also a political task of historical recovery. These Tiananmen parents endeavor to reestablish a connection not only with each other but also with their children's generation in order to keep alive familial as well as national memory, converting what is otherwise a purely biological and cultural relation of parenthood into an oppositional political identity.

In her work on the dynamics of cultural memory of the Holocaust, Marianne Hirsch proposes a resonant theory of *postmemory*—"the relationship of children of survivors of cultural or collective trauma to the experiences of their parents, experiences that they 'remember' only as the stories and images with which they grew up, but that are so powerful, so monumental, as to constitute memories in their own right" ("Projected" 8). As we saw in chapter 2, Hirsch's analysis focuses on photographs as one primary medium through which postmemory is produced, as later generations come to construct cultural narratives of their past via "encounters with images that have become generally familiar, perhaps even pervasive, in contemporary memory" ("Projected" 4). In the case of Tiananmen, the Tank Man photograph is surely one of those familiar and pervasive images of 1989, but as we saw in the last chapter, the contemporary Chinese encounter with it occurs within a framework significantly different from Hirsch's. Instead of instant identification with an overly familiar and iconic image, there is nonrecognition, hesitation, disidentification; instead of adoption of a prior generation's traumatic experiences as a social and political act of cultural memory, there is intergenerational separation, orphaning, forgetting. Whether or not the Tank Man image truly holds a memorial power for today's Chinese youths, the atmosphere bespeaks a breakdown of postmemory around Tiananmen.

It is in response to this situation that Ma Jian writes his novel *Beijing Coma*. He, too, perceives the generations growing up after June 4 as having neither personal nor cultural memory of Tiananmen, for their parents, whether out of fear or protectiveness or pure self-survival, have for the most part not passed down the legacy of this history to them. Like Ding Zilin and other activists, Ma invokes the trope of generationality as key to the political reclamation of Tiananmen, calling this breakdown of historical memory *duandai*, the severing of generations (qtd. in Zeng). As he asserts in one interview: "The Chinese people have been forced to forget the

Tiananmen massacre. There has been no public debate about the event, no official apology. The media aren't allowed to mention it. Still today people are being persecuted and imprisoned for disseminating information about it" ("China's Olympic"). In his own life, Ma has firsthand experience with *duandai* in relation to his own daughter, who refuses to visit him in his London home and disapproves of his democracy-leaning views, having, he believes, absorbed too much of the CCP's propaganda. "There is an inescapable bond," he notes. "But if I wasn't her father I would be the kind of person she would have nothing to do with" (qtd. in Edemariam). Yet for Ma, the phenomenon of *duandai* is not confined to the post-Tiananmen era but extends far back, beyond the Tiananmen generation and even his own, into his parents' generation. His grandfather was a landlord executed during the Cultural Revolution, but his father never spoke of this family history, a pattern of intergenerational silence not atypical of Cultural Revolution survivors. Ma recalls visiting his ancestral village but finding neither gravestone nor living witness to illuminate his grandfather's past: "I couldn't ask why was he arrested, who arrested him, where was he taken, how exactly did he die—there was no way of finding out. But it made me understand why my father lived in such fear all his life. And it was only when my father died that I found in his drawer a self-criticism he'd written, and realized that he lived in constant fear of being arrested" (qtd. in Edemariam).

This experience of recurrent familial severance will become the thematic entry point for Ma's portrait of his protagonist, Dai Wei, in *Beijing Coma*. Like Ma himself, Dai Wei is a pivotal character anchoring two vectors of *duandai* in communist history: as a son repulsed by and estranged from the broken man that his father was, he illustrates the post-Mao generation's backward amnesia about the Cultural Revolution and the suffering it spawned; as a minor student leader in the Tiananmen movement who gets shot in the head during the massacre and becomes a comatose patient for the next ten years, he personifies the forceful incapacitation of forward memory and the severing of knowledge in the post–June 4 period. In this novel, Tiananmen as history comes to fruition in literature. Although all the writers in my study address Tiananmen in their works, the movement and the massacre have largely been taken up as a vehicle for other concerns or critiques, whether existentialist or diasporic, feminist or capitalist. Of all the Tiananmen fictions, *Beijing Coma* is the most immanent to the student movement. It brings Tiananmen back full circle, from Gao Xingjian's intellectual-philosopher, Ha Jin's scholar-student, and Annie Wang's woman-hooligan back to the core of the movement's origins: student life. Moreover, where the other works emphasize the necessity or outcome of flight, Ma's alone insists on the geographical and conceptual return to, and reoccupation of, the Square as the symbolic place of the Communist Party's despotic past and present as well as of Chinese democracy's future struggle. In this sense, Ma is the diasporic writer who most fully embodies the brand of pro-democracy politics that has survived Tiananmen, both perilously within the PRC among such dissident intellectuals as the drafters of Charter 08, Liu Xiaobo chief among them, and also overseas in such activist groups as Human Rights in China. As such, Ma represents a significant mode of cultural politics in the Chinese literary diaspora, one that mediates discourses of democracy and human rights between the PRC and the West. Above all, Ma's is the fictional work that gives fullest significance to Tiananmen as a biopolitical event. As his novel argues, the genealogical scope of Tiananmen is not limited to the protests leading up to June 4 but extends back to Mao's time and forward into the post-1989 decade, beyond Deng Xiaoping's reign. Likewise, the boundaries of this half-century-long and still ongoing event stretch beyond the Square itself, fluidly constituted and dissolved in rural pockets during the Cultural Revolution and surreptitiously reconstituted in urban centers' private homes in the new millennium. The Square of 1989, however, remains the most visible site of the communist state's sovereign biopower, so it is here that Ma devotes the bulk of his novel to capturing, even as he increasingly unhinges this biopolitical paradigm from its material space and time and reproduces it as a general condition over China today. His central metaphor for this totalitarian biopolitics is cannibalism.

BIOPOLITICAL AND CAPITALIST CANNIBALS

Han Dongfang, the labor activist who helped to organize an independent workers' union during the Tiananmen demonstrations, has aptly compared the 1989 movement to the eating of something raw: "I compare the 1989 Democracy Movement to an unripe fruit. People were so hungry that they were desperate. When they suddenly discovered a fruit, they pounced on it, and swallowed it whole. Then they got a stomach ache and a bitter taste in the mouth. So should they have eaten the fruit? You can say they shouldn't have, but they were hungry. And if you say that they should have, what they ate was still green, inedible" ("*Gate*"). Neither naively heroizing nor complacently superior, Han sympathetically voices the quandary of those who are compelled to make a premature and ultimately self-wounding choice out of desperation. Literally in Chinese, the unripe fruit of Tiananmen is "a thing that cannot be eaten" (*bu keyi chi de yige dongxi*) but nonetheless is.

This portrait of a malnourished society's self-injury through the metaphor of bad ingestion may be traced to a more sinister literary antecedent:

Lu Xun's famous allegory, in the story "A Madman's Diary," of feudal China as a cannibalistic society where the strong devour the weak. As Gang Yue writes in his thematic study of hunger and cannibalism in twentieth-century Chinese literature, "In the grand narrative of revolution, the old China was a monstrous human-eating feast; only through revolution could the oppressed masses free themselves of that devouring system and transform it into egalitarian revelry" (2). It would be the ironic but double fate of Lu Xun to be enthroned as a communist national icon while his iconoclastic allegory comes to be appropriated by later writers to critique the exploitation, corruption, and cruelty of the communist state itself. As Perry Link elucidates, a number of PRC writers of the late 1970s and 1980s already began to raise anew the theme of cannibalism, in the form of organ harvesting, as part of the post–Cultural Revolution wave of exposé narratives about Party abuse of power (147). For instance, in Cao Guanlong's 1979 short story "Three Professors: Fire," a young death-row prisoner is fed on a specially rich diet so that his eyes may be kept healthy for their eventual transplant to a Public Security Bureau director. Mass cannibalism is further suggested in Hong Ying's 1997 memoir *Daughter of the River* (originally entitled *Daughter of Hunger*). Where Lu Xun ends his story with "save the children" as an impassioned plea for a more egalitarian future, Hong Ying underscores the failure of children's salvation when the human casualties of disastrous national policies such as the Great Leap Forward encompass not just the millions who died of starvation during the famine years but also, more obscurely and horrifically, those kidnapped children whose flesh was used as dumpling stuffings at local shops (68). In contemporary Chinese fiction both within the PRC and in the diaspora, cannibalism is no longer feudal but socialist, and more recently, capitalist—as in Mo Yan's *The Republic of Wine*—leading Michael Berry to aptly call Lu Xun's vision "as much a prophecy for the future as it is a commentary on tradition" (1).

In the wake of Tiananmen especially, there has been an intensified literary revival of the cannibalism theme. As I noted in the introduction, Mo Yan's novel is a prime example. In the diaspora, the seminal text may be Zheng Yi's *Scarlet Memorial*, a literary exposé that draws on local archives and firsthand interviews to detail the widespread, systematic, and Party-incited cannibalization of "class enemies" in the Guangxi Autonomous Region during the Cultural Revolution. Himself a former leader of the 1989 movement who has since fled into exile, Zheng Yi connects the innumerable cases of politicized murder and cannibalism during the Cultural Revolution with the June 4 massacre: both moments are awash in state-sanctioned blood, and both require witnessing and recording to "counter the cover-up" by the communist government (29–32). It is Zheng Yi's grisly investigative work, combined with his grim vision of a continuous thread of cannibalism throughout PRC history, that underlies *Beijing Coma*'s engagement with this theme. In this intertextual relation, we can in turn grasp the extent of Ma Jian's self-alignment with the dissident politics of post-Tiananmen pro-democracy activism.

"They ate Director Liu," a doctor tells Dai Wei in 1984, by way of recalling the events of 1968 in a Guangxi labor reform camp. Dai Wei's father, a professional violinist who had performed in the United States before repatriating to China after 1949, had been branded a rightist during the Cultural Revolution and been sent to the Guangxi Overseas Chinese Farm for two years. Now, some two decades later and three years after his father's death, Dai Wei is on a journey to learn more about his paternal past. Director Liu had been the farm's supervisor, a Malaysian Chinese who had likewise repatriated, and one of the few who befriended Dai Wei's father despite the latter's political branding.

At the doctor's words about Director Liu's fate, Dai Wei, instantly recoiling and groping for some familiar explanation, offers a moment from his father's journal: "My father told me that, of the three thousand rightists sent to the Gansu reform-through-labour camp, 1700 died of starvation. Sometimes the survivors became so famished that they had to resort to eating the corpses" (54). Hearing this account, we as readers will think to ourselves as Dai Wei does that, yes, cannibalism exists, but it is an instinctual act, motivated purely by the desperate will for biological survival; it is animalish behavior to which human beings become susceptible under extraordinarily dire privations. Some intellectual comfort can be derived from this appeal to instinct and circumstance, species drive and natural catastrophe, aberration and emergency. On this view, cannibalism, though horrific to the modern sensibility, can nonetheless happen anywhere, to any human community, for it is a fact of biology, but only one under extreme conditions.

Ma, however, does not rest with this view. Instead, he proceeds to outline, through the doctor's memorializing voice, a much more problematic category of cannibalism, one that is a direct consequence of state policies and properly *biopolitical*:

> "Here in Guangxi it wasn't starvation that drove people to cannibalism. It was hatred. . . .
>
> "It was in 1968, one of the most violent years of the Cultural Revolution. In Guangxi, it wasn't enough just to kill class enemies, the local revolutionary committees forced the people to eat them as well. In the beginning, the enemies' corpses were simmered in large vats together with legs of pork. But as the campaign progressed, there were

too many corpses to deal with, so only the heart, liver and brain were cooked. . . .

"Who were the murderers? You could argue that the only real murderer was Chairman Mao. But the fact is, everyone was involved. . . . During those years, the PLA soldiers sent to Wuxuan County were stationed here in Wuxuan Town. They were meant to carry out the executions, and the inhabitants of the surrounding villages were only supposed to make the arrests. But the villagers were eager to show their commitment to the revolution, so they took things into their own hands, and started executing the class enemies themselves. . . . When your father was sent down here, there were about a thousand people incarcerated on the farm. After a couple of years, the hundred or so rightists among them were transferred to other camps. Of the nine hundred labourers who remained, over a hundred belonged to the twenty-three undesirable types. All of them were killed. The corpses of the few who'd contracted diseases were buried, but the rest of them were eaten." (55–56)

In the doctor's narrative, cannibalism in the initial phase of the Cultural Revolution was "forced" upon the people by local Party cadres. This mode of coercive cannibalism, where human beings surrender to political pressure out of a will to survive, can be rationalized as a kind of biological urge toward self-preservation. Eventually, however, this mode gave way to one of consent and even fervor as villagers voluntarily and zealously took on the role of state executioners. We detect a shift in the psycho-political dynamics of cannibalism here: where the villagers reacted negatively and instinctively before, in order to negate the threat of death, they came to enact state agency positively and politically later on, as a way to prove their ideological mettle and "show their commitment to the revolution." With this shift, the village cannibals became political subjects proper; their cannibalism passed from an event in nature to one in political history. This mode of politicized cannibalism is premised not on individual or species necessity but national politics. The state exerts its power here by constructing cannibalism as a potent form of national agency, a local activity through which individuals can rid the country of its "bad elements," share in the power of the Party, and thereby produce, display, and authenticate themselves as good national subjects. Contrary to the doctor's diagnosis, then, his narrative suggests the villagers' gusto sprang not so much from a pathology of pure hatred as a transformed paradigm of biopolitical agency. For the first time, the act of consuming human flesh could itself signify revolutionary politics, national citizenship, and Party power-sharing for the villagers.[1] Within the chronology of Ma's novel, this is the first instance of the communist state's sovereign biopower.

In this newer cannibalistic formation, sovereign power need not materialize in Mao's person or the army's actual use of force. Instead of Mao's dictum that power grows out of the barrel of a gun, Ma's narrative conjures Michel Foucault's theory of biopower. On Foucault's analysis, populations are best controlled and dutiful subjects best produced not through threat of death but discourses of life. Where the sovereign of the classical or imperial age exercised his power through raw violence and "the right to decide life and death," the ruler of modern times—like Mao and later Deng—evidences his power by attempting to "administer, optimize, and multiply" life itself, "subjecting it to precise controls and comprehensive regulations. Wars are no longer waged in the name of a sovereign who must be defended; they are waged on behalf of the existence of everyone; entire populations are mobilized for the purpose of wholesale slaughter in the name of life necessity: massacres have become vital" (137). Foucault's explication resonates with surprising fit with Ma's portrait of the PRC. In the novel's retrospective on Guangxi and the Cultural Revolution, the masses were indeed "mobilized for the purpose of wholesale slaughter in the name of life necessity," in the name of ensuring the nation's life and safeguarding the people's ideological health. In this episode of Dai Wei's paternal root-seeking, by having his protagonist learn the fate of his father's generation, Ma implies that the Tiananmen generation succeeds the Cultural Revolution's "undesirable types" as the communist state's biopolitical victims, that the students' massacre belongs to the same biopolitical lineage, if not the same social order, as their parents' cannibalization. Yet Ma also intimates that this intergenerational connection may never come to public light. Even as the doctor narrates the biopolitical history that will similarly befall Dai Wei's future, even as he holds in his hands the ten-volume *Chronicles of the Cultural Revolution* that he and his team of researchers have compiled, he already knows to mourn this history's death. "The national government told us to carry out this research," he tells Dai Wei, "but the county authorities refused to cooperate because most of the people who organized the atrocities are now high officials in the local government. This whole project is a sham. Only five copies of these chronicles have been published. I doubt the public will ever get to read them. Once the victims we've listed have been rehabilitated, the chronicles will probably be locked away in the government vaults. None of the top officials will lose their jobs" (57–58). His elegy, too, foretells Tiananmen and its official erasure.

From this episode emerges the novel's first allusion to its Chinese title—*Routu,* "flesh earth" or "meat soil." As Dai Wei is departing Guangxi, he stumbles onto a crowd of foreign tourists happily pouring out of a bus. In this moment he has a ghastly epiphanic vision: "They put on multicoloured sun hats and smiled as they stood waiting for their photographs to be taken in front of the scenic backdrop. I wanted to tell them to run away, because the bodies of 100,000 massacred people were buried under their feet. They had no idea that China was a vast graveyard" (60). Dai Wei may be referring to Guilin's Elephant Trunk Hill in this passage, but the "scenic backdrop" cannot but proleptically evoke Tiananmen Square, where foreign tourists will likewise beam to flashing cameras at the whitewashed site of another state-directed carnage. Henceforth in the text, Guangxi's "vast graveyard"—an echo of Zheng Yi's "scarlet memorial covered with human blood" (21)—will become Ma's traveling signifier. As his title metaphor, the "flesh earth" first actualized by the Cultural Revolution will come to encompass all the moments of atrocity in PRC history which cannot be erased or buried adequately. It will surface again and again until it converges with the Tiananmen image of tanks flattening human bodies into the ground, an image Ma will hauntingly capture at the novel's end. But in this first textual detour from Beijing, the specter of the Square already appears outside of its space, ahead of its time. Zheng Yi too has made a similar point about Guangxi cannibalism as a national allegory: "Is Guangxi only Guangxi? Do those cannibals only number a few thousand? No! Guangxi is not only Guangxi. Guangxi is China! The cannibals were not merely individual cannibals, they were and they are our entire nation!" (119).

If Ma's novel presents the discourse of life and health on a crudely generic level in the Cultural Revolution's instances of actual cannibalism, it reverses this relation between real and metaphoric, the rhetoric of life and the politics of death, for the Deng Xiaoping era of economic liberalization. A few months after his Guangxi trip and return to university life in Guangzhou, Dai Wei marvels at the liberties afforded by capitalism:

> I thought back to my interrogation in the police station in 1982, and realized how much society had changed. Back then, you could get arrested for copying out a book that contained a few erotic passages. But now, just two years on, pornographic films were being shown in privately run video rooms on every street corner. . . . Students from Hong Kong and Macao could afford to rent rooms in the town, which gave them more privacy. When you have money, you have freedom. The government had recently announced that in the Special Economic Zone of Shenzhen, citizens were allowed to buy their flats. Private ownership had reared its head at last in Communist China. (62–63)

Dai Wei's assessment of social life in mid-1980s China seems to mimic a common view at the time, advanced by Deng himself, that freedom for the Chinese is economic, not political. Indeed, Dai Wei's belief that "when you have money, you have freedom" expresses just such a sentiment. Ma, though, is quick to undercut this argument.

In the scene immediately following the Guangxi episode, in the novel's only depiction of the classroom space, Ma raises again the apparition of the cannibal:

> On 1 October every year, prisoners on death row were executed in celebration of National Day. With the improvement of surgical skills and the liberalisation of the Chinese economy, any patient with enough money could now purchase themselves the organs of execut-ed prisoners. The organs of the corpse that was delivered to us that morning had been used for China's first successful heart-lung trans-plant. There had been an article about the operation in the newspaper the previous day, and now the heart and lungs were working away in-side the body of a Hong Kong businessman.
>
> We walked into the dissection lab. The room was stuffy and smelt of formalin.
>
> Professor Huang was a celebrated cardiovascular specialist. The successful heart transplants he performed were often reported by the press. His lectures were fascinating. Even the most squeamish of stu-dents would stay to the end. . . .
>
> "Last year's Ministry of Health guidelines allowed surgical opera-tions to be carried out in ambulances parked outside the execution grounds. But the success rate of the operations was low. The demand for organs has risen recently, especially from foreign patients who can pay in foreign currency, which is good for our economy. So to improve efficiency and meet demand, the government has now per-mitted executions to be carried out in the hospital where the organ transplant will be performed." (63–64)

While cannibalism during the Cultural Revolution was presented, with none of its horror muted, as brutal mass murder imposed by Party policy, it is seen to persist in a new permutation under Deng's rule—organ har-vesting. As such, cannibalism is not so much concealed as banalized, and whatever was demonstrably demonic about the cannibal disappears from view. Instead, the cannibal gets a facelift: the blood-mouthed peasant who stashes away Director Liu's liver for years to gnaw on as a medicinal tonic gives way to the wealthy urban businessman who can incorporate, without ever tainting his hands or conscience, the hearts and lungs of prisoners executed by the state's firing squad. The question of what crimes these prisoners committed, whether they were being punished for a social and moral offense such as homicide or a political one such as pro-democracy activism, is not asked, so long as the results promote the national economy. In Ma's acerbic portrait of Deng-era China, so-called liberalization and reform are exposed to be skin-deep, masking an overall biopolitical system that remains constant. The bodies of social and political offenders are still literally redistributed among and internalized by state-endorsed subjects for the maintenance of sociopolitical stability, and participation in this process still represents a way for individuals to locally produce themselves as loyal national subjects. Rather than politicizing life through actual cannibalism as on the Guangxi farm, however, the state's biopower has become diffuse, sinking beneath the surface of social practices. In its modernized, normalized incarnation, it operates not through biopolitical cannibalism but a network of cannibalistic biopolitics. Henceforth, social cannibalism will be ever less recognizable as such, receding as a metaphor for the primitive as medical discourses of organic life and public health become ever more sophisticated, techniques refined, procedures civilized. Organs are now meticulously transplanted rather than arbitrarily or fanatically consumed; peasant superstition is replaced by clinical expertise, local revolutionary committees by the Ministry of Health; and the messy "vast graveyard" of political purges contracts into the ordered, contained spaces of the execution ground and the hospital operation room. In this reconfigured biopolitical order, intermediate agents of state biopower multiply, not inside the Party machinery, but in the emerging ranks of middle-class professionals. The university as much as the hospital risks serving as not just alibi but instrument to the state's executions, since students and doctors alike, no longer labeled bourgeois or rightist, now have the Party's encouragement and society's blessing to train themselves in the science of life for the progress and profit of the nation. Perhaps, without Tiananmen, Dai Wei and his fellow students would have grown into another generation of Professor Huangs, uncritical pragmatists who face questions of medical ethics only with utilitarian interest: "Wouldn't it be a waste to cremate a corpse without making use of its organs first?" (65). On Ma's handling, this sterilized room of the university dissection lab, ostensibly so far from the Square's scene of bloodbath, nonetheless encapsulates the everyday mechanics of the same cannibalistic biopolitics.

Ma's suggestion here of the communist government's exploitation of prisoners' bodies for profit is no less grounded in documentary reports than his earlier episode of cannibalism on the Guangxi farm. Just as he integrates Zheng Yi's research on Cultural Revolution cannibalism into his Tiananmen narrative, so he invokes Harry Wu's work on organ harvesting in China's labor reform camps (*laogai*) as part of the massacre's more recent biopolitical prehistory. Wu, a political prisoner for nineteen years in twelve different labor camps before leaving China after his release in 1979, has been one of the most vocal diaspora critics of the PRC's state-sponsored organ-trading programs. In recent testimony to the Hawaii State Senate, he describes the circuit of profit between China's penal system and its human organ trafficking, where the government gains from multiplying executions and prisoners' bodies are reduced to a supply of ready cash crop:

> In China, there are currently 68 capital offenses, including non-violent crimes and political crimes. With throngs of poor economic migrants traveling from the Chinese countryside to its cities each year, and China's public security agencies responding to the resulting increases in crime with so-called "strike hard" (*yanda*) campaigns, the number of prisoners on China's death row has been immense. While the exact number of executions carried out each year is closely guarded as a State secret, several human rights groups estimate the annual figures to be in the thousands, more than all the other nations in the world combined. . . . Still, the Chinese continued to deny these allegations until confirmation finally came in 2006, when China's Vice-Minister of Health, Mr. Huang Jiefu, publicly admitted that more than 95% of the organs used in medical transplants in the country come from executed prisoners. Such an assertion is astounding, considering that China is now second only to the U.S. in the number of transplants performed each year. (1–2)

And in terms that hauntingly echo *Beijing Coma*'s depiction of medicine's complicity in the organ trade, Wu reports:

> In recent years, China has switched from executing prisoners with a bullet in the back of the head to using lethal injection, a method that facilitates the extraction of organs by medical personnel after death. My investigations, dating back to the early 1990's, have shown that Chinese hospitals regularly broker deals to supply privileged Chinese and foreign citizens with needed organs harvested from executed Chinese prisoners. . . . It is completely ordinary in China for an ambulance to be standing by at the site of an execution, with medical personnel ready to quickly remove needed organs and hurry them off to the waiting hospital. (2)

Most chilling of all is Wu's personal interview with a doctor who took part in a surgery in which two kidneys were removed from a living anesthetized prisoner before he was executed the next morning. As Wu comments, "Obviously, taking two kidneys from a person is tantamount to execution"

(*Troublemaker* 151). This case—"modern Chinese science at work," in Wu's wry phrase (148)—exemplifies the sovereign power of a network of state agents over the biological life of prisoners. By incorporating this newest manifestation of the state's cannibalistic biopolitics into his novel—an issue that, to be sure, has become a hotbed of contention between the PRC and international human rights groups in recent years—Ma once again demonstrably locates his cultural politics within the human rights discourse of dissident activists. Where Gao Xingjian purges himself of these dissident and diasporic affiliations, Ma synthesizes them. And he would likely agree with Nancy Scheper-Hughes's conclusion that organ transplantation "requires a reasonably democratic state in which basic human rights are guaranteed" (210). Organ harvesting, then, serves as a key node for him to link the June 4 massacre with the ongoing violations of human rights in post-Tiananmen China.

That the pre-Tiananmen decade of Deng-style economic liberalization, despite its superficial benefits and freedoms, stays entirely within the communist state's biopolitical regime is brought home by Ma's portrayal of the post-massacre years, particularly through the metaphor of Dai Wei's "comatose" body. Technically, Dai Wei is no longer in a coma at the time of his narration, since his mind has been reawakened and his memory now functions with extraordinary precision. His body, however, remains immobilized, stuck as it were in the time of the Square. (This is one instance in which Chinese and English do not have an easy linguistic correspondence, since the Chinese term for Dai Wei, *zhiwuren*, describes a physical condition and translates literally as "plant human," the rather indelicate English correlative being "human vegetable." On the other hand, the Chinese term for "coma," *hunmi*, suggests a state of unconsciousness contradictory to Dai Wei's mental vitality and perceptive acuity. A more accurate English term for Dai Wei may be "alert coma," the rare condition in which a coma patient exhibits some degree of sensory awareness. Still, linguistic and medical accuracy aside, we can appreciate how the English title felicitously foregrounds Dai Wei's peculiar state as a central trope for the novel.) With this mind-body split, Ma's *zhiwuren* comes to symbolize two sets of meanings. In post-Tiananmen China, where material evidence of the massacre has been largely obliterated, Dai Wei's body is a remnant, the massacre's sole preserved ruin and living tomb, its reluctant monument. At the same time, as Beijing residents and even student activists who witnessed the bloodshed collectively will themselves into political forgetfulness by plunging into the accelerated capitalism of the 1990s, Dai Wei's consciousness memorializes the event that has no memorial. His mind thus likewise anchors itself in the Square, which serves as the pivot to his reviving consciousness's compass.

Elsewhere, Ma repeatedly discusses the predicament and challenge of China's Tiananmen amnesia. In one recent interview, he comments: "The Chinese people have been forced to forget the Tiananmen massacre. . . . [They] are not aware of their own entrapment. They believe they live in a free society, but don't realize how much they are being monitored and controlled, how much the information they receive is restricted and warped, until they step out of line, that is, and feel the heavy hand of the state fall on them. Then they discover that the rights granted to them by the constitution are meaningless, and that the freedoms are a sham" ("China's Olympic"). In another article, he writes:

> Blinded by fear and bloated by prosperity, they have succumbed to a collective amnesia. . . . There is an expression in Chinese that says, "One can only stand up from the place where one fell." If China is to truly stand up and deserve its powerful position in the international community, it must return to the place where it fell. The regime must reveal the truth about past crackdowns and apologize to the victims and their families; release the hundred or so people still jailed for their connection to the Tiananmen movement, and the tens of thousands of other political prisoners languishing in jails and labor camps. And it must introduce democratic reforms. ("China's Grief")

For Ma Jian as much as Dai Wei, Tiananmen represents the moment when life divided, splintered. While the rest of the population becomes mercenary zombies, "*zhiwuren* that only know how to make money," Dai Wei embodies "the *zhiwuren* living within memory who is ultimately the only person alive" (qtd. in Zeng). As Dai Wei muses about his ironic condition at one point: "In this police state, I've managed to gain freedom of thought by pretending to be dead. My muteness is a protective cloak. . . . Do I really want to wake from this deep sleep and rejoin the comatose crowds outside?" (514–15). This situation of a comatose country blindly hurling itself forward on the tracks of development, Ma warns, signals "not merely a political crisis but also an ethical one": "The tanks of June 4 did not simply crush the students' bodies but also flattened the Chinese people's soul, making dim and confused their very conception of value" (qtd. in Zeng). Remembering Tiananmen thus stands as the absolute index to China's ethical future, the point at which cleft life may be reintegrated, the ethical spirit reanimated.

Meanwhile, though, life can only be sustained in partial or crippled form, as paralytic memory or mindless, robotic motion. Where Ha Jin uses the metaphor of the cocoon to suggest a kind of stagnant, suffocating worm life for pre-Tiananmen intellectuals like Professor Yang, Ma Jian appropriates the trope of dehumanized life but endows his post-Tiananmen student activist with even less mobility in the *zhiwuren*'s vegetable life. And where Tiananmen prompts flight to freedom and optimistically inaugurates diasporic afterlife for Jin's Jian and possibly for Wang's Lili, Ma's Dai Wei, by entombing the Square, marks the point at which diasporization fails. Indeed, if it has become a commonplace to observe of 1990s capitalist China, as for example Orville Schell does in his portrait of Wuer Kaixi, that "history always moves on" (440), Ma writes precisely the countertext to this image of inevitable progress. His is primarily a narrative of history's failure to move or move on, to diasporize, and of the struggle to live by those who remain, whether voluntarily or not, in the memorial space of the Square. Of all the Tiananmen fictions, Ma's is the only one to fully engage with this problem of survival in the symbolic space of the post-massacre Square.

It is from this perspective that we may understand *Beijing Coma* as distilling an alternative narrative of modern China, via not its political or socioeconomic or cultural history but its biopolitics. This biopolitical history, rarely isolated as a discrete narrative by either historians or writers, unfolds through Ma's novel as a thread that runs steadily through the PRC decades, notwithstanding changes in Party leadership, social structure, and economic policy. What his text exhorts us to witness, above all, is the continuity of the state's cannibalistic biopolitics even in the post-Tiananmen era of prosperity. Hence, just as the novel reenacts cannibalism from the Cultural Revolution in the altered form of medicalized executions during Deng's period, so it resurrects the criminal's cadaver from the dissection lab in the form of Dai Wei's comatose body. Superimposed onto Dai Wei's iron bed now is the past biopolitics of the village farm, the execution ground, the urban hospital, and Tiananmen Square itself—at the heart of each lies an immobilized body whose threshold of life and death is almost entirely determined by the state. Nor does this regime of biopower end with the 1989 crackdown or the 1990s' rise in socioeconomic freedoms. Again, Dai Wei's body functions optimally as an argumentative vehicle for Ma, for it is in relation to this Tiananmen body that he can lay bare most forcefully the state's intervention on the sustenance of life and the maintenance of death. This post-Tiananmen plot comes increasingly to the fore in the novel's second half, in the parallel narrative of Dai Wei's mother, Huizhen.

In the dozen or so years after June 4, Huizhen seeks out every avenue to keep her son's body alive and to wake him from his coma. Her efforts, though, are repeatedly thwarted by a now subtle yet sweeping network of state biopolitical control. Hospitals are forbidden to treat Tiananmen victims, and private doctors must be paid on the sly. Crematoriums are forbidden to keep the ashes of the Tiananmen dead, cemeteries to bury their bodies. But if, "in contravention of guidelines," some families succeed in burying their dead, the police place them under house arrest every Grave Sweeping Festival and June 4 anniversary to prevent any public display of mourning. Even insurance companies are forbidden to pay compensation to Tiananmen victims, leading Huizhen to bemoan despairingly, "What kind of country is it that punishes the victims of a massacre, rather than the people who fired the shots?" (178). Through this tightly controlled system that laces through institutions of health and finance as much as those of law, the state effectively foils every private effort at sustaining the biological and historical life of Tiananmen participants—even as it forces privatization by erasing all public records of the massacre and obliging families to confine the casualties, alive and dead, to their own homes, to domestic altars, coffins, beds. This is at once a biopolitics and a thanatopolitics. That these two structures become continuous to the point of indistinguishability marks Tiananmen as the principal symptomatic instance of what Giorgio Agamben would call "the biopolitical paradigm of the modern" (117).

In this post-Tiananmen capitalist period, state cannibalism is revived in its most unrecognizable form yet as black-market organ trading. Caught between Dai Wei's body and the state's biopower, the financial demands of preserving his life and the impossibility of obtaining government aid, Huizhen sets up a private urine bank out of Dai Wei's bedroom, selling his glucose-enhanced urine as a tonic to the occult-minded and the desperately sick (424–29). Although this episode of ingenious entrepreneurship has its comic elements and may even bespeak a kind of prevailing laissez-faire attitude toward private ventures, we learn that the urine bank is shut down by the authorities soon after its promising beginnings. More eerily, lurking behind the quaint and motley crew of urine consumers are the specters of the village cannibal and the corporate transplant patient. The latter figure is evoked with special pointedness in an ensuing and bleaker episode, in which folk magic bleeds into modern medicine: Huizhen, depleted once again by the costs of caring for Dai Wei's body, resorts to selling one of his kidneys to a wealthy colliery boss. In this latter-day marketplace of human organs, the communist state, far from interfering with Huizhen's private dealings, transforms instead into her commercial competitor. To secure the highest price for Dai Wei's kidney, Huizhen must time her sale in order not to overlap with the spate of public executions on National Day or the Spring Festival and their attendant organ glut. This new circumstance of biocapitalism may be the most efficient method of political control yet, since the dissident life now exists only in the accumulated value of its bodily fluids and organs. Like Dai Wei, it will wish for nothing more than to die on the operation table (456).

THE UBIQUITOUS SQUARE, THE NEOMORT'S TIME

We may be tempted to conclude here that the Tiananmen massacre represents a rupture, rather than a culmination, of communist China's biopolitical history as written by Ma. After all, if the Cultural Revolution's biopolitics operates through the feverish hands of peasants and the Deng-era one through the scalpels of celebrity surgeons, in neither scenario does the state exert its power from the barrel of a gun. Only in the Tiananmen moment does the system of everyday biopolitical control lapse and discourses of national life fail to produce state agents out of ordinary citizens; only in the Square do real soldiers need to be marshaled, tanks mobilized. It would seem, moreover, that "normal" biopolitics resumes after the crackdown, with pre-Tiananmen liberalization intensified as full-throttle hypercapitalism post–June 4. From the perspective of technique, of means, this conclusion would appear valid.

From the perspective of ends, of the fundamental hierarchy of political power, however, we see in Ma's theme of an ever-metamorphosing cannibalism precisely the endurance of a constant biopolitical order. Indeed, one of the most far-reaching propositions of his novel is that Tiananmen is not a historical exception but the starkest manifestation of a biopolitical norm for the PRC. Where Tiananmen represents a pivotal and inaugural point of diasporization for Ha Jin, it is by contrast the exception that has become the rule for Ma Jian. The picture of Tiananmen Ma captures is akin to a photograph developed from three superimposed negatives: (1) the Foucauldian theory of modern biopower and its micromechanics in everyday life; (2) the Benjaminian eighth thesis on the philosophy of history that "the tradition of the oppressed teaches us that the 'state of emergency' in which we live is not the exception but the rule" ("Theses" 257); and (3) Agamben's merging and escalation of the preceding two theses in his claim that "the camp, which is now securely lodged within the city's interior, is the new biopolitical *nomos* of the planet" (*Homo* 176). Already in the Guangxi episode, Ma behooves the reader to ask the very question Agamben raises:

> What happened in the camps so exceeds the juridical concept of crime that the specific juridico-political structure in which those events took place is often simply omitted from consideration. . . . Instead of deducing the definition of the camp from the events that took place there, we will ask: What is a camp, and what is its juridico-political structure, that such events could take place there? This will lead us to regard the camp not as a historical fact and an anomaly belonging to the past (even if still verifiable) but in some way as the

hidden matrix and *nomos* of the political space in which we are still living. (*Homo* 166)

In answer to this question, Agamben proposes that the camp is "the space that is opened when the state of exception begins to become the rule" (*Homo* 168–69). What characterizes Western modernity for Agamben is that the state of exception—"a zone of indistinction between outside and inside, chaos and the normal situation," and historically actualized only in extraordinary circumstances such as "martial law and the state of siege"—is no longer "unlocalizable" in theory alone but has become so in practice (*Homo* 19–20).

In Ma's novel, Agamben's model finds its nationally specific materialization in the ubiquitous Square. Ominously if dimly foreshadowed by the Guangxi farm and the dissection lab before the massacre, the Square proliferates in its images from the time of the demonstrations onward and succeeds the "vast graveyard" of the Cultural Revolution as the text's central metaphor. As Mou Sen, one of the more prescient student leaders in the novel (and the fictional counterpart of Zhang Boli), observes to Dai Wei early on: "But since we entered the Square, it's been impossible to step back. There are no escape routes. We're trapped here, in the spotlight" (357). And a bit later: "There's nowhere to hide in this country. Every home is as exposed as a public square, watched over by the police day and night" (375). Mou Sen's initial vision of the Square as an island prison, isolated but distinct, might yet imply a relation to normality through the idea of a delimited penal site. But his next vision of an all-pervasive prison over China—where "every home is as exposed as a public square" and no inside or outside space is imaginable—definitively signals the arrival of Agamben's camp. This camp may find its most visible manifestation in the physical space of the Square, but really, Mou Sen suggests, there is nowhere that is not symbolically the Square, nowhere that is not biopolitically suspended within a state of emergency. All of national life has been seized by exceptionality, all lives have become bare life. This iconic magnification of the Square is Ma's clearest deployment of a national allegory.

Trapped in the Square under martial law, other students will begin to echo Mou Sen's words, but it is Huizhen who, years later, will come to grasp his insight most fully. It is she who utters the resonant line: "China is one huge prison. Whether we're in a jail or in our homes, every one of us is a prisoner!" (511). Two post-Tiananmen events trigger this realization for her—the Falun Gong crackdown and the Beijing Olympics bid. At the heart of each, Ma places Huizhen as the most ordinary and accidental victim of state biopower. Unlike Dai Wei, she is a lifelong devout believer in and defender of the Communist Party, a pragmatic woman who fiercely protects her own family and scorns dissident activism. In the wake of Tiananmen, as a single elderly mother of a *zhiwuren* son, she becomes an avid practitioner of Falun Gong out of a need for spiritual comfort and communal support. Her fiery remark about the prison-house of China is directed at two police officers sent to investigate her involvement in the movement, and up to this point, the ever-high-tempered Huizhen feels brazen enough yet to openly scoff at the idea of a government clampdown. Her remark is prophetic, however, and in the ensuing large-scale manhunt, she is arrested. At the detention center she is beaten with electric batons, forced to renounce Falun Gong, and in exchange for her release so that she may return home to care for Dai Wei, driven to betray her Falun Gong friends. In the days that follow, we witness her descent into paranoia: "She often paces nervously around the flat, especially late at night. Sometimes she stands at the window and gazes out, listening to the distant roar of machinery as buildings are demolished or constructed, and mumbles, 'They'll be here any minute. They're coming to arrest us. It won't be long now . . .'" (525). Her home becomes increasingly stifling, imprisoning, with Dai Wei's bedroom turning into the central repository of trash within the larger rubbish heap of her apartment: "My mother hasn't thrown anything out of the flat for years, so she has trouble finding things. I imagine the flat is so crammed now that there isn't much room to stand. . . . She is continually changing our locks, but forgets to throw away the old keys, so they stay on the same ring with the new ones. . . . When she can't find space in the sitting room for something, she'll toss it into my room. The empty milk cartons, pill bottles and food packaging she's flung under my bed have attracted colonies of ants" (545). This self-imposed lockup is also a self-created shelter, for the only space outside of the general prison-house now is that of one's own making. With Kafkaesque humor, Ma paints Dai Wei as a Gregor Samsa figure, his room, like his body, "a corpse that's rotting from within" (564). But even this little private cell is not safe, for the state soon threatens with another intrusion. As part of Beijing's 2000 Olympics bid, Huizhen's compound is to be razed to make way for a giant shopping center. As one of her neighbors comments: "Listen, Auntie. You and I are just ordinary citizens. You can't refuse to move. Government officials will turn up here and squash you like a fly. And anyway, this demolition is important for our Olympic bid. If the old buildings aren't torn down, the new ones can't go up'" (535). Dai Wei then wryly notes: "So this building will become a public square. Ten years ago, I escaped from the nation's political center and retreated into my home. But soon my home will become a shopping center. Where can I retreat to then?" (536). In the name of the national good, and in the service of an event that touts international health and athleticism, the state exerts its sovereignty once again.

The symbolic Square, like Agamben's camp, has indeed lodged itself within the city's interior, not just in the smallest of domestic spaces but now in lieu of domestic space itself. In its latest incarnation of the mega shopping center, where modes of consumption will appear ever more remote from political struggle, the Square will be hardly identifiable as such. Yet Ma obliges exactly this identification, this witnessing. The final pages of the novel thus juxtapose two times, two scenes: that of the tanks rolling into Tiananmen Square on June 4, and that of the bulldozers rolling toward Huizhen's apartment on the eve of the new millennium. The crisis of livelihood, shelter, and life itself is no less jeopardized, but the elaborate emergency measures of old—like the declaration of martial law in 1989—can now be made utterly simple by the neocapitalist agenda of urban development as an eviction notice. Tanks are replaced by bulldozers, guns by construction equipments. Minor characters from Dai Wei's past resurface as the new agents of state biopower. Lulu, his childhood neighbor and first love interest, turns out to be the absentee landlady and chairwoman of the Hong Kong developing company in charge of the demolition of the apartments and the building of the shopping center. And while corporate heads like her can remain offstage in Dai Wei's ground-zero narrative, we are given a glimpse of the migrant workers deployed for the job, including one called the Drifter, a homeless man whom Dai Wei and his university dorm mates had charitably sheltered in the pre-Tiananmen years. In this 1990s era, then, state predation on the weak is no longer personified by Party cadres with overt political power but by former neighbors, lovers, and beneficiaries, all co-opted into the new ideology of business profits and annual bonuses. We are thrust back to the Cultural Revolution's Guangxi farm, with fellow villagers eagerly cannibalizing each other within a sanctioned sociopolitical order, but in ever more sanitized and normalized forms. It can be as clean as flipping a switch or two. As one neighbor tells Huizhen: "It's not like the old days. The government won't forcibly evict you. But think things through. If you stay here over the winter, how will you survive without water, electricity or heating?" (563).

Just as Dai Wei remains as the last relic of the massacre, so Huizhen stands as the last resident refusing to vacate her apartment. In another heated exchange, she now confronts relocation officers, another new set of agents of state biopower: "You businessmen are colluding with the government to oppress us ordinary citizens. But I'm not afraid of you! Go ahead and build your shopping centre, your public square, your Bird's Nest stadium, but don't push me out of my little nest!" (568). Despite her protests, though, the way to the Beijing Olympics will be paved over her flat, the national Bird's Nest stadium over the private "bird's nest" of her home. If Gaston Bachelard dreams of the nest as a primal image of intimacy, the "absolute refuge" of an "oneiric house" and a "first home" (103), here we encounter not simply the destruction of the experience of intimacy but the annihilation of a whole phenomenology of domestic space. The construction site outside Huizhen's building progressively evokes the zone surrounding Tiananmen Square, with "bulldozers everywhere and mountains of debris" (558), until her apartment is the only one left unrazed, she the only occupant not squeezed out:

> The bulldozer charges into the building like an army tank, making our walls shake and our floor-beams tremble and crack. It moves back, its tracks screeching over shattered glass and planks of wood. Beside it, a digger is shovelling broken tiles and metal frames into an open-back truck. The bulldozer rams again and our walls shudder. . . .
>
> My mother roars like an angry tigress. "This is my home! You Fascists! If you come any nearer, I will jump!" . . .
>
> The covered balcony and most of the outer walls and windows of the rest of the flat have fallen down. All the flats of our left and right have been demolished, as have the stairwell and landing behind us. Our flat is now no more than a windy corridor. It's like a bird's nest hanging in a tree. I can feel it shaking in the wind. (578–79)

By now, Ma's image of Huizhen is almost mythic. Not just a crazed widow, she is the Tiananmen Mother, a biopoliticized solitary figure blocking the path of bulldozers for the sake of her victimized son as much as her sheer tenacity of will to live. This image certainly does much to offset Ha Jin's disturbingly maternalized metaphor, in the closing pages of *The Crazed*, of China as "an old bitch that eats her own puppies," "an old hag so decrepit and brainsick that she would devour her children to sustain herself" (315). Aside from degendering Jin's trope of China's social cannibalism, Ma's heroic portrait of Huizhen also pointedly recalls another historical image: the Tank Man. For Huizhen is no Ding Zilin: she has neither the material resources nor the international cultural capital of the real-life founder of the Tiananmen Mothers organization. Unknown to and unprotected by the world, Huizhen is more akin to the anonymous and defenseless Tank Man, but now feminized. While we remain to this day ignorant of the Tank Man's fate, Ma informs us of Huizhen's, which tragically mirrors her son's. In her last scene in the novel, we see her half-deranged, possibly stroke-stricken and becoming a "vegetable" herself, muttering confusedly: "I want to go to the Square. I want to go on a hunger strike . . ." (583). The irony of this belated nostalgic invocation of Tiananmen biopolitics is made more terrible by our realization that, in the face of bulldozers and corporate developers, a hunger strike will be nothing more than an obsolete technique. That the hunger strike was a viable and efficacious form of protest in 1989 indicates that, inside the Square, there was still a general faith in a biopolitical contract between the state and its subjects, a common belief in the government's political responsibility toward the biological life of citizens when they exhibit it as pure sacrifice. For all that it symbolizes the place of massacre and encapsulates the negative limit-point of state biopower, the Square simultaneously delimits the space of an utopian biopolity. This is perhaps why Ma refuses to abandon the imagination of this space. This is also why he would have Huizhen recall for us, in the epochal threshold of the millennium's turning in the novel's final pages, the hunger strike. What he fears above all is not the Square's actual ubiquity but the permanent vanishing of its ideal potential—as a community of mutual biopolitical responsibility. But this vanishing is what we are menaced with in his vision of China in its contemporary moment, in the neocapitalist order of scattered agency and remote, invisible biopower.

By the novel's end, Huizhen's body is removed from the site of demolition, possibly transferred to a hospital or a sanitarium, so that, unlike the bodies of some Tiananmen students, hers is not directly crushed into the "flesh earth." Dai Wei's body, on the other hand, is abandoned to the bulldozers. Like the mysterious Tank Man, his fate remains undisclosed to us, wavering between death and miracle. In this sense, he epitomizes the bare life of Agamben's *homo sacer*, an utterly exposed life that may be killed with impunity by anyone, with everyone his sovereign. Unlike the students in the Square, whose life may perhaps be seen as a modern form of political sacrifice, a sacred offering of themselves to state power for the purpose of inciting revolutionary consciousness in the people, Dai Wei's killing may be deemed sacrificial only within the perimeters of a spectacular burlesque. Where the Tiananmen students had the army as their executioners and the world's cameras as their witnesses, Dai Wei has two or three migrant laborers, the Drifter among them, as onlookers to his deathbed scene—a chorus of fools in a most unheroic tragedy. Ma highlights this quality of burlesque in the only dialogue to take place at the apartment's demolition site: to Huizhen's "You Fascists!" one of the laborers turns puzzlingly to another with, "What does 'Fascist' mean?" To which the other responds, "Are you stupid? *Fa-shi-si*: It means 'punish-you-with-death.'" The first then hurls back at Huizhen, "Punish-you-with-death, old lady!" (579). There is even less dignity, albeit higher tragicomic spirit, granted Dai Wei's death than that of the cadaver on the operation table. What the new capitalism renders obsolete, then, is not only the hunger strike as biopolitical technique but sacrifice as a category of biopolitical control and protest. Henceforth, biopower will play its hand on the stage, not of revolutionary tragedy, but of vaudeville.

In his analysis of the modern avatars of *homo sacer*, Agamben identifies one called the "neomort." Attributing the term to Willard Gaylin's 1974 article on organ harvesting, Agamben defines it as a body that has the "legal status of corpses but would maintain some of the characteristics of life for the sake of possible future transplants." The neomort, like the comatose patient who is kept alive solely through life-support technology, exemplifies a modern biopolitics in which sovereign power comes increasingly to occupy the medical and biological sciences: "The hospital room in which the neomort, the overcomatose person, and the *faux vivant* waver between life and death delimits a space of exception in which a purely bare life, entirely controlled by man and his technology, appears for the first time" (*Homo* 164). We may realize here that what Ma suggests through Dai Wei's *zhiwuren* condition is a haunting portrait of Tiananmen's neomortic afterlife, as "purely bare life" caught in the nexus of state thanatopolitics, biomedical technology, and—the term which Agamben never adequately accounts for—global capital. This is a far cry from the exit strategies variously adopted by Gao Xingjian, Ha Jin, and Annie Wang in their Tiananmen narratives. Rather than routing the massacre's end toward existential death or catapulting the survivor toward diasporic or domestic revival, the neomort's life in the ever-expanding space of the massacre necessitates a different form from mere closure. And it entails a different time.

The neomort's time, like Benjamin's messianic instants, is aporetic, monadic. The neomort's death does not follow the linear clock of the diminishing body but belongs to another order of time altogether, one that unravels over the historical fate of bare life as such. Hence, Dai Wei's epiphanic self-dirge at the novel's end is at once belated and premature, too late for animated life's cessation but too early for its decay, suspended between paralysis and rot. "I see a public square," says Dai Wei in his final narrated paragraph. "It's a flattened expanse of broken bricks, shattered tiles, sand, dust and earth. Positioned at its centre is not a memorial, but me and my iron bed, lying inside this building that's been carved away like a pear eaten to its core" (585). In this ultimate vision—a vision that cannot be properly labeled "dying" in the usual sense, since its finality derives not from organic failure but epochal crisis and hence flashes up brilliantly rather than dimly flickers—Tiananmen reemerges once again. Not only is the besieged Square superimposed onto the home's iron bed and the neomort's inert body, but time itself is arrested, the intervening years emptied. That the actual massacre happened in 1989 does not mean, Ma intimates, that the tanks ever left the Square. On the contrary, a decade later, the Square is everywhere—except now bulldozers replace tanks, migrant laborers do the dirty work of army soldiers, and former neighbors turned entrepreneurs rather than Party hard-liners give the order for destruction.

The instant this vision dies and the last neomortic body gets pulverized will be the instant of decisive victory for this epoch's sovereign power.

In Ma's simile, Dai Wei's life on this cusp of impending obliteration and the new millennium is "like a bird's nest that's fallen to the ground" (585). This language summons again not just the Olympic stadium but Ma's proverbial comparison of Tiananmen to the fallen place where China must pick itself up: "If China is to truly stand up and deserve its powerful position in the international community, it must return to the place where it fell" ("China's Grief"). Here we come to grasp Ma's role as Benjamin's historical materialist par excellence. His broad biopolitical history of China aims at once toward a representational totality and a negative philosophy. As historical fiction, the novel approaches history not as data but evidence, and not of civilization's apotheoses but its barbarisms. As a counternarrative to the official discourse of national progress, the novel employs temporal as much as spatial structures of distortion and lapse to disrupt the sense of historical accumulation. Thus, just as the Square swells, loses its boundaries, and comes to engulf the whole country and century in the text, in Tiananmen historical time also "falls," or in Benjamin's description, "stands still and has come to a stop" ("Theses" 262). But Beijing Coma's model of stopped time is not to be confused with that found in the mainland genre of scar literature or the retrospective fiction of the 1980s. It may be the case that these works similarly lament time's stalling in the Cultural Revolution decade, but for the most part they do so by implicitly validating the need for national progress, without maintaining the need to continually inhabit the time of the fall itself; for these works, the very possibility of writing the Cultural Revolution's misfortunes typically signals hard times' passing and the onset of a better era. Ma's Tiananmen time, however, corresponds to the Benjaminian notion of an omnipresent now, the "monad" that can comprise an "entire history." As such, Tiananmen is not simply a tough period to be survived and surpassed or an isolated trauma to be remembered so as to be laid psychically to rest. Nothing lies so far from a sanguine attitude of survival and recovery as Ma's acknowledgment of an inescapable lingering. Yet, too, like Benjamin's time of the now, Ma wants to claim for Tiananmen's persistently arrested time a promise of futurity, a potential for "a revolutionary chance in the fight for the oppressed past" that is "shot through with chips of Messianic time" (Benjamin, "Theses" 263). Tiananmen time is hence both fallen and messianic: the student movement's collapse and the country's resuscitation will happen in the same instant, with Dai Wei its time capsule. Meanwhile, the in-between years of national prosperity—from the 1990s economic boom to the promise of a 2000 Beijing Olympics to the time of the novel's now, the moment around the 2008 Olympic Games that is alluded to anachronistically through Ma's images of the bird's nest—these years unfold in a "homogeneous, empty time" that only masks the ruins of communist history. Rather than progress, the angel of history presiding over *Beijing Coma*, like Benjamin's, sees "one single catastrophe which keeps piling wreckage upon wreckage." And though he, too, like Dai Wei, "would like to stay, awaken the dead, and make whole what has been smashed" ("Theses" 257–58), the bulldozers are closing in, the landscape of rising debris all too literal. For Ma, it is only by stopping here, by installing the Square's remnant in the center of the Olympics construction site and Tiananmen time in the interval of nation building, that we may come to see PRC biopower in the full light of comprehension. And this is not yet to imagine a biopolitical alternative.

Part II. Reclaiming Student Life and After

THE MASSACRE RECONSIDERED

Before we can imagine otherwise, however, we must return to the place and time of the massacre and abstract its historical significance anew. This at least seems to be Ma Jian's intimation, evident in his insistent focus on student life and especially his fictional reconstruction of the military crackdown. By the time of *Beijing Coma*'s English publication in 2008, historical assessment of Tiananmen has weathered several controversies. The debates splinter particularly over the fault line of the students' role in the massacre—whether a massacre indeed took place, who died in it, and who shared the blame. In the immediate aftermath of June 4, in the initial wave of international horror and sympathy, the prevailing view was that thousands of students heroically defended the Square to the last and that most of them were brutally slaughtered by the People's Liberation Army. This view, propagated by some eyewitness reports and suggestively supported by partial video footage taken by foreign camera crews, was subsequently reiterated by major world presses. For the general public in the West, it remains the standard understanding of the episode known as the "Tiananmen Square Massacre."

Three key testimonies at the time produced and sustained this version of events for world audiences. The first was a June 8 tape recording made by Chai Ling, high-profile student leader and one of the chief instigators of the hunger strike. "I think I am the most qualified person to comment on the events of June 4," she says on the recording. "In order to let the whole world know the truth, I have the responsibility to expose the whole course of the event" ("I'm" 266). Chai's account of the final evacuation from the Square mixes fact with insinuation to evoke a large-scale massacre:

Even at this time, some students still had faith in the government. They stayed, thinking that the army would at most arrest them. But who knew that tanks would run over them. Those students still sleeping in their tents were crushed into flesh pie. It was said that 200 people were killed. Others said 4000 people died in the square. At this point, it is still hard to have complete statistics of the death toll. . . . Later we were told that after the students left, tanks and armored personnel carriers crushed the tents. [The soldiers] then poured gasoline over the tents and cremated them together with the students' bodies. They then washed everything away with water. Those butchers! They wanted to cover up the truth of the massacre by leaving not a trace in the square. ("I'm" 268)

A second eyewitness statement that aligns well with Chai's narrative of butchery was the widely publicized account given by a putative twenty-year-old student from Qinghua University. Published first by the Hong Kong newspaper *Wen Wei Po* and later in translation by the *New York Times*, *Washington Post*, and *San Francisco Examiner*, this account describes in detail a final confrontation at the Monument of the People's Heroes between 4:40 and 5:00 a.m., when a swarm of PLA soldiers appeared at the top of the monument and began beating students down with electric cattle prods and rubber truncheons while another regiment of soldiers machine-gunned them from below. This widely circulated testimony quickly became a major source for other international reports on the massacre ("What").[2]

A third account that gained considerable international attention was put forward by John Simpson, renowned foreign affairs editor at the BBC and one of the "media stars of the Beijing spring" whose team later won a series of awards for its Tiananmen coverage (Black and Munro 247). In an oft-cited article in *Granta*, Simpson recounts how he and his crew witnessed and filmed the final massacre at the Monument of the People's Heroes from their hotel room:

We took up our position on the fourteenth floor of the Beijing Hotel. From there, everything seemed grey and distant. We saw most of what happened, but we were separated from the fear and the noise and the stench of it. We saw the troops pouring out of the Gate of Heavenly Peace, bayonets fixed, shooting first into the air and then straight ahead of them. They looked like automata, with their rounded dark helmets. We filmed them charging across and clearing the northern end of the Square. . . . We filmed the tanks as they drove over the tents where some of the students had taken refuge. . . . Dozens of people seem to have died in that way, and those who saw it said they could hear the screams of the people inside the tents over the noise of the tanks. We filmed as the lights in the Square were switched off at four a.m. They were switched on again forty minutes later, when the troops and the tanks moved towards the Monument itself, shooting first in the air and then, again, directly at the students themselves, so that the steps of the Monument and the heroic reliefs which decorated it were smashed by bullets. (23–24)

With histrionic bravado, Simpson prefaces this narrative with a declaration of remorse for having left the Square too early and not being present at ground zero during the massacre: "My colleagues and I wanted to save our pictures in case we were arrested, and I told the others that we should go back to the Beijing Hotel and come out again later. I now feel guilty about the decision; it was wrong: we ought to have stayed in the Square, even though the other camera crews had already left and it might have cost us our lives. Someone should have been there when the massacre took place, filming what happened, showing the courage of the students as they were surrounded by tanks and the army advancing, firing as it went" (23). Simpson's posture of personal responsibility and collective professional guilt does not necessarily augment the authenticity of his account, but it does buttress his moral authority as a conscientious and potentially self-sacrificing observer. Moreover, as some have pointed out, it strengthens the impression of a "student massacre without witnesses" (Black and Munro 247).[3]

A conflicting set of eyewitness and news reports, however, also emerged in the aftermath of June 4. Though initially eclipsed by more dramatic narratives of a bloodbath in the Square, they have since come to be regarded as providing a more accurate rendition of events, especially among historians and scholars. One chief spokesperson for this alternative view is Robin Munro, former director of the Hong Kong office of Human Rights Watch. By his own estimation, Munro was one of ten Western journalists in the vicinity of the Monument of the People's Heroes after 4:30 a.m. and, along with American journalist Richard Nations, the last foreigner to leave the Square, at about 6:15. In effect, contrary to Simpson's account, they composed the "someones" who stayed behind. According to Munro, those journalists who remained until the end, including a Spanish film crew that shot the only-known footage of the entire student evacuation, all submitted reports in line with his own: there was no mass killing in the Square during the final exodus. "A massacre did take place," Munro writes in a 1990 article in the *Nation*, "but not in Tiananmen Square, and not predominately of students" (811). He denounces the Qinghua student's testimony as "lurid invention" (820), and in a later work, he discredits Simpson's *Granta* story by noting that "the Monument and the entire lower half of Tiananmen Square are hidden from view from the Beijing Hotel, half a mile away" (Black and Munro 247), so that it would have been physically impossible for Simpson's team to observe what unfolded in the Square. Munro's narrative of a mostly bloodless retreat—aside from a few possible casualties when the tanks moved in to demolish the tents—accords not only with accounts by the foreign journalists he cites but also with those by a number of nonstudent evacuees, such as the Taiwanese rock star Hou Dejian, the novelist Lao Gui, and the People's University professor Yu Shuo, all of whom were among the last group to withdraw from the Square. Their testimonies, collected by Human Rights in China soon after the crackdown, also indicate there was no mass killing during the Square's evacuation (Human 158–79). Yi Mu, a Beijing journalist writing soon after June 4 in collaboration with Mark V. Thompson, likewise concludes: "It is generally believed that such a term as the 'Tiananmen Square Massacre' is not only inaccurate, but an exaggeration of what occurred. If by 'massacre' we mean large numbers of people being slaughtered, then the massacre took place along Changan Avenue, not in the square" (91). Finally, the volume *The Tiananmen Papers,* too, citing classified intelligence reports by the PRC State Security Ministry, upholds this account: "Yang Shangkun relayed Deng Xiaoping's instruction that in Tiananmen Square itself there must be no bloodshed. The government's internal reports claimed that this goal was achieved. Most of the deaths occurred as troops moved in from the western suburbs toward Tiananmen along Fuxingmenwai Boulevard at a location called Muxidi, where anxious soldiers reacted violently to popular anger. Troops moving on the Square negotiated a peaceful withdrawal of the people remaining there as dawn broke on June 4, but some killing of both citizens and soldiers continued during the morning hours" (Zhang L. 365).

Yet, despite this revisionist view, the phrase "Tiananmen Square Massacre," as George Black and Robin Munro point out several years after June 4, "is now fixed firmly in the political vocabulary of the late twentieth century"; it has become familiar "shorthand" for what happened in Beijing that spring (234). The inflated accounts of vicious carnage in the Square, though "all pure fabrication," have nonetheless become "enshrined in myth" (236). From the first, Munro has been a strong proponent for setting the record straight on "the geography of the killing." One recurring thrust in his argument is a recentering of critical attention away from student deaths, whether real or imagined, to the actual deaths of workers and ordinary citizens. In his *Nation* article, he underscores that the "great majority of those who died (perhaps as many as a thousand in all) were workers, or *laobaixing* ('common folk,' or 'old hundred names'), and they died mainly on the approach roads in western Beijing" rather than in the Square itself (811). Years later, he returns to this theme with even stronger emphasis: "To insist on this distinction is not splitting hairs. What took place was the slaughter not of students but of ordinary workers and residents—precisely the target that the Chinese government had intended" (Black and Munro 234). Black and Munro contend that the public's predisposition to believe in a student massacre, even one without convincing evidence, may be "the necessary consummation of an allegory of innocence, sacrifice, and redemption," a mythology that the students themselves skillfully cultivated through theatrics and rhetoric, but from the standpoint of historical understanding, one unfortunate consequence to the mythification of the students is a general neglectfulness of the "crucial role of the workers and the *laobaixing*" (235). On their final analysis, the students "were marginal to the threat" (237).

Certainly, this alternative view of Tiananmen carries with it more than just a geographical correction in the interest of what Munro calls the "unvarnished truth." It implicitly argues for a reappraisal of the movement and claims not only centrality for workers and citizens but also their higher place in the hierarchy of power and sacrifice—their greater potential threat to the Party's stability, their greater vulnerability to government force, and most of all, their greater suffering within the overall scheme of violence and persecution. In a sense, Munro makes a case for workers and citizens as the true *homo sacer* of Tiananmen, and this view of them as bearing the brunt of government attacks in 1989 has been variously echoed since (Calhoun x; Boren 218–20; Schell 156).[4] Munro himself is not disapproving of the students, and he makes a point of describing their withdrawal from the Square in sincerely admiring terms: "All looked shaken; many were trembling or unsteady on their feet. But all looked proud and unbeaten" (819–20). Yet one side effect of his argument on behalf of the *laobaixing* is that a growing number of commentators on Tiananmen, particularly in the West, have come to judge the students with moral harshness. By the mid-1990s, the initial image of the students as patriotic and brave noble youths, an image as much self-fashioned as externally constructed by the media, had become severely tarnished by a less flattering one of them as a protected and foolhardy elite that led the truly oppressed classes to their deaths. For these critics, most unforgiving perhaps is the fact, not always voiced explicitly, that those student leaders who cried the loudest for self-sacrifice lived, and lived on in relatively comfortable exile.

DIASPORIC IMAGE WARS

In the United States, the ensuing range of views on the student leaders can be gauged by two documentary films on Tiananmen, produced and released within a year of each other: Michael Apted's 1994 *Moving the Mountain* and Richard Gordon and Carma Hinton's 1995 *The Gate of Heavenly Peace*. As Orville Schell observes, these two films, by advancing competing images of the student movement, have helped to precipitate an image war over "which one is the right historical interpretation" (qtd. in Tyler). The first, based on Li Lu's ghostwritten memoir and narrated by him, offers an essentially favorable view of the former student leaders. Besides Li Lu himself, the film gathers together in a roundtable discussion Chai Ling, Wuer Kaixi, and Wang Chaohua. The film makes a point of incorporating several critical remarks by veteran activists such as Wei Jingsheng and John Sham: the former bluntly points out how the students as much as the government "behaved foolishly and acted out of selfishness," while the latter speaks more generously of the students as "just kids, kids who have heart for the country but who know very little about politics, who know very little about the art of staging a fight with the government." On the whole, though, these criticisms of the students' political inexperience and shortsightedness are overwhelmingly offset by the film's dominant tone of sympathy and admiration—sympathy for the students' idealism, admiration for their courage, and compassion toward their exilic homesickness. The film's final scenes portray the former students as nostalgic drifters in the United States, haunted by the massacre and condemning of the Communist Party, yet still wistful for the home country to which they can no longer return. In several wrenchingly emotional moments, Wang Chaohua breaks down as she confesses feelings of guilt: "I won't say I killed anybody. But there is a Chinese saying for thousands of years: the person may not be killed by you, but they might be killed because of your action, because of you. I always feel there might be many people who died because of me, because of my actions, because of the mistake I made." In another poignant moment in this last segment, the previously flamboyant Wuer Kaixi tells the interviewer with quiet and almost sheepish wistfulness: "I only wanted to be a teacher, a good teacher, and then all of a sudden it was all gone, all these possibilities are all gone. I have to face this life of the dissident, a top dissident, which I'm really not. Here, sitting here looking at the Pacific Ocean and the Golden Gate Bridge, I can let my mind just go. But every time it goes, most of the time it goes to China, across and to the end of this water, China." Above all, the film emphasizes the students' new identity as dissidents in exile and their continued commitment to the cause of promoting democracy and human rights in China. Wuer is featured in his radio show studio presumably explaining human rights issues over the airwaves to Chinese audiences; assorted clips exhibit Li speechifying at universities, political rallies, and other Western venues on the need for political change in China; and Chai is given some airtime to discuss her Democracy for China fund, her persistent desire to help the mainland Chinese people, and her continual struggle with her sense of responsibility for those who died. Given these affecting testimonies, even Wang Dan's gentle reproach—that "they should all come back . . . if they really want to work for democracy in China, only when they return will it be possible"—simply highlights more acutely the political and emotional double-binds around his former classmates. Some tactfully refer to *Moving the Mountain* as a "tribute" to the student leaders that makes no pretense to critical analysis (P. Chen), while others brand it as an "ornate, gauzy, reenactment-glutted documentary" (Abraham) and even more scornfully as a shameless "hagiography" and "ideological vehicle" for Li Lu (Woodward 35).

By contrast, *The Gate of Heavenly Peace*, produced by the Long Bow Group and codirected by Carma Hinton, adopts a much more scathing stance toward the same student leaders. In interview, Hinton has spoken of her motivation for making the film:

> Some of the reasons why I finally pushed myself to do the film involved the fact that I was in the United States watching television in 1989. What bothered me was that as the event became bigger, a lot of the Western reporters who had been in China for a long time and who knew Chinese were brushed aside. Big television personalities took over as the anchors. They did not know Chinese, they did not know China, but they knew how to package, they knew how to draw viewers, and they knew how to do the perfect sound bite. . . . The adventures of the American news personalities became the story, and it became ever more simplistic. . . .
>
> Also, presenting images of the students as these innocent, totally pure little angels and the government as this monolithic block of bad people does not illuminate what was really going on. In both camps, there were intense struggle. . . . If there was a nice-looking student who could speak good English, he or she would become a much more important subject than a worker who shied away from the camera. The worker may have been more afraid of retaliation than the student, or the worker did not know any English, or whatever. The media selected their own heroes and leaders of the Chinese movement. I was quite bothered by all of that. (qtd. in Marchetti 238)

While Hinton describes her project as primarily a corrective to the American media's simplistic and one-sided portrayal of Tiananmen, her explanation also reveals dissatisfaction with the popular mythologizing of the students. Her pointed invocation of the hypothetical worker, less glib than the better-educated student but more fearful of government retaliation, recalls Munro's argument about workers and *laobaixing* as the forgotten participants of the movement. However, rather than focus on these neglected subjects, her film seems principally aimed at not just revising but overturning the heroic myth of the student leaders. Whether the film falls shy of condemning the students for the massacre is open to debate, but most commentators have interpreted it as not merely raising the question of student leaders' culpability but actually arguing for it. *New York Times* reviewers variously attribute to the film the position that "moderation was swept aside during the final days of the demonstrations" by radical students who "pushed too far" (Tyler), and that "had moderation prevailed, there would have been no violent crackdown, and Deng Xiaoping's cautious reformist agenda might have been accelerated" (Holden). Among scholars, Pauline Chen sees the film as arguing that "student protestors in their fight for democracy adopted the same extremism and repression of alternate views that they opposed in the government," while Gina Marchetti reads the film as criticizing "the extremists in the dissident camp" who "actually have a lot in common with the hardliners in the government" (223). Ian Buruma outright calls the documentary a "polemic," one that specifically targets Chai Ling (11–12).

Undoubtedly, the most controversial portion of *Gate* is the lengthy footage, never publicly aired before, of a May 28 videotaped interview of Chai by the American journalist Philip Cunningham, just days before the crackdown. The centrality of this interview for the documentary is readily detectable, for Gordon and Hinton split it into a half-dozen segments so that the film script—and the viewer—continually return to this one scene of Chai's self-presentation. As a result of this editorial loop, the interview comes to signify not just one passing moment in the tumultuous weeks of Chai's leadership but the most telltale and damning of confessions. In the final and longest segment, a clearly exhausted and somewhat rambling Chai, speaking in Mandarin, says amid tears:

> I've been feeling very sad recently. The students themselves lack a developed sense of democracy. To be honest, from the day I called for a hunger strike I knew we would not get any results. Certain people, certain causes are bound to fail. I've been very clear about this all along, but I've made an effort to present a staunch image, to show that we were striving for victory. But deep down I knew it was all futile.
>
> The more involved I got, the sadder I became. I already felt this back in April. All along I've kept it to myself, because being Chinese

I felt I shouldn't bad-mouth the Chinese. But I can't help thinking sometimes—and I might as well say it—you, the Chinese, you are not worth my struggle! You are not worth my sacrifice! But then I can also see that in this movement there are many people who do have a conscience. There are many decent people among the students, workers, citizens, and intellectuals.

The students keep asking, "What should we do next? What can we accomplish?" I feel so sad, because how can I tell them that what we are actually *hoping for* is bloodshed, for the moment when the government has no choice but to brazenly butcher the people? Only when the Square is awash with blood will the people of China open their eyes. Only then will they really be united. But how can I explain any of this to my fellow students? . . . That's why I feel so sad, because I can't say all this to my fellow students. I can't tell them straight out that we must use our blood and our lives to call on the people to rise up. ("*Gate*," italics added)

Aside from her self-pitying resentment against "you Chinese" and disturbing call for "brazen butchery," Chai is also problematically recorded as saying that she herself did not intend to stay in the Square, despite being the self-proclaimed Commander in Chief of the Defend Tiananmen Square Headquarters: "Because my situation is different. My name is on the government's hit list. I'm not going to let myself be destroyed by this government. I want to live. Anyway, that's how I feel about it. I don't know if people will say I'm selfish. I believe that others have to continue the work I have started. A democracy movement can't succeed with only one person!" ("*Gate*").

The substance of these remarks sparked a heated controversy in the Chinese media in mid-1995, both in Hong Kong and Taiwan as well as in the overseas dissident community.[5] In response to accusations of her role in bringing about the massacre, Chai at first published a self-defense and rebuttal, claiming that the word she had used in the interview—*qidai*—meant not "hoping" but "expecting." In a counterattack, she went on to accuse Hinton of harboring pro–Communist Party sentiments because of the latter's family history (Hinton's father had been a Mao admirer and a land reform advocate in late 1940s and early 1950s China), of trying to curry favor with mainland authorities, and of "hawking [her] documentary film for crude commercial gain by taking things out of context" (qtd. in Barmé, *In the Red* 330–31). In uglier language still, another former student activist called the filmmakers "a bunch of opportunists," "a bunch of flies," "the true disease of our era" (qtd. in Woodward 30). On the opposing side, the activist journalist Dai Qing, one of the intellectual voices most frequently and vociferously marshaled by Gordon and Hinton's film, has grown ever more vitriolic in response. In her recently published prison memoirs, Dai writes: "Two kinds of people wanted the protest to escalate in the hope that some people would die and the protest might turn into an 'incident' of some magnitude. These two kinds of people were indispensable to the escalation. One kind was composed of student leaders and some intellectuals, shallow, rash, blind, who lacked a basic understanding of China's domestic situation and wishfully thought that a mass movement could change the entire political situation in the country overnight. The other breed consisted of politicians who wanted the then-general secretary of the Party Zhao Ziyang to step down" (104). Dai baldly equates "extremist" student leaders such as Chai Ling and Li Lu with Party hard-liners, holding the former as much as the latter group responsible for Tiananmen's bloody outcome. She will reiterate this criticism of Chai specifically many times over. On one occasion, she cites as evidence precisely the Cunningham interview and likens Chai's cohort to Cultural Revolution Red Guards: "Take Chai Ling for example, the activist who famously said that what her group of student leaders were 'actually hoping for is bloodshed' on the eve of June 4, 1989. . . . People show their true colors in extreme situations, and Chai Ling proved to be a good student of Chairman Mao's" (Dai and Barmé). On both sides, then, reasoned analysis has to some extent degenerated into invective. Ironically, the very subject of this debate—the escalation of tension during the Tiananmen protests—is now being played out among the former protest participants themselves as intellectuals and student leaders face off, directing ever-greater rhetorical rancor at each other.

Nor has the hostility died down fifteen years later, as Tiananmen commemorates its twentieth anniversary. In 2007, Chai and her husband filed a legal complaint against the Long Bow Group for defamation and trademark infringement, accusing the *Gate* producers of propagating "a misleading sample of statements from outdated articles to circulate half-truths and falsehoods" out of "malice toward Chai" (qtd. in Hinton et al.). The lawsuit has gone public since 2009, and the Long Bow Group has in turn responded by publishing an appeal on its website, signed by hundreds of supporters, charging Chai with the intention "to drain the limited resources of the Long Bow Group" with "demands and tactics [that] have dire implications not only for us, but more widely for free speech and independent scholarship" (Hinton et al.). In the latest twist of this diasporic drama, Wang Dan, who is invoked in *Gate* as a positive voice of moderation among the student leadership, has emerged as a galvanizing defender of Chai. In an open letter issued in May 2009 to Hinton and Gordon on behalf of "Tiananmen survivors, participants, and supporters," Wang urges the filmmakers "to correct the false reporting and editing" in *Gate*. His analysis of the film's mistakes is very close to Chai's, though couched in more temperate language. The letter is worth quoting at length:

> In your documentary, you used selective quotes and interpretive and erroneous translation leaving viewers with an impression that Chai Ling had run away from the danger while sending her other students to die, or that she and all of us student leaders had provoked and hoped for bloodshed. This impression was contradictory to the facts of what actually happened at Tiananmen.
>
> Clearly, Chai Ling's language ". . . *qidai liuxue*" was mistranslated by Carma Hinton, the producer, and taken out of context. "*qidai*" is properly translated as "hope for with anticipation or wait." Those of us who were there know that Chai Ling meant that we were anticipating a possible crackdown and hoping that the crackdown would happen in public, in front of the media, rather than being driven back to the darkness and disappearing from the world record, like so many other uprisings in China before and after 1989. It is important to note that we anticipated a crackdown, not a massacre. It also should have been noted that the student leaders made a major effort to make sure students who chose to stay at Tiananmen were volunteers who understood the risks of remaining in the square.
>
> Above all, our fellow student Chai Ling's language ". . . I want to live . . ." was also taken out of context, and gives a false impression that she ran away. In fact, she was there with her fellow student demonstrators until the last minute at Tiananmen, and led the last protestors on the Square retreating to campus in the morning of June 4th, 1989. . . .
>
> On the 20th anniversary remembering all of the Chinese students' and citizens' sacrifices, it has been 14 years since we first raised our concerns with you, but we have seen no action taken to correct misrepresentations in *The Gate of Heavenly Peace*. Again, we who took the risk and live in exile today because of it, urge you to post on your website this brief response and defense of our attempt to bring freedom and democracy to China, and of those students and citizens who risked or sacrifice their life and future to cry for a better future of China. (Wang D., "Defense")

The dispute generated by Gordon and Hinton's film underscores a shift in Tiananmen discourse in the last twenty years. For the most part, commentators agree on the importance of remembering Tiananmen, and all sides remain sympathetic to the pro-democracy cause for China. What has come under contestation, and what refuses to be settled in the ongoing memory reconstruction of the event, is the issue of student responsibility.

In the current phase of Tiananmen's historiography, we see realignments of formerly divergent student leaders such as Chai Ling and Wang Dan as well as new transnational linkages beyond the East-West divide between Chinese intellectuals such as Dai Qing and China observers and scholars in the West such as Carma Hinton and her league of supporters. In short, what emerges as a new fracture in Tiananmen discourse is defined less by ideology or nationality than by generationality and group identification, with the main rift cutting between self-identified intellectuals or scholars on the one hand and self-identified (ex-)students on the other. In the wake of *Gate*, it is almost de rigueur among commentators on Tiananmen to raise the topic of student radicalism and guilt. As Kay Schaffer and Sidonie Smith note, "In virtually every interview with dissident leaders in the United States after the release of *Gate*, dissident students were challenged about their behavior on the Square" (213). This large-scale shift can have a concrete and vital impact on Sino-American international relations. As Schaffer and Smith further point out, during President Bill Clinton's 1998 trip to China for talks on its most-favored-nation status, the U.S. media's intense refocusing of attention away from the communist government to the student leaders as a source of blame effectively "took pressure off Clinton to respond to exiled students' demands that he secure an apology for the Tiananmen Square Massacre in return for trade agreements" (214). Post-*Gate*, rare is the self-reflective critic who will admit, as Su Xiaokang has, that "we [intellectuals] created an atmosphere that encouraged the students to be radical, and then, when they did, we turned around and lectured them about their extremism" (qtd. in Buruma 57). So, it may indeed be the case that *Gate* at once stages and partakes of "struggles for control of the square and its political symbolic capital" in a more expanded transnational framework, as Gina Marchetti argues (220–21). But by accentuating the problem of student culpability without further probing the roots of student radicalism, and by doing so from a seemingly privileged distance of intellectual as well as moral assurance and self-righteousness, the film has had the unconstructive results of fueling existing flames among Chinese dissidents and activists alike, polarizing pro-democracy discourses along lines of blame, and shrinking the terms of discussion about Tiananmen to narrow categories of moral character.

SPOTLIGHT ON LIUBUKOU

Within this context of Tiananmen's troubled historiography, *Beijing Coma* works to steer critical attention away from moral critiques of the student leaders back to the historical impetus of the Tiananmen movement. As we have seen, for Ma Jian, this is inextricably tied to communist state biopower, the wide-ranging and durable biopolitical history that both culminates in and persists beyond Tiananmen. Thus, aside from delivering such proleptically prenatal apparitions of the new millennium as the Bird's Nest Stadium, the novel ends by revisiting, in its penultimate climactic scene, the Square in the early-morning hours of June 4. Through a calculated re-presentation of the massacre, *Beijing Coma* exemplifies the use of literature as an interventionist medium for what Arif Dirlik calls "critical remembering" and "the historicity of the present" ("Trapped" 300).

Enfolded within the present-time scenes of bulldozers surrounding Huizhen's apartment, embedded in between her defiant refusals to be evicted, are the novel's key scenes of the besieged Square in the controversial hours of its evacuation. By this point in the novel's 1989 time frame, tanks and armored personnel carriers have already enclosed and entered the Square, the slaughter on Changan Avenue during the army's approach has already occurred, and Mou Sen, Dai Wei's best friend, has been shot and killed, along with scores of others. The final contingent of a few thousand students huddle around the Monument of the People's Heroes, Dai Wei among them. Then, true to real-life reports of a largely bloodless withdrawal, the novel shows these students force-marched safely, if brutally and chaotically, out of the Square. At the same time, Ma attempts to reconcile contrary accounts of isolated violence by incorporating references to a panicked stampede where people are "knocked over or trampled underfoot"; to army abuse where soldiers beat the students "over the heads with the butts of their guns as though they were driving out a pack of dogs"; and most pointedly echoing the Qinghua student's testimony, to army and police brutality where they kick and club a last group of about three hundred students who refuse to leave (572–73). Still, up to this point in the narrative, fiction roughly accords with eyewitness accounts.

The moment outside the Square, however, is the point at which the novel paradoxically comes closest to and also departs farthest from history. As the students retreat and the crowd thins, Dai Wei manages to stay with his group of friends. Among them are Bai Ling and Wang Fei—the unmistakable fictional counterparts of Chai Ling and her then-husband Feng Congde. In real life, both survived June 4, and both went on to immigrate to the West, Chai becoming the CEO of a computer software company in Cambridge, Massachusetts, Feng pursuing a Ph.D. in anthropology in Paris. The parallel universe of *Beijing Coma*, however, confiscates from them these exilic afterlives. Instead, like Dai Wei, Bai Ling and Wang Fei fulfill for Ma the symbolic role of the state's most gruesome biopolitical victims:

Heading north, we reached the Liubukou intersection. . . . One of the tanks suddenly left the blockade, roared towards us and shot a

canister of tear gas which exploded with a great bang in the middle of
our crowd. A cloud of yellow smoke engulfed us. My throat burned
and my eyes stung. I felt dizzy and couldn't stand straight. . . .

While we were still trying to crawl our way out of the acrid smoke,
I heard another tank roar towards us. It paused for a moment in
the middle of the road, then rumbled forward again and circled us.
As it swerved round, its large central gun swung over my head and
knocked down a few students standing beside me. I got up and ran
onto the pavement. An armoured personnel carrier drove forward
too, and discharged a round of bullets. Everyone searched for cover. I
heard Wang Fei scream. I looked back, but the yellow smoke was still
too thick to see anything clearly. I waited. I knew the tank must have
driven over some people. As the smoke cleared, a scene appeared before me that singed the retinas of my eyes. On the strip of road which
the tank had just rolled over, between a few crushed bicycles, lay a
mass of silent, flattened bodies. I could see Bai Ling's yellow-and-
white-striped T-shirt and red banner drenched in blood. Her face was
completely flat. A mess of black hair obscured her elongated mouth.
An eyeball was floating in the pool of blood beside her. Wang Fei's
flattened black megaphone lay on her chest, next to a coil of steaming
intestine. Her right arm and hand were intact. Slowly two of the fingers clenched, testifying that a few moments before, she'd been alive.

Wang Fei was lying next to her. He propped himself up on his
elbow, tugged the strap he was holding and dragged his flattened
megaphone away from Bai Ling's chest. The bones of his legs were
splayed open like flattened sticks of bamboo. His blood-soaked trousers and lumps of his crushed leg were stuck to parts of Bai Ling. I
glanced at the stationary tank and saw pieces of Wang Fei's trousers
and leg caught in its metal tracks. (576–77)

This passage deserves quoting in full for several reasons. First and foremost, the sheer graphicness of Ma's description makes this one of the most
vivid and memorable moments in the novel. If the imagery is grotesque
and even lurid, if it has a kind of shocking or alienation effect on the
reader, then the text succeeds in reanimating from world memory some
of the initial raw agony of that Beijing spring. Like the morgue scenes in
Ha Jin's *The Crazed*, this passage is saturated with the evidential force of a
photograph, with the impulse to testify and authenticate.

At the same time, suggestively, this passage bears a formal resemblance
to the genre of reportage literature (*baogao wenxue*). Far from shrill, Dai
Wei's tone here is insistently objective: his first-person narration of a direct
experience of an atrocity and his meticulous attention to perceived details

imitate the conventions of not just eyewitness accounts but also report-age literature. In his illuminating study of this genre, Charles Laughlin has demonstrated how PRC-era reportage writing may be traced to the documentary literature of public demonstrations and student activism from the Republican period, such as narratives of May 4 protests (109–11). As Laughlin elaborates, reportage literature centers on "collectives rather than individual characters" (28), and it probes not the singularity of a narrator's psyche but the collective consciousness of a social, oftentimes national, event. Likewise, *Beijing Coma* can fruitfully be read in relation to reportage, as an attempt to realize the collective student consciousness of Tiananmen. Certainly, the novel is more than a traditional bildungsroman about an individual protagonist's development and struggle. Dai Wei, for all his uniqueness as a neomort, is ultimately Ma's vehicle for embodying, reflecting on, and critiquing the evolving life of national consciousness. It may be more accurate, then, to see the novel's fictional dimension as work-ing in dynamic concert with its historical one to create a hybrid reportage bildungsroman: this is a coming-of-age narrative of the whole Tiananmen student generation, its maturation cut short by state violence and its life henceforth reduced to coma, a literal fate for Dai Wei and a metaphori-cal one for his peers. Establishing this generic relation to reportage al-lows Ma to claim for his fiction a lineage in documentary writing highly invested in truth-telling as well as a Chinese history of student activism. This in turn allows him to better intervene on historical reconstructions of Tiananmen, to better redeem student life from communist erasure as much as moralist censure.

Intriguingly, Laughlin notes that reportage "declined sharply in quality and popularity after 1989" (21), that the Tiananmen crackdown "altered irrevocably" the "field of cultural production that conferred value on the discourse of the actual in the 1980s" (279). Given this situation, *Beijing Coma* may be said to give life to a censored content via a suppressed form: published within a protected diasporic space, the novel is able to draw upon the historical and political functions of the very genre that has suffered tighter official control within the PRC since Tiananmen. This, too, harkens back to what Laughlin posits as reportage's origins as a counterdiscourse, as that which yields "a true, corrective version" to the government's of-ficial history (84). In this regard, it is telling that, despite the novel's monu-mental scope, we never once glimpse inside the Zhongnanhai compound, are privy neither to Deng Xiaoping's inner contemplations and moral struggles as more psychological fiction would readily give us nor to the Politburo's and the Party Elders' daily conversations as the collection *The Tiananmen Papers* already richly documents. Indeed, if the novel's sprawl-ing form—almost six hundred pages of chapterless narration, the bulk of which methodically and sometimes ploddingly recounts the day-to-day developments and frictions within the student camps in the Square—can strike the reader as unnecessarily mired in the trivialities of student life, or else overly invested in mimesis and the spell of reality effects, it is perhaps more instructive to read this mode of thick realism as a discursive gesture to *The Tiananmen Papers* itself. As such, the novel may be regarded as the latter's fictional complement, providing the missing chronicle of Tiananmen via the micro operations of the student movement.

Attending to the formal elements of Dai Wei's reportage-like narration in this passage will moreover reveal the precision of Ma's imagined geography. Unlike the other fictional works discussed in previous chapters, *Beijing Coma* pinpoints an exact location for the massacre: the Liubukou intersection on west Changan Avenue, about a mile northwest of the Square. Ma's focus on this spot is crucial. For one, as we have noted, his novel harmonizes with testimonies that claim that no large-scale massacre occurred inside the Square. However, in sharp contrast to analyses that concentrate instead on the deaths of workers and civilians, Ma lingers on the students, following them in their evacuation beyond the Square to a site where they, too, were in life massacred.

Slowly and piecemeal after June 4, various survivors have surfaced to tell of this little-known but much-witnessed incident at Liubukou. As early as 1990, a student by the pseudonym of Liu Tang provided this account to Human Rights in China:

> As we moved out of the residential area and headed toward Liubukou intersection, few civilians met us along the road. . . .
>
> I was last in the line of Qinghua students. Behind us were students from the University of Law and Politics. When we arrived at Chang-an Avenue we saw about four rows of tanks stationed 300 feet east of the intersection. This was our first encounter with soldiers since leaving the square, so we couldn't contain our anger. We chanted "Beasts! Beasts! Murderers! Murderers!"
>
> I saw the first row of tanks, four of them, begin its charge. The one on the north side of the street led the attack and they quickly picked up speed.
>
> The students began to run in a panic—the ones in front of me ran north, while the ones behind me ran south. I ran north and quickly turned west but had trouble running because I was pushing my bike. The tanks kept gaining on us. I remembered someone screaming at me to hurry up. Another student helped me drag my bike onto the curb.
>
> The tank missed me by a few yards. As it passed, the soldiers inside opened the hatch and tossed out four gas canisters. Unlike the

gas canisters they had used the day before, which had made us cry, these containers spewed yellow fumes and choked us by irritating our lungs. . . .

Back up the street, about a dozen students had been trapped by burned buses and abandoned bicycles. They had been unable to escape the first charge of the tanks. The first body I saw was a girl dressed neatly in a white blouse and red skirt. She lay face down on the avenue. One of her legs was completely twisted around, the foot pointed up toward the sky.

Another, a male student, had his right arm completely severed from his shoulder, leaving a gaping black hole. The last body in the line of students was a young man on top of a flattened bicycle. He had been trying to climb over the bicycles to get away from the tank. His head was crushed: a pool of blood and brain lay on the pavement a few feet away.

Altogether, eleven students were crushed by this tank. Ten minutes later, an ambulance arrived and picked up three or four students who may still have been alive. (Human Rights 176–78)

Apocryphal or not, this account has since been corroborated by a number of others. Timothy Brook, relying on confidential interviews in the China Documentation Project, cites three anonymous eyewitnesses of the Liubukou assault, two of them Beijing students retreating from the Square and one an Associated Press reporter at the scene. As in Liu Tang's account, one of the students counted eleven bodies, as did the AP reporter: "Seven died instantly and four probably died later. They were like hamburger, like a dead animal flattened on the highway. Maybe the driver just lost control, though I assume it was on purpose" (qtd. in Brook 149).

The numbers fluctuate, however, depending on the time and place of the witnessing, and given the mutilated state of the bodies and the chaos of the moment, the true figure may never be known. The latest data on the Tiananmen Mothers Campaign website list eight casualties at Liubukou for the early morning of June 4; of these, seven were students, four of them crushed by tanks ("Liusi"). Feng Congde himself has created a website, June 4th Memoir (recently revamped and now hosted by Li Lu), that exhibits numerous graphic photographs of Liubukou. The website also includes a 2001 report by a student with the pen name Yu Yuan, who relates similar experiences as Liu Tang's and who recalls seeing the bodies of five students, two of them also flattened by tanks onto their bicycles. More recently in 2004, Ren Bumei, a former student who was part of the final evacuation and who has since become a prominent voice of dissidence in cyberspace, writes of his arrival at Liubukou moments after the attack, belated enough to have escaped the violence but early enough to witness the carnage:

> As I neared Liubukou I suddenly sensed that the group of students in front of me was dissolving in chaos and beginning to retreat. Advancing a few steps, I saw a group of people lying in pools of blood in Chang'an Avenue. I don't remember how many people there were, perhaps around 18. A student said that when the tanks saw the group of students approaching, they advanced on them and some students were crushed. I and some other students immediately began administering first aide. . . . In fact, some of the people were already dead at the scene, their intestines and brains spilling out. I was 21 years old at that time, and it was the first time that I had faced death in such a way. (66)

The Tiananmen Papers, too, cites a State Security Ministry intelligence report sent to the Party leadership at Zhongnanhai on the morning of June 4 that backs up this account: "Liubukou, roughly 6 A.M.: When some students and citizens who had withdrawn from Tiananmen Square reached Liubukou, soldiers opened fire and drove tanks into their midst, killing eleven. Six of the corpses were not removed until 7 A.M." (Zhang L. 383).

Most credible of all, perhaps, is the testimony given by Fang Zheng, a double amputee who was rolled over by a tank at Liubukou:

> Just after we turned from west Chang'an Boulevard to Liubukou, many grenades were fired towards the crowd from behind. They immediately exploded among the marching students. One went off just beside me. A two-to-three meter layer of smoke quickly engulfed us. A female student walking next to me suddenly fainted, choking and in shock. I rushed to pick her up and take her to the side of the street.
>
> At this time I realized that a tank was racing toward us, traveling from east to west. With all my force, I tried to push the woman towards the guard rail by the sidewalk. In the blink of an eye, the tank was approaching the sidewalk and closing in on me. It seemed as if the barrel of its gun was inches from my face. I could not dodge it in time. I threw myself to the ground and began to roll. But it was too late. My upper body fell between two treads of the tank, but both my legs were run over. The treads rolled over my legs and my pants, and I was dragged for a distance. I used all my strength to break free and to roll to the side of the road. At that time I lost consciousness. Only later did I learn that Beijing residents and students brought me to Jishuitan Hospital, where I underwent a double amputation. My right leg was amputated, leaving just two-thirds of my right thigh. My left leg was amputated five centimeters below the knee. ("Testimony")

Few things are more persuasive as evidence than a wounded body, and few emblems more illustrative of sovereign biopower than an army tank rolling over an unarmed man, literally inscribing the state's supremacy on the subject's bared life. Fang Zheng's testimony, given in 1999, itself has a revealing prehistory. A gifted athlete at the Beijing College of Sports in 1989, Fang was denied his graduation certificate and a job assignment after the crackdown. Nonetheless, he went on to train in sports, winning gold medals in discus and javelin throwing at a 1992 sports meet for the disabled and becoming China's national record holder at the time. When authorities discovered he had been injured at Tiananmen, however, he was disqualified from the 1994 Beijing Special Olympics, even though he had pledged to keep the circumstances of his injury confidential ("In Memory"). His story has periodically resurfaced in the American press in the years since, and it is in part through him that Liubukou continues to be conferred historical relevance for the post-Tiananmen world.

By endowing Fang Zheng with a fictional parallel life in the character of post-massacre Wang Fei, Ma Jian in turn brings to the fore this continual relevance, intricately linking up the biopolitics of Tiananmen with the politics of the Beijing Olympics. Just as Fang Zheng has become a spokesperson for government accountability for Tiananmen in the post-Deng era, so Wang Fei gives voice to the same position, underscoring its urgency in the age of China's economic ascendancy and global power. As Wang tells his friends and fellow survivors in a 1999 reunion in Dai Wei's apartment, in one of the most resonant speeches in the novel:

> "We're the 'Tiananmen Generation', but no one dares call us that,"
> Wang Fei says. "It's taboo. We've been crushed and silenced. If we
> don't take a stand now, we will be erased from the history books.
> The economy is developing at a frantic pace. In a few more years the
> country will be so strong, the government will have nothing to fear,
> and no need or desire to listen to us. So if we want to change our
> lives, we must take action now. This is our last chance. The Party
> is begging the world to give China the Olympics. We must beg the
> Party to give us basic human rights." Wang Fei's wheelchair rattles
> and squeaks as he twists from side to side. (505)

Wang Fei may be full of fighting spirit in this passage, but his fate will be bleaker than Fang Zheng's. The last reference to him in the novel, indirectly related through a phone call to Huizhen, is that he has been arrested and forcibly committed to a mental asylum. The response of Huizhen, herself half-mad after her Falun Gong arrest and torture, is an index of the spreading biopower of the state in Ma's vision: "A mental asylum? How nice. I wouldn't mind going in for a bit of treatment myself" (564).

Ma's spotlight on Liubukou, then, is a redirection of a redirection. Heeding Munro's call, he does essay to set the record straight on the geography of the killing. Yet his unswerving focus is on the students—the reality of student deaths, and the costs of student life. In this respect, his novel shows a deliberately cultivated relation to the ongoing constructions of history, not just in points of fact but also in the shifting terrains of interpretation. On the one hand, if some student leaders have come under heavy criticism for bringing death to those who defended and supported them, Ma stresses that students, too, were among the ranks of Tiananmen's victims, in death as in life, and nowhere more severely than at Liubukou. His text's amplification of this specific massacre may hence be read as a reclaiming of student casualties from the historian's footnote.[6] On the other hand, if the communist government has manipulated the fact of a largely bloodless evacuation to conceal massacres outside the Square proper, Ma does not answer this cover-up by fabricating a massacre where there was none. Nor does he simply conclude, as Orville Schell does and many may be inclined to do, that efforts at defining the boundaries of the Square are a "purely semantic" exercise, that "whatever the number of dead, and wherever they died," the event's ultimate significance lies in "state-sponsored terror" (156–57)—as if historical accuracy and historical meaning are mutually exclusive categories. What Ma's text proposes is the noncontradiction of the two. It remains meaningful for him to map the dead accurately, to not relegate them to the "whatever" and "wherever" of semantics. Given that he has Huizhen join the Tiananmen Mothers organization, we can further speculate on his mindfulness of the arduous labor of those like Ding Zilin who painstakingly track down, record, and authenticate each Tiananmen victim. At the same time, the fictional dimension of his novel makes possible a symbolic reordering of time and space, so that even as the text operates with topographical exactness on one level, it can simultaneously suspend the particularities of thick realism to illuminate the allegorical meanings of Tiananmen—the symbolic ubiquity of the Square as a biopolitical space and the unremitting presence of the massacre as a biopolitical time. And it is only by reactivating the operations of fiction that Ma can displace Chai Ling, that most vilified of student leaders in post-Tiananmen life, onto her fictional double's death at Liubukou.

Given that history is an omnipresent intertext for his novel, Ma's rewriting of Chai's fate takes on magnified meaning in the ongoing debate about student survival. From one angle, his fictional move can be interpreted as an evasive maneuver, an attempt to circumvent the thorny issue of assessing the former student leaders' current lives in exile. Especially on the heels of Gordon and Hinton's documentary, there has been no lack of commentators eager to disabuse the public of the mythology of valiantly self-sacrificing students. Yvonne Abraham, for example, in a seven-part series for the *Boston Phoenix* in 1997, begins her exposé thus: "After the bloody crackdown in China, a few brave student leaders escaped to carry on the fight from American shores. At least that was the story. Here's what really happened." Titling her piece "Cashing in on Tiananmen," she goes on with biting tenacity to paint a collective portrait of post-Tiananmen Li Lu, Wuer Kaixi, Shen Tong, and Chai Ling as not only bewildered young dissidents unexpectedly swept up by the American media circus but also, less flatteringly, as greedy opportunists capitalizing on their accidental fame. While it is understandable that the suddenly exiled students may have "traded on Tiananmen to make themselves darlings of the Western media," Abraham further insinuates that the students may have funneled millions of dollars in donation money toward their own use, to sustain their newfound extravagant lifestyles as cultural celebrities. The accusation, in effect, is that these student leaders have abandoned the cause of democracy and betrayed the people back in China even as they deceive the good-hearted if naive donors of the West. Abraham borrows her authority in part from Liu Binyan, whom she quotes as saying: "When [the students] were still in China, they were too radical and self-centered, and acted as stars before the world's media. When they arrived abroad, they behaved like aristocrats, seeming to forget the ordinary people at home." In a mutually enforcing and ever-amplifying representational loop, Abraham's article is in turn linked by Gordon and Hinton as resource material, specifically on Chai Ling, to their *Gate of Heavenly Peace* website. The limelight is again explicitly on Chai, and implicitly on the student leaders' moral fiber, their failure to live up to the image of heroic dissidents, and their not being "what they say they are."

Survival, after all, is far more complicated than death, at least from the standpoint of the living and the perspective of moral judgment. The cliché about life's inherent sacredness is rarely said of a person's manner of living, for *bios* does not lend itself to sentiments of the sacrosanct so readily as *zoē*. Ma shows ample recognition of this insight when he portrays some student survivors choosing to embrace the benefits of capitalism rather than continue the fight against political oppression. In life, this decision is reflected in Chai Ling's climb of the corporate ladder in America. Hers may be a choice less amenable to a romantic vision of melancholic exile than, say, Zhang Boli's to enter the church and become a pastor, but both paths bespeak a certain escapism. One renounces politics in the name of pragmatic self-advancement while the other renounces secular concerns altogether in the name of spiritual salvation, but both can be comprehended as reacting to an upbringing under a communist regime as much as disappointed idealism in the wake of the student movement's tragic failure. So it is almost with a sense of prophetic fulfillment that, in the latest twist of events, the paths of these two oppositely iconic figures of the student movement have merged. In 2009, after hearing a live testimony in Washington, D.C., of one woman's forced abortion under China's one-child policy, Chai Ling announced that she was converting to Christianity—for only God, she declares, can stop this "inhuman crime" done "in broad daylight" that is "hundreds of times more deadly than the Tiananmen Massacre" (Testimony). She was baptized on Easter the following year, to the warm and vocal support of Zhang Boli.

Ma, however, is not merely trying to excuse Chai Ling or rescue her from her critics by contriving a morally unassailable end for her fictional counterpart. He is careful not to enter into the zero-sum game of a biopolitical moral calculus, on which a horrific death converts into political credit and a comfortable life into political debt. Rather, his novel suggests it is simply inadequate to evaluate the student movement in the strictest terms of moral character. If reports such as Gordon and Hinton's or Abraham's have brought much evidence to light about the students' impetuosity and arrogance, self-interest and power-mongering, *Beijing Coma* does not sanitize its representation of the movement of these traits. On the contrary, in its methodically chronicle-like manner, the novel incorporates many reported episodes of the student leaders' disorganization, factious infighting, and power abuse. For instance, the "election" of student leaders at the movement's inception is depicted as haphazard and undemocratic, in the process of which Dai Wei, just by virtue of "standing by the tables with the other speakers," involuntarily becomes a founding member of Beijing University's organizing committee (162–65). As the same cliques of students assign themselves and their friends to multiple leadership roles, Dai Wei will be designated "head of security" (because of his unusual height) and then appointed to various other posts, some of which he himself forgets (202). Later, as student organizations proliferate and a flurry of appointments are made and unmade amid "many coups and reshuffles" (217), debates will devolve into quarrels, quarrels into power struggles, first between the hunger strike group and the dialogue delegation, then between Beijing students and provincial ones, and finally among a dizzying array of realigned factions.

Nor does the novel shirk from showcasing the student leaders' tendency toward authoritarian control—by shutting out opposing views, by monopolizing the loudspeaker system for propaganda purposes, periodically breaking into brawls over command of the megaphone or the broadcast station (323, 376–78, 399), and even by censoring student poll results about leaving the Square (359). In real life, these practices, as critics have pointed out, eerily replicate the Communist Party leadership's clandestine mode of operation, and Ma's text likewise suggests that the student leaders, once they assume power, swiftly adopt similar behavioral patterns of unilateral decision making, information suppression, bureaucratic governance, and forceful bullying. In their most self-protective and unheroic moment in the novel, they are shown in a 3:00 a.m. secret meeting, after the government has announced its intention to clear the Square by dawn (a false alarm, as it turns out), discussing plans for splitting the donation money and separately absconding from the Square without notifying the rest of the student body. Bai Ling here invokes the same argument as Chai Ling, in her Cunningham interview, about the privileged duty of student leaders: "If we want to keep the flame of the movement alive, we must leave the Square and go underground" (348). In this scene's ensuing dispute, she is scarcely the sterling example of self-sacrifice as she nervously entreats the others to "hurry up and share out the cash." Mou Sen, by contrast, emerges as a voice of conscience and unity: "This is too much! . . . We can't creep away without telling anyone. We must make an announcement and explain our actions" (348). Dai Wei also advocates for a general announcement and evacuation, but once his vote is defeated, he, too, despite twinges of guilt, takes the money and prepares to flee. It is a scene that starkly illustrates the gulf between the student leaders and those they represent. As Dai Wei thinks uneasily to himself, "it didn't seem right that the leaders were skulking away like this, especially since they'd been urging everyone else to stay" (350). A hierarchy now exists between student leaders and ordinary students, the same division of power they had presumably set out to democratize.

The novel, of course, does not stop at these moral nadirs in the student movement. Their inclusion is part of Ma's strategic rounding out of the students, perhaps best read in counterpoint to their flattened image as "counterrevolutionaries" by the communist government on the one hand and as reckless "extremists" by liberal critics on the other. Ultimately for Ma, the negative face of student life does not detract from Tiananmen's deepest meaning as a movement opposed to totalitarian biopower. By ending his reconstruction of student life at Liubukou, he shifts the analysis of Tiananmen away from the student leaders' moral character and political responsibility back to the biopolitical history that they, perhaps naively, sometimes selfishly but nonetheless earnestly, strived to disrupt and overthrow. Above all, he fixes attention on *the Square*'s mobility and reincarnation, *not the students*'. If Chai Ling and Zhang Boli are able to find metaphorical new life in exile and reinvent themselves as a corporate executive and a Christian minister respectively, Bai Ling and Mou Sen are not. Ma's rescripting of these two student leaders' fate highlights the failure of the movement to regenerate since 1989 and the symbolic end of the student leaders *as such*.

Most revealing of his view toward student life is the fact that Bai Ling and Mou Sen epitomize antithetical poles of the student movement but nevertheless meet with similar fates. Where Bai Ling leads the more radical student camp by championing the hunger strike and advocating suicide by fire (245), Mou Sen stands as the staunch intellectual who endorses more moderate student leaders (199, 247–48), believes in political education, gradual change, and peaceful resistance, and insists on opening his Democracy University even on the eve of the massacre (528–33). She is the accidental face and mouthpiece of the movement's revolutionary pathos, he the behind-the-scenes engineer of its intellectuality and logos. At times they come together in collaboration—as when she reads out the hunger strike declaration he drafts (230–31)—and when they do, they enormously amplify the movement's emotional and rational appeal. Fundamentally, though, they represent rival politics, and their joint presence in the novel foregrounds the range of political attitudes within the student movement. If some prominent intellectuals have characterized Tiananmen as a movement polarized between irrational, hotheaded, extremist students and rational, sober, reform-minded intellectuals (and here we can recall the voices of Wei Jingsheng as much as Dai Qing, Liu Binyan as much as Gao Xingjian), Ma marks a critical departure by delineating not only the spectrum of student positions but also their at times strategic collaborations and convergences. In *Beijing Coma*, the students too have their philosophers and reformers. Yet, by having Bai Ling and Mou Sen come to similar ends on June 4, Ma implies that the crux of history does not lie in the students' chosen political path. Reformism and radicalism alike are met by the state with force: the difference lies only in the degree and method of force, between a bullet and a tank. On Ma's final analysis, the student movement's failure is not to be traced to character flaws or political blunders but serves instead as an ever-present cause for continued vigilance to ever-newer permutations of state sovereign biopower.

Aside from the moral perspective, then, and in light of history's outcome, the student movement cannot be given its due if it is primarily assessed on the basis of political efficacy. To be sure, the students were inexperienced activists, more occasional agitators than professional dissidents, and Ma gives abundant support to this view in his novel. What then was the nature of the students' "democracy"? One notable hypothesis, as discussed in the previous chapter, is put forward by Joseph Esherick and Jeffrey Wasserstrom. As they note, it would be imprecise to characterize the student movement as a truly pro-democracy one if the term *minzhu* is taken to mean a Western-style pluralist political system, since few students at the time had any concrete knowledge of democratic governance. Moreover, Esherick and Wasserstrom point out that the students consistently displayed an "elitist reading of *minzhu*" and a "distrust of the *laobaixing* or untutored masses" as well as a "lack of concern for the needs of workers and peasants" (31). Ma, too, has no illusions on this score; at one point in the novel, when a worker approaches the student leaders seeking to join his petition to theirs, the students suspiciously and callously brush him aside, stating, "You do your thing and we'll do ours" (182). Certainly, many students took to the streets in 1989 out of not simply high-minded ideals but also a consciousness of their unique power precisely as students, as a group of cultural elite that, in modern times since May Fourth, has been perceived as bearing the moral conscience of the nation and hence enjoyed some measure of political immunity. Given this history, Esherick and Wasserstrom argue that we are less likely to understand the Tiananmen students if we regard them as political analysts or philosophers than if we focus on their actions as symbolic performances in a political theater, a "cultural performance before a mass audience . . . that expresses beliefs about the proper distribution and disposition of power . . . and other scarce resources" (39). If the students have been faulted for not having a "coherent political program," if they "rarely analyzed the failings of the Chinese political system or proposed a concrete program for political change," the reason is that "theirs was a performance designed to impress and move an audience, not a lecture designed to inform." Esherick and Wasserstrom thus maintain that it "makes little sense to ask whether these students really knew what 'freedom' and 'democracy' meant, and still less sense to ask whether they were truly prepared to die for their beliefs. These last testaments were power statements of great symbolic meaning. They revealed a fundamental alienation from the regime and a willingness to make great (perhaps even the ultimate) sacrifice for an alternative political future" (40). Such a hypothesis necessarily assumes that those like Mou Sen are in the minority.

The element of theatricality, as we have seen, is rampant in Annie Wang's portrayal of the Square, although she is less prone to analyze it as a traditionally rooted political performance than as a hybrid byproduct of Deng-era commodification culture and China's self-orientalism in its encounter with the capitalist West. Theatricality is also present in Ma's novel, if in more subdued form, through occasional references to rock bands (395) and rock stars (497–98) in the Square as well as the student leaders' posturing as "stars of th[e] movement" (323) and "actor[s] on the stage" (369). Indeed, how can theatricality not play a part in any representation of Tiananmen, with pop cultural icons such as Hou Dejian and Cui Jian so salient a part of that Beijing spring's spectacle? Yet in Ma's novel, the students' role-playing unfolds in an ever more terrifying allegory of a country with no exits. Again, Mou Sen's early premonition of the Square as a stage with "no escape routes," and of the students as "trapped here, in the spotlight" (357), succinctly captures Ma's larger thesis about the ubiquity of communist state biopower. As the tanks advance on the Square, minor characters in the movement become like "extra[s] in a fight scene" (542), and Dai Wei himself feels "as though we were standing behind the scenes in a theater, overhearing the noisy commotion taking place on the stage" (561). Ma is less invested than Wang in painting Tiananmen in the hyperreal terms of material commodification, nor is he interested in staging a critique of national politics as another manifestation of consumer culture's mass psychology. The hyperreal here is not pervasive but isolated, flashing up intermittently within the text's fabric of documentary realism, alarm signals of a biopolitical status quo above the mundane details of student activities. Despite some savviness about the theatricality of politics, the students in *Beijing Coma*, unlike those in *Lili*, tend to be more profoundly embedded in the bewildering chaos of experiential existence where history has yet to be made and meaning decided. Ma's students are more confused than calculating, and more earnestly keen for historical knowledge than shallowly captivated by material glitter. While they know enough of the "script" of political theater to stage all the dramatic acts of public protest, they bear out Esherick and Wasserstrom's analysis in that they show no real understanding of the meanings of democracy. In this sense they resemble more, perhaps ironically, the 1920s student revolutionaries in Mao Dun's early pro-communist fiction, a generation of young idealists likewise caught up in the tidal wave of political radicalism and armed with the intellectual imperative to oppose entrenched social habits and ideologies but sorely lacking in the tools to do so themselves.

Yet for Ma, what his students lack above all is knowledge of even the recent history of political dissent in their country. This ignorance is dramatized in a conversation in which Dai Wei, discussing politics with his friends on the eve of the 1986–87 student protests, admits to knowing little about the 1978–79 Democracy Wall movement (86). Ma focuses on this theme of historical amnesia as key to student life under communist totalitarian rule. His novel suggests that the Party wields and retains its power only by repeatedly rupturing intergenerational memory, by thwarting the transmission of historical memory from one generation to the next, not just about political dissent but also everyday suffering caused by national policies. Hence, Dai Wei knew almost nothing about his father's life prior to reading the latter's diary and little more about the Cultural Revolution prior to his Guangxi trip. It is this generational ignorance that Ma highlights as an essential determinant in the Tiananmen student leadership's eventual modus operandus. As we have seen, he calls this phenomenon *duandai*, the severing of generations: "When we look again at this [Tiananmen] generation, we can very clearly arrive at this conclusion: the students' ignorance is not merely a product of their own doing but also that of society's. What I try to do in my novel is also to show how society has allowed them to '*duandai*,' allowed them to fail, caused them to become something very close to the Communist Party itself—for instance, their power struggle, their mutual distrust, and their disbelief even toward the end, when they had been pushed to the brink of repression" (qtd. in Zeng). For Ma, what could be leveled at the students as criticism of their moral failings or political egotism is cast instead as the sociopsychic effects of totalitarian rule—how its forcible disruptions of intergenerational memory result in an ethos of foolhardy and self-aggrandizing politics. On his view, "the 1989 students as much as today's Chinese students are fundamentally victims" (qtd. in Zeng); both are severed generations without the benefit of inheriting their predecessors' richly instructive historical experiences.

If anything, the atmosphere of power struggle and mutual suspicion among the Tiananmen students can be understood as a direct legacy of the communist system and the social-psychological environment it produces. This legacy has trickled down to the post-Tiananmen generations in the form of Dai Wei's neomortic afterlife. Unlike Ha Jin's Jian or Annie Wang's Lili, Dai Wei is neither the befuddled outsider stumbling into Beijing at the last minute nor the jaded outsider who gets emotionally caught up in the activist mob. He is a minor insider all along, not the chief leader but a lesser figurehead with an impressive title but no real power. Indeed, he has no real desire for power and forgetfully eats during the hunger strikes (249, 255); he has passed the TOEFL exams and plans to study abroad (101) and thus has no lofty ambitions to save China; and by his own admission he is just "not fanatical" (203). At the margins of the movement's political idealism, emotional vortex, and power struggles, he is nonetheless the massacre's most enduring casualty to the letter. It is this lingering bare life that Ma relentlessly foregrounds as the most significant legacy of Tiananmen facing China's generations now. But Ma seems to realize, too, that in actual life even this neomortic body is withheld from some now, that afterlife can be attained only as metaphysical faith or else fiction. And so, perhaps in homage to this reality of the lived aftermath, and in a reversal from his fates for Chai Ling and Zhang Boli, he has elected in the end to name his protagonist after one of June 4's real victims: Dai Wei, native of Beijing, age twenty in 1989 when he was shot in the back outside Minzu Hotel a few blocks from Liubukou on the night of June 3, who was then rushed to a nearby hospital but died from loss of blood in the early-morning hours.

On the Tiananmen Mothers website is a photograph of his mother, Liu Xiuchen, holding a funereal photograph of him ("Dai Wei").

But in our afterlife, the most frightening circumstance may not be a repetition of history but the banishing of all repetition, not the reenactment of totalitarian biopower but the forgetting of all biopolitical action, not another massacre at Liubukou but a Square with no students hereafter.

Conclusion: The Square Comes Full Circle

Among Tiananmen's many revelations is that historical imagination may not always be literal. It may accrete through accidental suggestions and rumors, even inventions and errors, as much as facts. As George Black and Robin Munro justly put it, the term "Tiananmen Square Massacre" has firmly entered into the "political vocabulary of the late twentieth century," even though, technically speaking, no massacre happened inside the Square. At best the phrase is a "shorthand," but they will insist it is also a misnomer (234). Munro in particular has pleaded with passionate sincerity that "journalism may be only the rough draft of history, but if left uncorrected it can forever distort the future course of events" (811).

Given how Tiananmen's narratives have been told and its meanings produced, what seems to be at work with its historical imagination is undoubtedly something more literary than barely factual. The "Tiananmen Square Massacre" is at once a synecdoche, a myth, an allegory. The incident's potential meanings, from the first, have been fluid, pliable, and even now, more than twenty years later, they continue to be amenable to literary shaping. It is hard to dispute Munro's claim that the geography of the killing matters, that the demographic of the dead matters. But what then? What does and will Tiananmen mean for a time that exceeds, and a world that survives, the massacre? Contrary to what observers projected at the time, the "truth" of Tiananmen will not wait to be redeemed on some future horizon when knowledge meets history, when some fateful historian-seer comes into full possession of all knowable data. Rather, the time of historical imagination is ever present and open. It has been so in the Tiananmen literature, with all its ellipses, catachreses, even distortions.

This is the "future course" that our present moment occupies. Craig Calhoun articulates a similar insight for the mainland itself: "For most of the people of China, and for the future of democratic struggles in China, firsthand observations will be far less crucial than representations of the movement in photographs, narratives, news reporting, gossip, histories, sociological analyses, trials, speeches, and poetry" (203–4). Fiction constitutes only one slice of this future, but it derives unique power from its capacity to move between the concrete and the conceptual, to bring into dialectical concert history's actuality and the present's exigencies.

Ren Bumei, the former student activist and Liubukou survivor, once commented: "It would be fair to say that all of my writings have been influenced by this tragedy—to a greater or lesser extent, there is nothing that does not originate from that seething spring and that blood-soaked dawn" (65). This testimony to Tiananmen's omnipotent and enduring effect on an individual psyche can be taken as a distillation of Ma Jian's national allegory as much as Ha Jin's diasporic melancholia. In terms Ma will echo a few years later, Ren noted that "June 4th has not really led Chinese to a spiritual awakening.... For this reason I worry that the aftermath of the June 4th tragedy is an even greater tragedy: the bloodbath has not actually imparted to the Chinese spirit any sense of guilt or humiliation or personal growth, resulting in only more needless sacrifice of life. This easy retreat, this ready indulgence in mutual flattery over a little 'progress,' can only make one sigh in the depths of despair." Finally, deploring the "barrack-room boasting" and "mutual recrimination" that vex Tiananmen discourse on the Internet by parties both within and outside of the PRC, Ren concluded: "15 years without self-reflection, 15 years of callous indifference, 15 years of speechless rage or rageless speech—all of this shows that June 4 was not really a turning point for Chinese.... In a human tragedy of such massive scale, China did not produce a single book, film, mass commemorative movement or humanist champion worthy of the event" (68).

We can only speculate on what Ren might think of *Beijing Coma*, but here at last is a work that earnestly, fervently, epically attempts to be "worthy of the event," blow by blow. In sync with Ren's exhortations, Ma's novel calls for the Chinese people, whether within the PRC or in the diaspora, to move beyond "barrack-room boasting" and "mutual recrimination," beyond superficial self-congratulations about China's progress and self-exonerating criticisms of student leaders. His text resonates with Ren's declaration that "China urgently needs to enter an era of political self-reflection" (67). And, refreshingly, it does so without a drop of what Ren calls "maturity" (*chengshu*), the "overly practical or cynical attitude of the intellectual elite toward matters of principle" (68 n. 5). Annie Wang's

Lili, we might say, performs the same task with even greater "immaturity," from the ironic perspective of the female hooligan.

From another quarter, it is not unusual for us to hear today, from commentators disillusioned with liberal democracies but themselves snugly protected within the folds of nonauthoritarian states, the quip that global capital has annihilated the distinction between communism and democracy, that the advent of capitalism into the second world has neutralized the distinctive threat of Mao-style autocracy for our time. Of the writers here, Wang is most trenchant in undercutting this neoliberal fantasy and its complacent faith in the equalizing power of transnational capital. Ma, too, is adamant in his answer that, no mistake, the PRC "must introduce democratic reforms," not despite but precisely because of the country's economic development ("China's Grief"). That the communist state's market goals can be pursued in utter harmony with its totalitarian policies is repeatedly illustrated in Ma's novel, and his focus on the cannibalistic biopower of Deng-era liberalization and beyond represents his strongest argument on this score. In fact, Ma sees the urgency of political change escalating in recent years, as China emerges as a global economic power of the first order and the international community increasingly gives sanction to its politics out of economic interest. It is within this circumstance that he has been so outspoken a critic of the 2008 Beijing Olympics. He will not be one to scoff at democracy in the age of globalization. On the contrary, democracy remains for him a necessary anchor, holding in place a specific counterpolitics with determinant content.

This is the reason too that, as resonantly as his novel rings to Western theories of bare life and exceptional states, Ma would not so quickly dream—as does Giorgio Agamben—of Tiananmen as a "coming community," that utopia of pure belonging where the masses of "whatever singularity" rise up as one great humanity against state power (Agamben, *Coming* 85–87). Ma's idealism toward student life leans in a decidedly different direction; it is an idealism that cannot afford to be devoid of an affirmative identity and agenda. Indeed, we might observe that Agamben's writing is made possible only because the biopolitical situation he theorizes as a contemporary universal—the camp that has supposedly become the normative order of the planet—has not been politically realized in the very place and time of his writing. This discursive possibility arguably marks the pockets of the camp's nonrealization. Tellingly, then, he must reach out to Tiananmen for his empirical example, toward another state's biopolitical regime, in a conceptual move where the inside/outside demarcation still matters, and matters essentially. Conversely, that Ma can publish his biopolitical saga of Tiananmen only outside the place of its occurrence, outside the PRC's discursive jurisdiction, indicates the real state of exception has its strict boundaries still, and in this case, the boundaries remain firmly national. If the authority of the nation-state as a political unit has been attenuated in the age of globalization, Ma would maintain that, in the case of the PRC, its sovereign biopower stays very much alive, and in ever more insidiously pervasive forms, for its subjects.

In an adjacent theoretical direction, Ma would heartily agree with Michael Hardt and Antonio Negri that the Tiananmen movement, like other uprisings across the world at the close of the twentieth century, was "at once economic, political, and cultural—and hence . . . biopolitical" because it involved a contest over the multitudes' very "form of life" (Hardt and Negri 56). Indeed, Ma's magnum opus, insofar as it strives to translate a local event and render it intelligible, proximate, even neighborly to outsiders, helps to overcome what they diagnose as a mutual atomization and a "paradox of incommunicability" that have befallen contemporary social movements (54). This capacity to translate not just culture but sociopolitical life highlights another distinct efficacy of Tiananmen fictions. Nonetheless, vis-à-vis Hardt and Negri as much as Agamben, Ma would object to the conceptual leveling of Tiananmen as simply another instance in a series of world struggles against "the common enemy" of globalization, as if the latter were some leviathan whose immense power could stay intact even as its diverse political contents get eviscerated. Against their notion of Empire as a uniform planetary regime without boundaries or limits (xiv), Ma would insist on retaining a sense of the local polity, and the persistent weightiness of the nation-state, not as absolute singularity or radical alterity, but as the site where biopolitical differences are still enacted and lived out by many subjects today. Beijing for him is not so easily catalogable, as in the other two theorists' sentence, alongside "Los Angeles, Nablus, Chiapas, Paris, Seoul" (56).

By continually reminding the world of 1989 Beijing, all the Tiananmen fictions in this study present a collective challenge, moreover, to the optimistic view on the part of some Western intellectuals that China's economic rise will herald a new and brighter epoch of global cooperation and human recognition. Giovanni Arrighi, for one, has argued that "the Chinese ascent . . . can be taken as the harbinger of that greater equality and mutual respect among peoples of European and non-European descent that [Adam] Smith foresaw and advocated 230 years ago" (379). This projection, issued from an anticolonialist, antiracist, and labor-oriented position that takes as its central antagonist the long history of European imperialism and U.S. hegemony, understandably reaches for East Asia as the vehicle for an alternative, postimperial model of globalization. Yet such sanguine faith in the "extraordinary social achievements of the Mao era" (370) and in the Chinese communist government as truly one of "mass participation in shaping policies" (389) would strike the diaspora writers here as not only naïve and insupportable but woefully dismissive of the PRC's internal politics and its vast human costs. In what meaningful sense, the writers here might ask, can the communist state help usher in a "commonwealth of civilizations truly respectful of cultural differences" (389) when it cannot tolerate political dissent from within the nation and continues to maintain social stability and a semblance of cultural unity via measures of silencing and force? Is a government that repeatedly resorts to totalitarian tactics of domestic peacekeeping the entity on which we must pin our messianic hopes for a global future? The post-Tiananmen literary diaspora is particularly skeptical about this brand of exuberant Sinophilia, and its role in preserving the relevance of PRC political history may well become even more acute in the twenty-first century.

At the same time, the diaspora writers here are keenly aware that, given official censorship of June 4 on the mainland, they write Tiananmen primarily not for Chinese readers in the PRC but for Chinese and non-Chinese audiences around the world. They are hence not merely exhuming a buried history but also, whether voluntarily or not, contributing to an ongoing construction of Tiananmen's global discourse. They know they occupy a middle ground and perform a double task: not only are they overturning an oppressive government's historical erasure, they are simultaneously confronting a saturated consciousness of an international community for whom the massacre is an already overwritten or overimagined episode, facilely recallable through media images of tanks grinding down Changan Avenue. These writers know that, given the compulsory first circulation of their texts in countries outside the PRC, they are writing not on a tabula rasa of world memory but on a palimpsest of countless recycled images and narratives, from the Tank Man to lurid reports of a blood-bathed Square—even if they themselves remain ignorant of the actual casualty count.

Within this context, *Beijing Coma* marks the latest turn of the diasporic screw that brings us around full circle. Gao Xingjian's 1989 *Taowang*, the first full-length fictional work on Tiananmen, was written in Chinese at the behest of an overseas Chinese democracy group. Though frequently cited as a representative work in Gao's oeuvre, particularly in relation to his Nobel Prize, this play remains largely unscrutinized by critics, thus perpetuating his reputation as a dissident exilic writer. At the turn of the millennium and after ten years of halting writing, Ha Jin and Annie Wang both imaginatively resurrected the scene of Tiananmen but from the discursive space of Asian America, on the linguistic terrain of English. Both *The Crazed* and *Lili* convey in their textual endings a promise of survival and renewal outside the Square, whether in the diaspora or some unnamed utopian site, a promise materially delivered by the fact of the novels' publication in a language and a place outside of the narratives' national and linguistic milieu. Finally, in a reversal of the typical publication chronology, Ma Jian's *Beijing Coma*, though written in Chinese, was first published in English in 2008 and had to wait more than a year for its original Chinese version to appear. Even then, its dissemination in Chinese has been sporadic. The diasporic path that began with Gao might find itself routing through Jin's and Wang's self-translating detours into English, but with Ma's novel, the English translation now precedes the original, both in the material reproduction of the work as a cultural object and in the symbolic production of the work's meanings in world discourses on Tiananmen. A most telling sign of this obligatory translation circuit is that, in the year following the novel's English-language publication, Chinese-language media sources worldwide have come to refer to the book much more commonly as *Beijing zhiwuren* than *Routu*. Indeed, it would seem that Ma's original title is destined for the literary historian's footnote, since the press that now publishes the Chinese edition of the novel has also chosen to market the book under the reverse-translated title of *Beijing zhiwuren*.[1] In this latest phase of globalization and its ever more dislocated modes of cultural production and historical memorialization, not only does the PRC no longer have temporal or interpretive priority in its self-representation, but the Chinese literary diaspora itself becomes increasingly intertwined with the modes of representation and reproduction of China's cultural, linguistic, and national others. So, even as Ma insistently focuses on the Chinese students in the Square, in an attempt to reclaim the centrality of the place of origin and the agents of origin's politics, the moment in which he writes and publishes ironically behooves him to make this reclamation first and foremost in translation.

But the end results of this absorption of Chinese diasporic aesthetics into English, and of its politics into Western institutions, have yet to be fully played out. As we saw in chapter 1, Gao's dissident status was largely manufactured by the international media in the wake of his Nobel award, in part so that he could fulfill the role of native informant qua exilic critic of the PRC for the liberal West. Gao's fame, then, has fed an enduring Cold War discourse of Asian oppression and Western heroism, enabling the West to pursue its economic partnership with the PRC while exteriorizing criticism of the communist government by attributing it to one of China's own native sons, albeit a rejected and expelled one. And as we saw in chapters 2 and 3, Jin's corpus too plays a part in sustaining this discourse, while Wang's novel takes neo-orientalism as an explicit target of critique even as her English-language fictions capitalize on Western consumer trends that fetishize the sexuality of Asian women. It would appear that Ma's meteoric rise to literary prominence in the West is the latest instance of this global neo-orientalism surrounding the Chinese diaspora writer. In fact, Ma fits the liberal bill even more perfectly. Unlike Gao, he does not need to have his anticommunist stance mythologized, and unlike both Gao and Jin, he does not distance himself or his writing from politics but is only too vocal in his public denunciations of PRC policies. His penchant for the gothic may even serve to nurture Western readers' perception of Chinese atrocity and exceptionalism. *Beijing Coma*'s running metaphor of cannibalism, though derived from a familiar trope indigenous to the modern Chinese canon and meant as an argument for further political change, may resonate only too well with narratives of Chinese barbarity that continue to circulate in the West. For an example, we can invoke James Dobson, chairman of the American conservative evangelical organization Focus on the Family, who protested the 1995 United Nations Conference on Women in Beijing precisely by characterizing China as a cannibalistic state, using Harry Wu's book and the one-child policy to shore up exotic stereotypes and racialized hatred among his American right-wing supporters (Berglund 175–83). Against this backdrop, the image of Dai Wei's comatose and decaying body—the figure of the lone Chinese victim that plays the counterpart to the Chinese barbarian—may be read only too readily as the latest incarnation of what Eric Hayot calls the "hypothetical mandarin": the imaginary figure of a suffering Chinese stranger, with the accompanying trope of Chinese pain, that has been essential in structuring Western discourses of human sympathy and moral responsibility for the last two centuries (4–6). Viewed cynically within these contexts, the enthusiastic embrace of Ma by the West may signal the most heightened form of contemporary global neo-orientalism yet. From this perspective, the post-Tiananmen literary diaspora now carries the torch of Western imperialism by fetishizing the Chinese body in pain, with the grotesque image of Dai Wei's rotting body serving as the newest revival of the spectacle of *lingchi* that so erotically captivated Georges Bataille several decades ago.

In the end, however, such a critique can all too briskly lead us back to the dead end of an orientalist/anti-orientalist debate in which East and West, origin and diaspora, stay inexorably, ontologically polarized—a diasporic version of what Rey Chow calls the "deadlock of the anthropological situation" (*Primitive* 176). On such a view, the measure of a diaspora writer's integrity can only be his or her obscurity in the West, and any hint of popular success or recognition can only be a sign of his or her co-optation by the other. This is a moral double bind no less limiting than the Maoist injunction against Western appropriations. As we saw in chapter 3, this criticism has often been leveled, and often by diaspora critics, at diasporic memoirs of the Cultural Revolution, and Tiananmen fictions are all too easily construed as a successor to that genre. Indeed, my intuition is that the subtle cultural pressures exerted on diaspora writers by the diaspora itself operate as a strong literary deterrent for writing Tiananmen. Since June 4 has come to symbolize an intransigent political difference between communist China and the liberal West, any diaspora writer attempting to fictionalize the episode will unavoidably be caught up in a global cultural politics and a representational tug-of-war, in addition to the diasporic image wars I discussed in chapter 4. Many critics may be inclined to hold in contempt these creative efforts as self-orientalizing gestures pandering to the tastes of a global market. This attitude underlies, for instance, Michael Berry's parenthetical aside when he casually notes that Jin's *The Crazed* "fails to highlight (exploit?) the massacre in the way that many other works have" (354).

We can find another example in Shuyu Kong's otherwise astute review of *Beijing Coma* when she writes: "Not surprisingly, Ma's heroic self-image as a dissident, his controversial works, and his uncompromising criticism of China as a totalitarian society have enticed international publishers and readers, and led to comprehensive publication of his works in recent years. . . . Is it possible that such a situation, where Ma writes about China but must sell his work outside China, has influenced some of his ethical and political choices, in other words, the way that he writes about China, and what aspects of China he chooses to represent?" Is there a way to answer this question except in the affirmative, insofar as location and conditions of writing and publication inevitably influence a writer's choices? The question of what Ma's novel attempts to illumine about Tiananmen, however, is not asked. Instead of probing the discursive functions of a reportage style and what this might mean for a reinterpretation of June 4, the review complains of the novel's lack of "literary craftsmanship" and its "tedious and verbose display of unedited documentary footage"; instead of examining Ma's tactics at deflecting moral judgments on the student activists, the review reinstates morality as the yardstick of literary greatness, bemoaning that the novel lacks the "moral complexity that great works are often valued for." Habits of aesthetic appreciation and expectations for literature to serve as a moral guide are perhaps especially tenacious in Tiananmen discourse. Yet the task of mining deeper insights from Ma's book requires not just readerly patience and perseverance but an acknowledgment that we may not know the history of the massacre as well as we might think. Though Ma does not explicitly satirize Western orientalism as Wang does in *Lili*, Tiananmen through the lens of *Beijing Coma* is still far from a self-orientalizing history known many times over, flattened into already seen images and mediatized as an already attended spectacle. On the contrary, Ma presents us with an event whose significance is not simply excavated through a revisitation of its unfolding moment in slow time, in all its thick banalities, but constantly juxtaposed against an ever-accruing future that is our present. Without a recognition of these aesthetic effects and the political value they bear for a renewed understanding of Tiananmen in the circumstances of the now, one might indeed worry that the novel risks "fall[ing] into the usual political traps and cultural stereotypes that afflict other works written by Chinese émigré authors" (and among these Shuyu Kong includes *The Crazed*). Ultimately, the assumptions behind this judgment have the unfortunate effect of discouraging, perhaps even denigrating, serious efforts at historical reevaluation for purposes of critical memory and political advocacy. The plea for human rights may not always already be just another case of diasporic self-colonization.

As with Gao, we can begin to work out the problem of the Western commodification of Chinese diaspora writers, not by resorting to some notion of nativist integrity or loyalty, nor by fantasizing in the abstract about some radically non-orientalist aesthetics, but by tracing the lines of a cross-hemispheric theory of the polis, of political responsibility, and of politicized life. For one socialist version of this, we might look to the critical efforts of Wang Hui. Here the connection to Tiananmen becomes direct, historically as well as intellectually. Himself a former participant in the Beijing protests who was among the last group of students to leave the Square on June 4, Wang has since combined his training in Chinese literature with an inquiry into globalization's political economy. In his incisive tract on 1989 and its relation to contemporary China—an essay that has never been published in the mainland but that circulates widely on the Chinese Internet and in translations abroad (Huters 6)—Wang states his thesis about the global impact of Tiananmen right from the outset: "The 1989 social movement had a profound influence not just on China but on the whole world" (46). On his analysis, the 1989 movement represented the final instance of China's century-long tradition of revolutionary socialist politics: more than anything else, the populace's cry for democracy arose from a desire not for political deposition but for socioeconomic equality, not for "a set of political procedures and legal stipulations" but a "guaranteeing [of] social justice and the democraticization of economic life" (61). As he points out, in addition to its well-known calls for "democracy," the movement also invoked the socialist ideal of "the equality of everyday life," but unlike the older ideology under Mao, this concept had been transformed into "a force for the mobilization of social critique" (61–62). The key point for Wang is that the Chinese party-state under critique by the masses in this watershed moment was no longer socialist in spirit or practice but had become all too *neoliberal*—by 1989, the communist government had embraced globalization's "program of market totalization," in which "relations based on capital take possession of the social sphere" and priorities of markets and profits completely trump matters of social welfare (124, 127). Against the neoliberal paradigm, Wang argues that market reform and economic liberalization in the PRC have never been "spontaneous" affairs but are "normally . . . expressed through state policy and its reliance on coercion" (120); neoliberal tenets about the market's self-regulation and capital's free flows are not merely inaccurate but insidious and pernicious, masking the state's hand in the increasing monopolization of power within the nation while absolving the state's political responsibility in safeguarding social equality for its workers and subjects, both intranationally and transnationally. To my mind, the challenge Wang mounts for a contemporary rethinking of Tiananmen, whether on this or that side of the Pacific, is much more formidable than the one posed by neo-orientalism alone: the real danger today, he suggests, is not a reinvigorated cultural exoticism of China or even a geopolitical polarization between East and West but the actual incorporation of a supposed other polity into an already hugely unequal hegemonic world order dominated by the neoliberal logic, a world order in which the political duties of a so-called socialist state and the possibility of wide-scale socialist politics are rapidly disappearing everywhere. For Wang, the June 4 massacre, while it "shook the world" at the time, has unfortunately fed a historical evaluation of 1989 that promotes a neoliberal teleology, so that the very interest groups that colluded with state power could subsequently pass themselves off as "radical reformers" and "a progressive force moving toward the world market and democracy" (62). Post-1989, the West's habitual fixation on the massacre as the supreme meaning of Tiananmen as well as its eagerness to interpret the PRC's accelerated capitalism as a laudable mode of freedom only underscore neoliberalism's spreading dominion and socialism's epochal decline. In this situation, the "alternative globalizations" Wang seeks are emphatically not embodied by the laissez-faire market economies of the West, politically democratic or otherwise. Instead, he will look to Tiananmen again for the seed of a promise: the 1989 movement cannot be read "unidirectionally" as "the final victory of the Western social system, with China as merely an isolated and incomplete historical instance," for "once this single understanding becomes the world's predominant narrative, once it becomes ironclad proof of the superiority of the present system, once protest becomes merely praise for that system, then [the social movement's] true meaning, its critical potential, and its historical significance will all be lost" (65). In the absence of a "united world government to coordinate global industrial policy, financial security, and equitable economic distribution," Wang will continue to invest the unit of the nation-state with "broad political responsibility for the domestic economic order and for social justice" (129). Beyond the domestic, he also forecasts "the role of the state within a new trend of participatory internationalism," in which "various states organize a global force to reduce the polarization of north and south, protect the global ecology and push for a fair world order, rather than working to oppose those ends" (130). Such a bifocal envisioning of the nation-state as local polity and guarantor of social life as well as participatory actor for global equality and planetary preservation has yet to materialize in any Tiananmen fiction, though the literary diaspora would do well to heed this vision's potential in the age to come.

Finally, complementing Wang Hui's model, the importance of Ma Jian's novel can be cast as its attempt to redefine critical discourse away from a worldview of hemispheric dichotomy toward issues of totalitarian biopower on a grand scale. If the Square's ubiquity within *Beijing Coma* is interpreted metatextually as a telescoping of the PRC's present and future expansion in the global economy, then its sovereign biopower within its national domain can be imagined as starting to seep outside the Square, into a province of networked relations beyond China proper. In many ways, the PRC has already occupied center stage in international debates about biopower in the last decade, particularly around the topic of illegal organ trading of death-row prisoners and Falun Gong practitioners, hence extending beyond the nation's borders the long-standing world fascination with the one-child policy as a biopoliticization of everyday life. Indeed, the Chinese state's politicizing of its subjects' bodies historically precedes, and has been temporally coeval with, Western theories of biopower from Foucault to Agamben and Hardt and Negri onward, so that it could be deemed one unacknowledged origin point, material as well as discursive, for the other hemisphere's not-so-insular biopolitical speculations. If the PRC maintains its course toward global dominance, what may emerge as a paramount critical enterprise for world scholars in this millennium is the rethinking of totalitarianism as a condition for biopolitical exceptionality, with totalitarian biopower as a crux analytic category of globalization that intersects with imperialism and capitalism to generate new modes of interrogating scattered transnational power. What Dai Wei's body pinpoints, with negative utopianism, is one location where that global future can be halted—at the never-departed Square.

Notes

Introduction

1. See Michael Berry's chapter "Beijing 1989" in his *A History of Pain* for a discussion of Chinese literary and filmic representations of Tiananmen within the critical framework of trauma.

2. The climate in the PRC has changed in the past few years for these writers. Duo Duo was allowed back in China in 2004 and now teaches at Hainan University; Yang Lian has made frequent trips back to China since 1999 on a New Zealand passport; and Bei Dao, though still barred from China, now teaches at the City University of Hong Kong and is finally permitted to have his books published on the mainland.

3. Ha Jin is the pen name of Jin Xuefei, hereafter referred to as Jin.

4. The GCIM was launched in 2003 by the United Nations and a number of world governments to respond to these planetary realities, but its 2005 report forcefully concludes that "the international community has failed to capitalize on the opportunities and to meet the challenges associated with international migration," and that "new approaches are required to correct this situation" (2).

5. Of this group, Annie Wang is unique in that she now lives in both California and Shanghai, a point I will expand on in chapter 3.

6. For a survey of some Tiananmen films and documentaries, see Berry (319–52). For a study on the influences of June 4 on transnational Chinese cinema more generally, see Gina Marchetti's *From Tian'anmen to Times Square*.

7. Sheng Qi's art can be viewed on his website, Sheng Qi. From March to May 2011, eight of his paintings of Tiananmen Square comprised the solo exhibition *Square* at the Fabien Fryns Fine Art Gallery in Los Angeles.

8. One of the paintings in this series, which depicts crumpled tents and moving tanks under the misty floodlights of a square, is part of *Goya to Beijing*, an internationally traveling exhibition memorializing June 4, comprised of some twenty works by contemporary artists from around the world. The exhibition organizers hope to ultimately end the tour in Beijing, "to bring this collection of artwork to Beijing as a

memento," at a future point when the massacre has been officially acknowledged (P.-Y. Han).

9. For these reasons, too, I regrettably give short shrift to Tiananmen fictions that have not been translated, such as Hong Kong writer Li Bihua (Lilian Lee)'s *Tiananmen jiupo xinhun* (Tiananmen old souls and new spirits) (1990), and those works originally written in languages other than Chinese and English, such as the Japan-based novelist Yang Yi's recent prize-winning *Toki ga nijimu asa* (A morning steeped in time) (2008).

10. For this reason, I cite Gao's play throughout this book as *Taowang*—as opposed to my usual practice of citing Chinese-language texts first by their English titles, followed by the original Chinese in parentheses. In instances in which the Chinese text has not been published in English (as with *Liusi shiji* and *Tiananmen qingren*), I cite the Chinese title first, followed by a parenthetical translation of it in roman type.

1 / The Existentialist Square

1. Even the most casual sampling of one day's news in English will reveal this media pattern. The October 13 *Boston Globe* article "Nobel in Literature Awarded to Chinese Dissident" begins with "Gao Xingjian, a Chinese novelist and playwright whose works have been banned by the Chinese government, has been chosen to receive this year's Nobel Prize in Literature" (Feeney), while the same day's *Washington Post* likewise emphasizes Gao's exilic condition with the headline "Chinese Exile Wins Nobel for Literature" (Weeks). In Canada, the *Toronto Star* article "Exiled Novelist Wins Nobel" recounts how "the 60-year-old survivor of China's upheaval and oppression became its first Nobel Prize laureate for literature," while the *Montreal Gazette*, with greater sensationalist flare, runs the headline "Writing to Survive: Chinese Nobel Winner Was Forced to Destroy 'Kilos and Kilos' of His Works." Across the Atlantic, London's *Independent* reports on "Exiled Dissident Whose Works Are Banned in China Wins Nobel Prize" (Moyes), while the *Financial Times* begins its coverage by describing Gao as "a Chinese-born novelist branded persona non grata by Beijing's government" (Kynge). Similarly in Australia, Melbourne's *Herald Sun* calls Gao a "Chinese-born writer" who had his works "banned in his homeland" ("Chinese"), while the lead-in to the next day's *Sydney Morning Herald* article "Writer Could Trust No-one, Not Even My Family" histrionically relates how the writer "burnt his early writings to save himself from communist zealots, was denounced by his wife and eventually went into exile" (August). For a summary of similar media reportage on Gao's Nobel in languages other than English—in Taiwan, Hong Kong, and Europe—see Kwok-kan Tam's "Introduction" (4–7).

2. The exception is *The Other Shore* (1999), a collection of Gao's post-PRC experimental drama dating largely from the early 1990s. See appendix 1 in Henry Zhao's *Towards a Modern Zen Theatre* for a checklist of Gao's major works, in original Chinese and in various Western translations, up until 2000.

3. The publication of Gao's two novels, *Soul Mountain* (2000) and *One Man's Bible* (2002), has been followed swiftly by that of his plays: *Snow in August* (2003), *Escape & The Man Who Questions Death* (2007), and *Of Mountains and Seas* (2008). A collection of his short fiction in translation, *Buying a Fishing Rod for My Grandfather* (2004), has been succeeded by a multigenre bilingual anthology, *Cold Literature* (2005), as well as a collection of his essays in translation, *The Case for Literature* (2006). Even his visual art has been assembled into two volumes, *Ink Paintings by Gao Xingjian* (2002) and *Return to Painting* (2002). In addition, Gao is now the focus of numerous

journal articles and a scholarly anthology, Kwok-kan Tam's edited *Soul of Chaos* (2001), as well as the subject of several single-author critical studies: Sy Ren Quah's *Gao Xingjian and Transcultural Chinese Theater* (2004), Izabella Labedzka's *Gao Xingjian's Idea of Theatre* (2008), and Jessica Yeung's *Ink Dances in Limbo* (2008). One exception here is Henry Zhao's *Towards a Modern Zen Theatre* (2000), the first English-language book-length study of Gao's drama, which was first written in Chinese and published in Taipei in 1999 before its English version appeared just days before the Nobel announcement.

4. In his introductory sections to *Soul of Chaos*, Kwok-kan Tam argues that Gao Xingjian's "transcultural" aesthetics places him "in the forefront of world literature," marking a "transition from tradition to modernity" ("Introduction" 2). This claim is materially reproduced by the 2003 edition of *The Bedford Anthology of World Literature*, which has added Gao to its ranks, after Lu Xun and Bei Dao, as only the third representative twentieth-century Chinese writer of "world literature." More recently, at the December 2007 conference "Globalizing Modern Chinese Literature: Sinophone and Diasporic Writings," held at Harvard University, Gao was the name most frequently cited in conversations about Sinophone writers in the diaspora. Just a few months later in May 2008, the Chinese University of Hong Kong, the French Centre for Research on Contemporary China, and the University of Aix-Marseille I jointly organized an international conference in Hong Kong focused solely on Gao, this time to explore his relationship to "his culture," that is, Chinese cultural traditions.

5. Contrast Mabel Lee's passage with this more subdued account by Bonnie McDougall and Kam Louie: "The increasingly repressive atmosphere [in the PRC] after 1986 led to prohibitions on Gao's new work. After travelling to Europe in 1987, he settled in Paris where he continues to write fiction and drama" (365).

6. See Lovell too for a penetrating analysis of the larger cultural significance of the Nobel Prize for post-Mao intellectuals in their quest for international—that is, Western—recognition of Chinese national literary identity, a quest she diagnoses as an anxiety-ridden "intellectual marginality complex."

7. Throughout this chapter, where no translator is cited in the text or in the bibliography, the translation is my own.

8. Unless otherwise noted, quotations from "Without Isms" are based on Mabel Lee's translation of the essay in *The Case for Literature*.

9. The first term is adopted by Mabel Lee (64), the second by Winnie Lau, Deborah Sauviat, and Martin Williams in their earlier translation of the essay (105).

10. In Gao's post-1989 drama too, we discern a steady disappearance of social preoccupations. Of his PRC plays, *Alarm Signal* (*Juedui xinhao*) (1982) is the most overtly social, though *Bus Stop* (*Chezhan*) (1983) has also been widely read as an allegory of the Cultural Revolution decade. While Henry Zhao points out that, by the late 1980s, "Gao's positions of social engagement" were already becoming "gradually individualized," that "social issues no longer commanded his attention" (94), we can still see visible ties to contemporary social issues in his work of this period, and even *Wild Man* (*Yeren*) (1985), the last of his plays to be staged in the PRC, addresses a specific cultural crisis in China.

11. In his grand history of Western philosophy, Castoriadis identifies Plato as the one who "inaugurates the era of philosophers who wriggle out of the city" by conceiving of "a city removed from time and history, governed not by its own people but by 'philosophers'" (8). Castoriadis is critical of this philosophical tradition for emptying

the city of its political function and for absolving citizens of public service and civic responsibility.

12. The English translation history of this passage in *Mencius* indicates a divergence of interpretation over this very question: should Mencius be read as strictly a man of his time and an advocate of imperialism, or can we recuperate him as a more modern and egalitarian spirit? Waley suggests the latter, and he may well be supported by both James Legge's 1860s translation and Bryan Van Norden's more recent one in 2001. The key term here is *tianxia*—"under Heaven" for Waley, "all under heaven" for Legge, and the most secular of all, "the world" for Van Norden. D. C. Lau, by contrast, insists on the terminology of empire and translates the passage with colonial overtones: "When he saw a common man or woman who did not enjoy the benefit of the rule of Yao and Shun, Yi Yin felt as if he had pushed him or her into the gutter. This is the extent to which he considered the Empire his responsibility" (V.B.1).

13. See Peg Birmingham for a discussion of this dimension of Arendt's thought, particularly her principle of "common responsibility" premised on the human "capacity for both horror and gratitude, both violence and pleasure" (1–3).

14. Gregory Lee first translated *Taowang* into English as *Fugitives* in 1993, but this version was published in a little-circulated collection of conference papers. The recent retranslation of the play by Gilbert Fong, as the first title work in the independent volume *Escape & The Man Who Questions Death*, stands to gain a much wider readership for Gao. See Henry Zhao's appendix 1 for a list of *Taowang*'s translations and performances up until 2000.

15. Gao identifies the locale simply as *dushi yi feixu* (130), which Gregory Lee translates as "a ruin in a capital" (89) and Gilbert Fong as an "abandoned market in the city" (2). Lee's translation is more accurate in this instant, though with the translation of the female character's title, Fong's "Girl" is closer in connotation to Gao's *Guniang* than Lee's "Young Woman." For convenience of cross-reference, since Fong's version is now widely distributed and accessible, my quotations of *Taowang* are taken from his translation of it in *Escape & The Man Who Questions Death*.

16. Earlier in his career, Gao had adopted this allegorical figure of the passerby from Lu Xun's short play *Guoke* as the Silent Man in *The Bus Stop*. The point of disparity between the earlier play and *Taowang* is that, while the Middle-aged Man remains immobile, the Silent Man walks out on a situation of inertia and opens up the promise of an exit in an otherwise no-exit drama. Comparing these two works, we can appreciate how Gao's stance on nonaction has become solidified from the time he was in the PRC to the time he wrote his Tiananmen play.

2 / The Aporetic Square

1. "The House Behind a Weeping Cherry" was first published in the *New Yorker* in 2008 before its inclusion in *A Good Fall* in 2009.

2. See also my "Theorizing the Hyphen's Afterlife," in which I read the motifs of bodies in *The Crazed* through a theoretical framework of biopower and within the context of Asian American transnationalism (151–55).

3. For a reading of modern Chinese narratives of trauma via the conceptual dichotomy of "centripetal" versus "centrifugal," see Michael Berry. Borrowing from Bakhtin, Berry distinguishes between two types of traumatic narratives: the first involves episodes of violence occurring under the shadow of colonialism such as the Nanjing Massacre, which lead to a drive to "create and cement a new modern

conception of the 'Chinese nation,'" while the second involves episodes of "indigenous violence" propagated by the communist state itself such as the Cultural Revolution and Tiananmen, which lead to narratives seeking "alternatives to the nation in a new global landscape" (5–6).

4. See, for example, the website June 4th Memoir (Liusi dangan).

5. Several book-length studies are illustrative in this regard. Xiaobin Yang's *The Chinese Postmodern* is arguably closest to the psychoanalytic method. Yang uses the lens of trauma to read a host of contemporary mainland writers, linking their "postmodern" narrative strategies to the psychic effects of actual historical violence. Citing Freud's theory of deferred action, Yang proposes that trauma offers a broadly applicable basis for interpreting the "culturo-historical status of contemporary China," for it is "*Nachträglichkeit* of the deeply ingrained trauma that correlates the previously experienced historical violence with the current act of writing of Chinese avant-garde fiction" (49). Another example is Michael Berry's *A History of Pain*. Less psychoanalytically informed than Yang's book but likewise deploying trauma as an overarching rubric, this study surveys a wide array of contemporary Chinese literary and filmic texts, organized chronologically by the episodes of historical violence they depict, from the Musha Incident to the Hong Kong Handover. Berry treats historical violence chiefly as representational content rather than life experience or psychic outcome, and so, unlike Yang, he does not endeavor to provide a unified theory of trauma as such. Instead, he sketches an expansive picture of the imagination of national crisis for contemporary writers and filmmakers, in which the notion of "pain" becomes "a crucial component of our understanding of modern China." Against this backdrop, "historical crises have been continually renewed and re-created *not* in history, but through the lens of literature, film, and popular culture" (1–2). Berry thus mostly engages with trauma as artistic content and creative agency rather than psychic residue.

6. For an erudite exception to the rule, see Liangyan Ge. For another example, see Louis Parascandolathis, though the force of this latter is somewhat diluted by its generic comparison of Jin's *Waiting* to George Orwell's *1984*.

7. Within this milieu, there is a world of difference, I think, between the claiming of Jin by a historically minor canon such as Asian American literature, for the purpose of pushing beyond its own entrenched positions, and by contrast, the co-opting of Jin by an expansionist model of the Chinese national canon that seeks to assimilate its most far-flung and trenchant critics by emptying out their political content.

8. For example, one 2003 anthology of diaspora theories defines "diaspora" as above all a "contestatory" structure, at once putting into "question the rigidities of identity itself—religious, ethnic, gendered, national" and providing "myriad, dislocated sites of contestation to the hegemonic, homogenizing forces of globalization" as much as "nation and nationalism" (Braziel and Mannur 3, 7).

9. With some skepticism does Bruce Robbins call this celebratory stance an "ethically idealized internationalization" (99), one that naively posits "transnational mobility and the hybridity that results from it as simple and sufficient goods in themselves" (98). As he points out, diasporic discourse constitutes only one version of "U.S. internationalism" in the 1990s. Some critics, however, do at times demonstrate an awareness of this limitation to diaspora discourse. Ien Ang, for one, despite the overall tenor of her book, which treats "hybridity" as a good-in-itself, recommends a deconstruction of the idea of diaspora, advocating instead a recognition of "the double-edgedness

of diasporic identity: it can be the site of both support and oppression, emancipation and confinement" (12).

10. Hall's theory has disseminated widely within Caribbean and black intellectual discourses of diaspora, where the deconstructive prong takes precedence as well. For instance, Paul Gilroy advances a view of diasporic cultural identity that is closely analogous to Hall's second definition when he describes the "black Atlantic" through the language of "creolization, *métissage, mestizaje*, and hybridity" (*Black* 2). For a "tracking" of diaspora discourse, see James Clifford.

11. Aside from the macro narrative of *A Free Life*, arguably the most blatant example of Ha Jin's pro-Americanist views, see the chapter "The Abduction of General Bell" in *War Trash*, especially the phone conversation between General Bell and General Fulton (180–81). In a telling passage, the novel's narrator opposes two sets of political ethos, American friendship versus Chinese communist comradeship: "I was amazed by the phone call, not having expected that the American generals would talk in a casual, personal manner in the midst of such a crisis. They had treated each other as friends, not as comrades who shared the same ideal and who fought for the same cause. They hadn't mentioned any ideological stuff. What a contrast this was to Chinese officers, who, in a situation like this, would undoubtedly speak in the voice of revolutionaries, and one side would surely represent the Party" (181).

3 / The Globalized Square

1. According to Huang, "In the 1980s, FDI [foreign direct investment] and international trade were minuscule" for the PRC (54). Yet Huang is also unique in arguing, contrary to most studies, that the 1980s was the "true China miracle" in terms of the country's economic development, especially from the perspective of rural poverty reduction, whereas accounts of China's achievements in the 1990s are vastly overstated (54–55).

2. In interviews, Wang states that *Lili* took ten years to write, a period that spanned most of the 1990s ("Beijing's"; "Conversation").

3. The first day Wang's column became available online for *South China Morning Post* subscribers, the newspaper's website received more than one hundred thousand extra hits, and the column itself averaged about fifteen thousand hits per week by mid-2004 (Chhibber).

4. Wang perhaps tries to thematize this class privilege in one chapter in *The People's Republic of Desire* when she has her narrator report on factory workers in Shenzhen: although Niuniu proclaims the experience to be eye-opening, she devotes only one paragraph to the workers themselves, describing them as "an important part of the global economic chain that produces the goods that Wal-Mart or Nike stores sell in the United States," and then lamenting the pittance they get paid (263). The chapter then switches to detail Niuniu's romantic travails and her airplane conversation with a married engineer with a midlife crisis and a hankering for beautiful Shenzhen girls. In the next chapter, the only thing we hear about her Shenzhen article is a one-liner about her having spent three days doing interviews there (268), with no further reflections on how the products made by these very workers are invariably scorned by her and her yuppie friends.

4 / The Biopolitical Square

1. As Liu Binyan reports in his review of Zheng Yi's *Scarlet Memorial*: "In Qing-zhou District, with a population around 300,000, Zheng Yi found official Party surveys, done in 1983, of the grisly phenomenon of promotion as a reward for murder: 10,420 people were killed in Cultural Revolution violence; 1,153 people were admitted to the Communist Party after demonstrating credit for a killing; 458 officials received promotions; and 637 people were given urban work permits, on the same basis" ("Unnatural" 271).

2. See Albert Chang for a discussion of conflicting eyewitness accounts of the massacre's location and scope.

3. In its continual canonization, Simpson's piece has been republished in several anthologies, including a volume of his collected writings, *The Darkness Crumbles*, ever-newer editions of *The Granta Book of Reportage*, and an anthology of literary journalism entitled, ironically enough, *The Art of Fact*.

4. Shen Tong's memoir likewise reinforces this view: "I was not in Tiananmen Square, but I was at one of the two centers of the most brutal killings. Many have corroborated what I saw: most of the people who died were civilians and workers, and they were gunned down in Xidan and Muxudi areas, on the western approach of Changan Avenue to the square" (337).

5. For a discussion of this controversy, see Barmé's *In the Red* (328–33).

6. Aside from aforementioned sources that spotlight the deaths of workers and *laobaixing*, see Dingxin Zhao, who refers to the Liubukou massacre in a footnote as a tragic incident where "a speeding tank crashed into a crowd; several students who had just left the Square were killed or wounded as a result" (206 n. 177).

Conclusion

1. Mingjing Press, or Mirror Books, is itself a diasporic enterprise: founded in Toronto in 1991 by a China-born journalist, it is now based in New York with a Hong Kong office.

BIBLIOGRAPHY

Abraham, Yvonne. "Cashing in on Tiananmen." *Boston Phoenix,* 27 March–3 April 1997. Web.

Agamben, Giorgio. *The Coming Community.* Translated by Michael Hardt. Minneapolis: University of Minnesota Press, 1993.

———. *Homo Sacer: Sovereign Power and Bare Life.* Translated by Daniel Heller-Roazen. Stanford, Calif.: Stanford University Press, 1998.

An Tian. *Tiananmen qingren* [Tiananmen lover]. New York: Boxun chuban-she, 2004.

Ang, Ien. *On Not Speaking Chinese: Living Between Asia and the West.* London: Routledge, 2001.

Angel, Karen. "Reading the East Wind." *South China Morning Post,* 21 March 2004, 1.

Appadurai, Arjun. "Disjuncture and Difference in the Global Cultural Economy." *Public Culture* 2, no. 2 (1990): 1–24.

Appiah, Kwame Anthony. *Cosmopolitanism: Ethics in a World of Strangers.* New York: Norton, 2006.

Apted, Michael, dir. *Moving the Mountain.* Film. Hallmark Home Entertainment, 1995.

Arendt, Hannah. "Karl Jaspers: Citizen of the World?" In *Men in Dark Times,* by Arendt, 81–94. San Diego: Harcourt Brace, 1968.

———. *On Violence.* San Diego: Harcourt Brace, 1970.

———. "Organized Guilt and Universal Responsibility." In *Essays in Understanding, 1930–1954: Formation, Exile, and Totalitarianism,* edited by Jerome Kohn, 121–32. New York: Schocken, 1994.

———. *The Origins of Totalitarianism.* San Diego: Harcourt, 1968.

Arrighi, Giovanni. *Adam Smith in Beijing: Lineages of the Twenty-First Century.* London: Verso, 2007.

August, Marilyn. "Writer Could Trust No-one, Not Even My Family." *Sydney Morning Herald,* 14 October 2000, 7.

Bachelard, Gaston. *The Poetics of Space.* Translated by Maria Jolas. Boston: Beacon, 1969.

Barmé, Geremie R. "Confession, Redemption, and Death: Liu Xiaobo and the Protest Movement of 1989." In *The Broken Mirror: China after Tiananmen,* edited by George Hicks, 52–99. Chicago: St. James, 1990.

———. *In the Red: On Contemporary Chinese Culture.* New York: Columbia University Press, 1999.

Barmé, Geremie, and Linda Jaivin, eds. *New Ghosts, Old Dreams: Chinese Rebel Voices.* New York: Random House, 1992.

Barnstone, Tony. "Introduction: Chinese Poetry Through the Looking Glass." In *Out of the Howling Storm: The New Chinese Poetry,* edited by Tony Barnstone, 1–38. Hanover, N.H.: Wesleyan University Press, 1993.

Barthes, Roland. *Camera Lucida: Reflections on Photography.* Translated by Richard Howard. New York: Hill and Wang, 1981.

Bataille, Georges. *The Tears of Eros.* Translated by Peter Connor. San Francisco: City Lights, 1988.

Bates, Roy. *10,000 Chinese Names.* Beijing: China History, 2007.

Baum, Richard. "Tiananmen—The Inside Story?" Review of *The Tiananmen Papers,* compiled by Zhang Liang. *China Journal* 46 (July 2001): 119–34.

Bei Dao. "deny"/"Fouren." In *Landscape Over Zero,* translated by David Hinton with Yanbing Chen, 96–97. New York: New Directions, 1995.

———. "June"/"Liuyue." In *Unlock,* translated by Eliot Weinberger and Iona Man-Cheong, 2–3. New York: New Directions, 2000.

———. "Requiem"/"Diao wang." In *Old Snow,* translated by Bonnie S. McDougall and Chen Maiping, 10–11. New York: New Directions, 1991.

Beijing Comrade [Beijing tongzhi]. *Beijing gushi* [Beijing story]. Guangtong. org., 25 April 2001. Web.

———. *Beijing Story.* Nifty.org, 11 May 2005. Web.

Bell, William. *Forbidden City: A Novel of Modern China.* Toronto: Doubleday Canada, 1990.

Benjamin, Walter. "Critique of Violence." Translated by Edmund Jephcott. In *Selected Writings, Volume 1, 1913–1926,* edited by Marcus Bullock and Michael W. Jennings, 236–52. Cambridge: Belknap Press of Harvard University Press, 1996.

———. *Illuminations: Essays and Reflections.* Edited by Hannah Arendt. Translated by Harry Zohn. New York: Schocken, 1968.

———. "The Task of the Translator." In Benjamin, *Illuminations,* 69–82.

———. "Theses on the Philosophy of History." In Benjamin, *Illuminations,* 253–64.

Berglund, Jeff. *Cannibal Fictions: American Explorations of Colonialism, Race, Gender, and Sexuality.* Madison: University of Wisconsin Press, 2006.

Berry, Michael. *A History of Pain: Trauma in Modern Chinese Literature and Film.* New York: Columbia University Press, 2008.

Birmingham, Peg. *Hannah Arendt and Human Rights: The Predicament of Common Responsibility.* Bloomington: Indiana University Press, 2006.

Black, George, and Robin Munro. *Black Hands of Beijing: Lives of Defiance in China's Democracy Movement.* New York: Wiley, 1993.

Boren, Mark Edelman. *Student Resistance: A History of the Unruly Subject.* New York: Routledge, 2001.

Braziel, Jana Evans, and Anita Mannur. "Nation, Migration, Globalization: Points of Contention in Diaspora Studies." In *Theorizing Diaspora: A Reader,* edited by Jana Evans Braziel and Anita Mannur. Malden, Mass.: Blackwell, 2003.

Brook, Timothy. *Quelling the People: The Military Suppression of the Beijing Democracy Movement.* New York: Oxford University Press, 1992.

Buruma, Ian. *Bad Elements: Chinese Rebels from Los Angeles to Beijing.* New York: Vintage, 2001.

Calhoun, Craig. *Neither Gods nor Emperors: Students and the Struggle for Democracy in China.* Berkeley: University of California Press, 1994.

Cao Guanlong. "Three Professors: Fire." Translated by John Berninghausen. In *Roses and Thorns: The Second Blooming of the Hundred Flowers in Chinese Fiction 1979–1980,* edited by Perry Link, 130–45. Berkeley: University of California Press, 1984.

Castoriadis, Cornelius. *Philosophy, Politics, Autonomy: Essays in Political Philosophy.* New York: Oxford University Press, 1991.

Chai Ling. "I'm Chai Ling. I'm Still Alive." In *Crisis at Tiananmen: Reform and Reality in Modern China,* by Yi Mu and Mark V. Thompson, 265–69. San Francisco: China Books, 1989.

———. "Testimony." All Girls Allowed. May 2010. Web.

Chan, Alfred L., with rejoinder by Andrew J. Nathan. "The Tiananmen Papers Revisited." *China Quarterly* 177 (March 2004): 190–214.

Chan, Andrew. "*Lan Yu*: That Obscure Object of Desire." *Reverse Shot* 24 (2009). Web.

Chang, Albert. "Revisiting the Tiananmen Square Incident: A Distorted Image from Both Sides of the Lens." *Stanford Journal of East Asian Affairs* 5, no. 1 (2005): 9–25.

Chang, Leslie T. *Factory Girls: From Village to City in a Changing China.* New York: Spiegel and Grau, 2009.

Cheah, Pheng. *Inhuman Conditions: On Cosmopolitanism and Human Rights.* Cambridge: Harvard University Press, 2006.

Chen Guang. *Impulsion to Extremeness: Chen Guang Internet Exhibition.* Chen Guang Liao Art. Blogspot.com, 28 July 2008. Web.

———. "An Interview with Chen Guang: The Ruined Prospects in the Waves of History," by Shu Yang. 13 July 2008. Chen Guang Liao Art. Web.

Chen Li. "Gao Xingjian: Life as a Literature Laureate." *BBC World Service*, 17 March 2001. Web.

Chen, Lingchei Letty. "Translating Memory, Transforming Identity: Chinese Expatriates and Memoirs of the Cultural Revolution." *Tamkang Review* 38, no. 2 (2008): 25–40.

———. *Writing Chinese: Reshaping Chinese Cultural Identity*. New York: Palgrave Macmillan, 2006.

Chen, Pauline. "Screening History: New Documentaries on the Tiananmen Events in China." *Cineaste* 22, no. 1 (1996): 18. Web.

Chen Ran. *A Private Life*. Translated by John Howard-Gibbon. New York: Columbia University Press, 2004.

Cheng, Terrence. *Sons of Heaven*. New York: Morrow, 2002.

Chhibber, Kabir. "All the Rage in Hong Kong." *Financial Times*, 10 April 2004, weekend magazine, 12.

Chin, Marilyn. *The Phoenix Gone, The Terrace Empty*. Minneapolis: Milkweed, 1994.

"Chinese Author's Nobel." *Herald Sun* (Melbourne), 13 October 2000, 31.

Chow, Rey. *Primitive Passions: Visuality, Sexuality, Ethnography, and Contemporary Chinese Cinema*. New York: Columbia University Press, 1995.

———. *The Protestant Ethnic and the Spirit of Capitalism*. New York: Columbia University Press, 2002.

Clifford, James. "Diasporas." *Cultural Anthropology* 9, no. 3 (1994): 302–38.

Conceison, Claire. "Focus on Gao Xingjian: Review Article." Review of *Towards a Modern Zen Theatre: Gao Xingjian and Chinese Theatre Experimentalism*, by Henry Y. H. Zhao, and *The Other Shore: Plays by Gao Xingjian*, translated by Gilbert C. F. Fong. *China Quarterly* 167 (2001): 749–53.

Crampton, Thomas. "A Novel of Sex, Violence and Tiananmen Square." *International Herald Tribune*, 5 June 2001, 20.

Dai Qing. *Tiananmen Follies: Prison Memoirs and Other Writings*. Edited and translated by Nancy Yang Liu, Peter Rand, and Lawrence R. Sullivan. Norwalk, Ct.: EastBridge, 2005.

Dai Qing, and Geremie Barmé. "'Tiananmen Follies': An Exchange." *New York Review of Books*, 27 April 2006. Web.

"Dai Wei." Tiananmen muqin wangzhan: liusi zhaopian ziliao [Tiananmen mothers website: June 4 photographs and profiles]. The Tiananmen Mothers, 2011. Web.

Davis, Paul, et al. *The Bedford Anthology of World Literature Book 6: The Twentieth Century, 1900–The Present*. New York: Bedford/St. Martin's, 2003.

Derrida, Jacques. *On Cosmopolitanism and Forgiveness*. Translated by Mark Dooley and Michael Hughes. London: Routledge, 2001.

Dirlik, Arif. "Critical Reflections on 'Chinese Capitalism' as Paradigm." *Identities* 3, no. 3 (1997): 303–30.

———. "'Trapped in History' on the Way to Utopia: East Asia's 'Great War' Fifty Years Later." In *Perilous Memories: The Asia-Pacific War(s)*, edited by T. Fujitani, Geoffrey M. White, and Lisa Yoneyama, 299–322. Durham: Duke University Press, 2001.

Edemariam, Aida. "Playing with Fire." *Guardian*, 8 August 2008, 10.

Eng, David L. *Racial Castration: Managing Masculinity in Asian America*. Durham: Duke University Press, 2001.

Esherick, Joseph W., and Jeffrey N. Wasserstrom. "Acting out Democracy: Political Theater in Modern China." In *Popular Protest and Political Culture in Modern China: Learning from 1989*, edited by Jeffrey N. Wasserstrom and Elizabeth J. Perry, 28–66. Boulder: Westview, 1992.

"Exiled Novelist Wins Nobel." *Toronto Star*, 13 October 2000, A3.

Fang Lizhi. *Bringing Down the Great Wall: Writings on Science, Culture, and Democracy in China*. Edited and translated by James H. Williams. New York: Norton, 1990.

Fang Zheng. "In Memory of Tiananmen Massacre: Special Interview with Fang Zheng." *Epoch Times*, 6 June 2005. Web.

———. "Testimony of Fang Zheng, Wounded." Human Rights in China, 31 January 1999. Web.

Fanon, Frantz. *Black Skin, White Masks*. Translated by Charles Lam Markmann. New York: Grove, 1967.

Feeney, Mark. "Nobel in Literature Awarded to Chinese Dissident." *Boston Globe*, 13 October 2000, A18.

Feigon, Lee. "Gender and the Student Movement." In *Popular Protest and Political Culture in Modern China: Learning from 1989*, edited by Jeffrey N. Wasserstrom and Elizabeth J. Perry, 165–76. Boulder: Westview, 1992.

Fewsmith, Joseph. *China since Tiananmen: The Politics of Transition*. 1st ed. Cambridge: Cambridge University Press, 2001.

———. *China since Tiananmen: From Deng Xiaoping to Hu Jintao*. 2nd ed. Cambridge: Cambridge University Press, 2008.

Fong, Gilbert C. F. Introduction to Gao, *The Other Shore: Plays by Gao Xingjian*, translated by Fong. Hong Kong: Chinese University Press, 1999.

Foucault, Michel. *The History of Sexuality*. Vol. 1. Translated by Robert Hurley. New York: Vintage, 1990.

Gao Xingjian. "About *Escape*." Translated by Shelby K. Y. Chan. In Gao, *Escape*, 69–71.

———. *Alarm Signal*. In *Chinese Drama after the Cultural Revolution, 1979–1989*, edited and translated by Shiao-Ling S. Yu, 159–232. Lewiston, N.Y.: Edwin Mellen, 1996.

———. "Bali suibi" [Paris jottings]. 1991. In Gao, *Meiyou zhuyi*, 19–30.

———. *Bus Stop*. In *Chinese Drama after the Cultural Revolution, 1979–1989*, edited and translated by Shiao-Ling S. Yu, 233–89. Lewiston, N.Y.: Edwin Mellen, 1996.

———. *Buying a Fishing Rod for My Grandfather*. Translated by Mabel Lee. New York: HarperCollins, 2004.

——. *The Case for Literature.* Translated by Mabel Lee. New Haven: Yale University Press, 2007.

——. "The Case for Literature." In Gao, *Case for Literature,* 32–48.

——. *Cold Literature: Selected Works by Gao Xingjian / Lengde wenxue: Gao Xingjian zhuzuo xuan.* Translated by Gilbert C. F. Fong and Mabel Lee. Hong Kong: Chinese University Press, 2005.

——. *Escape.* In *Escape & The Man Who Questions Death,* translated by Gilbert C. F. Fong, 1–66. Hong Kong: Chinese University Press, 2007.

——. *Fugitives.* Translated by Gregory B. Lee. In *Chinese Writing and Exile,* edited by Gregory B. Lee, 89–137. Chicago: Center for East Asian Studies, University of Chicago, 1993.

——. "Guanyu *Taowang*" [About *Escape*]. 1991. In Gao, *Meiyou zhuyi,* 206–8.

——. *Ink Paintings by Gao Xingjian: Nobel Prize Winner.* Dumont, N.J.: Homa and Sekey, 2002.

——. "Literature Makes It Possible to Hold on to One's Awareness of Oneself as Human." Interview by Jean-Luc Douin. *Label France* 43 (2001). Web.

——. *Meiyou zhuyi* [Without isms]. 1996. Taipei: Lianjing chuban shiye gongsi, 2001.

——. "Meiyou zhuyi" [Without isms]. 1993. In Gao, *Meiyou zhuyi* 3–14.

——. *Of Mountains and Seas: A Tragicomedy of the Gods in Three Acts.* Translated by Gilbert C. F. Fong. Hong Kong: Chinese University Press, 2008.

——. *One Man's Bible.* Translated by Mabel Lee. New York: HarperCollins, 2002.

——. *The Other Shore: Plays by Gao Xingjian.* Translated by Gilbert C. F. Fong. Hong Kong: Chinese University Press, 1999.

——. *Return to Painting.* Translated by Nadia Benabid. New York: Harper Perennial, 2002.

——. *Snow in August.* Translated by Gilbert C. F. Fong. Hong Kong: Chinese University Press, 2003.

——. *Soul Mountain.* Translated by Mabel Lee. New York: HarperCollins, 2000.

——. *Taowang* [Escape]. 1990. In *Gao Xingjian juzuo xuan* [Selected plays by Gao Xingjian], 129–96. Hong Kong: Mingbao chubanshe, 2001.

——. "Without Isms." In Gao, *Case for Literature,* 64–77.

——. "Without Isms." Translated by Winnie Lau, Deborah Sauviat, and Martin Williams. *Journal of Oriental Society of Australia* 27–28 (1995–96): 105–14.

——. "Wo zhuzhang yizhong lengde wenxue" [I advocate a cold literature]. 1990. In Gao, *Meiyou zhuyi,* 15–18.

——. Zixu [Preface]. 1995. In Gao, *Meiyou zhuyi.*

"*The Gate of Heavenly Peace* Transcript." The Gate of Heavenly Peace. Long Bow Group, 1995. Web.

Ge, Liangyan. "The Tiger-Killing Hero and the Hero-Killing Tiger." *Comparative Literature Studies* 43, no. 1–2 (2006): 39–56.

Gilroy, Paul. *The Black Atlantic: Modernity and Double Consciousness*. Cambridge: Harvard University Press, 1993.

———. *Postcolonial Melancholia*. New York: Columbia University Press, 2005.

Global Commission on International Migration (GCIM). "Migration in an Interconnected World: New Directions for Action—Report of the Global Commission on International Migration." Global Commission on International Migration, 5 October 2005. Web.

Goh, Robbie B. H. "The Culture of Asian Diasporas: Integrating/Interrogating (Im)migration, Habitus, Textuality." In *Asian Diasporas: Cultures, Identities, Representations*, edited by Goh and Shawn Wong, 1–13. Hong Kong: Hong Kong University Press, 2004.

Goldblatt, Howard. Translator's Note. In *The Republic of Wine*, by Mo Yan. New York: Arcade, 2000.

Gordon, Richard, and Carma Hinton, dirs. *The Gate of Heavenly Peace*. Film. Long Bow Group, 1995.

Grice, Helena. *Negotiating Identities: An Introduction to Asian American Women's Writing*. Manchester, U.K.: Manchester University Press, 2002.

Gu Zhaosen. "Plain Moon." Translated by Michelle Yeh. In *Running Wild: New Chinese Writers*, edited by David Der-wei Wang with Jeanne Tai, 137–57. New York: Columbia University Press, 1994.

Hall, Stuart. "Cultural Identity and Diaspora." In *Identity: Community, Culture, Difference*, edited by Jonathan Rutherford, 222–37. London: Lawrence and Wishart, 1990.

Han Hsiang-ning. Erju dangdai meishuguan [Nomadic contemporary art gallery]. Sina.com.cn, June 2011. Web.

———. "Lao zhaopian huagao" [Old photographs and sketchbook]. Erju dangdai meishuguan. 3 June 2010. Web.

Han, Pei-Yuan. "Foreword—Twenty Years Later." Goya to Beijing 1990–2030??, *Goya to Beijing* exhibit, 4 June 2009. Web.

Hardt, Michael, and Antonio Negri. *Empire*. Cambridge: Harvard University Press, 2000.

Harmsen, Peter. "Former Tiananmen Soldier Depicts Crackdown through Art." Agence France Presse, 7 June 2009. Web.

Hassan, Ihab. "Janglican: National Literatures in the Age of Globalization." *Philosophy and Literature* 34, no. 2 (2010): 271–80.

Hayot, Eric. *The Hypothetical Mandarin: Sympathy, Modernity, and Chinese Pain*. Oxford: Oxford University Press, 2009.

Hinton, Carma, et al. "An Appeal." The Gate of Heavenly Peace. Long Bow Group, 15 April 2009. Web.

Hirsch, Marianne. "Projected Memory: Holocaust Photographs in Personal and Public Fantasy." In *Acts of Memory: Cultural Recall in the Present*, edited by Mieke Bal, Jonathan Crewe, and Leo Spitzer, 2–23. Hanover, N.H.: University Press of New England, 1999.

———. "Surviving Images: Holocaust Photographs and the Work of Postmemory." *Yale Journal of Criticism* 14, no. 1 (2001): 5–37.

Holden, Stephen. "Assessing Both Sides in Tiananmen Square Massacre." *New York Times,* 14 October 1995, 14.

Hom, Sharon K. "Introduction: Points of No Return." In *Chinese Women Traversing Diaspora: Memoirs, Essays, and Poetry,* edited by Hom, 3–28. New York: Garland, 1999.

Hong Ying. *Daughter of the River.* Translated by Howard Goldblatt. New York: Grove, 1997.

———. *Summer of Betrayal.* Translated by Martha Avery. New York: Grove, 1997.

Hsia, C. T. *A History of Modern Chinese Fiction.* Bloomington: Indiana University Press, 1999.

Huang, Wen. "Introduction: The Voice of China's Social Outcasts." In *The Corpse Walker: Real-Life Stories, China from the Bottom Up,* by Liao Yiwu, translated by Wen Huang. New York: Pantheon, 2008.

Huang, Yasheng. *Capitalism with Chinese Characteristics: Entrepreneurship and the State.* New York: Cambridge University Press, 2008.

Huang, Yibing. *Contemporary Chinese Literature: From the Cultural Revolution to the Future.* New York: Palgrave Macmillan, 2007.

Human Rights in China. *Children of the Dragon: The Story of Tiananmen Square.* New York: Macmillan, 1990.

Huters, Theodore. Introduction to *China's New Order: Society, Politics, and Economy in Transition,* by Wang Hui, edited by Huters. Cambridge: Harvard University Press, 2003.

Jacobs, Andrew. "Tiananmen Square Scars Soldier Turned Artist." *New York Times,* 3 June 2009, A1.

Jameson, Fredric. "Third-World Literature in the Era of Multinational Capitalism." *Social Text* 15 (Autumn 1986): 65–88.

Jiang Pinchao, ed. *Liusi shiji* [June 4 collected poetry]. Hong Kong: Boda chubanshe, 2007.

Jin, Ha. "The Art of Fiction No. 202." Interview by Sarah Fay. *Paris Review* 191 (Winter 2009). Web.

———. *The Bridegroom: Stories.* New York: Vintage, 2001.

———. *The Crazed.* New York: Vintage, 2002.

———. *Dengdai* [Waiting]. Translated by Jin Liang. Changsha: Hunan wenyi chubanshe, 2002.

———. *Fengkuang* [The crazed]. Translated by Huang Canran. Taipei: Shibao wenhua chuban gongsi, 2004.

———. *A Free Life.* New York: Pantheon, 2007.

———. *A Good Fall.* New York: Pantheon, 2009.

———. "The House Behind a Weeping Cherry." *New Yorker,* 7 April 2008, 66–75.

———. *In the Pond.* New York: Vintage, 2000.

———. "An Individual's Homeland." In Jin, *Writer as Migrant,* 61–86.

———. Interview by Jana Siciliano. Bookreporter.com, 13 October 2000. Web.

———. "Introduction: Lu Hsun as a Man." In *Selected Stories*, by Lu Hsun [Lu Xun], translated by Yang Hsien-yi and Gladys Yang. New York: Norton: 2003.

———. *Luodi* [A fall]. Translated by Ha Jin. Taipei: Shibao wenhua chuban gongsi, 2010.

———. "Man to Be." In Jin, *Under the Red Flag*, 17–30.

———. *Nanjing Requiem*. New York: Pantheon, 2011.

———. *Ocean of Words: Stories*. New York: Vintage, 1998.

———. "The Spokesman and the Tribe." In Jin, *Writer as Migrant*, 3–30.

———. "A Tiger-Fighter Is Hard to Find." In Jin, *Bridegroom*, 54–70.

———. *Under the Red Flag*. Cambridge, Mass.: Zoland, 1998.

———. *Waiting*. New York: Vintage, 2000.

———. *War Trash*. New York: Vintage, 2004.

———. *The Writer as Migrant*. Chicago: University of Chicago Press, 2008.

Joyce, James. *A Portrait of the Artist as a Young Man*. New York: Penguin, 1991.

June 4th Memoir [Liusi dangan]. China Truth Foundation, 2009. Web.

Kellman, Steven G., ed. "Interview with Ha Jin." In *Switching Languages: Translingual Writers Reflect on Their Craft*, 81–84. Lincoln: University of Nebraska Press, 2003.

Khoo, Olivia. *The Chinese Exotic: Modern Diasporic Femininity*. Hong Kong: Hong Kong University Press, 2007.

Kong, Belinda. "Theorizing the Hyphen's Afterlife in Post-Tiananmen Asian-America." *Modern Fiction Studies* 56, no. 1 (Spring 2010): 136–59.

Kong, Shuyu. "Diaspora Literature." In *Columbia Companion to Modern East Asian Literature*, edited by Joshua Mostow and Kirk A. Denton, 546–53. New York: Columbia University Press, 2003.

———. Review of *Beijing Coma*, by Ma Jian. In *Modern Chinese Literature and Culture*. MCLC Resource Center, August 2009. Web.

Kristeva, Julia. *Strangers to Ourselves*. Translated by Leon S. Roudiez. New York: Columbia University Press, 1991.

Kuo, Alex. *Chinese Opera*. Hong Kong: Asia 2000, 1998.

Kwan, Stanley, dir. *Lan Yu*. Film. Strand Releasing, 2001.

Kynge, James. "Asia-Pacific: Chinese Writer Wins Nobel Prize." *Financial Times*, 13 October 2000, 12.

Labedzka, Izabella. *Gao Xingjian's Idea of Theatre: From the Word to the Image*. Leiden: Brill, 2008.

Laughlin, Charles A. *Chinese Reportage: The Aesthetics of Historical Experience*. Durham: Duke University Press, 2002.

Lee, C. Y. *Gate of Rage: A Novel of One Family Trapped by the Events of Tiananmen Square*. New York: Morrow, 1991.

Lee, Gregory B., ed. *Chinese Writing and Exile*. Chicago: Center for East Asian Studies, University of Chicago, 1993.

———. "Contemporary Chinese Poetry, Exile and the Potential of Modernism." In G. Lee, *Chinese Writing*, 55–77.

———. Introduction to *Chinese Writing*, by G. Lee.

Lee, Gregory B., and Noël Dutrait. "Conversations with Gao Xingjian: The First 'Chinese' Winner of the Nobel Prize for Literature." *China Quarterly* 167 (2001): 738–48.

Lee, Leo Ou-fan. "On the Margins of the Chinese Discourse: Some Personal Thoughts on the Cultural Meaning of the Periphery." In *The Living Tree: The Changing Meaning of Being Chinese Today*, by Tu Wei-ming, 221–38. Stanford: Stanford University Press, 1994.

Lee, Mabel. "Gao Xingjian on the Issue of Literary Creation for the Modern Writer." In *Soul of Chaos: Critical Perspectives on Gao Xingjian*, edited by Kwok-kan Tam, 21–41. Hong Kong: Chinese University Press, 2001.

———. "Gao Xingjian's Dialogue with Two Dead Poets from Shaoxing: Xu Wei and Lu Xun." In *Soul of Chaos: Critical Perspectives on Gao Xingjian*, edited by Kwok-kan Tam, 277–91. Hong Kong: Chinese University Press, 2001.

———. "Nobel in Literature 2000 Gao Xingjian's Aesthetics of Fleeing." *Comparative Literature and Culture* 5, no. 1 (2003). Web.

———. "Of Writers and Translators." Paper presented at the conference "The Flight of the Mind: Writing and the Creative Imagination." National Library of Australia, Canberra, Australia, 25 October 2009.

———. "Pronouns as Protagonists: On Gao Xingjian's Theories of Narration." In *Soul of Chaos: Critical Perspectives on Gao Xingjian*, edited by Kwok-kan Tam, 235–56. Hong Kong: Chinese University Press, 2001.

———. "Walking out of Other People's Prisons: Liu Zaifu and Gao Xingjian on Chinese Literature in the 1990s." *Asian and African Studies* 5 (1996): 98–112.

Li Lu. *Moving the Mountain: My Life in China from the Cultural Revolution to Tiananmen Square*. Film. London: Macmillan, 1990.

Li, Yiyun. "Found in Translation." *Guardian*, 6 December 2006, G2: 8.

Liang, Diane Wei. *Paper Butterfly*. London: Picador, 2008.

Liao Yiwu. *The Corpse Walker: Real-Life Stories, China from the Bottom Up*. Translated by Wen Huang. New York: Pantheon, 2008.

———. "Datusha" [Massacre]. In *Liusi shiji* [June 4 collected poetry], edited by Jiang Pinchao, 74–78. Hong Kong: Boda chubanshe, 2007.

———[as Anonymous]. "The Howl." In *New Ghosts, Old Dreams: Chinese Rebel Voices*, edited by Geremie Barmé, and Linda Jaivin, 100–105. New York: Random House, 1992.

Link, Perry. *The Uses of Literature: Life in the Socialist Chinese Literary System*. Princeton: Princeton University Press, 2000.

Liu Binyan. "An Unnatural Disaster." Review of *Hongse jinianbei* [Red Memorial], by Zheng Yi. In *Two Kinds of Truth: Stories and Reportage from China*, edited and translated by Perry Link, 267–80. Bloomington: Indiana University Press, 2006.

Liu Binyan, with Ruan Ming and Xu Gang. *"Tell the World": What Happened in China and Why*. Translated by Henry L. Epstein. New York: Pantheon, 1989.

Liu Hong. *Startling Moon*. London: Review, 2001.

Liu Xiaobo. "On Solitude." In *New Ghosts, Old Dreams: Chinese Rebel Voices*, edited by Geremie Barmé and Linda Jaivin, 207–9. New York: Random House, 1992.

Liu Yiqing. "Na chengshi zuojiaoyi: Ha Jin he tade xiaoshuo *Dengdai*" [Trading on honesty: Ha Jin and his novel *Waiting*]. *Gaungming ribao* [Guangming Daily], 14 June 2000. Web.

"Liusi sinanzhe mingdan" [June 4 victims list]. Tiananmen muqin yundong [Tiananmen mothers campaign]. The Tiananmen Mothers, 2009. Web.

Lo Kwai Cheung. "The Myth of 'Chinese' Literature: Ha Jin and the Globalization of 'National' Literary Writing." David C. Lam Institute for East-West Studies (LEWI) Working Paper Series 23 (2004).

Lou Ye, dir. *Summer Palace* [*Yiheyuan*]. Film. Palm Pictures, 2006.

Lovell, Julia. "Filthy Fiction: The Writings of Zhu Wen." The China Beat. Blogspot.com, 5 August 2009. Web.

———. "Gao Xingjian, the Nobel Prize, and Chinese Intellectuals: Notes on the Aftermath of the Nobel Prize 2000." *Modern Chinese Literature and Culture* 14, no. 2 (2000): 1–50.

———. Translator's Afterword. In *I Love Dollars and Other Stories of China*, by Zhu Wen, translated by Lovell, 229–40. New York: Penguin, 2008.

Lu Hsun [Lu Xun]. *Selected Stories*. Translated by Yang Hsien-yi and Gladys Yang. New York: Norton: 2003.

Ma Jian. *Beijing Coma*. Translated by Flora Drew. New York: Farrar, Straus, and Giroux, 2008.

———. *Beijing zhiwuren* [Beijing coma]. New York: Mingjing chubanshe, 2009.

———. "China's Grief, Unearthed." Translated by Flora Drew. *New York Times*, 4 June 2008, A25.

———. "China's Olympic Crossroads: Author Ma Jian on Beijing, Spectacle and Reality." Interview by Flora Zhang. *New York Times*, 5 August 2008. Web.

———. "The Great Tiananmen Taboo." *Guardian*, 2 June 2009 G2: 6.

Ma, Laurence J. C. "Space, Place, and Transnationalism in the Chinese Diaspora." In *The Chinese Diaspora: Space, Place, Mobility, and Identity*, edited by Ma and Carolyn Cartier, 1–49. Lanham, Md.: Rowman and Littlefield, 2003.

Ma, Laurence J. C., and Carolyn Cartier, eds. *The Chinese Diaspora: Space, Place, Mobility, and Identity*. Lanham, Md.: Rowman and Littlefield, 2003.

Marchetti, Gina. *From Tian'anmen to Times Square: Transnational China and the Chinese Diaspora on Global Screens, 1989–1997*. Philadelphia: Temple University Press, 2006.

McDougall, Bonnie S., and Kam Louie. *The Literature of China in the Twentieth Century*. New York: Columbia University Press, 1997.

Mencius. *Mencius*. Translated by D. C. Lau. Baltimore: Penguin, 1970.

———. "*Mengzi (Mencius)*." Translated by Bryan W. Van Norden. In *Readings in Classical Chinese Philosophy*, edited by Philip J. Ivanhoe and Bryan W. Van Norden, 110–55. New York: Seven Bridges, 2001.

———. *The Works of Mencius.* Translated by James Legge. Hong Kong, 1861. Vol. 2 of *The Chinese Classics.* 7 vols. 1861–76.

Mo Yan. *The Republic of Wine.* Translated by Howard Goldblatt. New York: Arcade, 2000.

Moyes, Jojo. "Exiled Dissident Whose Works Are Banned in China Wins Nobel Prize." *Independent,* 13 October 2000, 15.

Mu, Yi, and Mark V. Thompson. *Crisis at Tiananmen: Reform and Reality in Modern China.* San Francisco: China Books, 1989.

Munro, Robin. "Remembering Tiananmen Square: Who Died in Beijing, and Why." *Nation,* 11 June 1990, 811–22.

Nathan, Andrew J. "Introduction: The Documents and Their Significance." In *The Tiananmen Papers,* compiled by Zhang Liang, edited by Nathan and Perry Link. New York: PublicAffairs, 2001.

———. "Preface to the Paperback Edition: The Tiananmen Papers—An Editor's Reflections." In *The Tiananmen Papers,* compiled by Zhang Liang, edited by Nathan and Perry Link. New York: PublicAffairs, 2001.

Ng, Maria N., and Philip Holden, eds. *Reading Chinese Transnationalisms: Society, Literature, Film.* Hong Kong: Hong Kong University Press, 2006.

"Nobel Literature Prize Politically Used: Official." *Xinhua News Agency,* 13 October 2000.

Nonini, Donald M., and Aihwa Ong. "Chinese Transnationalism as an Alternative Modernity." In *Ungrounded Empires: The Cultural Politics of Modern Chinese Transnationalism,* edited by Ong and Nonini, 3–33. New York: Routledge, 1997.

Oh, Seiwoong. "Cultural Translation in Ha Jin's *Waiting.*" In *Querying the Genealogy: Comparative and Transnational Studies in Chinese American Literature,* edited by Jennie Wang, 420–27. Shanghai: Shanghai yiwen chubanshe, 2006.

Ommundsen, Wenche. "From China with Love: Chick Lit and the New Crossover Fiction." In *China Fictions/English Language: Literary Essays in Diaspora, Memory, Story,* edited by A. Robert Lee, 327–45. Amsterdam: Rodopi, 2008.

Ong, Aihwa. "Chinese Modernities: Narratives of Nation and of Capitalism." In *Ungrounded Empires: The Cultural Politics of Modern Chinese Transnationalism,* edited by Ong and Donald M. Nonini, 171–202. New York: Routledge, 1997.

———. *Flexible Citizenship: The Cultural Logics of Transnationality.* Durham: Duke University Press, 1999.

Ong, Aihwa, and Donald M. Nonini, eds. *Ungrounded Empires: The Cultural Politics of Modern Chinese Transnationalism.* New York: Routledge, 1997.

Overseas Compatriot Affairs Commission, R.O.C. (Taiwan). *Overseas Compatriot Population Distribution, Table 1: Overseas Chinese Population Count.* Overseas Compatriot Affairs Commission, R.O.C. (Taiwan), n.d. Web.

Parascandola, Louis J. "Love and Sex in a Totalitarian Society: An Exploration of Ha Jin and George Orwell." *Studies in the Humanities* 32, no. 1 (2005): 38–49.

Parreñas, Rhacel Salazar, and Lok C. D. Siu. "Introduction: Asian Diasporas— New Conceptions, New Frameworks." In *Asian Diasporas: New Formations, New Conceptions,* edited by Rhacel Salazar Parreñas and Lok C. D. Siu, 1–27. Stanford: Stanford University Press, 2007.

Perry, Elizabeth J. "Casting a Chinese 'Democracy' Movement: The Roles of Students, Workers, and Entrepreneurs." In *Popular Protest and Political Culture in Modern China: Learning from 1989,* edited by Jeffrey N. Wasserstrom and Perry, 146–64. Boulder: Westview, 1992.

Quah, Sy Ren. *Gao Xingjian and Transcultural Chinese Theater.* Honolulu: University of Hawaii Press, 2004.

Ren Bumei. "A Time for Self-Reflection." *China Rights Forum* 2 (2004): 65–69.

Rightmyer, Jack. "Author Ha Jin to Read, Talk at UAlbany on Life in China." *Daily Gazette,* 21 September 2003. Web.

Riley, Jo, and Michael Gissenwehrer. "The Myth of Gao Xingjian." In *Soul of Chaos: Critical Perspectives on Gao Xingjian,* edited by Kwok-kan Tam, 111–32. Hong Kong: Chinese University Press, 2001.

Riminton, Hugh. "Women Take a Great Leap Forward." CNN.com, 18 May 2005. Web.

Robbins, Bruce. "Some Versions of U.S. Internationalism." *Social Text* 45 (1995): 97–123.

Rojas, Carlos. "Without [Femin]ism: Femininity as Axis of Alterity and Desire in Gao Xingjian's *One Man's Bible.*" *Modern Chinese Literature and Culture* 14, no. 2 (2000): 163–206.

Ruan Ming. *Deng Xiaoping: Chronicle of an Empire.* Edited and translated by Nancy Liu, Peter Rand, and Lawrence R. Sullivan. Boulder: Westview, 1994.

Said, Edward W. *Culture and Imperialism.* New York: Vintage, 1994.

———. *Representations of the Intellectual: The 1993 Reith Lectures.* New York: Vintage, 1994.

Schaffer, Kay, and Sidonie Smith. *Human Rights and Narrated Lives: The Ethics of Recognition.* New York: Palgrave Macmillan, 2004.

Schaffer, Kay, and Xianlin Song. "Narrative, Trauma and Memory: Chen Ran's *A Private Life,* Tiananmen Square and Female Embodiment." *Asian Studies Review* 30, no. 2 (June 2006): 161–73.

———. "Writing Beyond the Wall: Translation, Cross-cultural Exchange and Chen Ran's *A Private Life.*" *PORTAL: Journal of Multidisciplinary International Studies* 3, no. 2 (2006): 1–20. Web.

Schell, Orville. *Mandate of Heaven: The Legacy of Tiananmen Square and the Next Generation of China's Leaders.* New York: Simon and Schuster, 1994.

Scheper-Hughes, Nancy. "The Global Traffic in Human Organs." *Current Anthropology* 41, no. 2 (2000): 191–224.

Shen, Shuang. *Cosmopolitan Publics: Anglophone Print Culture in Semi-Colonial Shanghai.* New Brunswick, N.J.: Rutgers University Press, 2009.

Shen Tong, with Marianne Yen. *Almost a Revolution*. New York: Houghton Mifflin, 1990.

Sheng Qi. Sheng Qi. 2011. Web.

Shih, Shu-mei. *Visuality and Identity: Sinophone Articulations across the Pacific*. Berkeley: University of California Press, 2007.

Shu Yang. Preface. "Impulsion to Extremeness: Chen Guang Internet Exhibition." Chen Guang Liao Art. 28 July 2008. Web.

Simpson, John. "Tiananmen Square." *Granta*, Autumn 1989, 9–25.

Spence, Jonathan D. "Tiananmen." In *Chinese Roundabout: Essays in History and Culture*, 293–303. New York: Norton, 1992.

Stanford, Peter. "Books Etc: The East Is Read—All over Again." *Independent* (London), 27 January 2002, Sunday ed., 13.

Su Xiaokang. *A Memoir of Misfortune*. Translated by Zhu Hong. New York: Knopf, 2001.

Swedish Academy. "The Nobel Prize for Literature 2000: Gao Xingjian." Press release. 12 October 2000.

Tam, Kwok-kan. "Introduction: Gao Xingjian, the Nobel Prize and the Politics of Recognition." In Tam, *Soul of Chaos*, 1–20.

———. Preface toTam, *Soul of Chaos*.

———, ed. *Soul of Chaos: Critical Perspectives on Gao Xingjian*. Hong Kong: Chinese University Press, 2001.

"*The Tank Man* Transcript." *The Tank Man*. PBS Frontline, 2006. Web.

"*The Tank Man*: Making the Film: Q&A with Filmmaker Antony Thomas." *The Tank Man*. PBS Frontline, 2006. Web.

Thomas, Antony. "PBS Frontline: 'The Tank Man'." *Washington Post*, 12 April 2006. Web.

———, dir. *The Tank Man*. Film. PBS Video, 2006.

Thomas, John D. "Across an Ocean of Words." *Emory Magazine* 74, no. 1 (Spring 1998). Web.

Tiananmen muqin [Tiananmen mother]. The Tiananmen Mothers, 2011. Web.

Tsai, Kellee S. *Capitalism without Democracy: The Private Sector in Contemporary China*. Ithaca: Cornell University Press, 2007.

Tsu, Jing. *Sound and Script in Chinese Diaspora*. Cambridge: Harvard University Press, 2011.

Tsu, Jing, and David Der-wei Wang, eds. *Global Chinese Literature: Critical Essays*. Leiden: Brill, 2010.

Tu Wei-ming. "Cultural China." In Tu, *Living Tree*, 1–34.

———. Preface to the Standard Edition. In Tu, *Living Tree*.

———, ed. *The Living Tree: The Changing Meaning of Being Chinese Today*. Stanford: Stanford University Press, 1994.

Tyler, Patrick E. "6 Years after the Tiananmen Massacre, Survivors Clash Anew on Tactics." *New York Times*, 30 April 1995, 12.

Uno, Roberta, ed. *Unbroken Thread: An Anthology of Plays by Asian American Women*. Amherst: University of Massachusetts Press, 1993.

Van Hear, Nicholas. *New Diasporas: The Mass Exodus, Dispersal, and Regrouping of Migrant Communities.* Seattle: University of Washington Press, 1998.

Virilio, Paul. *Open Sky.* Translated by Julie Rose. London: Verso, 2008.

Waley, Arthur. *Three Ways of Thought in Ancient China.* Stanford, Calif.: Stanford University Press, 1982.

Wang, Annie. "Beijing's Badgirl of Letters." Interview by Genessee Kim. *Gold-Sea,* n.d. Web.

———. "A Conversation with Annie Wang." Bold Type. Random House.com, June 2002. Web.

———. *Lili.* New York: Anchor, 2001.

———. "A New Chapter." *Time Asia,* 20 January 2003. Web.

———. *The People's Republic of Desire.* New York: Harper, 2006.

———. "People's Republic of Desire? Sex and Money in Today's China." Interview by Pueng Vongs. New America Media, 14 August 2006. Web.

———. *PostGlobal.* Washington Post.com. 10 July 2007. Web.

Wang, Ban. *Illuminations from the Past: Trauma, Memory, and History from Modern China.* Stanford: Stanford University Press, 2004.

Wang Dan. "Defense of Chai Ling." June 4th Memoir. 28 May 2009. Web.

———. "*Liusi shiji* chuban de yiyi" [The significance of the publication of June 4 collected poetry]. In *Liusi shiji* [June 4 collected poetry], edited by Jiang Pinchao, iii–iv. Hong Kong: Boda chubanshe, 2007.

Wang, David Der-wei. "Chinese Fiction for the Nineties." In *Running Wild: New Chinese Writers,* edited by Wang with Jeanne Tai, 238–58. New York: Columbia University Press, 1994.

———. *The Monster That Is History: History, Violence, and Fictional Writing in Twentieth-Century China.* Berkeley: University of California Press, 2004.

Wang, David Der-wei, with Jeanne Tai, eds. *Running Wild: New Chinese Writers.* New York: Columbia University Press, 1994.

Wang Gungwu. "Chineseness: The Dilemmas of Place and Practice." In *Cosmopolitan Capitalists: Hong Kong and the Chinese Diaspora at the End of the Twentieth Century,* edited by Gary G. Hamilton, 118–34. Seattle: University of Washington Press, 1999.

———. *Don't Leave Home: Migration and the Chinese.* Singapore: Times Academic Press, 2001.

———. "A Single Chinese Diaspora?" In *Joining the Modern World: Inside and Outside China,* 37–70. Singapore: Singapore University Press, 2000.

Wang Hui. *China's New Order: Society, Politics, and Economy in Transition.* Edited by Theodore Huters. Cambridge: Harvard University Press, 2003.

Wang, Jing. *High Culture Fever: Politics, Aesthetics, and Ideology in Deng's China.* Berkeley: University of California Press, 1996.

Wang, L. Ling-chi. "Roots and the Changing Identity of the Chinese in the United States." In *The Living Tree: The Changing Meaning of Being Chinese Today,* by Tu Wei-ming, 185–212. Stanford: Stanford University Press, 1994.

Wang, Lulu. *The Lili Theater: A Novel of Modern China*. Translated by Hester Velmans. New York: Talese, 2000.

Wang Shuo. *Please Don't Call Me Human*. Translated by Howard Goldblatt. Boston: Cheng and Tsui, 2003.

Wang Wei, Wang Fei, and Wang Rui. *Three Wang Sisters' Skies and Dreams*. Beijing: Culture and Art Press, 1997.

Wasserstrom, Jeffrey N., and Elizabeth J. Perry, eds. *Popular Protest and Political Culture in Modern China: Learning from 1989*. Boulder: Westview, 1992.

Weeks, Linton. "Chinese Exile Wins Nobel for Literature." *Washington Post*, 13 October 2000, C1.

Weisenhaus, Doreen. "Arts Abroad: Asia's Writers Turning to English to Gain Readers." *New York Times*, 25 December 2001, late ed., E2.

"What Happened at Tiananmen?" In *Crisis at Tiananmen: Reform and Reality in Modern China*, by Yi Mu and Mark V. Thompson, 249–55. San Francisco: China Books, 1989.

Wong, Elizabeth. *Letters to a Student Revolutionary*. In *Unbroken Thread: An Anthology of Plays by Asian American Women*, edited by Roberta Uno, 267–308. Amherst: University of Massachusetts Press, 1993.

Woodward, Richard B. "Anatomy of a Massacre." *Village Voice*, 4 June 1996, 29–35.

"Writing to Survive: Chinese Nobel Winner Was Forced to Destroy 'Kilos and Kilos' of His Works." *Montreal Gazette*, 13 October 2000, B14.

Wu, Harry. Testimony to Hawaii State Senate: Hearing of the Committee on Judiciary and Government Operations. Hawaii State Legislature Website. Hawaii State Legislature, 2 April 2009. Web.

Wu Harry, and George Vecsey. *Troublemaker: One Man's Crusade against China's Cruelty*. New York: Ballantine, 1996.

Wu Hung. *Remaking Beijing: Tiananmen Square and the Creation of a Political Space*. Chicago: University of Chicago Press, 2005.

"Xianggang zhuandian: Nuobei'er wenxuejiang bu tuo zhengzhi wei" [Hong Kong special report: Nobel Literature Prize is not without political flavor]. *Renmin ribao* [People's Daily], 13 October 2000.

Xu, Gang Gary. "My Writing, Your Pain, and Her Trauma: Pronouns as (Gendered) Subjectivity in Gao Xingjian's *Soul Mountain* and *One Man's Bible*." *Modern Chinese Literature and Culture* 14, no. 2 (2000): 99–129.

Xu Xi. "Manky's Tale." In *History's Fiction: Stories from the City of Hong Kong*, 40–50. Hong Kong: Chameleon Press, 2001.

Yamauchi, Wakako. *The Chairman's Wife*. In *The Politics of Life: Four Plays by Asian American Women*. Edited by Velina Hasu Houston, 101–49. Philadelphia: Temple University Press, 1993.

Yan, Haiping. "Theater and Society: An Introduction to Contemporary Chinese Drama." In *Theater and Society: An Anthology of Contemporary Chinese Drama*, edited by Yan Haiping, ix–xlvi. Armonk, N.Y.: M. E. Sharpe: 1998.

Yang, Xiaobin. *The Chinese Postmodern: Trauma and Irony in Chinese Avant-Garde Fiction*. Ann Arbor: University of Michigan Press, 2002.

———. "*The Republic of Wine*: An Extravaganza of Decline." *positions* 6, no. 1 (1998): 7–31.

Yao, Steven G. *Foreign Accents: Chinese American Verse from Exclusion to Post-ethnicity*. Oxford: Oxford University Press, 2010.

Ye, Ting-xing, with William Bell. *Throwaway Daughter*. Toronto: Doubleday Canada, 2004.

Yeh, Michelle. "Contemporary Chinese Poetry Scenes." *Chicago Review* 39, no. 3/4 (1993): 279–83.

Yeung, Jessica. *Ink Dances in Limbo: Gao Xingjian's Writing as Cultural Transition*. Hong Kong: Hong Kong University Press, 2008.

Yip, Terry Siu-han. "A Chronology of Gao Xingjian." In *Soul of Chaos: Critical Perspectives on Gao Xingjian*, edited by Kwok-kan Tam, 311–39. Hong Kong: Chinese University Press, 2001.

Yu Yuan. "Liusi tanke nianren zhenxiang" [The truth about June 4 tanks crushing people]. Liusi dangan [June 4th memoir]. April 2001. Web.

Yue, Gang. *The Mouth That Begs: Hunger, Cannibalism, and the Politics of Eating in Modern China*. Durham: Duke University Press, 1999.

Zeng Huiyan. "*Beijing zhiwuren* Ma Jian shinian zhu yijian" [*Beijing Coma*'s Ma Jian takes ten years to cast his sword]. *Dajiyuan* [Epoch Times] 4 June 2008. Web.

Zhang Boli. *Escape from China: The Long Journey from Tiananmen to Freedom*. Translated by Kwee Kian Low. New York: Washington Square, 2002.

Zhang, Hang. "Bilingual Creativity in Chinese English: Ha Jin's *In the Pond*." *World Englishes* 21, no. 2 (2002): 305–15.

Zhang Liang. "Preface: Reflections on June Fourth." In Zhang L., comp., *Tiananmen Papers*.

———. "'The Tiananmen Papers' Compiler Discusses His Actions." CNN.com, 3 June 2001. Web.

———, comp. *The Tiananmen Papers*. Edited by Andrew J. Nathan and Perry Link. New York: PublicAffairs, 2001.

Zhao, Dingxin. *The Power of Tiananmen: State-Society Relations and the 1989 Beijing Student Movement*. Chicago: University of Chicago Press, 2001.

Zhao, Henry Y. H. *Towards a Modern Zen Theatre: Gao Xingjian and Chinese Theatre Experimentalism*. London: School of Oriental and African Studies, University of London, 2000.

Zheng Yi. *Scarlet Memorial: Tales of Cannibalism in Modern China*. Translated by T. P. Sym. Boulder: Westview, 1996.

Zhong, Xueping, Wang Zheng, and Bai Di. Introduction to *Some of Us: Chinese Women Growing Up in the Mao Era*, edited by Xueping Zhong, Wang Zheng, and Bai Di. New Brunswick, N.J.: Rutgers University Press, 2001.

"Zhongguozuo xiefuzeren jieshou jizhe caifang zhichu: Nuobei'er wenxuejiang bei yongyu zhengzhi mudi shiqu quanweixing" [Assistant head of Chinese writers points out in interview: Nobel Prize for Literature is being used for political purposes and has lost its authority]. *Renmin ribao* [People's Daily], 13 October 2000.

Zhou Xiaojing. "Writing Otherwise Than as a 'Native Informant.'" In *Transnational Asian American Literature: Sites and Transits,* edited by Shirley Geoklin Lim et al., 274–94. Philadelphia: Temple University Press, 2006.

Zhu Wen. *Didi de yanzou* [Little brother's performance]. Shanghai: Shanghai renmin chubanshe [Shanghai People's Publishing House], 2007.

———. *I Love Dollars and Other Stories of China.* Translated by Julia Lovell. New York: Penguin, 2008.

INDEX

ABOUT THE AUTHOR

Belinda Kong is Assistant Professor of Asian Studies and English at Bowdoin College.